THE WORLD MILITARY ORDER

Also by Mary Kaldor

THE ARMS TRADE WITH THE THIRD WORLD
THE DISINTEGRATING WEST

The World Military Order

The Impact of Military Technology on the Third World

Edited by
Mary Kaldor and Asbjørn Eide

First published 1979 by
THE MACMILLAN PRESS LTD
London and Basingstoke
Associated companies in Delhi
Dublin Hong Kong Johannesburg Lagos
Melbourne New York Singapore Tokyo

Printed in Great Britain by
Unwin Brothers Limited
The Gresham Press
Old Woking, Surrey

British Library Cataloguing in Publication Data

The world military order
  1. Underdeveloped areas—
Military policy
I. Kaldor, Mary   II. Eide, Asbjørn
355.2'90172'4   UA11

ISBN 0-333-25394-9

Contents

Acknowledgements   vi

Notes on the Contributors   vii

Introduction   1
Ulrich Albrecht and Mary Kaldor

1   The Technological Imperative in US War Strategy in Vietnam   17
    David Marr

2   Blanket Coverage: Two Case Studies of Area Weapons in   49
    Indochina
    Michael Krepon

3   Qualitative Trends in Conventional Munitions: the Vietnam   64
    War and After
    Julian Perry Robinson

4   Counter-insurgency: the French War in Algeria   110
    Hartmut Elsenhans

5   Military Technology and Conflict Dynamics: the Bangladesh   136
    Crisis of 1971
    Javed Ansari and Mary Kaldor

6   Militarised Sub-imperialism: the Case of Iran   157
    Ulrich Albrecht

7   South Africa: Repression and the Transfer of Arms and   180
    Arms Technology
    Asbjørn Eide

8   The Economic Consequences of the Transfer of Military-   210
    oriented Technology
    Peter Lock and Herbert Wulf

9   Militarism: Force, Class and International Conflict   232
    Robin Luckham

    Conclusion   257
    Asbjørn Eide and Mary Kaldor

Selected Bibliography   277
Index   291

Acknowledgements

We are grateful to the Berghof-Stiftung for generous financial support in the preparation of the book; to Sandy Merritt, Karen Payne and Radha Kumar for making sense of some of our foreign English; and to Gillian Joyce for typing the manuscript.

Notes on the Contributors

ULRICH ALBRECHT is Professor of Peace and Conflict Studies at the Free University of Berlin. He left East Germany in 1956 and was trained as an aviation engineer and economist. He is the author of *Der Waffen Handel* (Munich, 1971).

JAVED ANSARI is Lecturer in Economics at City University, London, and was brought up in Bangladesh. He was educated at Karachi and Sussex Universities.

ASBJØRN EIDE is an international lawyer working for the International Peace Research Institute in Oslo. He has been a member of the Norwegian delegation to the CDDH in Geneva, and was General Secretary of the International Peace Research Association from 1971 to 1975.

HARTMUT ELSENHANS is a junior professor at the University of Marburg, West Germany. He is the author of *Frankreichs Algerienkrieg* (Munich, 1975).

MARY KALDOR is a Fellow of the Science Policy Research Unit, University of Sussex. She formerly worked for the Stockholm International Peace Research Institute. She is co-author of *The Arms Trade with the Third World* (Stockholm, 1971) and author of *The Disintegrating West* (London, 1978).

MICHAEL KREPON works for the United States Arms Control and Disarmament Agency and was until recently on the staff of Representative Hicks in the US Congress. He has written on the subject of weapons in *Foreign Affairs*.

PETER LOCK was formerly head of the West German assistance programme in Ecuador. Currently he lectures at the University of Hamburg.

DAVID MARR is a fellow of the Research School of Pacific Studies, Australian National University, Canberra.

JULIAN PERRY ROBINSON is a Fellow of the Science Policy Research Unit. He formerly worked for SIPRI where he wrote much of *The Problem of Chemical and Biological Warfare* (6 vols, Stockholm, 1971–73). He has acted as a consultant on weapons questions to the United Nations Secretariat and the World Health Organization.

HERBERT WULF formerly worked for the West German technical assistance programme in India. He currently works, together with Ulrich Albrecht and Peter Lock, for the *Arbeitsgruppe für Rüstung und Unterentwicklung* in Hamburg and they have co-authored a book *Rüstung und Unterentwicklung* (Rowohlt, 1976).

Introduction

Ulrich Albrecht and Mary Kaldor

> The modern principality was built with blood and steel. Its strength
> and might developed both at home and abroad as far as the sword
> could reach. The modern state and the modern army arose together.
> Thus any discussion of the modern state has to make reference to
> the special characteristics of military institutions.
> But this is not the only reason why I speak about the composition
> and growth of modern armies. Basically and above all it is
> because of the crucial role they played in the promotion and spread of
> capitalism and, hence, the advent of militarism appears to be
> a fundamental premise of capitalism.
> In the early stages of capitalism, force of arms, by and large,
> decided the fate of European states as well as the colonies, and it is true
> to say that, in the beginning, there were armed forces.

> Werner Sombart: *Der moderne Kapitalismus* (1913; authors' translation)

Sombart's observations in 1916 on the function of militarism within
capitalism in general, and in colonial societies in particular, apply with
great force to present day military-technical relations between poor
countries (or 'developing nations' in the current euphemism) and
advanced industrial powers. The end of the Vietnam war and the
Portuguese colonial wars, the burgeoning of arms trade since 1973, the
establishment of arms manufacturing facilities in the more advanced
third-world countries, particularly in the Middle East, and the
emergence of a militarism hitherto rarely noticed in the third world,
all contribute to a growing consciousness of what we describe as the
World Military Order. To understand the many problems characterised by underdevelopment, dependence, national poverty and
distress, it is necessary to analyse the world military order and to
identify the connections between military, economic, social, and
political developments in the third world. Neither research into
development, nor political-science studies dealing with the third world,
nor the efforts of peace researchers have been able to encompass the
dynamic aspect of this problem. It was in order to remedy some of the
inadequacies of current analyses of the role of armaments in the third
world that the International Peace Research Association convened a
group of concerned scholars; this book is one of the results of their
discussions.

The essays deal with the impact of foreign military technology in all
its various forms: arms trade, licensed arms production, the transfer of

1

military skills through training or personnel, and direct foreign military intervention as in Vietnam or Algeria. A major theme of the book is the weakness of orthodox interpretations which hold that such transfer of military technology are justified by 'defence' requirements as defined by conventional strategists; that military efficiency is synonymous with technical sophistication; and that power relationships can be assessed on the basis of technical–military criteria. These are interpretations which carry sinister implications; in Vietnam for example, they led to the confusion of strategic objectives with the number of casualties, so that killing became more important than winning, and the means of killing improved dramatically. They have also led to immeasurable economic wastage. Some of the essays put forward alternative explanations that deal with the role of military technology in integrating third-world armies and élites into an international system dominated by the super powers, and with the relation of military technology to domestic political and economic issues as well as to intervention in various forms by outside powers.

In this introduction, we describe the scale of the problem and set out a conceptual framework for the chapters that follow.

The arms build-up

All wars since 1945 have been fought in the third world, with weapons designed and generally produced in advanced industrial nations. By far the most sophisticated technology has been operated by the armies of outside powers; the Dutch, the French, the British, the Portuguese and above all the Americans have all been involved directly in third-world conflicts and, compared with the size and cost of their military efforts, the arsenals of third-world nations seem almost puny. The Americans were spending $25,000 million a year on the war in Vietnam, five times as much as the total world arms trade in that period. New and devastating military technologies emerged out of the direct fighting experience of the rich countries and continued to be developed long after military withdrawal. Some of the new conventional weapons originally designed for Vietnam, such as controlled fireballs or cluster-bombs, threaten to inflict a scale of destruction in a future conventional war that is not so far removed from what is generally anticipated to be the outcome of nuclear warfare.

The American defeat in Vietnam and the liberation of the former Portuguese colonies has led to a lull, perhaps temporary, in the active military involvement of the industrial nations. The arming of local forces in the third world can perhaps be viewed as a substitute: a less direct, less unpopular, and less expensive form of intervention, one which other advanced industrial countries, notably the USSR, have long practised. The withdrawal of foreign military forces, combined with the oil crisis and its attendant consequences, may perhaps explain the explosion in the transfer of arms from rich to poor countries since 1973.

Arms transfers represent an expanding share of international economic transfers, especially in third-world countries.[1] Arms and munitions are only the more visible aspects of military trade, which predominantly consists of spare parts and auxiliary equipment, and, more recently, costly equipment for the production of weapons in third-world facilities. For the purpose of trade statistics, government licensing policies, etc., these goods are often presented as harmless civilian merchandise; yet they may be instrumental in establishing an impressive military potential, often outside the institutions which traditionally command the use of force. Military fuels and stores for military consumption, facilities for military research and development, equipment needed to test and evaluate military hardware, are added to the burden peripheral economies have to bear. Trade statistics also exclude the experts who swarm in from industrialised countries alongside the complex technical products, to operate the newly acquired weapons, erect plant, establish design teams, organise the assembly and production of advanced weapons, and teach nationals to take over in the future: the new white-collar mercenaries.

The extent of this militarisation of world trade is generally unknown to the public because of the paucity of sources. Even the best known research institutes (the Stockholm International Peace Research Institute, the US Arms Control and Disarmament Agency, and the International Institute for Strategic Studies in London) provide only information on arms transfers, and ignore transfers of equipment to produce arms and expert personnel to run the equipment or its production.[2] Recently the Stockholm International Peace Research Institute (SIPRI) has begun to study arms production in peripheral countries, but none of the research institutes analyse small arms transfers or electronics and communications systems.[3]

Weaponry, production equipment, and personnel are only the concrete aspects of a more general philosophy which is transferred from industrial countries to the third world. This includes ideas about military tactics and doctrine (around which, of course, the weapons have been designed), as well as industrialisation strategies and attitudes towards social systems—all of which, as we shall argue, have profound implications for the role of third-world countries in the international system.

In the 1950s and 1960s, the Americans supplied huge quantities of arms and associated services, such as training, repair and maintenance, and technical advice, as part of a policy of 'communist containment'. Even today, the United States is the largest supplier of arms to the third world. The excuse that American military aid is given to stabilise democratic governments in the third world is belied by the high correlation between such aid and military *coups d'état* in the recipient countries.[4] Decisions taken in the United States, the Soviet Union, and China have all contributed to the increase in third-world military potential, but the desire for power and control is not a sufficient explanation for their massive investments. Economically, military transfers to the third world are important in maintaining as large as possible a capacity for military production, especially production of the most advanced and sophisticated equipments. Transfers to under-developed countries are necessary to justify the financial burden of the global arms race. Since so many arms now go from industrialised countries to the third world, the third world is bearing a major part of this burden.[5]

In Western countries, the need to utilise surplus military-industrial capacity has been combined with other motives for the arms trade. In the United States, great emphasis has been laid on the need to offset the foreign exchange cost of overseas military intervention. The McNamara reforms of the military aid programme included a new guideline for the provision of military aid, that military aid should help to promote future military sales.[6] The US had as an objective the mobilisation of 'inexpensive auxiliary forces for global US interests under the umbrella of generous "development aid" '.[7] Pentagon cost-effectiveness experts demonstrated how cheap, non-American personnel could be used to fulfil military tasks in the American strategy.[8] More generally military transfers benefit the American economy and American foreign policy through direct political leverage and influence on the orientation of the recipient regimes; the transfer of arms to sympathetic regimes is one of the mechanisms which brings about support for urban-industrial concepts and integration of third-world countries into the Western dominated world market. Finally, arms transfers have a pre-emptive function as part of the overall US–Soviet competition. They keep protagonists out of the business and impose additional economic constraints on the USSR: 'Military aid represents a more effective use of American resources when open aggression and subversion are made more costly for our opponents.'[9]

Medium-sized industrial powers like Britain, France, and West Germany seem economically even more dependent on military transfers than the super powers. They have attempted to preserve a capacity for the development and production of some categories of advanced military technology (e.g. manned air warfare, army equipment), while —predominantly for financial reasons— they have been forced to opt out in others (strategic missiles, particularly complex guidance technology like MIRV; aircraft carriers and other large means of naval warfare). Continued participation at some level of the arms race requires the repeated payment of entry costs into areas of innovative technology—a burden which can be lessened by substantial exports.

In the case of France, where military transfers have been estimated to account for as much as 30 per cent of exports, these sales are vital not only for the continued existence of the domestic arms industry, but for the economy as a whole. An abrupt halt in military export orders could lead to a severe economic crisis. The renaissance of French arms manufacturing based on exports led the general manager of USIAS, the union of French aerospace producers, to say in 1974: 'The military sector remains the main pillar of our exports.'[10] In Britain, exports allow for the retention of a fairly independent and technologically competent arms industry. The contribution of military production to the balance of payments has often been stressed by British industrial organisations. West Germany is the world's second biggest overall exporter, but the West German government claims to be restrictive with export licences for military goods. However, West Germany does provide military production support and technical expertise, and it uses co-production arrangements to conceal exports.

The USSR has less than half as many clients as the United States:[11] in 1973 the Soviet Union supplied arms to thirty-two third-world countries, while the United States supplied arms to seventy. According to the US Arms Control and Disarmament Agency, the Soviet Union was the second largest supplier of arms on the world market during the last fifteen years. More than half of these transfers went to five third-world countries—Egypt, North Vietnam, North Korea, Iran, and Indonesia. And a third of the transfers went to Soviet allies in the Warsaw Pact. The size and sophistication of Soviet arms transfers does not appear to be subject to as much restriction as in the West. Rather, costly arms technology is only exported to allies and friendly countries of a semi-socialist nature. The number of French arms clients (sixty) is nearly double the number of Soviet clients; Britain also sells arms to many more countries than does the USSR. The political significance, particularly for the student of international affairs, seems to be more relevant for Soviet arms transfers than does the economic impact, particularly the impact on industrialisation strategies (compared with the many countries which produce Western arms, only India and China make Soviet weapons). This is why, in a book which is primarily about the impact of the military upon development and political life in third-world countries, Soviet and Chinese arms transfers are treated as secondary issues.

Statistics about the world arms trade are unreliable, and, as we have seen, exclude important transfers of a military nature. It is, however, possible to ascertain to some degree the growing importance of deliveries to the third world. In 1963, third-world nations absorbed around 50 per cent, or US $1,600 million, of the world arms transfers. A decade later nearly two-thirds of this business went to the third world; and in 1975 the proportion reached a peak of 75 per cent. The total volume of transfers also expanded rapidly, from $3,200 million in 1963 to $9,700 million in 1975.[12] *Time* magazine correctly described the arms trade as 'the world's fastest growing business'.[13] Yet civilian trade (as the magazine failed to mention) is stagnant; third-world countries account for less than 25 per cent of the total.[14] The third-world share of transfers of machinery of special importance for economic growth has dropped slightly to 24 per cent.

The weapons that these numbers obscure cover a wide range, from second-hand small arms sold by private dealers, to the most sophisticated weapon systems that oil money can buy and governments are prepared to sell. These might include the Iranian Chieftain tank embodying the new Chobham armour, the latest American F-15 fighter, or even the technology of nuclear warfare.

The driving forces behind this military build-up are not only to be found in metropolitan areas. Some third-world governments actively co-operate with industrial powers, and have also taken decisive initiatives for the expansion of arms transfers. One better-known reason is the massive increase in the price of crude oil imposed by producers and dealers (multinational corporations) upon world consumers. Oil revenues are used to finance acquisition of arms, or, to put it more precisely, the additional income generated by oil is largely absorbed by the purchase of unproductive goods. A second factor is the sale of second-hand weapons within the third world, generally taken from the surplus stocks of US war materiel left behind in South-East Asia. Private firms, especially in Taiwan and South Korea, are apparently making fortunes by selling refurbished US equipment on world markets (continuing to operate at full capacity what were formerly repair and overhaul facilities for US forces deployed in those areas). A US government report lists thirty countries which acquired equipment disposed of after the Vietnam and Cambodia wars.[15] A third and—in the long run—more important factor which explains the role of third-world governments in the global military build-up ought to be mentioned: the demand for instruments of repression in peripheral countries has grown enormously. It stems from the popular reaction to industrialisation—a process which involves increased inequality and exploitation, the expulsion of peasants from their lands, the explosion of an unemployed urban population, hunger and violence. An industrial development strategy may also exacerbate external tensions, stemming from uneven development within the third world, the rise of sub-imperial powers like Brazil, Israel, Iran, or India, and the inculcation of an anti-foreign nationalist ideology which holds together a divided society. Even if third-world élites are opposed to authoritarian methods of rule and external warmongering, a forced process of industrialisation and modernisation following the Western pattern or its Soviet copy must inevitably place severe political and social constraints on government.

A conceptual approach to military technology

Among the military attitudes that pervade modern society is a kind of technology fetishism. In the statements of political leaders or military commentators, in the learned assessments of specialist publications or in many public pronouncements of the media, there is to be found a widespread belief that military power consists of superior military technology measured in quantitative and qualitative terms and that political power derives from military power.

The conventional criteria for measuring military power include such things as the dollar size of military budgets and the quantities of men, tanks, and aircraft. Considerable weight is attached to the sophistication and modernity of military equipment, assessed according to the date and type of equipment and to performance characteristics such as speed, payload, or electronic capabilities. A particularly high value is assigned to nuclear weapons. Using such global indicators, one would have had to conclude that the United States enjoyed an overwhelming military superiority over its enemies in Indochina, and that the Arabs enjoyed a similar advantage over Israel. But military power of course is not about quantities; it is about the ability to achieve specific political or strategic objectives through military means. Even for advanced industrial nations it is not at all clear that the two meanings of military power are compatible, that the sophisticated arsenals of East or West will necessarily prove an advantage in actual battlefield conditions. Improvements in the accuracy and destructiveness of conventional munitions suggest that the dispersal tactics of Vietnam may be a more apt precedent than the more orthodox battles of the Second World War. The increased vulnerability of all weapon platforms—ships, tanks, aircraft—call into question the utility of equipment which is difficult to hide and expensive to replace. In addition, complex modern equipment entails considerable logistical problems. A squadron of F-4 Phantoms, for example, requires an inventory of 70,000 spare parts to be kept operational under wartime conditions. Despite the unprecedented scale and sophistication of logistical operations in Vietnam, there were perennial shortages.

The first chapter on Vietnam in this book shows how the very political weakness of the United States in Vietnam—its unpopularity which stemmed from its role in upholding an exploitative social system and unwillingness, for domestic reasons, to fight a labour-intensive war—forced American strategy into ever-increasing dependence on technology. Gradually, all forms of political control gave way to the dynamic imperatives of military technology. As each American technological fix was countered by a well organised and socially committed opposition, so new and more horrific forms of killing were invented by the technicians. The way in which decisions about important new technologies were taken is the subject of Chapter 2, while Chapter 3 describes the technological impulse set in motion by the war. Yet in the end, despite the unprecedented scale of physical destruction, social dislocation, and personal misery, the technology was decisively defeated in Vietnam and the social content of power relationships was reasserted. The Algerian study, Chapter 4, makes the same point; technology, it is argued, was of little relevance in the French military victory in Algeria; moreover, military struggle gave rise to new social and economic developments in France as well as Algeria, which resulted in political defeat.

For third-world countries, such doubts about the military value of modern armaments are magnified. First of all, sophisticated weapon systems are highly capital-intensive requiring an advanced industrial base for repair, maintenance, and operation. The shortage of skilled industrial manpower, the inadequacy of roads and airfields, etc., is bound to impair military efficiency. Indeed, in some cases, equipment confidently accredited to third-world countries actually lies rusting, often uncrated, in ports. One of the themes of the chapter on the Bangladesh crisis is the argument that, in the Indo/Pakistani wars, where the education and skills of the soldiers were roughly matched, sophisticated military equipment actually proved a handicap. For example, in 1965, Pakistani soldiers were unable to operate the automatic control needed to fire the guns of their Patton tanks, and this considerably hampered their offensive. More important perhaps is the fact that the relative scarcity of those factors of production needed to operate a modern military machine adhering to the standards set by advanced industrial countries means that third-world countries are heavily dependent on their suppliers for spare parts and for services.

All this suggests that the acquisition of modern armaments may not contribute to military power in the true sense of the expression. It may be that a clearer focus on military tasks as opposed to military means would result in alternative, possibly labour-intensive, solutions. Such an argument would also imply that political power based on the size and sophistication of arsenals is no more than a matter of perception. Indeed the military dependence induced by the acquisition of modern armaments may actually reduce political power. For example, both the United States and the Soviet Union have been able to use arms supplies to the Middle East as a way of bargaining for short-term diplomatic objectives;[16] this would not be possible if the demand for armaments were less. Furthermore, in wartime military dependence means that suppliers have the power of military veto. There are several instances in which an embargo on spares has grounded third-world air forces within a period of weeks. Supplier involvement, the inevitable consequence of dependence, is the mechanism through which local and particular events are transformed into the substance of global conflict.

If one takes into account the economic basis of political power, the dissociation between political power and modern military technology is all the greater. For military dependence is associated with economic dependence and economic dependence may well be an important factor in explaining continued poverty.

The fact that current assumptions about military power are so widely accepted suggests that their significance is more than military. If one accepts the connection between beliefs and social setting, and its corollary that every society has its own military ideology, then the pervasive nature of modern attitudes towards armament has profound implications for the unity of the international system. In seeking to portray an alternative view of the significance of military technology, we might start with an analysis of the form of force that characterises different societies.

The form of force can be defined as comprising the techniques of force and the relations of force. The techniques of force are the weapons and the way they are used. The relations of force are the organisation of men, the nature of military hierarchy, the way men are drawn into the armed forces. The techniques of force are at once the product of the level of technology in society and the appropriate tool for a particular set of military relations. The relations of force are those most convenient for organising a body of men in a given society, and those most likely to generate loyalty to the social formation, that is to say, to generate assent among soldiers for the unenviable risk of fighting wars.

It is evident that the techniques of force are only one element in the determination of military power and that theories which fail to take into account the social organisation of the military, the relations of force, and the social basis for technology are inadequate. It took the introduction of a market for soldiers, i.e. mercenaries, before guns, the product of urban technology, were accepted into the armed forces. Similarly, the fact that the Vietnamese were able to make use of imported weapons (often more effectively than the Americans) was due to their social organisation.

The form of force is thus a reflection of society as a whole. But it is not an exact replica. The form of force and the social formation are divided by time—military developments may proceed at a different rate from economic and social developments—and by differing exposure to the outside world. Hence the form of force may, in some circumstances, serve to transmit the influence of one society on another. This may be the consequence of war. The German response to the Napoleonic Wars contributed to the democratisation of Germany. Equally, the counter-insurgency operations of the United States and France might be termed radicalising experience with profound economic and political implications for society. Or it may be the consequence of peaceful military exchange, the export of arms and military know-how. This dynamic tension between the form of force and the social formation, a tension which is expressed in the role of force as an instrument of destruction and in the absorption and mobilisation of resources for destructive purposes, is perhaps the most important theme of this book—a link between the different studies.

The form of force that characterises advanced capitalist societies is the industrial army. One feature of the industrial army is the weapons system concept. The armed forces, with the possible exception of the infantry, are organised around the weapons system, which comprises the weapons platform (the ship, aircraft, tank, etc.), the weapon, and the means of communication. Formerly, the weapon was the instrument of the soldier. Today, the soldier appears to be the instrument of the weapons system. The resulting organisation is hierarchical, atomistic, and dehumanising. It reflects the importance accorded to industrial products, particularly machines, in society as a whole. Furthermore, the weapons systems are themselves ranked and subdivided into a hierarchical military organisation, minimising the possibilities for individual or small group action. At the apex of the navy is the aircraft carrier making it possible for aircraft to operate from its deck, destroyers, frigates, and submarines to defend it, and supply ships to replenish it. The bomber and the battle tank have similar functions in the air force and army. The liberal ideal of the fighter pilot as the modern hero of individual combat is a convenient myth. In reality, fifty men are required to operate each combat aircraft, together with the men required to operate supporting aircraft, so that the special importance accorded to the pilot is merely symbolic.

The second feature of the industrial army is the built-in tendency for expansion. Permanent technical progress implies a permanent process of obsolescence. The continuous development of new weapons, incorporating improved firepower, mobility, or communication, necessitates the continuous replacement of existing weapons. The process can be entirely autonomous, requiring nothing more than the existence of an external enemy. It can be assumed that any plausible military developments will be applied by the enemy (the 'worst case analysis'), and because of the long gestation of modern weapons systems, the response must be adopted as quickly as possible. The new technology involves expansion, the technical improvements are more complex to manufacture and operate, requiring more labour for both production and use.

In one sense, however, the technical progress is conservative. It is socially circumscribed by the structure imposed by the weapons system. A revolutionary technology, involving perhaps less expenditure, is inhibited by the organisation of the armed forces. The development of missile technology could have implications that are as revolutionary as was the development of firearms. The vulnerability of all weapons platforms (until antisubmarine detection is improved, the submarine escapes this generalisation) threatens to reduce the grandiose marvels of modern technology—the aircraft carrier, bomber, or battle tank— to expensive absurdities. Indeed, the obsolescence of the capital ship, of which the aircraft carrier is the current example, was demonstrated as long ago as the First World War. Yet the concept is defended, in the vague terms of modern strategy, as 'flexible response' (US) or a 'balance of forces' across the 'whole spectrum of operations' (UK), because the weapons-system-based force structure is intimately connected to the structure of modern industry and of society as a whole.

The industrial army can be traced back to the Anglo-German naval arms race before the First World War. In the 1880s the manufacture of arms, mainly ships, was contracted out to private companies, in the words of a British government committee 'to stimulate inventors and manufacturers to vie with one another to produce the best possible article'.[17] Berghahn has shown how, in Germany, the Tirpitz plan for naval procurement was closely related to the concern in shipbuilding and heavy industry about the deepening of recessions and the problems of excess capacity.[18]

Through the twentieth century, the development of the armed forces proceeded alongside the development of the arms industry. Each weapons system was the product of a particular company and the centre of a military unit. The manufacturing capabilities of a company were at one and the same time the performance characteristics of a weapons system and the operational doctrine of a military unit. The relationship between different military units exactly paralleled the structure of industry. Changes in the structure of industry, as in Britain in the late 1950s and early 1960s, were associated with changes in the relations of force. A more current example is the trend towards multi-national defence companies in Europe, which is accompanied by new doctrines about the need to standardise and integrate European armed forces.

But, in general, these changes are resisted because the armed forces are frozen in the industrial structure which created their current form. Thus the navy and naval shipbuilding have a relatively predominant role in Britain, reflecting their zenith in the late nineteenth century. The US armed forces are a Second World War creation, dominated by the structure of aerospace. The new military technologies which challenge these decaying military establishments are the product of new dynamic industries, like electronics, and are most liable to be adopted by countries dominated by those industries, such as Germany and Japan.

The significance of the weapons system concept, lies, therefore, not so much in their use, but in the commitment they create to use force in defence of certain interests. For the armed forces, the preservation of their own structure also means the preservation of a particular industrial structure and the social organisation on which the structure is founded. Quite apart from its direct importance to the production process, in creating employment for example, the significance of this elaborate form of force is political. The direct military aspects are minor.

What is the consequence of the transfer of military technology—the export of techniques of force? Force played a central role in the imperialist process; imperialism meaning not necessarily territorial annexation, but the absorption of peripheral economies into the world capitalist system. The success of the industrial army in imposing the conditions under which this process could take place reflected the dominance of the capitalist social formation. The failure of the industrial army, in Vietnam, for example, or Southern Africa, might be said to reflect the decadence of the weapon system concept. But these are cases in which the transfer of technology involved the transfer of relations of force, the use of techniques by the industrial armies for which they were designed. The consequences of the export of techniques alone, the export of arms to local élites in the third world are currently the major topic for debate.

It is useful to draw a distinction between two model forms of force to be found in the third world. Obviously much more refined distinctions can be made, corresponding to complex class structures. The first model is the pre-industrial army—the Bedouin levies of the Middle East, the retinue armies of pre-colonial Africa, the nineteenth-century militia and Caudillos of Latin America.[19] Typically, these are infantry- or cavalry-based; the weapon being still the instrument of the soldier. The weapons are largely imported although the choice of weapons is delineated by the relations of force. In some cases, quite sophisticated weapons prove appropriate; the White Guard of Saudi Arabia has, since 1963, made use of Vigilant man-portable anti-tank missiles.

This form of force does not necessarily involve capitalist relations of force, but it is dependent on capitalist techniques. In this it corresponds to the social formation in which it operates. This is generally characterised by the production of one or two basic commodities for export, sometimes by wage labour and sometimes on a slave or feudal based mode of production. The revenue from these exports is spent on necessities (where not produced alongside the export commodity) and on prestige goods and arms for the ruling class. The arms are used directly for repression, to preserve the position of the ruling class.[20] Thus the social formation may not be capitalist, in the sense of employing capitalist techniques and utilising a free market for labour, but it is dependent upon and essential to a capitalist world system.

The second model form of force is the industrial army. This is the consequence of the import of modern military technology on an extensive scale. It is associated with the beginnings of industrialisation, the rise of an urban élite, the spread of a multinational manufacturing capital, and the development of authoritarian forms of rule. Because the weapons system concept limits the possible variations in the relations of force, it gives rise to a form of force that is an imitation of the metropolis. A primary concern of this book is the impact of the industrial army on third-world societies.

In the early sixties, it was fashionable to argue that the army as a modern institution could make a positive contribution to industrialisation and economic growth in underdeveloped countries.[21] Support for these ideas came from Professor Benoit's attempt to demonstrate, not altogether convincingly, a positive correlation between the share of GNP devoted to military spending and the rate of growth of civilian GNP.[22] In recent years, however, people have begun to question whether 'modernisation', industrialisation, and economic growth can be said to constitute economic and social development. Indeed it is argued that economic growth involves increased foreign dependence, and that modernisation, meaning the introduction of modern attitudes and modern technology, may conflict with the satisfaction of basic needs.

The connection between the level of military technology and the level of industrialisation is fairly well established. It is the more industrialised third-world countries like India, Egypt, Argentina, Brazil, or South Korea that possess the most sophisticated armaments, and even a rudimentary capacity for the manufacture of arms. For most underdeveloped countries, armaments represent a very high proportion of total capital imports. And in many countries, industrial capacity is reserved for the repair of weapons. Chapter 8 describes these linkages and argues that it is the requirement of the modern industrial army that shapes the whole pattern of industrialisation.

It is a capital-intensive pattern of industrialisation which is heavily dependent on foreign technology and on foreign aid and foreign investment. This is consistent with other empirical studies. Philippe Schmitter, in a survey of Latin American countries for the period 1950–67, found that the association between militarism and high rates of economic growth could be explained by foreign dependence.[23]

It is also a pattern of industrialisation that tends to generate inequality. In addition to foreign aid and investment, the foreign exchange and savings needed to finance industrialisation are extracted from the production of primary products for the world market in the countryside. The benefits of industrialisation are not redistributed but are spent on luxury consumption by the élite, on arms, re-invested in further industrialisation, repatriated by foreign investors as profits or to aid donors as debt repayment. Because industry is capital-intensive, it does not generate sufficient employment to absorb the surplus rural population. Unfortunately there is very little empirical evidence about economic inequality. The rate of infant mortality could be taken as a rough indicator of the standard of living of the mass of the population. Countries like Brazil, Iran, or South Korea which are characterised by high levels of military spending and by a dependent pattern of industrialisation tend to have a rate of infant mortality that is above the regional average.[24]

These features of so-called development strategies which are associated with heavy military spending—industrialisation, foreign dependence, and inequality—emerge clearly from the chapters on Iran, Bangladesh, and South Africa. These studies deal with the way in which military technology served to link such development strategies with international interests in fairly direct ways. In Iran the transfer of military technology was the pacemaker for the entry of multinational corporations and the establishment of industrial facilities in the Iranian economy. And military ways of doing things infected other fields of economic and social endeavour, like education or health. In Pakistan, military aid and membership in Western military alliances led to American influence over economic planning and provided the basis for pro-Western military governments, setting in motion the very problems of dependence and inequality which led to the crisis of 1971. And in South Africa, the position of the white minority depends to a large extent on imported military technology which has been accompanied by the growing importance of foreign investment and defence production in the South African economy.

But the role of armaments in these cases does not only result from economic linkages. On the contrary, these development strategies necessarily lead to popular dissatisfaction which may often warrant military repression. The sophisticated instruments of the modern industrial army may not be the most appropriate for this purpose. In Pakistan, the armed forces tend to resort to lathis (big sticks) when suppressing riots. But Chieftain tanks are used to terrorise villagers in Southern Iran and the use of imported military technology for repression in South Africa has led to international condemnation and hence, as Chapter 7 demonstrates, to the contradictory role of South Africa within the international system.

Popular dissatisfaction may also rule out democratic legitimation. Perhaps the most significant implication of the modern weapon system is ideological, for the import of modern armaments may provide the military with a vested interest in a strategy of industrialisation on the Western model so that elections can be replaced by the military *coup*. This is, undoubtedly, important in explaining the prominent role of the armed forces in Pakistan and Iran. Chapter 9 is about this wider political role of military technology in the spread of militarism and repression.

If this interpretation is correct, then armaments play a critical role in cementing the current international system; the World Military Order now prevailing serves to uphold current hierarchies of international political and economic relationships. The ideology of political power, based on a fetishism of military technology, offers third-world nations an opportunity to raise their status within the international system by imitation; yet imitation must of necessity always lag behind. This then is a fundamental contradiction. For every attempt by third-world countries to increase their political power and independence on the basis of this ideology must recoil in increased dependence. The acquisition of modern military technology is one mechanism whereby third-world countries are drawn into the global confrontation between the super powers and a world division of labour that limits the full potential of development.

It is out of this contradiction that the possibility for change emerges. The chapter on militarism demonstrates the cleavages within the armed forces, the complexity of society. The dominant military ideology serves to suppress these cleavages. But the actual experience of war, as indeed in the case of Bangladesh, and the growing emiseration of the mass of the population in consequence of 'modern' industrialisation strategies, expose the mythical nature of the ideology. And, in this, arises the possibility of alternative forms of power and consequently of new and meaningful approaches to disarmament and development. These issues are raised in the concluding chapter.

NOTES

1. The term 'transfers' is used to indicate all types of transfer, whether they are financed by the recipient or not, and whether they cover goods or services.
2. US Arms Control and Disarmament Agency, *World Military Expenditures and Arms Trade*, 1963–73 and 1965–75 (Washington, D.C., 1974 and 1976); International Institute for Strategic Studies, *The Military Balance* (London, annual) Table: 'Major Identified Arms Agreements' in the appendix; SIPRI (Stockholm International Peace Research Institute), *The Arms Trade with the Third World* (Stockholm: Almquist and Wicksell, 1971); and *Arms Trade Registers. The Arms Trade with the Third World* (Stockholm:Almquist and Wicksell, 1975). (See also the tables in the annual yearbook, *World Armaments and Disarmament*, details below.)
3. SIPRI, *World Armaments and Disarmament, SIPRI Yearbook 1974* (Stockholm: Almquist and Wicksell, 1974) Appendices 8D and E, Ch. II.
4. The US army *Military Review* contains two contributions which discuss such correlations. Cf. also Edward Thomas Rowe, 'Aid and coups d'état', *International Studies Quarterly*, Vol. 18, no. 2 (June 1974).
5. See H. Bühl, 'Frankreichs Sicherheitspolitik der siebziger Jahre', *Wehrkunde*, no. 3 (1974) p. 126.

6. J. E. Lynch, 'Analysis of Military Assistance', *Military Review* (May 1968) p. 41.

7. Hans Dieter Boris, 'Zur politischen Ökonomie der Beziehungen zwischen Entwicklungsländern und westlichen Industriegesellschaften', *Das Argument,* vol. 8, no. 3 (June 1966) p. 184.

8. Lynch, op. cit., p. 42.

9. Lynch, op. cit., p. 45.

10. Quoted from *Le Monde*, 28 Sep 1974.

11. US ACDA, *World Military Expenditures and Arms Trade,* 1963–73, op. cit.

12. US ACDA, *World Military Expenditures and Arms Transfers,* 1965–75, op. cit.

13. *Time Magazine,* 3 Mar 1975 (cover story).

14. Non-military export figures from *Standard Industrial Trade Classification* 715–29.5; UN Statistical Papers, Series M, no. 34, rev. 2 (1975).

15. Sources on excess US arms, NACLA articles and documents, from *Newsletter* 1970 (special off print). Cf. also F. C. Weyand, 'The Army in the Pacific is a Visible Presence for Peace', *Army,* vol. 23, no. 10 (1973) pp. 48–51.

16. See Leslie Gelb, 'Arms Sales', *Foreign Policy,* no. 25 (winter 1976–7).

17. Quoted in Philip Noel Baker, *The Private Manufacture of Arms* (London: Gollancz, 1936).

18. V. R. Berghahn, *Germany and the Approach of War in 1914* (London: Macmillan, 1973).

19. These last might be better described as absence of form, reflecting perhaps profound social and economic disorder. The irregular guerilla bands and bandits of modern Bangladesh and Burma might be placed in a similar category.

20. This model has much in common with Terray's description of Gyaman in pre-colonial Africa. Here, long-distance trade, including arms, led to the introduction of slavery, alongside a kin-base mode of subsistence production. The slaves were used to produce gold for export and the revenue was spent on prestige goods and guns to capture and maintain more slaves. (E. Terray, 'Long Distance Exchange and the Formation of the State: The Case of the Abron Kingdom of Gyaman', *Economy and Society,* Vol. 3, no. 3.)

21. Essays on this theme can be found in H. Bienen (ed.), *The Military and Modernisation* (Chicago: Aldine Atherton Inc., 1971) and John J. Johnson, *The Role of the Military in Underdeveloped Countries* (Princeton: Rand Corporation, 1962).

22. See Emile Benoit, *Defence and Economic Growth in Developing Countries* (Lexington, Mass.: Lexington Books, 1973).

23. See P. C. Schmitter, 'Military Intervention, Political Competitiveness and Public Policy in Latin America: 1950–1967', in Maurice Janovitz and Jack Van Doorn (eds.), *On Military Intervention* (Rotterdam University Press, 1971).

24. See M. Kaldor and J. P. Perry Robinson, 'War', in C. Freeman and M. Jahoda (eds.), *World Futures: The Great Debate* (Martin Robertson, forthcoming). A discussion about the relationship between inequality and military spending in Brazil by the Brazilian Marxist Cardoso and by Philippe Schmitter can be found in Alfred Stepan, *Authoritarian Brazil: Origins, Policies and Future* (Yale University Press, 1973).

1 The Technological Imperative in US War Strategy in Vietnam

David Marr

In May 1845 the captain of the USS *Constitution*, John Percival, took it upon himself to seize three Vietnamese court representatives meeting with him in Da-Nang harbour. A French Catholic priest was under sentence of death by the Vietnamese royal authorities, and Captain Percival felt he had to do his duty as a fellow Christian and white man. As further persuasion Captain Percival sent ashore a Marine raiding detachment which proceeded to kill and wound Vietnamese civilians. Although refusing to relinquish the French priest to Captain Percival, the Vietnamese court did promise eventual expulsion. The Americans released the hostages and sailed off to other waters.[1]

Almost exactly one hundred years later the US government permitted the French government to transfer many tons of valuable US lend-lease military equipment from Europe to Indochina, thus implicitly sanctioning the systematic French effort to turn back the clock and destroy the newly formed Democratic Republic of Vietnam (DRVN). In 1950 the United States sealed this alliance with the French by formally recognising the puppet Bao Dai regime. By early 1954 the US was providing 80 per cent of France's military and pacification costs in Indochina.[2] The endeavour failed. Beaten at Dienbienphu in May 1954 by a combination of over-confidence, exasperation, Viet-Minh artillery and Viet-Minh logistical skills, France withdrew below the 17th Parallel and attempted to patch together a more modest satellite regime in Saigon.

The United States, however, had far more ambitious ideas for what was already titled the Republic of Vietnam (RVN). The RVN in the American view was to be the south-east Asian bulwark against international totalitarian communism. Beyond that, if conditions permitted, the Army of the Republic of Vietnam (ARVN) was to be assisted in counter-attacking north of the 17th Parallel and thus rolling back the sinister red carpet. To these ends the ARVN was re-equipped with modern US tanks, trucks, artillery, and engineering and communications gear. French military officers were replaced as 'advisors' by American officers fresh from the Korean War experience and by a sprinkling of counter-insurgency specialists from the Philippines and Malaya. Ngo Dinh Diem, the American choice as premier, was encouraged to use this new weaponry first against alternative non-

17

communist power blocs (Binh Xuyen, Hao Hao, Cao Dai), then against
Viet-Minh political cadres and former activists who, quite legitimately
according to the 1954 Geneva Accords, had remained in their home
provinces rather than re-group north of the 17th Parallel. It was a grim,
agonising period for all of these groups, with tens of thousands of
people killed or imprisoned. The ARVN was assisted in its brutal task
by the RVN National Police, newly equipped and trained by personnel
from Michigan State University.[3] Meanwhile, American leaders spread
the message around the world of President Diem, the great Asian anti-
communist messiah.[4]

US/Saigon successes proved transitory. In 1959 people began
striking back at the Diem regime with whatever came to hand. On
20 December 1960 the National Front for the Liberation of South
Vietnam (NLF) was formed, and within months it appeared that the
entire repressive network put together by the Americans and their
Vietnamese clients was unravelling. NLF units of platoon or mere
squad size, armed only with a few captured American M-1 rifles, even
older French single-shot weapons, often a sprinkling of spears,
machetes, or crossbows, somehow succeeded in driving RVN soldiers,
police, and administrators out of large reaches of the fertile Mekong
delta and the strategic highland areas. When heavily armed ARVN
battalions counter-attacked they found no one except peaceful,
seemingly apolitical farmers who said they knew nothing about the
'Viet-Cong'. Meanwhile, in an adjacent district yet another small post
was being attacked and overrun, and ARVN tanks and trucks were
soon being ordered to lumber off in that direction. By late 1961 the
NLF had captured enough automatic rifles, 30 calibre machine guns,
and 60 mm mortars to be able to ambush Saigon supply columns and
keep main roads cut for weeks at a time.

Then in early January 1963, at Ap Bac, an NLF battalion dug in and
fought a position battle for the first time, in the process mangling three
ARVN battalions and destroying five US helicopters, before with-
drawing skilfully at dawn the next day.

Having touted the RVN as a showcase of democracy, a model of
what Asian anti-communists could do for themselves if they really
tried, US political leaders and global security strategists were clearly
upset. Kennedy administration fears were multiplied by the Bay of Pigs
fiasco in Cuba, by a seeming inability to resolve the Berlin Crisis short
of nuclear holocaust, and by the increasing awareness that US-supported
elements in Laos would be lucky to get off with part membership in a
shaky neutralist coalition. In short, by a combination of policy design
and historical chance, South Vietnam became America's most
important self-imposed test of international virility in its 200-year
existence. Whatever the obstacles, the United States had to demonstrate that this war of national liberation—and thus by implication all

such wars—could not succeed.

Many Kennedy administration policy makers were aware, at least in the most general terms, that the communist-led movement for independence had been since the 1930s the dominant political force in Vietnam.[5] Indeed, this is one reason why serious diplomacy and political compromise as a means of resolving the conflict had been spurned by the Eisenhower administration and continued to get little attention from four later presidents. On the other hand, the euphoria that seized many Americans during the Kennedy years included a belief that just about any problem was capable of resolution if enough enthusiasm, grit, and money were mobilised for the job. Although compromise with the communists was out of the question, at least until they had been 'contained', it seemed ridiculous to most Kennedy-era enthusiasts to argue that a small, underdeveloped state like Vietnam could resist the weight of American ingenuity, resources and, if necessary, direct military power.

Thus large numbers of high-level US missions were despatched to Saigon, ranking White House and Pentagon officials began reading Mao Tse-tung and Vo Nguyen Giap, and contracts were let to a wide variety of think-tanks and engineering firms to speculate wildly on new counter-guerrilla tactics and techniques. Rather early in this crash programme, however, a division developed between those who put relatively more emphasis on responding to the perceived grievances of the populace—for land reform, clean administration, schooling, and medical care, for example—and those who continued to talk in terms of better weaponry, more highly trained and motivated military personnel, and more refined methods for surveillance and control of the civilian population. Throughout the 1960s there were representatives of both viewpoints in every US military branch and civilian agency, but proponents of physical security and control had the upper hand from the very beginning and by 1967 they completely dominated policy making.

This was no accident. After all, the logic of perceived grievance response led inexorably to condemnation of most of the existing RVN bureaucracy, the ARVN generals and colonels, and the growing class of civilian war profiteers. Although searching for alternative leaders became a favourite pastime of certain American policy makers and embassy assistants, the individuals they produced tended to be long on eagerness to speak English and woefully short on mass following, practical rural experience, or solid revolutionary ideology. Besides, the more time that truly sensitive Americans spent looking into popular grievances the more they came to suspect that foreign involvement in the political and social process was part of the *problem*, not the solution. Even more unsettling, it seemed that only the communist-led Viet-Minh and its successor in the South, the NLF, had been able to address themselves effectively to both foreign aggression and social revolution. All others were either tainted by intimate association with the French, Japanese, and Americans, or they thought that social revolution consisted of vague speeches, slogans, and occasional fraternising with their 'backward' rural cousins.

The US government, however, was committed to fighting communists everywhere and was not at all interested in sanctioning heretical ideas about certain communist-led movements enjoying popular legitimacy. Then too, how could one accept the idea of foreigners, in this case Americans, causing part of the trouble and expect actively to change events in favour of the anti-communists? Most Americans in the 1960s believed deeply in their own good intentions and their ability to solve world problems, and could not accept any other view of events in Vietnam or elsewhere in the world. Vietnam would suffer untold death and destruction as a result.

Those Americans who wanted to take an active role in Vietnam had to deny the logic of communist legitimacy and foreign meddling and to create alternative images of what was happening. For example, the NLF was researched on the basis of inadequate and highly questionable data and discovered to be a hydra-headed organisational machine dependent on terrorism, completely unresponsive to democratic initiatives.[6] Other studies attempted to sidestep matters of political legitimacy and foreign interference by simply assuming that Vietnamese peasants were apolitical, worrying about their next bowl of rice, or about how they personally could prosper from new techniques and material aid (provided by foreigners, naturally), rather than about national independence, freedom, and social equality. Vietnamese peasants, it was argued, found little meaning or value in political ideology, except perhaps in some archaic Confucian maxims. Those who accepted communist ideology had been duped or coerced, or perhaps attracted by promises of larger rice bowls. In short, Vietnamese peasants were mere reeds in the wind, who would lean towards whomever was pointing the gun.[7]

The inevitable conclusion was that the outside élite with the best techniques of organised violence would inevitably triumph. Once this essentially reactionary outlook on human nature—or at least Vietnamese nature—was accepted, a vast array of possibilities, both primitive and sophisticated, could be envisaged. And no one was more capable of applying them than the richest, most powerful nation in the world. By 1962 even Kennedy administration policy makers like Roger Hilsman, who continued to emphasise that the NLF was more a political than a military threat, had accepted the argument that physical security, which later came to be called population control, was an essential prerequisite to 'civic action' programmes.[8] It was necessary to build a counter-revolutionary system to monitor and supervise people's daily activities, and begin forcibly to isolate the NLF from the people, before major attention could be devoted to popular needs and grievances.

Not surprisingly, this is what the small corps of professional counter-insurgency specialists had been saying all along. Colonel Edward Lansdale, having won his spurs by helping to suppress the Huk movement in Luzon, brought a combined US CIA and Filipino mercenary team to Saigon at a very early date.[9] Sir Robert Thompson who helped engineer a repression of communists in Malaya, was next to bring his experts and tools-of-the trade to South Vietnam, and took a leading role in designing the 'strategic hamlet' programme for forcibly resettling and 'protecting' hundreds of thousands of rural people living in 'insecure' areas.[10] Then came a series of young, eager US Special Forces teams, concentrating particularly on minority tribal groups living along the South Vietnam frontier with Laos and Cambodia. They were followed by CIA personnel, working under the ill-disguised cover of several US civilian agencies, who had the mission of selecting and training Vietnamese assassination and counter-terror squads and directing them against the NLF 'infrastructure'.

Counter-insurgency strategies

For all the excitement and high-level attention given to 'unconventional warfare' during the early 1960s, probably a majority of ranking US army and US Air Force officers had strong doubts about its efficacy. Products of the Second World War and Korean War experiences, they doubted that razzle-dazzle counter-guerrilla squads, police networks, 'psywar' leaflets, and civic action teams could do the job against well organised, truly dedicated opponents. Rather than attempting to 'meet the enemy on his own terms', they felt that strategies should be developed to force the enemy on to different terms, inherently more advantageous to the US and ARVN. As one military writer said, 'Limited conflicts can be remoulded, by means of basic and applied research.'[11]

The counter-insurgent aimed to outwit, outmanoeuvre, and perpetually harass the guerrilla enemy into submission, whereas more conventional practitioners believed it necessary to force the enemy into ultimate confrontations of one kind or another. The image of victory for the counter-insurgent was a situation where guerrilla casualties slowly mounted, morale slipped, food and water became short, rest was impossible, counter-guerrilla ambushes succeeded, medical support was increasingly weak, people did not help as before, and the government received better intelligence from which to fashion a permanently downward spiral for the anti-government elements. Ultimately the latter would become manageable, at worst a problem of social banditry, at best accepting disarmament and amnesty.

By contrast, more conventional officers long had hopes of luring the enemy's main force units into the open and destroying them. When the NLF failed to oblige US conventional war strategists, they focused increasingly on sealing off the borders and coastline. When this too failed to prevent the RVN's decline, attention shifted to the modulated bombing of North Vietnam to force a complete policy reversal by the revolutionaries. Meanwhile the first US ground combat units were sent into South Vietnam to ward off imminent disaster for the ARVN. From then on counter-insurgency had little relevance and conventional concepts were dominant.

In retrospect it was an inevitable sequence. With RVN and ARVN the counter-insurgents had poor material with which to work. And the NLF was hardly a group of inexperienced upstarts. One American expert, realising these grave deficiencies yet still totally committed to intervention, concluded that the RVN 'must be *forced* to accept US judgment and direction', not only at the highest level but also, more importantly, by means of a complete American control apparatus right down to the local level. This apparatus involved the so-called advisors, who in effect held the purse-strings on 'all reconstruction and pacification type expenditures', and who directly commanded their Vietnamese counterparts unless countermanded by the next higher echelon.[12] Ironically, American and British specialists could not provide their Vietnamese clients with counter-insurgency techniques or expertise superior to what the NLF already possessed, and could only provide superior technological gadgetry. In 1961 Pentagon sources leaked to the American press hints about 'new techniques and weapons specially developed to meet local needs', ranging from a 'microjet' rocket to a 'silent killing device fired from a plastic tube no longer than a drinking straw'. They also mentioned a 'heavier-than-air explosive gas' that could be dumped over the enemy and ignited by a mere spark—a weapon that required another decade or more of testing before being used in any quantity.[13]

In the same year, at a US National Security Council meeting presided over by President Kennedy, it was decided that a major new technologically-oriented effort would be mounted to halt enemy movement back and forth across the rugged, ill-defined Laotian and Cambodian borders. Ground operations were to be bolstered by 'regular aerial border surveillance and the application of technological area-denial techniques (e.g. CW, BW, light plastic, air droppable land mines, fluorescent materials, etc.).'[14] Authorisation was also provided for establishing in Vietnam a combined US–Vietnamese Combat Development and Test Centre, which would 'devise practical application of the latest scientific techniques to the conditions of sub-limited warfare now being waged throughout Southeast Asia'.[15] If the counter-insurgency specialists complained about this essentially palliative

approach to problems, there is no record of it. The nose of the technological camel was under the tent, and within a few years it would walk
away with the tent entirely.

By far the most important piece of machinery imported by the
Americans during the entire war was the helicopter. On 11 December
1961 two US Army helicopter companies of 36 Shawnee helicopters
and 370 officers and men landed in Saigon.[16] In later years literally
thousands of American helicopters roamed South Vietnamese skies,
transporting infantry, supplying outposts, evacuating dead and
wounded, serving as gun platforms, rocket launchers, command
centres, reconnaissance probes—indeed doing just about every military
job imaginable. Helicopters became the new status symbol for
ambitious, aggressive generals and colonels, in the same way that
commanders had looked to close air support during the Korean War
and tanks in the Second World War. 'The sky is a highway without
roadblocks', rhapsodised Senator Henry Jackson in 1963 after briefings
from the Pentagon. 'The helicopter', he continued, 'frees the government forces from dependence on the poor road system and the canals
which are the usual arteries of communication.'[17] Later General William
Westmoreland was quoted as saying that without the helicopter the
US would have required in South Vietnam one million more men than
the 540,000 he eventually obtained.[18]

During 1962 and early 1963 the helicopter gravely disrupted NLF
operations, particularly when ten or fifteen craft were able to fly in a
heavily armed company of ARVN rangers or marines to block normal
retreat and dispersion tactics. Indeed, Dr Nguyen Khac Vien,
prominent DRVN interpreter of contemporary historical events,
recently gave 1962 helicopter tactics grudging credit as the third most
difficult problem faced by modern Vietnamese revolutionaries.[19]
Eventually partial counter-measures were worked out by the NLF,
including quicker alerts, diversionary tactics, 50 calibre and 20 mm
anti-aircraft guns and assorted ground obstacles. Nevertheless, the
helicopter remained a major problem until 1974, when the combined
impact of SA-7 heat-seeking missiles and the steadily declining
maintenance capabilities of the RVN air force finally reduced it to
manageable proportions.[20]

In the long run, such US and ARVN air mobility had a very serious,
if hidden deficiency. Since about 80 per cent of the people of Vietnam
happened to live along the 'poor' roads and canals that Senator Jackson
had been so proud to bypass, and since even a thousand or more
perfectly maintained helicopters could never hope to tie in all of South
Vietnam's villages and hamlets on a day-to-day basis, increased air
travel tended inevitably to draw the RVN even further from the
humdrum realities of creating political and social credibility at the
local level. It did not even truly resolve the problem of establishing local

physical control, since ARVN units at the village level knew they could always call on massive firepower from the outside rather than develop their own skills for expanding an effective village intelligence and surveillance network. It was part of a political degeneration that had begun in early French colonial times, was accentuated by the French introduction of road-bound truck and armoured vehicle convoys against the Viet-Minh, and now culminated with American helicopters floating across the monsoon clouds, swooping down occasionally to wreak destruction or supply an isolated blockhouse.

By early 1964 it was apparent to US strategists that neither the counter-insurgency specialists nor the multiple squadrons of American helicopters were stopping the NLF. Indeed, the NLF was now using those same roads and canals ignored by air power proponents to move personnel, equipment and supplies at night, gradually surrounding the districts and provincial towns, mobilising tens of thousands of new, eager fighters and support groups for larger political and military actions.[21]

Each US adviser had his own list of reasons why the ARVN was doing so poorly. Almost none of them dared to re-examine the deeper historical and motivational causes of NLF success. To have done so might have led to the conclusion that further support for the RVN was senseless, and under the new Johnson administration that was still a taboo.

Conventional strategies, 1965–8
Instead, US analysts and policy makers chose to focus even more attention on cadres and supplies coming to the NLF from North Vietnam. This may have been the worst American strategic blunder of the war, since it concentrated tremendous resources and intellectual energy for the next eight years on what was essentially a secondary problem. While communist cadres had been moving in both directions since 1955, their numbers were so small and the borders so long and mountainous that even an RVN frontier control system as sophisticated as those devised in East Germany could not have stopped them. The quantity of supplies moving south in 1963 and early 1964, even according to US intelligence analysts, was still minute, the equivalent of one C-130 Hercules flight per month by contemporary reckonings. By 1965 this situation had changed, of course, but only as part of a decision to fight incoming American troops immediately rather than to retreat and reduce operations back to small-unit guerrilla proportions. Whatever the case, the movement back and forth along what came in the West to be called the Ho Chi Minh Trail remained a supporting leg of the liberation struggle, not the heart of it.

Completely frustrated in counter-insurgency, frantically searching for new strategies, a consensus rapidly developed in the new Johnson administration that it might well be possible to force the leaders of North Vietnam to call off the struggle in the South. What to do about the North thus became the great American preoccupation. An amphibious assault on North Vietnam might risk massive Chinese counter-action; stretching a wall of ground troops and fortifications below the 17th Parallel from the Gulf of Tonkin across southern Laos to the Thai border would be too costly and debilitating. Throughout late 1964 and early 1965 the primary strategy was to threaten and implement a modulated bombing of the North, with the expectation that Hanoi would eventually terminate the struggle in the South. When this failed, a more complicated strategy of attrition involving intensive bombings, electronic detection, anti-personnel devices, and ground and naval gunfire was instituted. US capital-intensive warfare had truly arrived in Indochina, although it was another six years before it reached its peak technological complexity in the Igloo White system.

Meanwhile, also in early 1965, the grave demoralisation among ARVN forces, the pathetic *coups* and counter-*coups* among Saigon's generals, and the regimental scale attacks by the People's Liberation Armed Forces (PLAF), the increasingly well-armed and competent NLF main force units, convinced President Johnson to begin a massive transfer of American ground combat units to South Vietnam. By January 1966 there were nearly 200,000 US troops in South Vietnam and the numbers eventually reached their peak at 540,000 in 1968. Huge offensive operations were mounted to either smash the PLAF physically or break its will to fight.[22] Even the most cautious military analysts, both in the US and elsewhere, expected the Vietnamese revolutionaries temporarily to concede the overwhelming impact of American technology and firepower and retreat to minor skirmishing and political proselytising, hoping for better times later.

The key American battle concepts in South Vietnam in 1965–7 were constant mobility and unprecedented firepower, a combination of movement and mass that strategists clearly considered invincible. Air power held everything together. C-130 Hercules transports shifted whole regiments from one end of the country to another in a matter of hours.[23] Within tactical sectors swarms of helicopters dropped battalions in and pulled them out, a leapfrogging technique aimed at exploiting the tiniest hint of battle opportunity. Small O-1 and O-2 reconnaissance aircraft floated back and forth over the hills and plains, checking for any evidence of the enemy. When they found something, no matter how questionable, attack aircraft were requested and could arrive within 5–15 minutes, dropping 500- or 750-pound high explosive bombs, napalm, white phosphorus, and anti-personnel fragmentation and cluster-bomb units, and shooting rockets or 20 mm cannon at anything that spoke of human existence.[24]

Because high performance jets were too fast and lacking in

manoeuvreability for many close air support requirements, the US Army built up a large fleet of UH-1 (Huey) helicopter gunships to loiter over 'Indian country' and spray death on anything that moved. Soon the USAF introduced a competitor: old C-47 transports converted to side-firing weapons systems, the infamous 'Puff the Magic Dragon' which could circle lazily, particularly at night, and dispense up to 18,000 rounds per minute from three 7.62 mm Gatling guns mounted in the doors.[25]

Such air and ground activity called for incredibly complex command and communications arrangements. The first complete air-ground control system was activated in autumn 1965. There were six by 1968, and air space over South Vietnam became the most crowded in the world, traffic exceeding that of even the north-east corridor in the United States. That year, in the ten largest fields in South Vietnam, there were more than five million takeoffs and landings. Three airfields, Bien Hao, Da Nang, and Tan Son Nhut (Saigon), each averaged 70,000 per month, 15,000 more than Chicago's O'Hare International, the busiest in the United States.[26] At times it was necessary to put a general or a colonel in an airborne transport equipped as a circling command post. The USAF was extremely proud of having been granted control of seven different air arms operating in the Khe Sanh battle zone between mid-January and the end of March 1968, and during that period they used an airborne post to direct 24,654 air strikes and 4,000 reconnaissance, forward air control and airlift flights.[27]

Meanwhile, on the ground, communications specialists constructed the most modern grid of wide-band troopscatter facilities for long-range use, microwave stations for traffic inside South Vietnam, and intricate telephone linkups at every base and command post. A US Signal Corps general explained, 'To watch every hole and tree in the country and be able to do something about enemy action when it takes place, you need a big, organised and complicated communications system. You have to blanket the whole country with communications.'[28] Between early 1962 and the end of 1968 US Army Signal Corps personnel in Vietnam jumped from under 1000 to over 23,000 men, by far the largest communications organisation ever deployed in a combat theatre. In the same period message traffic through two theatre-level communication centres, at Phu Lam (Saigon) and Nha Trang, ballooned from 35,000 per month to 3,000,000 per month. The next year, 1969, an ultra-modern, commercially installed automatic dial telephone system was handling one million calls per day, and division commanders found themselves in the seemingly envious position of being able to call the smallest subordinate installation or the most distant US base in the world, anywhere, any time.[29] In the same way, staff officers in the Pentagon, or even the President himself, could talk with local commanders in Vietnam and receive an almost infinite quantity of computerised data on what was happening, or said to be happening. In the opinion of one CIA intelligence specialist, this ready availability of minutiae about the war 'provided the generals and admirals an opportunity to avoid the kind of strategic thinking they were being paid to do. Instead, they could immerse themselves in the tactical nitty-gritty of the war and, in effect, serve as rather high-paid company or squadron commanders.'[30]

Parkinson's Law may be especially applicable to communications systems, since the more radios and telephones that were available, the more military personnel at all levels tended to use them for decreasingly meaningful purposes. Creighton Abrams once told combat signalmen, 'You fellows belong to something that is almost a bottomless pit. No matter how big you make the system, there are more people going to want to send things over it.'[31] He might have added that they would usually want to send it faster than the next person, so that precedence indicators on messages would undergo a rapid inflation. In Vietnam 50 per cent of all traffic came to be classed as 'flash' or 'immediate', and the Joint Chiefs of Staff had to create a new category, 'super flash', to make sure that what was truly flash action was effectively disseminated.[32]

The cost of these antenna arrays, transmitting and receiving stations, humidity-free temperature-controlled buildings, diesel generators, and endless wired circuits ranged into billions of dollars. One-third of all major items of equipment in Vietnam were communications-electronics items, and over 50,000 different types of communications-electronics replacement and repair parts were stocked by the US supply system in Vietnam.[33]

Yet, in the end, even this vast system could not meet the technocratic fantasy of the Signal Corps general who wanted to service a system watching 'every hole and tree in the country.' The PLAF and NLF remained intact and capable of functioning efficiently with only the smallest fraction of the modern communications equipment available to the Americans.

Given the manner in which US forces were accustomed to fighting and living, a tremendous amount of effort and manpower had to go into elaborate base construction logistics and rear area maintenance and service operations. Most important was the construction and constant improvement of aircraft facilities, including eight 10,000-foot jet bases, 100 airfields to accommodate a huge fleet of C-130 Hercules transports, and literally thousands of semi-permanent landing zones for helicopters. In line with the strategic concept of moving anywhere by air in the shortest possible time, the concrete objective was to have 'every point in South Vietnam within twenty-five kilometers of an airfield.'[34] Since the Second World War-style pierced steel planting was not strong or smooth enough for high performance aircraft, a new combination of landing mats and waterproof membranes was devised.

Ninety million square feet were laid in 1966-7 alone. Nevertheless, dust whipped up by aircraft still proved destructive to delicate engines and electronics gear, and also settled into food and open wounds, causing problems of infection. Thus an additional 40 million square yards of bituminous binder were spread over the ground beyond the mats and membranes. This operation had to be repeated every few weeks, so in the end it was considerably less expensive to bypass portable matting entirely and spend the time constructing permanent hardstands of concrete or asphalt.[35]

Almost as significant as the airfields was the building of six entirely new deep-water port complexes to supplement the single, extremely constricted port of Saigon available in 1965. These massive facilities included not only deep-draught berths for ocean-going ships but also wharfs for barges, hydraulic dredges, endless rows of warehousing, petroleum storage tanks, ammunition dumps, electric generator ships, maintenance shops, personnel cantonments, access roads, water and sewage treatment stations, and even ice production and milk recombination plants. Ninety per cent of all US military supplies and equipment arrived at these ports by deep-draught vessels, and were then either stockpiled or transported to hundreds of secondary depots and operational bases around South Vietnam.[36]

Yet even while the supply train constantly expanded, American forces never seemed to have enough of what they requisitioned. Ironically, one reason was oversupply, the undisciplined pouring of material into Vietnam and then its loss within the system or pilferage by American and Vietnamese personnel. The more basic reason, however, was the incredibly intricate nature of the US war machine collectively and most items of equipment individually. As one army officer admitted, 'If you look around this country, you will see a lot of expensive US engineering equipment which is idle because the part it needs is big, expensive, and can only be had in Detroit.'[37]

Electric power seemed in perennial short supply. Again it was Parkinson's Law with a vengeance, demand always catching up with and attempting to surpass availability. The real problem here was not basic military needs (communication equipment, lighting, maintenance shops, etc.), but rather the unprecedented creature comforts provided for the American soldier in Vietnam. Early units had lived in open tents or barracks and eaten B-rations supplemented by locally purchased fruits and vegetables and a variety of dairy products. Generators were just beginning to catch up with these demands when individual personnel were permitted to buy and install television sets, room-size air conditioners, electric fans, hot plates, small refrigerators, toasters, and electric percolators—creating another huge demand for electricity. Power requirements increased to 2000 watts per man, four times that of the Second World War. Up to 100 gallons of water per man per day was pumped into US cantonments, mostly for showers. This entire system failed to produce contented GIs, despite costing the American taxpayer an estimated $3000 per man to put together and operate—not including individual purchases from salary and material acquired through 'moonlight requisitioning', i.e. tolerated theft.[38]

Fuel was another serious bottleneck, but for somewhat different reasons. Even though it was well known that aircraft, trucks, tanks, boats, bulldozers, generators, and bituminous spreaders are insatiable fuel guzzlers, the Pentagon continued to rely heavily on commercial operators, namely Esso, Shell, and Caltex, to supply, store, and (for several years at least) distribute this indispensable military item. Such corporations were extremely reluctant to expand their facilities beyond likely post-war demand, and they asked for more compensation for the immediate physical hazards involved than the Pentagon was prepared or able to provide. Nonetheless, in 1965, 92 per cent of fuel storage was still at the two commercial tank farms of Nha Be (nine miles south of Saigon) and Da Nang. Not surprisingly, PLAF commanders directed numerous attacks on these two locations and US fuel losses were considerable. In 1966 at least 30 of the 50 areas where US forces were located had no bulk fuel storage capability, not even collapsible bladders. Although the Joint Chiefs of Staff in February 1967 finally ordered construction of 4.4 million barrels of military storage capacity in Vietnam, the actual amount apparently never exceeded 2.6 million barrels. Considering that US military consumption alone rose to more than three million barrels *per month* in 1968, US forces were extremely lucky not to have been forced to reduce operations due to fuel short-ages.[39] In early 1975 the ARVN was not so fortunate.

US private corporations had an operational impact far beyond petroleum logistics. President Johnson's decision in November 1965 not to order a general call-up of the Reserve and National Guard was a major reason. Apart from the Air Force, the majority of organised military construction, facilities engineering, and base services units were in the Reserve and National Guard. Somebody had to be found who would take their place, preferably people who, for a price, would stay longer than the twelve months specified for military personnel. The Pentagon quickly negotiated contracts with a handful of American corporations, the fortunate recipients simply agreeing to furnish labour, organisation, and management while the US government supplied all equipment, repair parts, tools, materials, and even housing quarters and eating facilities. As political pressures began to grow at home there was an executive effort to limit the total number of American servicemen in Vietnam, and to pay civilian contractors to do the same jobs. Construction operations alone employed 51,000 civilian personnel in 1966, 10 per cent of them American. Costs were about two-and-a-half times greater than for similar construction projects in the US, not only because of transportation costs but also because corporations demanded and received outlandish amounts of money in the name of 'expediting completion'. The same was true of design and manufacturing companies who had equipment badly needed by the Pentagon.[40] By 1968, the emphasis had shifted to facilities engineering and base services, with a single corporation, Pacific Architects and Engineers (PA and E), receiving over £100 million per year (plus government supplies) to employ and direct 24,000 civilians, 5 per cent American, 15 per cent 'third country nationals' (mostly from the Philippines, South Korea, and Taiwan), and 80 per cent Vietnamese.[41]

To the surprise of almost everyone, including some socialist allies of the DRV and NLF, Vietnam's revolutionary leadership did not order a strategic retreat to try to avoid the unprecedented impact of this modern US juggernaut. Rather, they sent in tens of thousands of well equipped, extensively trained troops from the North, combined them with the experienced, highly motivated NLF main force units, and attempted to counter-attack the American troops vigorously wherever conditions were remotely favourable. They did not expect to achieve a general military victory over US forces, or even necessarily to win a single crucial battle, but rather to frustrate American plans for creating a steamroller effect, a strategic initiative that could not be parried. Given the limited geographical size of Vietnam and the magnitude of the American invasion, the option of constant withdrawal and reduction of unit size might have proved disastrous. Instead, offence was the best form of defence, the sole objective being the creation of a situation in which Americans would finally realise they could not win. Only then could diplomatic negotiations begin.[42]

Attacking the Americans in this manner obviously had its liabilities. Casualty rates were very heavy. US forces wiped out whole villages as they tried to retaliate effectively. Far more supplies and personnel had to come from North Vietnam, running the bombing gauntlet all the way. Most seriously, the DRV and NLF ran the risk of seeing the entire conflict remoulded in ways advantageous to US capital-intensive warfare and disadvantageous to people's war, the multi-faceted political and military campaigns in which the NLF excelled. The US Army Limited War Laboratory had said that it 'strongly believes that the technological superiority of the United States is an advantage which should be fully exploited by forces in the field'.[43] But the principles of judo could be employed by the smaller power against the larger, using the movements of the opponent to defeat him, whacking his sensitive areas and reflex points rather than punching him head on.[44]

One of the key Vietnamese strategies for avoiding this American-devised technological pitfall was to continue to retain a potent capability for individual political proselytising, village mobilisation, and district- and province-level guerrilla actions *even while* constantly rebuilding and launching main force attacks against US forces. Over the years, as PLAF main force units slowly increased in size and complexity, acquiring ever more sophisticated military technology in their own right, the NLF ability to attract a grass-roots following and thus to counter RVN pacification efforts with local resources and initiatives was never really lost. In any given tactical region or province it was possible for the revolutionary forces to shift back and forth across the military spectrum, depending on the degree of enemy pressure or sudden weakness in enemy dispositions. Sometimes the situation was so grim in a given district or province that only a few underground cadres could survive, while others were forced to flee and join operations elsewhere. But the objective always was to rejuvenate locally while constantly improving the equipment and sophistication of main force units.

By mid-1967 US troop levels had already reached 470,000 but field commanders were unable to report any definitive success. Indeed, General Westmoreland was forced to admit privately to President Johnson that 'unless the will of the enemy is broken or unless there was unravelling of the VC infrastructure the war could go on for five years'.[45] Given American casualty figures and the huge financial deficits already being incurred this was bad news for Johnson. There were others who looked at continuing RVN corruption and ARVN ineffectiveness and wondered if it would ever end.

Area denial strategies
Partly in response to such disturbing realities, American attention shifted slowly away from large-scale sorties against PLAF main force units and towards the development of position defences around a number of strategic locations. An integral part of this strategy was the forced depopulation of vast areas of rural South Vietnam. Early American designation of large 'free fire zones', followed by B-52 raids, F-4 Phantom attacks on vague 'targets of opportunity', long-range artillery and naval 'harassment and interdiction' fire, and movement of villagers at gunpoint during 'search and destroy' missions, had already sent millions of South Vietnamese citizens to guarded resettlement camps or to pitiful urban ghettos and shanty towns adjacent to American bases. Now US counter-revolutionary theorists put an approving name on it, 'forced urbanisation', and US commanders proceeded to co-ordinate every weapon in their arsenal to separate the remaining Vietnamese rural populace from the armed liberation forces. Mao Tse-tung had once said that revolutionaries were to the people as fish to the sea. Having failed to annihilate the fish or even locate them properly, US strategists proposed to drain the water from the fish and leave the latter floundering, finally vulnerable to identification and destruction.

One large-scale technique of 'area denial' was defoliation, using C-123 transports equipped with multiple wing nozzles to spray various types of herbicides. Defoliation was first employed by the British in Malaya. The US began defoliation operations in South Vietnam no later than January 1962. In late 1966 there was a major expansion to 18 C-123 spray aircraft and accompanying fighter escorts.[46] By the time mounting pressure from national and world public opinion forced the Nixon administration to abandon the programme in 1970, US pilots had sprayed about one-tenth of South Vietnam's cropland and nearly one-third of the country's total forest acreage.[47]

Seeking a more total technique than defoliation, US Army engineers came up with fleets of 20-ton caterpillar tractors fitted with 11-foot wide, 2.5-ton blades to smash down and plough under all vegetation. Encased with an extra 14 tons of steel armour to ward off enemy fire, these 'Rome ploughs' began in 1965–7 by clearing 300- to 600-foot-wide swathes on both sides of many roadways. In 1968, Rome ploughs were directed against whole zones of potential enemy concentration, for example the 7000-acre Boi Loi woods in Tay Ninh and the 9000-acre Ho Bo woods in Binh Duong. By mid-1971 it is estimated they had obliterated 750,000 acres of vegetation, roughly the size of the state of Rhode Island.[48] In 1974 the Provisional Revolutionary Government of the Republic of South Vietnam (PRG) reported continuing extensive use of bulldozers by the ARVN, including the flattening of villages reconstructed since the January 1973 Paris Agreement.[49]

Several serious American efforts to produce huge firestorms in areas previously dried up by defoliation were made during 1966–8. US military commanders studied the Second World War Allied fire-bombing of Hamburg, Dresden, and Tokyo, then invited US Forest Service specialists in to convert the technique to non-urban conditions in Vietnam. Magnesium incendiary bombs were dropped at the precise times and places most conducive to producing vast self-feeding conflagrations, although many uncontrollable variables, in particular residual tropical moisture during the dry season, affected the fires. One fire, begun in March 1968 as a by-product of conventional bombing of the U Minh Forest near the southernmost tip of Vietnam, was successfully expanded and prolonged for several months by rocket fire from US Navy vessels lying offshore.[50]

Weather modification, in this case large-scale rainmaking, was another area denial and area harassing technique on which US specialists spent much time and achieved only partial results. It was first attempted by the CIA in South Vietnam in 1963, and the USAF subsequently greatly expanded the research and testing and then flew innumerable cloud seeding missions over parts of central Vietnam and southern Laos. While the main objectives were to slow down PLAF transport and divert people to road repair, rainmaking at certain times also waterlogged crops and increased the danger of valley flooding. It may have been a factor in the 1971 Red River floods in North Vietnam, although this was never admitted by US officials.[51]

The planting of vast zones in South and North Vietnam, Laos and Cambodia with air-delivered mines and time-delay bombs was another form of area denial. American scientists spent considerable time, money, and ingenuity perfecting weapons that would cover the largest area, instil the most fear, and produce the most intractable injuries. Some bombs were timed to explode when medical personnel were likely to be evacuating earlier casualties. The Dragontooth anti-personnel mine was artfully camouflaged and constructed partly of plastic, the jagged slivers of which surgeons found very hard to detect in the limbs of victims. The Spider mine sent trip threads out in eight directions after landing, the better to catch anyone walking in the area. Such weapons remain scattered on the ground throughout Indochina and will threaten the population for decades to come.

It was often argued by apologists of US operations that defoliation, ploughing, burning, rainmaking, and mine sowing were aimed at enemy combatants and not at the civilian populace. But millions of people lived and farmed in the areas affected. Once most of them were forced to leave, continuation of such programmes made it more likely they would not dare to return. Even those whose lands had not been affected thought twice before returning, for fear of subsequent operations.

While technologically sophisticated programmes were important, more conventional techniques of constant air attack and artillery and naval gunfire created most of the refugees in South Vietnam. As early as 1965, a US officer advocating the establishment of a large new free-strike zone in a populated area said, 'If these people want to stay there and support the communists, then they can expect to be bombed'.[52] Emphasis was placed on the perpetual threat of death and destruction. Many civilians were prepared to build underground shelters and try to survive one, five, or even ten such attacks, but American tactics became so refined that rural inhabitants in many areas were kept in almost constant terror, afraid to till their fields, to sleep above ground, or to sit down together around the cooking fire. With increased use of B-52s from 1968 onwards, a single raid could blanket an entire valley with high explosive bombs, often without even a minute's warning. In such conditions millions more fled, and indeed often were encouraged to do so by NLF cadres.

Those who chose to remain had to function with what amounted to military precision, farming at night, sleeping by day in (or beside) reinforced bunkers, running long distances to secondary hiding places in the event of NLF intelligence alerts of search and destroy operations or B-52 raids. This result had been foreseen and warned against by counter-insurgency specialists such as John P. Vann, who argued that 'by leaving the enemy in unchallenged control of such [free strike] areas, we encourage and assist him in the decision to move most of his forces into other contested areas, leaving behind only that cadre needed to control the remaining population and their agricultural output'.[53] Although it has never been confirmed publicly, intelligence intercept vessels from the Soviet Union hovered at various points between Guam and the Vietnam coastline to provide general vectoring and monitoring information to locations in both North and South Vietnam. B-52s coming from Thailand may have been tracked by PLAF ground radar stations in Laos and Cambodia. Exactly how much of this intelligence reached specific localities in time to do much good is unknown, although Vietnamese in a position to know have spoken of receiving 15–20 minutes' warning of B-52 attacks in many cases.

In contrast to the PLAF, which almost never lacked military intelligence from a wide variety of sources, US and ARVN forces faced a constant paucity of reliable information on enemy activities. Much money was spent on recruiting and paying agents, but their information was often 'soft', too general, or too late, and many of them were never really trusted. Since people did not often willingly tell US and ARVN troops who the NLF cadres were, where they hid, or what sort of ties existed, there was a tendency to try to force it out of them in one way or another, but that only made things worse the next time around.

Lacking a popular base in the countryside, US strategists began searching for alternative methods of locating the enemy. Tremendous amounts of money and research time went into this problem. Many devices were carried to Vietnam and tested extensively, only to be proved inadequate in some way. For example, one laboratory devised marker dye capsules to be left unobtrusively on village perimeters. People leaving the village after curfew would stain their feet and be picked up as VC suspects. At another point kits were distributed locally to test people's hands for gunpowder traces.[54] Perhaps the ultimate in technological brainstorming involved placing a small colony of live bedbugs in a container fitted with a sensitive microphone to catch the bugs' nervous anticipation whenever the scent of human beings came in the vents, for example when searching underground tunnels. Unresolved problems included how to exclude the scent of the American soldier carrying the contraption, or if it was deposited somewhere and monitored, how to keep the bedbugs alive.[55]

Most detection techniques were less humourous. The US Army Limited War Laboratory attempted almost anything that ambitious, creative engineers brought to them. As they advertised, 'solutions involving technological breakthrough and unique, different or novel approaches are particularly desired.' They tried to create a situation where 'even a solitary, motionless, camouflaged enemy is a "discontinuity". He can be identified by Uhf (ultra-high frequency) radiometry, dialectric loading, olfactory analysis, ir (infra-red) illumination and nucleonic sensing.'[56] Testing new gadgets meant ordering artillery to fire on whatever the instrument sensed, or was believed to sense. Detection systems were eventually accepted or rejected according to physical body counts in the experimental area.[57] There is no record of test personnel ever proving that bodies were those of soldiers rather than civilians.

By the late 1960s in Indochina prodigious numbers of new sensing and collection devices were being employed, from tape recorders and ground radars to aircraft-mounted cameras, infra-red instruments and side-looking radar. Although none of these instruments could really distinguish an armed opponent from an unarmed civilian, a decision had already been made to attack and try to kill any 'discontinuity'. Thus, men, women, and children going about their daily chores often became body count statistics; they had been unlucky enough to live in an area subject to total electronic warfare.

On the other hand, knowledgeable, disciplined PLAF soldiers and support forces were often very quick to perceive that a new search technique was being used against them and to develop ingenious responses. The head of the Pentagon's south-east Asia research and development effort once admitted, 'The enemy has shown extraordinary cleverness in countering some new things we have introduced. It is seldom more than a few months after we introduce something new before we capture a document that tells the enemy, in essence, how to counter the new device.'[58] When helicopters were rigged up to sense the smell of urine, PLAF units were reported to have responded effectively by hanging pots full of urine in trees well away from their camps. Infra-red cameras were used with considerable success at night, particularly along main truck routes later in the air war, but it was still possible to build diversionary fires, to let bomb fires burn indeterminably, to spread trucks out and hope that the warm, rain-soaked jungle foliage would disperse the heat, or, as a last resort, to switch back temporarily to fleets of specially reinforced bicycles capable of carrying up to 800 pounds per load. A variety of sensitive airborne metal detectors were introduced by US forces, but they often became confused by the plethora of bomb fragments and disabled vehicles.

The Lockheed Aircraft Corporation developed sensors to catch electro-emissions of motor ignitions and these were being employed widely by 1970–1. But once again deception procedures won out. Somehow, 600–1000 T-54 tanks were in fact available in three disparate locations for the PLAF 1972 Spring Offensive, compared to the prior US intelligence estimate of 50.[59] Before that campaign, General Westmoreland had declared publicly that the communist forces were incapable of a high level of fighting for more than a few days at a time, before having to re-group, re-supply and re-equip.[60] In reality, the offensive lasted for more than six months. The PLAF proved itself light enough and flexible enough to alter tactics and basic operating procedures rapidly, yet heavy enough and well enough trained and equipped to incorporate tanks, 130 mm artillery, heavy trucks, and long fuel pipelines into its overall offensive strategy.

The Nixon era

Looking back on events throughout Indochina, 1972 was the culmination of some seven years of searching by Vietnamese, Lao, and (after March 1970) Cambodian revolutionaries for ways to withstand, outmanoeuvre and eventually outperform the American technological juggernaut. The 1968 Tet Offensive throughout South Vietnam induced the US to begin gradual troop withdrawals and to accept the concept of a negotiated compromise. But it was extremely costly, especially in local cadres and experienced soldiers. In the late summer of 1968 the PLAF shifted temporarily to a military posture of strategic defence, abandoning the 'continuous offence' concept.[61] Throughout 1969 the US and ARVN 'accelerated pacification' programme made some headway, particularly in the Mekong delta. Meanwhile, the bombing in Laos was at its height, and the highly secret B-52 bombing of Cambodia was initiated—often involving more than half the total B-52 sorties in south-east Asia.[62] It was a time to fend and parry, waiting for the enemy to expose himself.

Realising that the time for US ground initiatives was running short, the Nixon administration decided in spring 1970 to assault the PLAF sanctuaries in eastern Cambodia, hoping to smash main force divisions that had withdrawn there as part of the late 1968 defensive shift. When the PLAF eluded this trap US troops spent considerable time trying to locate hidden supply dumps before being ordered to withdraw as a result of massive popular protests at home. Then, in what may have been the most serious US tactical error of the war, ARVN forces with American air support were launched into southern Laos in early 1971, hoping again to destroy elusive main force enemy units and perhaps to cut the Ho Chi Minh Trail by means of a series of fortifications—the very plan that had been discarded in 1964–5. Unlike the year before in Cambodia, on this occasion the combined PLAF and Pathet Lao divisions counter-attacked in force, for the first time employing tanks, long-range artillery, and radar-guided anti-aircraft guns in a large-scale mobile confrontation. The well trained, heavily equipped ARVN units cracked and ran, leaving their own tanks, trucks, and artillery behind. US helicopter losses were also heavy. The groundwork for the 1972 Spring Offensive had been laid.

Upon taking office in January 1969, Richard Nixon had had little choice but to accept the outgoing Johnson's policy of negotiations and troop withdrawals. His insistence on a policy of negotiating from strength, however, meant that some potent force had to replace outgoing American troops. While some advisors may have honestly believed that 'vietnamisation' would provide an eventual solution, it seems clear that neither Nixon nor ranking Pentagon officers were willing to depend on the ARVN, hardly the model of reliability, to preserve the prestige and power of 'the greatest nation on earth'. Thus more and more attention focussed on new and larger technological solutions, creating the most capital-intensive war machine yet imagined.

Perhaps most hope was placed in a programme code-named Igloo White, an automated air war system directed at the Ho Chi Minh Trail network. The earliest coherent effort of this kind had aimed to draw a line at the 17th Parallel and across southern Laos, to sprinkle sensors everywhere along that line, and then to try to kill anything that was detected. Nicknamed the McNamara Wall and installed in 1967, this system apparently was plagued with a number of malfunctions. In early 1968 air-dropped sensors around the fortress of Khe Sanh were credited with significantly improving detection of the PLAF in that one battle zone for a period of less than three months. Helping to protect such a point of defence was not the sort of tactical situation, however, that electronic and intelligence specialists would be expected to master. Rather, they were ordered to expand the McNamara Wall concept over the enemy's entire north–south logistical complex.[63] By early 1971 some $3 billion had been spent on the electronic components alone.[64]

At its peak operation in 1971–2, Igloo White was a tremendously ambitious, intricate system for seeking out and destroying truck convoys, supply depots, bivouacs, anti-aircraft sites, construction crews, repair teams, and just about any other signs of life in the hundreds of miles between the Mu Gia Pass on the North Vietnamese border and the general area where the borders of Laos, Vietnam and Cambodia converge. Ground sensors, airborne 'people sniffers', and infra-red detection equipment pinpointed local activity and transmitted this information automatically to a battery of IBM computers in Nakorn Phanom, Thailand. Depending on the nature of the alleged target, operational commanders at Nakorn Phanom ordered B-52s, fighter bombers, transports with side-firing weapons, or helicopters to vector in and attack, often on the basis of automatic firing signals. Much of this activity occurred at night, without pilots ever actually seeing the target. Meanwhile, during the day they increasingly unloaded 'smart bombs', guided in by diverse means usually beyond the reach of the pilot. As one commentator rhapsodised, 'The entire process, "from beep to bang", may take less than five minutes'.[55] The whole operation seemed like a wild scientist's dream come true.[66]

But as the 1972 Spring Offensive demonstrated, something had gone wrong with American planning. Researchers and operational commanders had failed to understand the enemy or give him enough credit for ingenuity. Once again, by making the termination or drastic curtailment of north–south traffic a pre-eminent measure of success, they had continued to ignore or downgrade other critical elements of the struggle throughout Indochina. The Ho Chi Minh Trail had become an obsession. Yet even within the terms of that obsession, US planners never fully appreciated how tens of thousands of men and women along the Ho Chi Minh Trail in 1971–2 could outwit the electronic battlefield or, when that failed, reconstruct with alacrity, multiply the number of roads and paths available for alternative travel, and strip the most damaged trucks for repair of the least damaged. Although the USAF predicted publicly that it would destroy 25,000 trucks on the Ho Chi Minh Trail in 1971, and later claimed to have destroyed at least 12,000, it seems likely that it put out of action permanently less than half that number. Meanwhile, China, the Soviet Union, Czechoslovakia, Poland, and the German Democratic Republic were making up those losses and more than making them up.[67] In the words of one CIA official, North Vietnam theoretically 'ran out of trucks at least seven or eight times while I worked on the North Vietnam desk. Each time this happened the JCS (Joint Chiefs of Staff) demanded to know why we were still seeing trucks in North Vietnam.[68] By early 1972 the Vietnamese and Lao forces had also significantly increased their anti-aircraft defences along the trail, to include SA-2 missile installations. Occasionally MiG-21 fighters made feints and challenges over Laos, enough to force tactical revisions and drain off some US aircraft for fighter cover.

Ground sensors were probably the least effective part of the Igloo White system, and when the 1972 Spring Offensive showed the weakness of the overall operation, it was decided to ignore most of the ground sensors and distant control mechanisms in favour of aircraft operating in the immediate target area. This involved placing diverse detection equipment, a computer, operators, and weaponry all in one aeroplane. As linear descendants of the C-47 and C-119 side-firing systems, C-130 transports were packed full of infra-red sensor equipment, powerful external spotlights, parachute flares, a computer, numerous operators, four 7.62 Gatling guns, four 20 mm guns, and the large amounts of ammunition needed to feed these rapid-firing weapons, and then let loose over the Ho Chi Minh Trail. By late 1971 the USAF had installed 40 mm rapid-firing cannon designed by a Swedish company in some C-130s, and in 1972 there were reports of 105 mm howitzers being tested, presumably firing out of rear cargo doors.[69]

By 1971 Igloo White was already running into another serious obstacle, the desire of the US Congress to further reduce the tremendous costs of the Indochina War. Although Pentagon witnesses tried to point out that the combination of vietnamisation and US air bombardment was significantly less expensive than maintaining half a million US ground troops in Vietnam (subject to much higher casualties, demoralisation, and domestic political opposition), Congress was looking at continuing inflation, balance of payments difficulties, and poor industrial productivity and searching hard for further cuts. Some congressmen were frankly sceptical of claimed bombing results, and in 1972 they were proved largely correct. A few even tried to turn Pentagon arguments on their head, pointing out that if the US bombing really accounted for 85 per cent of enemy war materiel destroyed, as claimed, then North Vietnam had what amounted to an indefinite hold on US policy, since the RVN would be immediately threatened if the bombing were terminated.

By mid-1972 even the military realised that the Igloo White system was not working and began dismantling a number of components.[70] A retired USAF colonel admitted that civilian and military officials alike 'are unable to understand and explain how forty-ton tanks and other heavy equipment have been able to penetrate so far south in the face of the massive air attacks that have been launched'. The effectiveness of the Ho Chi Minh Trail interdiction effort, he said, was being 'seriously questioned'.[71] Other officials, months earlier, had been even more severe in their analysis, arguing that 'the problem with the air war is that it has never been based on the needs of the war here but on the American economy. All those incredibly expensive defence contracts kept the economy hypoed up for years. But they didn't produce weapons that were useful for fighting a war in Southeast Asia'.[72]

American fascination with highly depersonalised space-age gadgetry such as Igloo White reinforced the tendency to neglect long-standing deficiencies in more mundane individual and crew-served weapons and ammunition, upon which ground combat troops depended for day-to-day survival. In a 1969 internal staff study, Army Material Command was severely criticised for failing to realise that some US weapons and most US ordnance were decidedly inferior to comparable Soviet, Chinese, and other types being used by the PLAF. 'The Soviet 130 mm gun is no doubt the finest artillery piece in existence in the world today in its class', commented the study, adding that even the US 175 mm gun had difficulty maintaining effective counter-battery fire because of relatively greater inaccuracy. This deficiency became obvious to anyone who observed the PLAF 1972 Spring Offensive, and it continued to undermine ARVN confidence right up to the final débâcle of early 1975. Perhaps even more important was the general inability of US fuses to withstand the mud and water of Indochina's monsoons. The resulting high incidence of duds in US grenades, mortar shells, rockets, and bombs was doubly disconcerting: it demoralised American and ARVN combat troops, even to the point where they ignored or discarded certain key weapons; and it allowed meticulous, highly efficient NLF and PLAF recovery teams to collect unexploded ordnance and use the components in a wide variety of ways. In contrast to US fuses, PLAF-employed fuses apparently withstood environmental conditions quite well, and ammunition was routinely stored in underwater caches.[73]

With the highly intricate Igloo White system failing to prevent massive PLAF attacks, more emphasis was placed on B-52 bombers as a terror weapon and means to force the DRV to make major diplomatic concessions. Short of nuclear weapons this was the only military option left to the Nixon administration. Political opposition to the indis-criminate use of B-52s was not strong enough prior to December 1972, either domestically or internationally, to prevent this technique from being employed with unprecedented ferocity, especially against Haiphong and Hanoi.

Although the Soviet Union had provided the DRV with increasing quantities of anti-aircraft equipment and the Vietnamese were using it in ever more sophisticated fashion, US electronic counter-measures (ECM) were still far enough ahead in summer 1972 to keep aircraft losses down to levels acceptable to the US. Another factor in this deadly electronic warfare was US remotely piloted vehicles (RPVs), small, fast, highly manoeuvreable drones capable of very low or very high flight and presenting minimum radar and infra-red signatures. Some RPVs were used for reconnaissance work over heavily defended targets, while others served as decoys and distributors of metal chaff to lead North Vietnamese radar operators away from the B-52s and fighter bombers (all of which were also equipped with elaborate ECM gear).[74] In addition, anti-radiation missiles (shrikes) were capable of locking in on Vietnamese anti-aircraft radar emissions, forcing operators to choose between temporarily shutting down their sets or enduring very accurate explosions.

This seeming predominance undoubtedly influenced President Nixon's decision to order the December 1972 B-52 raids over Hanoi and Haiphong, after having agreed to halt all attacks as part of the October negotiated settlement. His intention was to bomb the Vietna-mese back to the negotiating table on American terms. But North Vietnamese electronics specialists had made certain small but crucial modifications to their Soviet-supplied equipment, and these were combined with barrage firings of SA-2 missiles aimed at the B-52s. According to a knowledgeable DRV source the modifications involved adding one or more bands to their radar sets which US ECM gear was not prepared to jam.[75] An American aerospace journal claimed that Vietnamese radar operators computed the B-52 flight paths from emissions of the devices used to jam the radars.[76] Pentagon officials admitted to losing at least 16 B-52s in 12 days, the DRV asserted they had shot down 34, and the figure may well have been closer to the latter than the former, since USAF sources admitted they did not count aircraft that went down at sea or over Laos or Thailand, or planes that managed to land but were too badly damaged to repair.

Such losses could not have been sustained much longer without cutting permanently into Strategic Air Command (SAC) worldwide capabilities, since B-52s were no longer being manufactured. Equally important, the international outcry at the US scrapping of the October agreement and wanton destruction of urban centres, including hospitals, schools, and market-places, convinced Nixon to send Henry Kissinger back to Paris on diplomatic terms almost identical to those arranged earlier. Many Americans could not believe what had happened. When the chairman of the Joint Chiefs of Staff, Admiral Thomas Moorer, came before a congressional committee ten days after the termination of the bombing, Representative Daniel Flood, an outspoken hawk, expressed open bewilderment and frustration. 'My, my, my,' he exclaimed, 'that the . . . Department of Defence, the Pentagon, that they were going to be handcuffed by some little backward country called North Vietnam and completely knocked off balance, good gravy . . . here this little backward, these gooks . . . are knocking down your B-52s like clay pigeons, with all the sophisticated hardware which was beyond our own ken, being run by gooks. This is some kind of lesson.'[77] Indeed it was, although neither Representative Flood nor Admiral Moorer understood the full political and historical meaning. Nor did the American people, since many of them believed Richard Nixon when he claimed that the Christmas 1972 bombings had contributed to the peace settlement.[78] A new myth of air power as the decisive factor was on its way to being created.

But myths do not equal reality. True, US air power had managed to stave off complete ARVN defeat in spring 1972. True, wanton US B-52 targeting of North Vietnam's cities was one factor which the DRV and PRG had to take into serious account when formulating their negotiating position leading to the January 1973 Paris Agreement. However, it was not a preponderance of air power that caused President Nixon and his client, Nguyen Van Thieu, to refuse to implement key provisions of this same Paris Agreement. Rather it was the reverse, the disconcerting knowledge that if they *did* recognise the legitimacy of the PRG, did permit local commanders to arrange truces, did release political prisoners, did allow democratic freedoms, and did negotiate a tripartite National Council, then air power would quickly become irrelevant. The PRG could achieve its goals—non-violently, and US and ARVN air power would essentially be finished. In short, not to remain politically intransigent would almost certainly produce the results the US had been trying to prevent for more than 20 years, namely victory of a Vietnamese movement for national liberation led by a communist party.

The final defeat

Such American obduracy made further large-scale military confrontation almost inevitable, as each of the parties probably realised by late 1973. The only remaining question was exactly when it would happen, and, as a closely related factor, whether President Nixon or his appointed successor, Gerald Ford, would be able to order massive US air re-intervention. Watergate seriously reduced that threat, but did not altogether eliminate it. President Ford did not shift position towards serious implementation of the Paris Agreement, since no action was preferable to inherently self-defeating political action. When the DRV and PRG issued several clear warnings in late 1974, the US continued to bluff and bluster. In January 1975 the PLAF took the provincial capital of Phuoc Long in smooth, decisive fashion. The ARVN was so outclassed that Thieu did not even attempt a serious counter-attack.

Then, in March and April 1975, the war finally ended. Beginning with the central highlands, reaching the climax in the flatlands around Hue, Quang Ngai, and Da-Nang, and terminating on the access routes to Saigon, the PLAF showed themselves masters of that technology which they had chosen to integrate into their overall struggle concept. The ARVN, still enjoying a considerable quantitative technological edge as the result of continuing large-scale US military assistance and advisory support, found itself outmatched in every engagement. Although there were numerous reports of ARVN units lacking in close air support, helicopter mobility, adequate fuel, or artillery ammunition, these were more the product of gross mismanagement, failure to practise preventative maintenance, or just plain corruption, than the result of reduced US military aid. Aircraft, repair parts, fuel, and ammunition were all available somewhere in South Vietnam, but not at the right place at the right time. It was the first time in recent memory, certainly since 1948–9 in China, that an entire army enjoying complete air and sea superiority had been thrown into total rout. Casualties on both sides were fortunately rather light, since the essence of the campaign after 29 March was a series of efficient PLAF logistical manoeuvres to sustain momentum and follow the vanishing, panic-stricken ARVN.

Why did it happen so quickly, so decisively? Clearly the will to fight had gone out of even the 60,000–100,000 élite ARVN soldiers who had borne the brunt of serious combat since 1971. This loss of will did not occur primarily because of material conditions favouring one side or the other, but because of the fundamental political and historical advantages enjoyed by the revolutionary forces from 1945 onward. American strategists had talked in quasi-religious terms about establishing a military presence everywhere, of seeing everything.[79] The only conceivable way of accomplishing this task in any 'practical' sense was first to break the back of PLAF main force and regional units, then somehow to convert the entire effort into a massive, minutely organised campaign of police repression, with perhaps 100,000 teams of ten men each stationed every 500 yards or so across the entire face of South Vietnam. The PLAF and NLF stubbornly refused to permit the Americans to execute this strategy. Given American troop failure, there was no conceivable way that their sidekicks in ARVN could accomplish it on their own.

Such revolutionary success was not the work of angry farmers simply picking up their hoes and marching on the district chief's office, or of saintly grandmothers putting up their hands and stopping advancing American or ARVN tanks. Confrontations like this did indeed happen, but it was the *combination* of this anger and heroism with an understanding of politics, culture, history, and—not least—military arts and sciences, that brought the revolution on 30 April 1975 to the steps of Independence Palace in Saigon. The Viet-Minh and later PLAF commanders did not downgrade technology, but they incorporated it on their own terms and into their own schedule of training, repair, and logistical capabilities, not those of foreign military experts who had been raised on other traditions and who had their own policy motives for urging particular solutions.

ARVN commanders, by contrast, had mostly been reared in the French colonial army and tended to be awed by the physical power of a Western tank, aeroplane, or warship. When the Americans replaced the French and brought in even more military machinery, topped with a supreme self-confidence, it seemed they could not lose. After all, was not the US the most powerful nation on earth?

An American colonel, in the face of obvious declining US and ARVN fortunes in early 1975, began to fathom the enormity of the error:

They (ARVN) adopted tactics based on U.S. technology and wealth, without question. Their military ranks swelled—hardly a family would escape participation. Together we uprooted the people and erased their hamlets for the better employment of U.S. tactics. . . . After years of U.S. resistance, South Vietnam's only defense is cast in our image. The country is now tied inexorably to U.S. tactics, but, minus wealth, remains our dependent. Its economy is a shambles; agricultural plenty is a memory. Its manpower must defend everything, every place all the time. Vietnamization indeed! The very heart of that program was American. [80]

Eight weeks later an ARVN officer, facing imminent defeat, focused on some of the psychological implications of this US strategy:

You give an army the means to get around in helicopters or on roads, you accustom them to unlimited artillery and air support for long enough, you get them used to sleeping in bed at night, and what happens? I will tell you what happens. At a certain point neither the troops nor the officers are willing any longer to walk to battle, tracking their way through jungles if necessary. So they stay in their helicopters and get shot down or cut off from American rescue, or they drive along the road, where they get shelled or ambushed, and cut to pieces. Every officer knows this, but our army has become flabby and lazy over the years, and we owe some of that to the kind of luxury aid you gave us.[81]

An ARVN officer presumably either fled to the United States, or stayed in South Vietnam and learned that there was more to such demoralisation than misguided military decisions. It was a lesson to be learned not only by ARVN officers, but by Americans—civilian and military alike—and by the world.

NOTES

1. Tran Van Dinh, 'Did the U.S. stumble into the Vietnam War?', *The Christian Century* (5 June 1968) p. 755. Four years later, President Zachary Taylor sent a letter to the Vietnamese king apologising for the affair, but also threatening further action if Vietnam dared to retaliate.
2. George McT. Kahin and John W. Lewis, *The United States in Vietnam* (New York, 1969) p. 32.
3. Ralph H. Smuckler *et al., Report on the Police of Vietnam* (East Lansing, Mich., 1955).
4. For example, John F. Kennedy, 'America's Stake in Vietnam', *Vital Speeches* (1 Aug 1956) pp. 617–19; O. K. Armstrong, 'Biggest Little Man in Asia'. *Reader's Digest* (Feb. 1956) pp. 144–8.
5. See, for example, the assessment made by John Kenneth Galbraith at the request of President Kennedy, *Pentagon Papers*, Gravel edition, II, pp. 121–4.
6. Douglas Pike, *Viet Cong* (Cambridge, Mass., 1966).
7. See, for example, Denis J. Duncanson, *Government and Revolution in Vietnam* (London, 1968) pp. 21, 174–8, 297–8.
8. *The Pentagon Papers,* Gravel edition, II, p. 142.
9. Edward G. Lansdale. *In the Midst of Wars* (New York, 1972).
10. Duncanson, op. cit., pp. 311–27.
11. Lt.-Col. Robert B. Kalisch, 'DoD Basic Research and Limited Conflict', *OAR Research Review* (July 1968) pp. 10–11. I would like to take this occasion to thank Dr Milton Leitenberg of the Center for International Studies, Cornell University, for making available to me hundreds of technical articles and documents, without which this study would have been impossible. Eric Prokosch of the American Friends Service Committee, Philadelphia, was also extremely helpful in drawing my attention to certain specialised materials and in commenting on a preliminary draft of this study.

12. John P. Vann, 'Harnessing the Revolution in South Vietnam', 10 Sep 1965, internal policy paper circulated in Saigon. Vann estimated that 'over half the population is not accessible without a military operation', which led him to the classical apology of counter-revolutionary theorists that 'We are therefore faced with the dichotomy of having to maintain an autocratic government while laying the foundation for a democratically oriented one'.
13. *The Reporter* (14 Sep 1961). This 'Fuel Air Explosive' (FAX) gas was mentioned many times subsequently, and was reported as having been used in the last weeks of the US–Lon Nol effort in Cambodia. AP report from Phnom Penh, *Los Angeles Times* (2 Mar 1975).
14. 'CW' stands for chemical warfare, 'BW' for biological warfare. *Vietnam Commitments, 1961*. Prepared for the use of the Committee on Foreign Relations, US Senate, 20 Mar 1972, pp. 16, 23.
15. Ibid. See also *Pentagon Papers*, Gravel edition, II, p. 50.
16. For an account of operations by the first marine helicopter squadron in Vietnam, see Lt.-Col. Archie J. Clapp, 'Shu-Fly Diary', *US Naval Institute Proceedings* (Oct 1963) pp. 41–53.
17. Henry Jackson, 'A Key to Victory in Vietnam', *Army* (Mar 1963), p. 62.
18. Brig.-Gen. Lynn D. Smith, 'Facts, Not Opinions', *Army* (Dec. 1969) pp. 24–31.
19. The first was 1945–6, responding to terrible famine, consolidating an independent government and resisting French re-entry. The second was 1955–9, responding to the American replacement of the French in the South while trying to build socialism in the North. Discussion with the author, 31 Dec. 1974.
20. The SA-7, or 'Strela', is a shoulder-fired infra-red guided missile produced in the Soviet Union and somewhat similar to earlier models of the 'Redeye' missile produced by General Dynamics in the US.
21. Jeffrey Race, *War Comes to Long An* (Berkeley, 1972).
22. For example, in April 1965 military commanders in the field predicted that in 'perhaps a year or two' the US could 'break the will of the DRV/VC by depriving them of victory'. Report by McNamara on meeting with Ambassador Taylor and US military leaders in Honolulu, dated 21 April 1965. *Pentagon Papers,* Gravel edition, III, pp. 705–6.
23. Prior to massive US entry ARVN had already been provided with C-47, C-123, and C-7 (Caribou) transports, in addition to the US helicopter units mentioned previously. Maintenance, training and some flying time were provided by USAF 'Air Commando' crews, first sent as an 'advisory mission' in autumn 1961. George Weiss, 'Tac Air: Present and Future lessons, Problems and Needs', *Armed Forces Journal* (Sep 1971) pp. 30–6.
24. Prior to 1965, T-28 trainers and A-1 attack planes, both propeller-driven, had been flown in close air support missions by American and Vietnamese pilots. They often took an hour or more to arrive, the slowness actually due more to air control restrictions and confusion than to their slower air speeds. Contrary to later public relations sensitivities, up until 1966 there was no unwillingness to release photos of prop aircraft napalming villages. See, for example, *Aviation Week and Space Technology* (21 Feb 1966) p. 69.
25. Robert M. Loebelson, 'The US Military Chopper—A Prognosis', *Aerospace International* (Mar–Apr 1971) pp. 22–5; Lt.-Col. Ross E. Hamlin, 'Side-

Firing Weapons Systems', *Air University Review* (Jan/Feb 1970) pp. 76–88.
26. *Air Force/Space Digest* (June 1969).
27. Weiss, op. cit. The seven air arms were Royal Australian Air Force, Air America, US Army, Navy, Marines, VNAF, and US Seventh Air Force.
28. Quoting Brig.-Gen. Walter E. Lotz in 'The War that Needs Electronics', *Electronics* (16 May 1966) pp. 96–118.
29. Maj.-Gen. Thomas M. Rienzi, *Communications-Electronics, 1962–1970*, Vietnam Studies Series, Dept. of the Army (Washington D.C., 1972) pp. v, 10, 14, 134.
30. Patrick J. McGarvey, *C.I.A.—The Myth and the Madness* (Baltimore, 1973) p. 114.
31. Rienz, op. cit., p. 157.
32. Ibid., p. 91.
33. Ibid., pp. 139, 172.
34. Lt.-Gen. Carroll H. Dunn, *Base Development in South Vietnam, 1965–1970*, Vietnam Studies Series, Dept. of the Army (Washington, D.C., 1972) p. 63.
35. Ibid., pp. 12, 65; Maj.-Gen. Robert R. Ploger, 'The Lessons of Vietnam', *Army* (Sep 1968) pp. 70–75.
36. Dunn, op. cit., pp. 37–41, 50, 54–63, 68–72, 120.
37. Ploger, op. cit., p. 70.
38. Dunn, op. cit., pp. 44–7, 84.
39. Ibid., pp. 124–31.
40. Rienzi, op. cit., pp. 80–1.
41. Other major contract recipients included RMK–BRJ (Raymond International, Morrison-Knudson, Brown & Root, J. A. Jones), Philco-Ford, and the Vinnell Corporation. Dunn, op. cit., pp. 25–7, 42–3, 89–93, 134.
42. Vo Nguyen Giap, *Big Victory Great Task* (New York, 1968) esp. pp. 24, 100.
43. Frank Leary, 'Finding the Enemy', *Space/Aeronautics* (Apr. 1967).
44. This concept is discussed briefly by Dr Nguyen Khac Vien in 'The Judo Lesson', *Tradition and Revolution in Vietnam*, Indochina Resource Center (Berkeley, 1974) pp. 9–13.
45. *Pentagon Papers*, Gravel edition, IV, pp. 348–89.
46. Lt.-Col. Arthur F. McConnell Jr, 'Mission Ranch Hand', *Air University Review* (Jan–Feb 1970) pp. 89–94.
47. *Newsweek* (7 Aug 1972).
48. Lt.-Col. Joseph M. Kiernan, 'Combat Engineers in the Iron Triangle', *Army* (June 1967) pp. 42–5; 'Land Clearing Emerges as a Top Tactic of the War', *Engineering News Record* (15 June 1970) p. 27; E. W. Pfeiffer and Arthur H. Westing, 'Land War: Three Reports', *Environment* (Nov 1971) pp. 2–15.
49. 'Check the Hands of the Saboteurs of the Paris Agreement' (Giai Phong Publishing House, Aug 1974) p. 5.
50. *St Louis Post-Dispatch* (28 Jan 1967 and 12 Apr 1968); *Time* (26 Apr 1968); *New York Times* (21 July 1972); D. Shapley, 'Technology in Vietnam: Fire Storm Project Fizzled Out', *Science* (21 July 1972) pp. 239–41. Although truly a forest area, U Minh often sheltered tens of thousands of civilians in addition to main force PLAF units.
51. *New York Times* (3 July 1972); John Gliedman, *Terror from the Sky* (Berkeley: Vietnam Resource Center, Aug 1972) pp. 69–82; Deborah Shapley, 'Weather Warfare: Pentagon Concedes Seven-year Vietnam Effort', *Science* (7 June

1974); *Weather Modification*, Hearings before the Subcommittee on Oceans and International Environment, Committee on Foreign Relations, US Senate (25 Jan and 20 Mar 1974).

52. Vann, op. cit., p. 9.
53. Ibid.
54. *Missiles and Rockets* (28 Mar 1966), p. 46.
55. This was a joint University of Florida and US Department of Agriculture innovation and testing effort, reported in the *New York Times* (6 June 1966) and *St Louis Post-Dispatch* (6 Oct 1966).
56. Leary, op. cit., pp. 92–104.
57. *Investigation into Electronic Battlefield Program*, Hearings before the Electronic Battlefield Subcommittee, Committee on Armed Services, US Senate (1971) p. 49.
58. Leonard Sullivan, quoted in *Science and Technology* (Oct 1968).
59. *US News and World Report* (15 May 1972) p. 23.
60. Associated Press dispatch from Saigon (1 Feb 1972).
61. Truong Chinh speech, published in *Vietnam Documents and Research Notes*, no. 51 (Sep 1968), p. 2.
62. *Bombings in Cambodia*. Hearings before the Committee on Armed Service, US Senate, 93rd Congress, First Session (1973).
63. 'Southeast Asia Sensor Fields: More Eyes and Ears', *Armed Forces Journal* (1 Mar 1971) pp. 38–9; Michael Malloy, 'The Death Harvesters', *Far Eastern Economic Review* (29 Jan 1972).
64. Speech by Sen. William Proxmire, *Congressional Record* (23 Mar 1971) S. 3618.
65. Malloy, op. cit. See also G. Heiman, 'Beep to Bang', *Armed Forces Management* (July 1970) pp. 36–9.
66. For an excellent discussion of the automated battlefield concept, see Michael Klare, *War Without End* (New York, 1973).
67. *Armed Forces Journal* (3 May 1971); Malloy, op. cit.
68. McGarvey, op. cit., p. 113.
69. Department of Defense letter, 21 Dec 1971, in response to enquiry by Carl Kukkonen, Indochina Resource Center; *Aviation Week and Space Technology* (26 June 1972) pp. 129–33; *International Herald Tribune* (31 Mar 1972).
70. John Strauss, compiler, 'Components and Contractors of the Automated Air War', National Action/Research on the Military Industrial Complex (Philadelphia, Dec 1972) pp. 1–3.
71. Col. Walter P. Glover, 'Air Armament', *Ordnance* (July–Aug 1972) p. 10.
72. US official in Thailand, interviewed by T. D. Allman, 'The Blind Bombers', *Far Eastern Economic Review* (29 Jan 1972).
73. Chief Warrant Officer Swerrington, USMC, 'Staff Study on Pernicious Characteristics of U.S. Explosive Ordnance' (Oct 1969).
74. 'RPVs in Combat', *Aerospace International* (July–Aug 1972) pp. 5–11.
75. Discussions with the author in Hanoi (2 Jan 1975).
76. Robert Hotz, 'B-52s over Hanoi', *Aviation Week and Space Technology* (Feb 1973).
77. *Department of Defense Appropriations*, Hearings before the Subcommittee of the Committee on Appropriations, House of Representatives, 93rd Congress, First Session (1973) p. 30.

78. A Gallup poll taken soon after the Paris Agreement revealed that 57 per cent believed that the bombing of Hanoi and Haiphong had contributed to the peace settlement.
79. Dunn, op. cit., p. 12. A hint of the problems involved is contained in Rienzi, op. cit., p. 62, where it is revealed that even at the height of American troop availability a combat division had an area of responsibility covering 3000–5000 square miles, compared to the 200–300 square miles they were organised and trained to cover in conventional warfare.
80. Lt.-Col. Robert C. Jarvis, *New York Times*, letter to the editor (3 Mar 1975). Ironically, Col. Jarvis made his argument *in favour* of continued indefinite military aid to the RVN since, he said, their 'only crime was trusting us'.
81. Quoted by Malcolm W. Browne, *New York Times* (24 Apr 1975).

2 Blanket Coverage: Two Case Studies of Area Weapons in Indochina*

Michael Krepon

> When they decided to use planes [in Indochina],
> they were, in effect, deciding to use napalm.
> *Dr. Alexander H. Flax,*
> *Assistant Secretary of the Air Force,*
> *Research & Development, 1963–9*

Of all the area weapons used in Indochina, napalm caused the most uproar. Dow Chemical was boycotted, indignant speeches were made in the US Congress, and lurid pictures of badly burned victims flashed across the media. Despite this attention, napalm and the entire family of incendiary weapons are firmly lodged in American military doctrine and procurement. The US is not alone in this regard; incendiaries have found their niche in military arsenals on all sides of the ideological spectrum.

The US political and military officials who prosecuted the Vietnam war were well acquainted with the possible uses of incendiary weapons. Scores of Japanese and German cities were subjected to firebomb attacks during the Second World War. Air strikes against Hamburg and Dresden created monstrous firestorms, but even they were eclipsed by the firebombing on Tokyo in March 1945. In the Korean War, incendiaries were used primarily against battlefield targets, as opposed to population centres. In all, 32,315 tons of napalm were used in Korea.[1]

---

*These case studies are based primarily on interviews with officials who served the US government in various capacities relating to weapons development and use. Wherever possible sources have been attributed, but the wishes of those who have requested anonymity have been respected. Gary Gilbert assisted in the research. The research and writing of these chapters was conducted under the auspices of the Student Advisory Committee on International Affairs. The section on Cluster Bomb Units is based on an article by Michael Krepon published in *Foreign Affairs,* entitled 'Weapons Potentially Inhuman: The Case of Cluster Bombs'. Reprinted by permission of *Foreign Affairs,* April 1974. © 1974 by Council on Foreign Relations, Inc. The views expressed are the author's and do not necessarily reflect those of the United States Arms Control and Disarmament Agency or of the United States Government.

Against this background and under the prodding of the International Committee of the Red Cross and the government of Sweden, the role of incendiaries in future wars is being re-evaluated. As the case study of napalm use in Indochina shows, re-evaluation is certainly needed. A fine line prevents weapons with indiscriminate characteristics from causing indiscriminate damage in wartime. Among developed countries, the capability to produce and expend questionable weapons in quantity further complicates the problem of political and military control. In one seven-month period alone, US forces dropped more napalm on Indochina than in the entire course of the Korean War.[2]

The napalm story begins with the US military assistance programme to South Vietnam. At first, the Diem government received only aged T-28s, delivered in November 1961. American advisors came along with the planes, and with the advisors began the US bombing of Indochina. For ordnance, 'they used whatever we gave them', according to one former Pentagon logistics officer, and that 'regularly and routinely' included napalm. Introducing napalm into the air war merely involved taking it off the shelf as a standard air-to-ground weapon. Nor was any special attention paid to research and development of incendiary weapons. R&D activity on napalm prior to and during the war was slight. Advancements were made on reducing dangers in shipment and increasing the intensity of the fireball, but most R&D energy was devoted to more innovative weapons.

The first T-28s could carry nothing—they were old, propeller-driven trainers, not bombers. Delivered to Vietnam without modification, their original purpose was to give the fledgling Vietnamese Air Force pilots immediate flying time. Five months later, two additional squadrons arrived with strengthened wings fitted with external bomb racks and 50-calibre machine guns.

The T-28s were replaced two years later by A-1s, which became involved in the first sustained air operations over Indochina—Operation Farmgate, a training programme conducted by the US Air Force. As part of their training, Vietnamese flew combat operations over enemy-held areas. According to one former Pentagon official 'it was an assumption around the building' that US Air Force instructors flew alongside on combat operations, to observe and assist their Vietnamese students. According to the same source, it was 'only a supposition' that if they were over targets, they 'probably' joined the Vietnamese in dropping ordnance. These suppositions took on added meaning with reports of US losses over South Vietnam flying 'inferior' aircraft, and with Defence Secretary McNamara's declaration to the Saigon generals in May 1964, that Farmgate should be viewed 'as a specific, reluctantly approved exception to US policy that fighting in Vietnam should be done by the Vietnamese , a supplementary effort transitory in nature'.[3] Ordnance restrictions for Farmgate related to tonnage rather than kind; A-1s could only carry a tiny bomb load.

President Kennedy authorised the use of napalm in these air operations over South Vietnam, but there is some confusion as to what ground rules were placed on its use. Military sources claim that napalm was authorised for search and rescue operations; ex-State and Defence Department officials claim there were categorical rules for using napalm against military targets only. Whatever differences existed on the ground rules, there is unanimity among those interviewed that no discernible evaluation procedures were established for napalm use.

As long as US air activity over South Vietnam was at an insignificant level, the Joint Chiefs of Staff did not press the napalm issue. From their standpoint, it was important that a precedent had been set placing the use of napalm in South Vietnam under a 'military ground rule'— that is, at the discretion of military commanders. According to Vice-Admiral Lloyd Mustin, USN (Ret.), director of operations for the Joint Chiefs of Staff, some people in the Joint Staff let field commanders know that, in a tight situation, their men could use napalm but were not to advertise the fact. Figures on napalm use by the South Vietnamese are not available. Prior to 1965, US aircraft dropped approximately 4000 tons.[4]

Some napalm earmarked for the South Vietnamese Air Force reportedly was used over Laos as well.[5] But for the most part, US policy on using incendiaries differentiated between South Vietnam and Laos.

The napalm issue could be sidestepped in Vietnam during the summer of 1964, but in neighbouring Laos, there were more questions to be answered. As long as the air war was ostensibly a South Vietnamese operation, and as long as the South Vietnamese leadership readily approved, bureaucratic opposition to napalm use could not get very far. But Laotian Premier Souvanna Phouma was more sensitive about these matters. Although the Royal Laotian Air Force as ill-trained and ill-equipped as that of South Vietnam, could certainly have used the same kind of 'advisory' support, diplomatic niceties prevented it. To train the Royal Laotian Air Force and to stock their bombing runs with incendiaries would blatantly violate the Geneva Accords, and this both governments were hesitant to do.

Systematic US air operations in Laos were under way in March 1964, with high-altitude photo reconnaissance, authorised by National Security Action Memorandum 288. In May, low-level tactical reconnaissance operations began over the Laotian corridor. Tactical reconnaissance aircraft carried sensors and photographic equipment, but no ordnance. They were sitting ducks for anti-aircraft fire, and within two weeks, the first tactical reconnaissance aircraft was shot down. Urgent requests from the Joint Chiefs then followed for armed escorts over Laos. In June, Souvanna approved US armed escorts of reconnaissance planes, on condition that they only return fire, and not initiate combat operations. Another ground rule was added from

Washington: napalm was forbidden. Under these restrictions, Yankee Team operations were under way in June 1964.

Impetus for the napalm restriction came from Vientiane and Washington, with US Ambassador Leonard Unger and Assistant Secretary of Defence John McNaughton leading the way. Unger was strongly against the use of napalm. He did not accept military assurances that it would be effective, and he also knew that napalm would make his job of maintaining some semblance of respect for the Geneva Accords more difficult. According to military officials close to US policy, Unger was operating under a 'plausibly deniable' set of instructions. That is, US policy was, 'If you can't plausibly deny it, don't do it.' Something as politically and materially combustible as napalm could not be denied very plausibly.

All these arguments surfaced in Washington, with one notable addition. State and Defence Department officials opposed to napalm use called attention to possible adverse 'world opinion' (but not the inhumanity of the weapon *per se*). Of all the arguments, this one bothered the Joint Chiefs the most. The Joint Chiefs countered the political argument with two responses: first, that napalm was a standard, conventional weapon, and second, that it was a very *effective* standard, conventional weapon. They argued that napalm was especially appropriate for countering resistance in heavily dug-in areas, and in silencing anti-aircraft fire. They raised the question of napalm use most pointedly with regard to search-and-rescue operations. Standard military procedure required that everything possible be done to rescue downed pilots, and napalm was seen as an essential instrument in accomplishing this mission. Moreover, napalm was being used for precisely this purpose in South Vietnam. There could be no effective political argument against this position. But with the exception of search-and-rescue missions, the napalm restriction for US air operations over Laos held. The Chiefs voiced oral objections, but did not take a strong stand. According to Mustin, who was privy to most of their discussions, the Chiefs were grateful that at least the wraps had been partially taken off US aircraft operating over Laos and that 'something was better than nothing'.

As for Laotian air operations, discretionary power to use napalm was placed in the hands of Ambassador Unger. Unger was virtually the air marshal of the Royal Laotian Air Force. He selected targets, proposed increases in the inventory, and selected ordnance. On 25 July 1964, his superiors at the State Department cabled 'preliminary views' on proposed Vietnamese Air Force cross-border operations against infiltration routes in the Laotian corridor: 'Armament would be napalm unless politically unacceptable in which case armament would be less effective conventional bombs, rockets and 20 mm.'[6]

By extrapolation from various documents in the Pentagon Papers and interviews with former officials, we can piece together the State

Department's priorities on napalm use in Laos: it would be best if napalm were not used at all, but if it had to be used for military effectiveness, better that it be used by the Royal Lao Air Force than by the Vietnamese Air Force, and better by the Vietnamese Air Force than by the US Air Force. If it had to be used, better that it be used in the corridor area (beyond the control of Souvanna) than in the entire Panhandle, and better in the Panhandle than in the populated Plain of Jars.

Unger apparently saw the logical extension of this train of thought, and took the position that the best way to avoid this slippery slope would be to bar napalm entirely from all Laotian T-28 operations.[7] But events were not moving in his favour. During the summer, the Pathet Lao captured the Plain of Jars, and its recapture became the focal point of military operations. The town of Phou Kout was a particularly strong enemy point. In August, Unger was given discretionary power to use napalm to recapture Phou Kout,[8] and here, for the first time, he used it, seeing no other way to dislodge an enemy deeply dug into defensive positions. The T-28 operations around Phou Kout were successful. The extent to which napalm was used on subsequent T-28 missions is somewhat uncertain. What is undeniable is that authorisation came from the American ambassador at all times. For the time being, the Royal Laotian Air Force, in McGeorge Bundy's words, 'would be the only appropriate user' of napalm within Laotian borders.[9]

This principle was tested once again in December 1964, with planning for another US air operation, Barrel Roll. Months of military deterioration in South Vietnam prompted negotiations with Souvanna to allow permission for cross-border operations to punish enemy infiltration routes through Laos. Unlike the Yankee Team operations which allowed aircraft to fire only when fired upon, Barrel Roll operations would be true armed reconnaissance in the US Army definition of the term: 'An air mission flown with the primary purpose of locating and attacking targets of opportunity, i.e. enemy material, personnel, and facilities in assigned general areas or along assigned ground communications routes and not for the purpose of attacking briefed targets.'

Deputy Secretary of Defence Cyrus Vance chaired the meeting on 12 December which discussed the Barrel Roll programme. The air force representative brought up the question of napalm use, and the by now familiar arguments pro and con were put forward. At this point, McNaughton still had the support of White House and State Department representatives. One new argument was added to the discussions: Barrel Roll was a signal of graduated pressure, and the US could always use napalm later on, if a stronger signal were needed. As a consensus decision, Vance amended the ordnance instruction to the theatre to exclude the use of napalm. McGeorge Bundy then informed the participants that the amended orders 'filled precisely the President's wishes.'[10] McNaughton still had the support of the man in charge.

In the first strikes against the North, the political arguments of McNaughton and his supporters continued to hold. Retaliatory strikes carried out in February 1965, called Flaming Dart, were armed with 'optimal conventional ordnance for the target to be attacked, excluding napalm.'[11] When the same ground rules were carried over to the initial Rolling Thunder operations, the sustained bombing campaign against the North beginning in March, the Joint Chiefs were incensed.

The Chiefs were under pressure from two fronts. From the field came reports of pilot dissatisfaction; pilots were facing anti-aircraft fire (flak) without napalm, an effective flak-suppression weapon, and in a terrain perfectly suited to that weapon. From the office of the Secretary of Defence, McNamara wanted to know why the air strikes were not more effective. He asked General Earle Wheeler, Chairman of the Joint Chiefs, to explain the poor performance of Flaming Dart, and to offer recommendations for action. Wheeler's first recommendation was to authorise napalm use.[12]

McNamara was sensitive to the political arguments against napalm, but he was more sensitive to poor field performance and the loss of aircraft and pilots. He must also have been sensitive to the fact that the Chiefs, in Mustin's words, had been making 'the most emphatic representations' to the President on this matter. McNaughton's support at the top slipped away; President Johnson authorised the use of napalm on 9 March 1965.[13]

With the air war in high gear, political checks on all aspects of the bombing began to melt away before military imperatives. The attention of civilian officials turned to target selection rather than ordnance selection. One by one, restrictions on bombing, and with it, the use of napalm, were stripped away. In April 1965, authorisation was given for Rolling Thunder missions to hit 'broadly defined geographical areas' and targets of specific routes; in May, pilots were given the authority to drop unexpended ordnance in various target areas; and in June, the first of a long series of B-52 bombing raids (Arc light) was authorised.[14] From 1965 on, approximately 8–9 per cent of the yearly bomb tonnage dropped in Indochina was napalm; in all, over 338,000 tons of napalm were dropped in the course of the war.[15]

Removed from political control, 'conventional' ordnance can be put to use in extraordinary ways. Incendiaries were occasionally used in conjunction with defoliants in South Vietnam for crop destruction purposes. Firestorming attempts using napalm after defoliation missions were also tried, though with virtually no success.[16] An offshoot of the firestorming concept, utilising napalm and aviation fuel, also failed.[17]

Napalm use opened the door for other incendiaries as well. Phosphorus-based incendiaries were first reported in the theatre in March and April 1965,[18] and magnesium-based incendiaries were introduced in August 1966.[19] New developments in incendiaries escaped civilian criticism because they appeared to be changes in technique rather than changes in the ground rules. After the war escalated in March 1965, political channels effectively yielded control to the military on this issue. And with the change-over from Military Assistance Programme funds to the Defence Department's Military Assistance Service Funding in 1965, the State Department yielded complete control over the supply side as well.

Inexorably, napalm became a staple part of US military tactics in Indochina, despite misgivings by some political officials. This was partly because different rules for napalm use applied in different countries, and restrictions tended to drop to the lowest common denominator. Close political monitoring procedures were never instituted; in any event, monitoring became lax once the war escalated to full-scale US involvement. But primarily, napalm was used because it had a proven record. In the words of one participant in counter-insurgency decision-making, 'It's not a question of who in the bureaucracy pushed napalm. It's more impersonal than that. It's like a doctor prescribing set medicines for set diseases.'

On one side, the highest official in government weighed adverse domestic and international political repercussions, as well as personal distaste for using fire-based weapons in combat. On the other side were military presumptions of saving American lives and prosecuting a frustrating war more effectively. In effect, both military and civilian officials were asked to perform impossible tasks in south-east Asia. But the military was paying in blood as well as in reputation; civilian war planners only had their reputations to lose. Reputations on both sides rested on hard-line advice, and the napalm issue soon got lost in the larger framework of punishing adversaries. And so the political line of restraint could not hold. The State Department, in the words of one direct observer, was reduced to 'much feeble protestation' against napalm use. It had already lost the opening round of the debate on tactical issues with the decision to use herbicides, and its energy and influence on subsequent issues was clearly on the wane.

A variety of fora might have been used to evaluate the use of incendiaries in Indochina; none was. The succession of inter-agency task forces and working groups shied away from questions of military tactics and ordnance selection. The Secretary of State, as was his custom, refrained from raising the issue as he believed it to be essentially a military matter. When questions on napalm use were raised in the Special Group-Counter-insurgency meetings, especially after reports of heavy civilian casualties, the dynamics were the same as within the State Department. In the words of one Special Group participant,

'These weapons already had a track record and a momentum of their own.'

Cluster Bomb Units (CBUs)

CBUs are conventional ironmongery.
Vice-Admiral Lloyd M. Mustin, USN(Ret.)
Director of Operations,
Joint Chiefs of Staff, 1964–7

The most indiscriminate and lethal area weapon developed for the Vietnam war was deployed without political control or review. Known as the Cluster Bomb Unit (CBU), it soon became, in the words of a former Pentagon official 'the darling of the aviators', and was used at the discretion of field commanders. The primary constraint lay in lack of production facilities.

CBUs use the principle of 'controlled fragmentation' to deny an area to the enemy. Hundreds of bomblets, each slightly larger than a tennis ball, are lodged within a hollow dispenser. Dropped from fighter aircraft like a conventional bomb, the dispenser splits apart, releasing its contents. The small bomblets, known as bomb live units (BLUs), are grooved to fragment before, during, or after impact, depending on the fuse employed. When jettisoned from an aircraft, each dispenser covers a designated area on the ground. Depending on the weapon used, the shower of controlled fragmentation can be effective against light military targets. But for the most part, CBUs are effective only against human beings, who are killed or wounded, depending on where they are within the fragmentation pattern.

The use of fragmentation to cripple an enemy is not a new concept. The hand grenade is perhaps the most simple example; even conventional blast bombs employ the fragmentation principle to a limited extent. But the ability to control a fragmentation pattern for tactical use is strictly an outgrowth of the war in Indochina.

Munitions designers developed fragmentation bombs during the Second World War, but the results showed more promise than sophistication. Major developments in fragmentation after the Korean War centred around new land mine techniques, such as the Claymore mine, which employed a curved metal plate which fragmented upon detonation. Later versions, projecting steel balls rather than a fragmented metal plate, were used in Vietnam. The real breakthrough in fragmentation weapons, however, related to air-dropped munitions. Working at the Development Centre at China Lake, California, and at Eglin Air Force Base, Florida, the navy and the air force designed a bomb live unit with fragmentation characteristics far superior to anything previously used by US armed forces. Later versions of this BLU, nicknamed 'pineapples' by the North Vietnamese, were the first to be used in Vietnam. But the overall weapons system, designated the CBU-2, still had major disadvantages.[20] Early dispenser models remained fixed to the wing of the aircraft, relying on ram air pressure entering the nose of the dispenser to force bomblets out of the tail. Dispensers had to be mounted at the outermost stations of the aircraft wings, so that the bomblets would not brush against the fuselage after dispersion. Pilots had to fly low and level, otherwise bomblets would not eject from the dispenser. CBU-2s were in the military inventory before a single plane made a sortie over Vietnam. Limited numbers of CBU-2s were deployed on aircraft carriers off the coast of Vietnam, and some were no doubt used in combat. But there was no particular support for their use, primarily because of the low and level tactic required to deliver them.

Sometime prior to 1963, work began within the airforce R&D division at Eglin to modify the dispensing system, to meet field demands for a dive-release mechanism so that CBUs could be dropped in a way that did not invite anti-aircraft fire.

The finished product, CBU-24, not only included the dive-release mechanism, but also delivered far more destructive bomblets. Nick-named 'guavas' by the North Vietnamese, they were the most widely used cluster bombs of the war. They contained far more fragments than any previous weapon of this kind, and above all were able to cover a much wider area. The exact range of destruction of the CBU-24 remains a classified military secret not publicly disclosed by the Pentagon. However, a Japanese team of experts travelling in North Vietnam and observing the effects estimated that a single CBU dropped in a linear pattern and detonated at an altitude of 600 feet was able to disperse its fragments so as to kill or wound people at an effective range of 300 metres by 1000 metres.[21] A report by the International Committee of the Red Cross placed the figure at 300 by 900 metres.[22] A Swedish team of experts agreed with the Red Cross figures, estimating further that a single fighter aircraft carrying CBUs could cover an area anywhere from one to 15 square kilometres.[23] While these figures are generally halved by American experts (noting the possible bias of the sources), the area coverage remains extraordinary, bearing in mind that the ordnance package for a single F-4 Phantom can include eight CBUs or, with special racks, as many as fifteen to twenty.

Operational tests in April 1966 proved beyond any shadow of doubt the flak suppression capabilities of the weapon. Soviet anti-aircraft units used by the North Vietnamese were only about ten to twelve feet across, an extremely difficult target to knock out even though only a small amount of damage could render them inoperative. CBUs, by literally pockmarking an entire area, could provide the maximum amount of cover for US aircraft, surpassing even napalm in effectiveness—although the introduction of CBUs into the war apparently did not affect the use of napalm in any way. It did not take a great deal of imagination to envisage other tactical uses for CBUs unrelated to flak suppression. Almost overnight, CBUs became *the* weapon for area denial. Vice-Admiral Lloyd M. Mustin, in his capacity as director of operations for the Joint Chiefs of Staff, became involved in the logistics of CBU deployment. 'Once we tested them,' he said in an interview, 'the immediate question became "How many can we make?"' CBU-24s were regularly used against North Vietnam from the summer of 1966 on, with an enthusiastic response from American pilots.

CBUs were not criticised in political channels. The little debate that did take place was within military circles, and according to participants, it concentrated on the extraordinary military effect of controlled fragmentation. No one discussed the inhumane or indiscriminate nature of the weapon; their concern was with revealing the weapon to the enemy.

The technology of controlled fragmentation had advanced to such a degree that the CBU represented one of the infrequent advances below the nuclear threshold acceptable for use on the battlefield. 'We thought', said a high-ranking military officer, 'these weapons could give us a quantum leap on the enemy, but not break the unwritten rules.' Yet the production techniques behind CBUs were relatively easy to copy and once deployed, weapons have no copyrights. As any weapon of this type was sure to be duplicated by the Soviets and Chinese, some Pentagon officials were reluctant to use it.

Reluctance should not be confused with indecision. The arguments within the Pentagon to deploy CBUs were compelling. CBUs were extraordinarily effective in flak suppression, they would complicate the enemy's task of rebuilding lines of communication, and they would strike a blow at his morale. Potential enemies would develop CBUs soon enough, if they did not already possess them, the arguments ran.

Discussions about revealing controlled fragmentation were drawn-out, apparently because decisions to deploy CBUs in principle were made on a model-by-model basis. Some models were never deployed, and their status as 'classified munitions' remains intact for future engagements. A classified munition is non-nuclear, but believed to be of special importance or effectiveness. A weapon is classified to keep its production techniques or its battlefield applications secret. Classified munitions, almost by definition, would result in serious political repercussions if deployed. Although the CBU-24 seems to fall within the definition of a classified munition, it was never so designated. One reason for this may have been a strong reluctance on the part of the Joint Chiefs to create another political controversy. The decision to use CBU-24 followed the drawn-out bureaucratic debate over the use of napalm. When the CBUs were ready for operational use, the Joint

Chiefs were in no mood to engage in another debate over ordnance selection.

According to Mustin, the Joint Chiefs never made any formal request to a political authority about the use of CBUs.

> In our view, they were a purely conventional weapon, and we regarded them as available, and the less said, the better. Somebody somewhere would want to raise the argument, 'Well, do we or don't we want to authorise the use of this weapon? . . .' We in J-3 [Directorate for Operations, Joint Staff of the Joint Chiefs of Staff] had ways of exchanging information with our subordinate echelons all the way out to pilots on the line, and we just said, 'As far as we know, that's authorised to you, you've got 'em, use 'em when you want, and keep your mouth shut, or somebody will tell you that you can't.'

The Pentagon played down CBUs, to avoid the political–military confrontations that were occurring over the use of napalm. CBUs were categorised and explained as a standard weapon—'conventional iron-mongery', in Mustin's words—and as flak-suppression ordnance, demonstrably effective in protecting the lives of US pilots. Controversy was also avoided because CBUs were never a headline-type weapon, either in the R&D stage or after deployment. Civilian assistant secretaries for R&D in the navy and air force had more pressing problems to consider. CBUs did not run into engineering problems; on the contrary, they were developed without major cost overruns or defects. Controlled fragmentation, from an R&D standpoint, was purely a technical matter. A former participant in the review process said with some disdain, 'They made decisions on a cost-effective basis. They compared CBUs to blast bombs for cost and weight of effort.' Because no political questions were raised, civilian heads of R&D programmes turned their attention elsewhere. 'We knew they were being developed', said another former official, 'but they weren't a high-profile item.' The Joint Chiefs continued the low profile inherited from the R&D community. They did not volunteer anything about their political repercussions, and they were never deeply questioned about CBUs through political channels.

When representations were made to the Secretary of Defence, they concerned the use and resupply of this conventional ordnance needed to cut aircraft losses. Indeed, the major political question about CBUs arose over inadequate resupply. CBUs may have been cost-effective, but they were still costly. In the military's estimation, the US never achieved a manufacturing capability to meet demand adequately—and not because the Joint Chiefs never pressed the point. McNamara's reluctance to approve new production facilities was notorious. There are two schools of thought about McNamara's motivation for limiting CBU, as well as other production. The first is economic: that McNamara was determined not to end the Vietnam war with a huge surplus of military equipment, as previous wars had ended. Furthermore, he was suspicious of bloated and vague requirements brought to him by the Joint Chiefs. So it was natural that his practice for cutting requests for material by the Chiefs would carry over to CBUs. The second possibility, less likely than the first, hints that McNamara used his resupply power to place restrictions on CBU use in the field. This argument is somewhat weakened by McNamara's personal choice of CBU-24 as the kill weapon for his scheme to build an infiltration barrier to protect South Vietnam.[24]

For whatever reasons, the supply problem was real. Demand was so great that there were regular airlifts of CBUs from one base to another to share limited supplies. Although no formal rules of engagement were placed on where, when, and how CBUs were to be used, Mustin assumes there were oral instructions 'of the most stringent variety' from field commanders to pilots not to use them 'unless you've got a flak target'. In addition, there were instructions to bring unexpended munitions back to base, instead of dropping them in designated areas, as was the case for standard blast bombs. The extent to which individual pilots exercised such restraint necessarily varied, given assertions by the press and foreign observers of their use in built-up areas.

Lack of supply proved to be the most effective political check on indiscriminate use, because once operational, civilian officials had little to say about CBUs. Political involvement at the State Department and in the office of the Secretary of Defence was very shallow. They too viewed these munitions in conventional terms, and could not argue convincingly for the banning of CBUs for flak suppression, when napalm, much more politically sensitive, had previously been authorised for just this task. By the time CBUs were deployed, there had already been protracted debates about herbicides and napalm, and political advisors were reluctant to begin another such bureaucratic discussion. The question of CBUs only arose after significant numbers of US troops had been committed to the war, when political considerations were much less important than military imperatives. Consequently political input on CBU use related mostly to the question of revealing or not revealing the weapons in question. Again, there was virtually no debate at technical or policy-making levels about the indiscriminate nature of the munition and mechanics for monitoring its use.

And so, CBUs went into extensive use by the US Air Force. They were employed primarily in North Vietnam and against the trail complex in eastern Laos. The most common targets were anti-aircraft installations (flak suppression), truck parks, and on occasion the areas around a downed American pilot when rescue attempts were under way. They also appear to have been employed in connection with B-52 raids, primarily in key supply areas in Laos and the southern part of North Vietnam, and in connection with the final B-52 raids against the Hanoi area in December 1972 and early January 1973.

So far as the South was concerned, the restraints appear to have been more severe and the employment more limited. Perhaps the most hard-hit province was Quang Tri, adjacent to the border with the North, where an observation team led by the staff of the Senate Judiciary Subcommittee on Refugees and Escapees obtained considerable testimony of their use during the Easter Offensive of 1972. News reports since the war have indicated that in some areas unexploded CBU bomblets form a significant part of the vast problem created by unexploded weapons littering the countryside.[25]

No knowledge is available on whether CBUs caused extensive civilian casualties in the trail areas of Laos; although no special restraints were apparently applied to their use in these areas, the general ground rules required that targets be at a significant distance from known villages.

In North Vietnam, however, extensive evidence exists. 'Guavas' became a prime exhibit of the North Vietnamese to visitors, and the best descriptions of the range of CBU effectiveness have come from foreign observers who were given the opportunity to examine its effects extensively—in a situation where these could be readily separated from the very different impact of other types of bombs. The North Vietnamese routine took visitors to see traces of cluster bombing in Quang Binh and Phu Tho provinces, while reports of cluster bombing drops against six North Vietnamese cities—Hanoi, Haiphong, Nam Dinh, Thai Binh, Vinh, and especially Viet Tri—filtered out in various media during the course of the war.[26] Given a weapon with a damage radius of several square kilometres, CBUs must have caused extensive civilian casualties, and in a high ratio to the military damage unquestionably inflicted on their intended targets.

In the South, CBUs were much less extensively employed in proportion to other munitions. By and large, North Vietnamese anti-aircraft activity in the South was mostly in direct connection with substantial military units and used at some distance from populated areas. On the other hand, in a few cases at the high point of the fighting, North Vietnamese units were active in areas largely under enemy control, and these included some of the highly populated provinces along the border and central coast. In general, efforts to separate out what proportion of civilian casualties was due to action by the Viet Cong and North Vietnamese rather than to action by American, South Vietnamese, and allied forces have been able to produce only the roughest sort of estimates.[27]

What is certain is that the CBU established itself during the Vietnam war as a highly effective weapon. Although the models used were not able to destroy well-placed guns or missiles, their total effect within the designated area did succeed in silencing the weapons and doubtless inflicted substantial casualties on their crews. Accordingly, from a military standpoint the CBU is now an established weapon in the US arsenal. South Vietnamese forces were also reported to be using CBUs in the final battles of the Vietnam war.[28]

Moreover, since the Vietnam experience is widely known, it appears certain the controlled fragmentation weapons of the CBU type will become a staple in arsenals on all sides of the ideological spectrum. It has been reported that CBUs were rushed to Israel during the October 1973 war to combat Soviet-supplied SAM missile sites.[29] This war, and the subsequent military build-up in the Middle East, gave great impetus to CBU programmes. The CBU-24 became a weapon of the past, surpassed by improved versions—CBU-52, CBU-58, and CBU-71—which were mass produced to increase US war reserve stockpiles.[30]

Among the new CBUs is the CBU-59B, which has 717 bomblets, each of which can discriminate between 'soft' and 'hard' targets. When a bomblet hits a soft spot, such as the ground, it pops up 3–10 feet in the air and bursts into fragments, thereby maximising its damage potential. When a bomblet hits a hard target, such as a lorry, it explodes instantaneously.[31]

Further recent developments include the mating of CBU technology to fuel air explosive and 'smart bomb' technology. The CBU-72B uses fuel air explosive techniques, releasing only three bomblets, each of which releases a cloud of ethylene oxide, which is then detonated by a delayed fuse. The resulting blast is effective against human targets, land mines, and some light material targets.[32]

Under Operation Pave Strike, the air force quickened eleven interrupted programmes deemed of high priority as a result of the October 1973 Middle East war. One of these programmes, Pave Storm, constitutes another major advance in controlled fragmentation. Pave Storm utilises the GBU-2, a 'glide bomb unit', adding smart bomb guidance packages to the basic CBU technology. Instead of being a free fall, unguided weapon, the GBU allows for far greater precision in weapons technology by the use of laser or imaging infra-red guidance techniques. GBUs are expensive; they will not replace CBUs in weapons inventories. In all probability, they will be used only against high value targets. GBUs will undoubtedly provide some measure of relief to decision-makers who wish to avoid collateral damage. But as long as CBUs constitute an integral part of weapons inventories, the problem of indiscriminate use of indiscriminate weapons will remain.

NOTES

1. UN Secretary General, *Napalm and Other Incendiary Weapons* (New York, (1972).
2. Ibid., p. 48.
3. *Pentagon Papers,* Gravel edition, III, p. 70.
4. SIPRI, *Napalm and Incendiary Weapons,* Interim Report (Stockholm, 1974) p. 84.
5. Marek Thee, the Polish delegate to the International Control Commission, claims fighter squadrons 'probably based in South Vietnam' used incendiaries for the first time in Laos in late October 1961, against Pathet Lao positions. *Notes of a Witness, Laos and the Second Indochina War* (New York, 1972) p. 189.
6. *Pentagon Papers,* Gravel edition, III, p. 514.
7. Ibid., pp. 515–6.
8. Ibid., p. 534.
9. Ibid., p. 254.
10. Ibid., p. 254.
11. Ibid., p. 300.
12. Ibid., p. 334.
13. Ibid., p. 284.
14. Ibid., pp. 285, 286, 384.
15. SIPRI, *Napalm and Incendiary Weapons,* pp. 51, 84.
16. *New York Times* (14 Mar 1970).
17. *Congressional Record* (1 Mar 1971) H 987.
18. *Wall Street Journal* (22 Mar 1965).
19. *New York Times* (19 Jan 1967).
20. Each variation or improvement in cluster bombs received a higher numbered classification.
21. John Duffett (ed.), *Against the Crime of Silence: Proceedings of the Russell International War Crimes Tribunal* (Flanders, N.J., 1968) p. 260.
22. International Committee of the Red Cross, *Weapons That May Cause Unnecessary Suffering or Have Indiscriminate Effects* (Geneva, 1973) p. 44.
23. Torgil Wulff, *et al., Conventional Weapons: The Deployment and Effects from a Humanitarian Aspect* (Stockholm, 1973) p. 122.
24. *Pentagon Papers,* Gravel edition, IV, pp. 121–2.
25. The *Washington Post* reported on 8 July 1973 that undetonated 'guavas' were acting like miniature land mines in the effort to reclaim fields for farming.
26. The most detailed and comprehensive account of this evidence of CBU use is in Duffett, op. cit., pp. 147–270.
27. A senate Judiciary Subcommittee report estimates that 'well over 50 % of the civilian casualties were attributable to GVN and US firepower.' *Hearing on the Relief and Rehabilitation of War Victims in Indochina* (Washington D.C., 1973) IV, p. 9.
28. *Baltimore Sun* (25 Apr 1975).
29. *Washington Post* (10 Nov 1973).
30. Department of Defence Appropriations (Senate, 1975), IV, p. 718.
31. Ibid., III, p. 860.
32. Ibid.

3 Qualitative Trends in Conventional Munitions: the Vietnam War and After*

Julian Perry Robinson

There is now a ferment in the design of routine weapon systems which many commentators believe is revolutionising the nature of conventional warfare. It is providing field commanders with capacities for destruction that have hitherto been available only with nuclear weapons. The most spectacular aspect, and the one that has attracted most of the commentary, is the extraordinary increase in capability for locating distant targets and then accurately directing weapons against them. Less noted have been the developments in what weapon-designers call 'kill mechanisms' and in the ways in which these can be packaged as munitions for weapons. The developments have been major; and it is important, not least for the future of arms limitation, to understand what they are. The present chapter is therefore an attempt to piece together the scattered information which the open literature contains on munition design so as to identify significant trends.

The focus is on destructiveness. There is a curious statistic that is to be found in some military writings which can be used as a yardstick: the 'lethality index'.[1] It reflects the area of ground per unit of time over which a weapon can create a mortal hazard to people or destroy whatever other types of target it may be designed against. The parameters of the index allow very different types of weapon to be compared, provided such matters as logistical constraint are ignored. Table 3.1, taken from a study commissioned by the US Army Combat Developments Command,[2] shows anti-personnel lethality indices for successive major weapons from the sword to the hydrogen bomb. We may observe from this that it took pre-twentieth-century weapons designers some three millennia to achieve a thousand-fold increase in lethality, but the next thousand-fold increase came within a bare half-century. Nuclear-fission technology provided the final order-of-magnitude jump; but in Table 3.2, which shows anti-personnel lethality indices calculated on exactly the same basis for present-day weapons, we see that the lethality of non-nuclear weapons now overlaps with that of nuclear weapons.

---

* This chapter is taken from a longer study, 'Trends in conventional munitions and their implications for qualitative arms limitation', Science Policy Research Unit, University of Sussex, May 1977, currently being revised for publication in the *SPRU Occasional Papers* series.

TABLE 3.1   A comparison of the lethalities of successive major weapons

Weapon	Lethality index
Sword	20
Javelin	18
Bow and arrow	20
Longbow	34
Crossbow	32
Arquebus, 16th century	10
Musket, 17th century	19
Flintlock, 18th century	47
Rifle, Minie bullet, mid-19th century	150
Rifle, breechloading, late 19th century	230
Rifle, magazine, World War I	780
Machine gun, World War I	13 000
Machine gun, World War II	18 000
Tank, World War I (armament: two machine guns)	68 000
Tank, World War II (one 3-inch gun, one machine gun)	2 200 000
Field gun, 16th century, ca. 12-lb round shot	43
Field gun, 17th century, ca. 12-lb round shot	230
Field gun, 18th century, Gribeauval, 12-lb shell	4 000
Field gun, late 19th century, 75 mm high-explosive shell	34 000
Field gun, World War I, 155 mm high-explosive shell	470 000
Howitzer, World War II, 155 mm high-explosive shell with proximity fuse	660 000
Fighter-bomber, World War I (one machine gun, two 50-lb high-explosive bombs)	230 000
Fighter-bomber, World War II (eight machine guns, two 100-lb high explosive bombs)	3 000 000
Ballistic missile, World War II, high-explosive warhead (V-2)	860 000
Fission explosive, 20 Kt airburst	49 000 000
Fusion explosive, 1 Mt airburst	660 000 000

Source   Col. T. N. Dupuy, 'Quantification of factors related to weapon lethality', annex III-H in R. Sunderland *et al.*, *Historical trends related to weapon lethality*, contract report from the Historical Evaluation and Research Organisation to the US Army Combat Developments Command (Oct 1964).

TABLE 3.2 Lethality indices of some modern weapons

Type of weapon	Specific weapon* for which index is calculated	Lethality index†
NON-NUCLEAR WEAPONS		
Assault rifle	5.56 mm M16	4 200
Light machine gun	7.62 mm M60	21 000
Medium howitzer, HE shell	155 mm M109 with M107 HE projectiles	89 000
Shoulder-fired TPA flame-rocket launcher	66 mm M202 with 4-rocket M74 clip	1 200 000
Medium howitzer, nerve-gas shell	155 mm M109 with M121 GB projectiles	1 400 000
Automatic grenade launcher, HE/frag grenades	40 mm XM174 with M406 grenades	1 500 000
Fighter-bomber with napalm firebombs	Phantom with 19 × BLU-1 750-lb firebombs	1 900 000
Main battle tank	M60 with a 105 mm gun, a light MG and a heavy MG	3 200 000
Medium howitzer, HE/frag submunition shell	155 mm M109 with M449 'improved conventional munitions'	3 500 000
Multiple rocket launcher, nerve-gas rockets	Lance with M251 warhead	6 800 000
Tactical guided missile, HE/frag bomblet warhead	Lance with M251 warhead	7 200 000
Fighter-bomber with HE general-purpose bombs	Phantom with 19 × M117 750-lb bombs	9 600 000
Multiple rocket launcher, HE/frag rockets	140 mm RAP-14 (French) with 21 rockets	12 000 000
Fighter-bomber (1950s) with FAE cluster bombs	Skyraider with 14 × CBU-55 cluster bombs	20 000 000
Heavy bomber with HE general-purpose bombs	B52 with 108 × Mk 82 500-lb bombs	23 000 000
Fighter-bomber with nerve-gas bombs	Phantom with 19 × MC-1 750-lb GB bombs	28 000 000
Bomber with blockbuster light-case HE bombs	Hercules with 2 × BLU-82 15,000-lb bombs	52 000 000
Tactical guided missile, nerve-gas warhead	Lance with E27 GB warhead	91 000 000
Fighter-bomber with HE/frag cluster bombs	Phantom with 19 × CBU-58 cluster bombs	150 000 000
Heavy bomber with HE/frag grenade clusters	B52 with 2 × SUU-24 dispensers for ADU-256 clusters	207 000 000
NUCLEAR WEAPONS		
Tactical guided missile, 'mininuke' warhead	Lance with developmental 0.05 Kt whd, airburst	60 000 000
Tactical guided missile, 1 Kt warhead	Lance with M234 whd, airburst at middle yield option	170 000 000
Medium howitzer, 'mininuke' shell	155 mm M109 with 0.1 Kt shell, airburst	680 000 000
Tactical guided missile, 20 Kt warhead	Pluton (French) with AN-52 warhead, airburst	830 000 000
Fighter-bomber with 350 Kt bomb	Phantom with one B-61 bomb at highest yield option	6 200 000 000
Strategic guided missile, 1 Mt warhead	Submarine-launched M-20 missile (French)	18 000 000 000
Strategic guided missile, 25 Mt warhead	SS-18 (Soviet) intercontinental ballistic missile	210 000 000 000

Conventions (FAE) fuel-air explosive; (frag) fragmentation; (HE) high explosive; (LC) light case; (MG) machine gun; (TPA) thickened pyrophoric agent, a napalm follow-on.

Notes * US weapons unless otherwise indicated. † Calculated from available area-of-effectiveness data according to the method of Col. Dupuy as in Table 3.1.

The origins of the present upsurge in the power of conventional weapons may be located in the Korean War.[3] This stimulated in the rich countries a search for technological ways of coping with military-manpower inferiorities on the battlefield. Several of the anti-personnel weapon concepts which, much later, were developed into operational weapons, emerged at that time, primarily—though by no means exclusively—in the United States. But they were overtaken in the R&D laboratories by battlefield nuclear weapons, and pressure to develop them did not recover until the early 1960s when the emphasis in military requirements shifted to 'limited war'. Thereafter the pressure became intense, at least in the West, and the great resources of technological skill and R&D capacity that were invested in support of the US war effort in Vietnam yielded several more weapon concepts, many of which still remain in development. It now seems inevitable that, over the coming years and in different parts of the world, these concepts will become fully reduced to practice for the arsenals of the rich countries, their dependents, and their clients.

Categories of munition
In the final resolve, battle (of any type) is and always has been a matter of taking and holding ground. The use of foot-soldiers continues to be the preferred way of doing this. By the same token, infantry force remains the basic element in an overall defence against territorial invasion or armed insurrection. This means that weapons for killing troops, or at least putting them out of action, are the primary armament of armed forces. Historically, anti-personnel weapons have indeed formed the bulk of national arsenals. But the counters to firepower are manoeuvre and protection, which therefore enter into the design of the weapons. If a moving force is to be attacked, the choices are either to out-manoeuvre it, to use weapons that can be brought to bear accurately and rapidly on moving targets, or to use area weapons that saturate terrain across which the force is moving. There are two variants on the last alternative: the use of massed delivery systems, each weapon delivering munitions with relatively small areas of effectiveness; or the use of a small number of weapons to deliver munitions with a large area of effect ('area munitions').

If a protected force is to be attacked, the type of protection dictates the choice of weapon. Protection through concealment within natural cover may be countered with one or other form of area weapon, or with special weapons (such as fire or chemical defoliants) that strip away cover. Protection by terrain may be countered with 'indirect-fire' weapons— ones capable of reaching over obstacles to direct fire—used for area effects unless the target is observable. The protection afforded to static forces by field fortifications or to mobile forces by armour, demands special weapons capable of destroying materiel. Just as the

sword and the spear are the archetypal anti-personnel weapons, so too
are the battering-ram and the sap and archetypal anti-materiel
weapons. As weapons technology developed, it came to provide anti-
personnel weapons that could also be used to breach light fortifications
or armour, simultaneously killing people inside them. This was the
primary feature of the first gunpowder weapons with firearms, especially
cannon firing exploding-shell projectiles, being among the first of what
are now known as 'general purpose' or 'anti-personnel/anti-materiel'
('anti-PAM') weapons. In Europe by the seventeenth century, anti-
PAM rather than anti-personnel weapons were becoming the dominant
armament. Further shifts came with the introduction of 'high' explosives
and machine-guns towards the end of the nineteenth century, for these
had the effect of making weapon systems *per se* primary targets of
attack. Indirect-fire weapons in particular became increasingly important targets, for with their long reach, their relative invulnerability
except to other indirect-fire weapons, their ease of supply and their
capacity for saturation attacks on area targets, they had become
formidable obstacles to attacking forces, and formidable threats to
defending ones.[4] Herein lay part of the stimulus behind the development of tactical ground-attack aircraft and, to a lesser extent, of tanks.
The emergence of these and other such weapons created a demand for
further counter-measures in the form of special anti-tank and anti-
aircraft weapons, these in turn demanding special counter-counter-
measures.

As a consequence of all this, the major preoccupation of weapons
designers over the last forty years or so has been the development of a
large variety of anti-weapon or anti-counter-measure weapons. Three
categories can be distinguished. The first comprises updated forms of
traditional anti-PAM weapons: multi-purpose weapons considered
cost-effective against a wide range of personnel and materiel targets,
including lightly protected weapons. They include napalm and the
routine types of high-explosive (HE) artillery shell and bomb. The
second category comprises anti-PAM weapons in which most of the
destructive energy is harnessed for penetrating armour or degrading
materiel, the anti-personnel effects being subsidiary. Examples include
weapons dispensing the many varieties of anti-tank warhead: heavy
projectiles made of tungsten or depleted uranium, HE in squash-head
or hollow-charge configurations, and so on. Although they are
intended as anti-materiel weapons, and would not be considered cost-
effective against unprotected personnel targets, their objective of
disabling enemy weapons systems is in fact met by killing the people
operating these systems; and for reasons associated with the requirement of prior penetration of protection, their anti-personnel kill
mechanisms are often extraordinarily horrible. The third category
comprises true anti-materiel weapons, ones that are designed to disable

enemy weapons systems or counter-measures, not necessarily by killing their occupants, but by destroying components or machinery. Weapons which are powerful enough to do this will certainly also kill people; and some of them have particular anti-personnel applications which are considered cost-effective. Fuel-air explosive mine-clearing weapons are one example; some types of anti-vehicle or anti-flak incendiary and fragmentation weapons are others.

A good taxonomy should impose order on a subject, but it may also have value in exposing disorder. The foregoing attempt demonstrates that a simple categorisation of modern weapons as either anti-personnel or anti-materiel is not possible. Ways of using weapons may perhaps be so categorised, but not the weapons themselves. All that can be said is that most weapons have anti-personnel effects; a few are designed for this alone (e.g. small-calibre assault rifles or some multiple-flechette warheads); but the majority are intended to have varying degrees and kinds of anti-materiel effectiveness as well. And if weapons are ranked according to the gravity of their effects on the human body, those designed purely for anti-personnel uses may in fact be nearer the less hideous than the more hideous end of the scale.

Within each of the foregoing categories, maximum lethality is provided by indirect-fire weapons. This follows from characteristics already noted, namely range performance, concertability and ease of replenishment, which together enable large weights of munitions to be delivered over a wide front. It is therefore on trends in the design of munitions for indirect-fire weapons—tube artillery, rocket artillery and ground-attack aircraft—that this chapter concentrates, first on the form of the munitions and then on their kill mechanisms.

The cheapest indirect-fire weapons to maintain and use are mortars; the most costly, supersonic ground-attack aircraft. If the latter are to be worthwhile, the effectiveness of their ammunition has a great deal of expense to justify. It follows that of all indirect-fire munitions those dispensed by aircraft are likely to be the most advanced. A pattern may be observed of novel concepts first appearing in air munitions and then, as experience is gained and production costs diminish, filtering down to less elaborate weapons systems. This is true of, for example, cluster munitions, which appeared first as cluster bombs, then as warheads for large battlefield rockets, and now as artillery shells of smaller and smaller calibres.

The latest trends in indirect-fire munitions are obscured from the public eye by military secrecy. We may, however, learn much—as the weapons designers did themselves—from the experience of the Vietnam war. Thus, if we can identify time-trends in the expenditures of different varieties of air munition over Indochina, we may be able to judge in broad outline which way indirect-fire munitions in general have since been developing.

Munition trends during the Vietnam war

We know from US Defense Department releases the annual tonnages of air munitions dropped on targets in Indochina either by US aircraft or by other aircraft carrying US-supplied munitions. Lumsden provides a collection of such data.[5] This tells us nothing about the different varieties of air munition used, but on this we have another source of information, namely what appears to be a complete year-by-year Defense Department record of the numbers (and costs) of all the different munitions procured or programmed for procurement by the US armed services during 1964–73.[6] If the figures on air munitions are extracted from these records (omitting the nuclear, biological and casualty-chemical munitions) and the total tonnage of the different procurements then calculated from what is known, or can be estimated, about the individual weights of the 80-odd different munitions, annual air-munition procurement can be compared with annual air-munition expenditure over Indochina. This is the procedure which underlies Table 3.3. We note from the table that procurement and use ran closely in step, the former exceeding the latter in 1966, 1968–9, and 1973, though not by much. This bears out what may be inferred from other sources and what Defense Department witnesses had testified to Congressional committees at the time: that the initial air operations over Indochina were supplied from war-reserve stocks of munitions of Second World War and Korean War vintage; that these stocks were 'largely expended' by 1967;[7] that standby production-lines for old munitions were then reopened and production-lines for new munitions built; and that not until 1973 did consumption rates slacken so as to allow replenishment of the denuded war-reserve stockpile.

There are many different varieties of air-to-ground munition, and some are more heavily relied upon than others. The US procurement record provides evidence on relative degrees of importance. Five broad categories of munition may be distinguished. The first two are the traditional armament of ground-support aircraft: machine guns, and free-fall bombs dropped individually. Then there are unguided rockets, an innovation (for aircraft) of the Second World War which, in the air-to-ground rather than the air-to-air role, languished after the war and did not fully recover until rockets became popular as a means for arming helicopters, which happened early in the Vietnam war. Munitions dispensing clusters of small free-fall sub-munitions constitute the fourth category; the simplest forms go back to the First World War but, during the 1950s, development programmes commenced which subsequently yielded a wide variety of bomblet and minelet cluster munitions, some of extraordinary complexity. Finally, there is the category of guided weapons: air-to-ground guided missiles and glide bombs fitted with target-homing devices that permit exceptionally accurate delivery. The latter are the 'smart' bombs which came into

TABLE 3.3 Tonnages of US conventional air-to-ground munitions used over Indochina, and tonnages procured by the US Air Force and US Navy, each year during 1963–73

	1964	1965	1966	1967	1968	1969	1970	1971	1972	1973	Total
US Air Force procurements (megadollars, by fiscal year)	58.6	175.9	839.2	1016.0	1063.4	1109.6	730.4	540.4	586.5	664.8*	6784.8
US Air Force procurements (kilotonnes, by fiscal year)	15.4	81.5	565.0	542.5	997.5	1089.5	649.5	540.3	638.7	678.0*	5797.4
US Navy procurements (kilotonnes, by fiscal year)	7.0	51.4	138.8	224.6	322.6	353.6	164.5	63.5	108.8	161.7*	1596.5
Total US procurements (kilotonnes, by fiscal year)	22.4	132.9	703.8	767.1	1320.1	1443.1	814.0	603.8	747.5	839.7*	7393.9
Quantities used in Indochina (kilotonnes, by calendar year)	?	285.8	458.4	845.6	1304.0	1258.5	886.7	692.3	983.7	378.1†	7039.1

Notes   * Programmed procurement as of 31 Dec 1972.   † January through June only.

Sources   On procurement: Figures calculated from data contained in US Defense Department annual returns on types, numbers and costs of munitions procured or programmed for procurement during fiscal years 1964–73.

On use: M. Lumsden, *Antipersonnel weapons* (Stockholm: SIPRI, forthcoming).

TABLE 3.4   Relative importance of different categories of air-to-ground munition as indicated by annual US Air Force procurements during fiscal years 1964–73

Category of weapon	Percentage of total annual procurement, by weight of munitions										
	1964	1965	1966	1967	1968	1969	1970	1971	1972	1973*	1964–73
PERCENTAGES BY WEIGHT OF MUNITIONS											
Massive bombs and mines	57.5	81.1	91.4	86.9	93.8	92.1	86.4	86.2	90.4	91.6	90.2
Precision guided bombs	np	np		0.3	0.1	0.4	1.0	2.5	2.6	0.8	0.8
Machine-gun ammunition	2.6	3.9	2.8	2.8	1.2	1.0	0.7	1.1	1.1	1.0	1.4
2.75 inch rockets	np	5.2	1.7	3.0	1.6	1.6	1.5	0.8	1.3	1.4	1.6
Cluster munitions	39.9	9.8	4.0	7.0	3.4	4.7	10.5	9.4	4.8	5.1	5.9
PERCENTAGES BY COST OF MUNITIONS											
Massive bombs and mines	6.7	32.7	56.2	44.7	63.1	61.3	46.1	49.8	56.8	57.8	53.9
Precision guided bombs	np	np	0.1	3.9	3.0	4.0	5.9	12.3	11.3	6.6	5.1
Machine-gun ammunition	5.3	12.3	14.6	11.9	8.2	4.6	2.7	5.1	5.1	4.5	7.6
2.75 inch rockets	np	12.2	6.5	7.7	6.5	6.8	5.1	3.6	5.6	7.5	6.5
Cluster munitions	88.1	42.9	21.7	31.8	19.3	23.3	40.3	29.2	22.1	23.6	26.9

Conventions   (np) no procurement; (. .) less than 0.05%.
Note   * Programmed procurement as of 31 Dec 1972.
Source   Figures calculated from data contained in US Defense Department annual returns on types, numbers and costs of munitions procured or programmed for procurement during fiscal years 1964–73.

increasing use in Indochina from 1967 until the USAF withdrew from direct operations.

Table 3.4 shows annual US Air Force procurements of each of these categories. The data are presented as percentages of total annual procurements, both by tonnage and by dollar cost. There are two major omissions: guided air-to-ground missiles other than smart bombs; and the fuzes for those munitions for which fuzes are supplied separately. These omissions probably do not greatly affect the overall tonnages, but they could make a substantial difference to the relative dollar costs per unit weight of each category of munition. Be that as it may, the table clearly indicates that the two categories in which innovation both burgeoned and was applied were those of smart bombs (which are beyond the scope of this essay) and of cluster munitions.

Cluster munitions

Table 3.4 indicates that cluster munitions—the 'CBUs' of Vietnam war reporting—were in production as War Readiness Materiel before the US Air Force had begun operations over Indochina. By 1966 requirements for cluster munitions were apparently exceeding supplies, a user-demand which subsequently, it would seem, both increased and was met. Somewhere between 50 and 100 different cluster munitions were studied in US R&D laboratories during the war,[8] and of those more than 30 went into production and were presumably used in Indochina.

The US Air Force procured about 350,000 tonnes of cluster munitions during 1964–73, and the US Navy another 40,000 tonnes. Though this was less than six per cent of the total weight of air munitions procured during that period, it accounted for more than a quarter of the procurement expenditure. This gives some idea of the importance attached to cluster munitions.

The logic behind cluster munitions is that the smaller a munition the greater is the area-effectiveness of a given total weight. This is because the destructive effects of a single munition, whatever its kill mechanism, diminish rapidly with distance from its point of function. Hence, if a munition is to exert destructive effects over an area, kills at the periphery necessitate overkill at the centre. Cluster munitions allow killing agents to be distributed more evenly over a target, thereby reducing net overkill and providing greater economy. They may, in some cases, allow attacks on area targets which, for logistical reasons, would otherwise be impossible to engage.

From the standpoint of design, the chief problem is to ensure that the cluster munition dispenses its sub-munitions evenly over the target. The design of the dispenser and the design of the sub-munitions are the two basic variables. Thus, some of the requisite dispersion may be achieved by having the dispenser forcibly eject the sub-munitions over

TABLE 3.5 Cluster munitions procured by the US Air Force and US Navy, 1964–73

Cluster munition	Type of sub-munition used
HIGH-SPEED REARWARD-EJECTION DISPENSER MUNITIONS............................	
Dispenser w/anti-personnel bomblets, CBU-1	Fragmentation, BLU-4
Dispenser w/anti-vehicle bomblets, CBU-2	Heavy pellet, BLU-3
Dispenser w/anti-tank bomblets, CBU-3	Hollow charge, BLU-7
Dispenser w/apers-smoke bomblets, CBU-12 & CBU-13	WP, BLU-17 & BLU-17 + BLU-16 (HC)
Dispenser w/apers jungle bomblets, CBU-46	Fragmentation, BLU-66
LOW-SPEED REARWARD-EJECTION DISPENSER MUNITIONS...........................	
Dispenser w/anti-vehicle bomblets, CBU-14	Heavy pellet, BLU-3
Dispenser w/apers-smoke bomblets, CBU-22	White phosphorus, BLU-17
Dispenser w/apers jungle bomblets, CBU-25	Fragmentation, BLU-24
DOWNWARD-EJECTION DISPENSER MUNITIONS...........................	
Re-usable dispenser, Gladeye	(unloaded)
Re-usable Tactical Fighter Dispenser (TFD), SUU-41	(unloaded)
Disp w/clustered anti-personnel bomblets, CBU-7	Fragmentation, BLU-18
Strongback w/clustered apers-irritant blets, CBU-19	CS irritant, BLU-39
Disp w/clustered apers minelets, CBU-28 & CBU-37	Blast, BLU-43 & BLU-44 Dragontooth
Disp w/clustered apers-irritant bomblets, CBU-30	CS irritant, BLU-39
TFD w/anti-tank mines, CBU-33	Hollow charge, BLU-45
TFD w/clustered apers minelets (WAAPM), CBU-34 & -42	Fragmentation, BLU-42 & BLU-54
Dispenser w/anti-PAM bombs, CBU-38	Fragmentation, BLU-49
TFD w/clustered ?apers jungle bomblets, CBU-43	Fragmentation, BLU-48
TFD w/apers bomblets, CBU-44	?
TFD w/multi-purpose minelets, CBU-45	?
CANISTER-CLUSTERS FOR INTERNALLY-MOUNTED DISPENSERS (FOR B-52 BOMBERS, &C.).................	
Re-usable dispenser, SUU-24	(unloaded)
Canister w/anti-personnel jungle bomblets	Fragmentation, BLU-24
Canister w/apers grenades, ?ADU-256 (*et al.*)	Fragmentation, M40 (and other grens)
Canister w/anti-vehicle bomblets, ADU-253	Heavy pellet, BLU-3
Canister w/anti-PAM bomblets, ADU-272	Pellet, BLU-26
Canister, anti-PAM, ?BLU-29	Napalm-B
Canister w/anti-PAM bomblets, CDU-22	Fragmentation, BLU-63
CLUSTER BOMBS	
125-lb, clustered anti-PAM bombs, M1A2 & M1A4	Fragmentation, M41
750-lb, clustered anti-PAM bomblets, M36	Incendiary, M126
500-lb, Rockeye w/anti-tank-apers bomblets, Mk20	Hollow-charge/frag, Mk118
750-lb, Sadeye w/anti-PAM blets, CBU-24, -29 & -49	Pellet, BLU-26, BLU-36 & BLU-59
750-lb, Sadeye w/anti-PAM bomblets, CBU-52	Frag/incendiary, BLU-61
750-lb, Sadeye w/anti-personnel bomblets, CBU-53	Incendiary, BLU-70
750-lb, Sadeye, w/anti-PAM bomblets, CBU-54	Incendiary, BLU-68
500-lb, clustered anti-PAM bombs, CBU-55	Fuel-air explosive, BLU-73
750-lb, Sadeye w/anti-PAM bomblets, CBU-58	Fragmentation, BLU-63
500-lb, Rockeye w/discr AT-apers blets, CBU-59	Hollow-charge/frag, BLU-77
750-lb, Sadeye w/sub-munitions, CBU-70	?

Conventions (*) incls US Navy procurement; ( ) number procured; (...) procurement without acquisition: (..) planned procurement not effected; (w/) with.

| | *Annual procurements (weight of munitions purchased, kilotonnes)* | | | | | | | | | |
	1964	*1965*	*1966*	*1967*	*1968*	*1969*	*1970*	*1971*	*1972*	*1973*
..TOTAL, percent wt:	82.6	16.9	5.8	15.7	19.7	2.9	0	0	0	0
	1.29	0	0	0	0	0	0	0	0	0
	4.06	0	0.07*	5.81	3.84	0	0	0	0	0
	0.77	1.03	0.33	...	0	0	0	0	0	0
	0	0.41	0.96	0.56	..	0	0	0	0	0
	0	0	0	0	3.71	1.92	0	0	0	0
TOTAL:	6.12	1.44	1.36	6.37	7.55	1.92	0	0	0	0
..TOTAL, percent wt:	0	32.7	19.1	10.5	0.6	5.6	7.0	4.0	11.2	9.7
	0	2.79	3.44	2.27	..	1.41	2.45	0.72	0	0
	0	0	0.12	0.29	0.16	0	0	0.14	0	0
	0	0	0.92	1.71	0.07	2.30	2.89	1.28	4.09	3.56
TOTAL:	0	2.79	4.48	4.27	0.23	3.71	5.34	2.14	4.09	3.56
..TOTAL, percent wt:	0	12.4	8.6	4.9	5.5	3.5	4.1	1.0	10.6	0
	(..)	(0)	(0)	(0)	(0)	(0)	(0)	(0)	(0)	(0)
	(0)	(0)	(0)	(2792)	(2088)	(..)	(0)	(0)	(0)	(0)
	0	1.06	1.68	...	0	0	0	0	0	0
	0	0	0.13	0.09	0	0	0	0	0	0
	0	0	0.16	1.29	0.85	..	0	0	0	0
	0	0	0	0.13	0.55	0.89	..	0	0	0
	0	·0	...	0.23	..	..	0	0	0	0
	0	0	0.06	0.27	0.70	1.38	2.57	0	0	0
	0	0	0	0	0	0.04	0.55	0.52	3.89	0
	0	0	0	0	0	..	0	0	0	0
	0	0	0	0	..	0	0	0	0	0
	0	0	0	0	..	0	0	0	0	0
TOTAL:	0	1.06	2.02	2.01	2.09	2.31	3.13	0.52	3.89	0
..TOTAL, percent wt:	0	13.3	50.1	9.9	0.2	0.1	4.4	0	2.8	0
	(0)	(80)	(84)	(0)	(0)	(0)	(0)	(0)	(0)	(0)
	0	0	1.14	..	0	0	0	0	0	0
	0	0.16	0.05	0.13	0.09	0.07	..	0	0	0
	0	0.98	7.04	2.47	..	0	0	0	0	0
	0	0	2.94	1.44	..	0	3.36	0	1.02	0
	0	0	0.58	0	0	0	0	0	0	0
	0	0	0	0	0	0	...	..	0	0
TOTAL:	0	1.14	11.75	4.03	0.09	0.07	3.36	0	1.02	0
..TOTAL, percent wt:	17.4	24.7	16.4	59.0	74.0	87.8	84.4	95.1	75.5	90.3
	0	1.23	2.02	0.56	1.73	3.38	0.75	0.55	0	0
	0	0	0	0	0	2.81	4.26	6.21	..	0
	0	0	0.12*	0.31*	0.63*	1.90*	3.65*	5.80*	7.65*	4.39*
	1.29*	0.87*	1.71*	23.16*	25.79*	49.53*	50.73*	22.10	..	0
	0	0	0	0	0	0	1.07	1.72	6.64	8.03
	0	0	0	0	0.24	..	0	0	0	0
	0	0	0	0	0.02	..	0	0	0	0
	0	0	0	0	0	0.07*	1.42*	0.50*	0.86*	4.12*
	0	0	0	0	0	0	2.28	14.24	12.54	16.42
	0	0	0	0	0	0	0	0.08	0	0
	0	0	0	0	0	0	0	0.13	0	0
TOTAL:	1.29	2.10	3.85	24.03	28.40	57.69	64.15	51.32	27.68	32.96
GRAND TOTAL:	7.41	8.52	23.46	40.70	38.37	65.69	75.97	53.98	36.68	36.52

an area, rather as artillery may be used for pattern fire. Alternatively, the sub-munitions may be fitted with some sort of self-dispersing mechanism so that they distribute themselves over the target area after release from the dispenser. The more sophisticated types of cluster munition combine both methods.

Table 3.5 shows the total US air cluster munition procurement during 1964–73 grouped into different categories according to the type of dispenser. It will be seen that procurement was initially directed towards rearward-ejection dispenser munitions (REDMs). These comprise an externally carried sheaf of tubes, looking rather like a rocket-pod pointing backwards. There are large streamlined versions for use from tactical ground-support aircraft at high speed; and there are smaller, simpler versions for helicopters and light aircraft. Each tube of an REDM—about 70 mm calibre in the early US ones—is loaded with several bomblets which are ejected in a rapid stream at a rearward velocity roughly the same as the forward velocity of the aircraft; they thus fall in a tight pattern along the flight path. Over the 1964–73 time period, procurement of REDMs increasingly concentrated on systems for low-performance aircraft. For high-performance aircraft, downward ejecting systems evidently came to be considered more attractive. Sub-munitions for these DEDMs could be larger than those for rearward-ejecting systems, for attacks on hard targets, as in the CBU-33 and CBU-38. Or they could be much smaller, thus enabling very wide area coverage. The latter property was exploited in Indochina in support of new mine-warfare techniques, DEDMs being used to scatter enormous numbers of small anti-personnel mines over areas across which passage was to be denied. Thus, the CBU-28/37 Dragontooth, the CBU-34/42 WAAPM, and the SUU-41 Gravel anti-personnel mining systems were extensively used during Air Force Igloo White operations in support of the 'McNamara Wall'. This is now an international growth area in indirect-fire weaponry.

In that DEDMs provided a means for dropping free-fall clusters of sub-munitions in quick succession, they have their antecedents in devices used during the Second World War for dropping small incendiary bombs from bomber aircraft. Among these the Soviet AK-2 Aerial Release Case may be noted. When B-52 and other bombers came to be used over Indochina, modernised versions of these devices, chiefly the SUU-24 Hayes Dispenser, were procured so as to allow the latest types of bomblet and grenade to be used in high-altitude area bombing attacks. The dispensers dropped large canisters—boxes commonly weighing about 150 lbs and with no special aerodynamic shaping—of bomblets or grenades, the boxes opening some way above the target to scatter their contents. The preferred payloads were evidently self-dispersing sub-munitions: spherical bomblets with vanes built into their outer surface shaped so as to impart rotation as the bomblet fell through the air and then Magnus lift to give the desired lateral motion. Two Hayes Dispensers can be carried in a B-52; each dispenser can hold 72 canisters; and each canister can hold some hundreds of sub-munitions depending on their size (more than 500 in the case of the small M40 grenades). Table 3.5 shows that procurement of Hayes Dispensers took place during 1965–6, and of canister-clusters for them intermittently during 1965–72. Press reports of B-52 cluster-bombing did not begin to appear in the outside world until the end of this period.

Canister clusters for Hayes Dispensers and the like accounted for about half of the tonnage of cluster munitions procured during 1966, but thereafter true cluster bombs became far the most heavily procured of all cluster munitions. In these, such as the Sadeye and Rockeye, the dispenser does not remain attached to the aircraft, but is dropped as an aimable free-fall unit resembling a general-purpose bomb; the casing opens in mid-air to release the bomblets. In the commonest variety, based on the navy's Sadeye dispenser which opens like a cockle-shell, the bomblets are of the spherical self-dispensing type, no special ejection mechanism being used to scatter them other than the spin imparted to the falling dispenser by its tailfins. The smaller but more elaborate Rockeye dispenser, also a navy innovation, does not use self-dispersing bomblets but appears instead to spin out its payload by means of a rocket motor. Loaded with hollow-charge bomblets, the Rockeye dispenser is the principal US air-delivered anti-tank munition. Cluster bombs of various types are included in US arms exports; certain NATO countries, Iran, and Israel have been among the recipients. Cluster bombs were used in the Israeli air-raid on Damascus on 9 October 1973 (a reprisal for the earlier Syrian FROG-missile attacks on Israeli kibbutzim).[9]

Several of the air-delivered cluster munitions used over Indochina were still in development at the time of their use, their procurement being for operational evaluation. There were probably others also, purchased out of R&D appropriations (and therefore not showing in the procurement tables): examples from among non-cluster munitions include the big Air Force fuel-air explosive bombs (BLU-72 and BLU-76) described later. Some of these developmental cluster munitions may later have been abandoned, but there is little published information either on this or on new types that have emerged since.

The 1972 and 1973 procurement data give some idea of which of the many cluster munitions were considered the most satisfactory and most appropriate for the post-Vietnam war-reserve stockpile. The US Defense Secretary's 1972 Defense Report states that these were the first two years of a

> 5-year procurement program to build an inventory of more sophisti-cated, more effective air munitions. When completed, this modernised

air munitions inventory will, through a higher degree of effectiveness per sortie, improve the ability of our fighter/attack aircraft to achieve desirable effectiveness with fewer sorties and less exposure to anti-aircraft defenses. This air munitions modernisation program calls for significant additions of new munitions with better target destruction capability than those currently in the inventory.[10]

Of the $187 million sought in the FY 1973 budget for procurement of cluster munitions, 75 per cent was to be spent on the stockpile.[11]

Recent writings continue to emphasise the importance of three roles which air cluster munitions played during the Vietnam war: the suppression of anti-aircraft defences; wide-area scatter mining; and tank destruction. For all of these, a new and much larger free-fall dispenser has been developed: the SUU-54, which is in the 2000-lb class. It is used in a variety of munitions that are still in development: examples include the GBU-2 Pave Storm flak-suppression munition; the Gator wide-area anti-personnel and anti-tank mining system; the Grasshopper anti-vehicle mine system; and the Piranha anti-tank mine system for use in shallow water.[12] For direct attack of tanks there is a 1974 report of a conceptual weapon in which the SUU-54 would be used to dispense independently-homing anti-tank sub-munitions.

The United States does not, of course, have a monopoly in cluster munitions. Very little seems to be known about Soviet cluster munitions, except that they exist. Among air-delivered anti-tank munitions, the Rockeye cluster bomb has at least two foreign competitors of similar size. There is the British Mk 1 No 1 Cluster Bomb (the BL755) which was conceived in 1964, shortly after the Rockeye, but which did not enter production until 1971; it dispenses a larger hollow-charge/frag-mentation bomblet with, so it is said, greater precision and reliability.[13] Foreign sales of the BL755 are being actively promoted: customers already include five other NATO air forces and at least one African country (Kenya), and there are hopes of US purchases also. Then there is the French Belouga cluster bomb, which seems similar to the BL755 but was still in development in 1976.[14] Three different types of sub-munition are available for it: anti-tank and anti-personnel bomb-lets, and a sub-munition for area-interdiction. There is an Australian cluster bomb, reported to be in development in the 1972 Defence Report. Finally there are West German developmental cluster-bombs within the Strebo programme on fixed and free-fall dispenser munitions.

The West German work on cluster munitions was kept secret until late 1970, when information on three types of sub-munition was released: the Pandora anti-tank minelet, designed to destroy the tracks of a tank but incapable of being triggered by wheeled vehicles or by unwary footsteps; the Medusa, a larger and more destructive magnetic anti-tank (hollow-charge) minelet; and two varieties of Dragon Seed bomblet, one anti-personnel and the other hollow-charge armour piercing.[15] One of the design considerations in the Strebo programme is the fact that Soviet tank-warfare doctrine envisages a massing of tanks into 500 metre squares prior to attack; certain of the developmental Strebo munitions—presumably including cluster bombs loaded with Dragon Seed—are said to be capable of enabling a single aircraft (e.g. a Starfighter or a Tornado) to attack such a square; other Strebo cluster munitions are being developed to give still larger area-coverage.[16] These systems are not confined to cluster bombs. There is what appears to be a DEDM dispensing Medusa minelets; and there is the Streuwaffen, a 19-tube REDM dispensing 409 half-kilogram bomblets (presumably Dragon Seed). The French Giboulée system, in development since 1966, is also an REDM, dispensing 50 mm anti-personnel (fragmentation) or anti-tank (hollow-charge) bomblets.[17]

The progression of cluster munitions from aircraft to missile to artillery to mortar systems is clearly displayed in the US arsenal. The non-nuclear warheads developed by the US Army for its battlefield-support guided missiles and heavy artillery rockets have all been of the clustered-bomblet type: first, since the 1950s, warheads containing spherical self-dispersing bomblets charged with chemical-warfare or biological-warfare agents, and then warheads containing fragmentation bomblets, some of them of types originally developed for air force cluster bombs. The latest version, the 1000 lb M251 warhead for Lance, standardised in 1974, contains 833 BLU-63 bomblets. The unit cost of a Lance fitted with this warhead was stated, in March 1976, to be $207,000. US production has so far been entirely confined to fulfilling foreign military sales orders: 200 for Israel (deliveries began in February 1976), and others for Belgium and the Netherlands. The M251 warhead is optimised for use against personnel and light materiel targets; still in development in 1977 was a warhead effective against personnel carriers and tanks.[18] Bomblet warheads have also been developed for air-to-ground missiles, but little information has been released about them. The Bullpup missile, in its AGM-12E variant developed for the Vietnam war, is said to have a warhead containing 830 BLU-26/36 fragmentation bomblets.

Bomblet and minelet payloads for cannon-artillery projectiles of 8-inch, 155 mm, and 105 mm calibre have been in development since the early 1960s. Bomblet shells have been one of the two main foci in the US Army's 'Improved Conventional Munition' (ICM) programme (the other focus evidently being the development of special high-fragmenting iron alloys for shell casings).[19] Minelet shells are the basis of the closely-related Army programme on Artillery-Delivered Target-Activated

Munitions (ADTAM), another manifestation of the current interest in new offensive mine-warfare techniques.

Field evaluation of ICM artillery clusters in comparison with current general-purpose HE shell took place in South Vietnam during 1968. It is reported that against like targets—presumably soldiers in the open—up to 55 per cent fewer ICM rounds were needed.[20] US Army Congressional testimony in 1974 spoke of the 105 mm ICM round as being ten times more lethal than the normal HE round; and it was said that the follow-on round then in engineering development would be more lethal still.[21] The US Army and US Marine Corps procured about 50,000 tonnes of cluster-shell projectiles during 1964–73.

As to mortar systems, the US Army has standardised an anti-personnel cluster round, the M453, for its 107 mm mortar.[22] There does not appear to have been any major procurement of this prior to 1974.

Outside the United States, it seems that the main interest in ground-launched cluster munitions has to do with offensive mine-warfare systems. Most of the available information is on West German developments: a 1971 report refers to 155 mm artillery rounds loaded with Pandora anti-tank minelets; a 1973 report, to development of warheads containing Pandora, Medusa, or Dragon Seed sub-munitions for the LAR 110 mm multiple rocket launcher (MRL) system.[23] The latter project now seems to have culminated in the Minenstreumittel-Werfer (MSM/W), which was undergoing final evaluation in 1976;[24] derived from LAR, it comprises a 15-tube truck-mounted launcher, each tube firing a canister containing five AT-II anti-tank minelets to within a range bracket of 800–3000 metres. There are signs that the French Army is developing cluster warheads for its own MRL system, the 140 mm RAP-14. Around 1970, the British Foil MRL project was subsumed into the nascent trilateral British–German–Italian RS-80 project on the joint development of a long-range (40–60 km) heavy-calibre (250–75 mm) MRL system; cluster warheads of anti-personnel and anti-armour minelets are envisaged for this. Britain withdrew from RS-80 in 1975.

Cluster munitions are, as described above, primarily intended for area weapons. Their quantitative area-effectiveness is therefore an important factor in decisions about their development and acquisition. Such information is also directly relevant to those questions of discriminateness and indiscriminateness which imbue much of the present international consideration of qualitative limitations on conventional weapons. But military authorities tend to keep this information secret, and it is difficult for outsiders to form a clear picture; there is also much unreliable information in circulation.

Table 3.6 provides estimates in respect of particular cluster munitions and certain other area munitions.

TABLE 3.6   Rough estimates of maximum effective areas of representative area munitions

Type of munition	Effective area coverage (hectares)	Actual munition on which the estimate is based
750-lb napalm firebomb	0.2	BLU-1 (US)
750-lb general-purpose HE bomb	0.4	M117 (US)
155 mm cluster shell with apers fragmentation bomblets	0.5	M449 (US)
Light RE dispenser munition with apers frag bomblets	0.6	CBU-25 (US)
600-lb anti-tank cluster bomb	0.7	Belouga (French)
Heavy RE dispenser munition with apers frag bomblets	1.0	Giboulée (French)
2000-lb general-purpose HE bomb	1.1	Mk84 (US)
500-lb fuel-air explosive cluster bomb	2.6	CBU-72 (US)
155 mm battalion fire, HE shell	5.8	M114/M1 (US)
External-carriage DE dispenser munition, apers frag bomblets	6.6	CBU-7 (US)
750-lb anti-PAM fragmentation cluster bomb	7.0	CBU-24 (US)
Anti-PAM frag bomblet warhead for battlefield-support missile	8.7	Lance/M251 (US)
Ground-launched anti-tank minelet cluster	9.0	MSM/W (West German)
Ground-launched apers frag warhead cluster	10	RAP-14 (French)
2000-lb anti-PAM fragmentation cluster bomb	19	Pave Storm (US)
15,000-lb light-case HE bomb	49	BLU-82 (US)
0.1 kiloton airburst nuclear-fission warhead	92	(hypothetical)
Nerve-gas bomblet warhead for heavy artillery rocket	110	Honest John/M190 (US)
Bomb-bay DE dispenser munition, clustered apers frag bomblets	150	SUU-24/ADU-256 (US)

Source The bases of the estimates, and the published sources on which they rely, are set out in J. P. Perry Robinson, 'Trends in conventional munitions...', *op. cit.* Actual effective area coverage of course depends on such factors as target-protectedness, delivery mode, etc. The estimates given here are roughly comparable points within ranges varying widely in breadth.

It should also be said in relation to Table 3.6 that the area of effect sought from an area weapon will depend on the type of target the munition is intended to attack and the type of operation in which it is to be used. In some cases only a limited area coverage will be sought.

For an anti-tank cluster bomb, for example, the desired coverage might be defined by the area of ground over which a tank might move during the time-of-fall of the bomb, plus an additional area to compensate for delivery errors. In other cases, maximum area effectiveness will be a primary objective, either as a means for reducing the weight of munitions needed to attack certain types of target or to provide special wide-area attack capabilities. For the latter there seems at present to be a marked growth in military requirements. The proliferation of ground-force precision guided munitions, particularly the new highly mobile anti-tank and anti-aircraft guided weapons, is undoubtedly stimulating greater interest in area-saturation weapons for the defence of armour and ground-support aircraft. Again, the increasing interest, noted earlier, in scatter-mining as an adjunct to offensive manoeuvre has created requirements for new wide-area target-activated weapons.

CATEGORIES OF KILL MECHANISM

The area of effectiveness of a munition is a measure of the area of ground over which the 'hit-kill probability' exceeds a specified level. This probability defines the combined probabilities of a target-element at which the munition is directed being struck (the 'hit probability') and of being put out of action by a strike (the 'kill probability'): a person killed or disabled, or a piece of equipment destroyed. Older types of munition tended to have either high hit probabilities or high kill probabilities, but not both. The basic anti-personnel weapon of the Second World War, the infantryman's rifle, is an example: during the war something like 50,000 bullets were fired for each hit, but every third or fourth hit killed. Cluster munitions represent an attempt at trading-off hit and kill probabilities against each other so as to achieve a greater overall hit-kill probability.

To this same end, the actual kill mechanism that is built into a munition or sub-munition has offered much scope to the ingenuity of weapons designers. For killing, the military have always preferred to hack, pierce, or shatter. Other possibilities have been less well regarded, but trends of fashion may be discerned, loosely connected with technical change. Flame, for example, has become increasingly popular during the present century; and, in the package of different kill mechanisms proffered by nuclear fission and nuclear fusion, the military are now seeing particular attractions in ionising radiation. In contrast, toxicity evidently has little allure, and infectivity even less. Physical methods of destruction, centred on bullets and explosives, remain in the ascendancy.

Chemical explosives provide two basic kill mechanisms: energy transfer by blast wave or by moving fragments. The latter, when exploited by detonating an explosive within a metal casing, is especially conducive to area effectiveness; the former, to high kill probabilities over limited areas. Fragmentation munitions come in three broad categories according to the type of casing used to surround the explosive. In the original type, going back to the early days of gunpowder, the casings did not incorporate any special aids to fragmentation: they shattered into a broad spectrum of fragment sizes, some large and excessively destructive, others so small as to be harmless. The trade-off between hit and kill probabilities was therefore poor. To improve this, techniques of 'controlled fragmentation' emerged which sought to narrow the fragment spectrum by scoring the casing so as to create a multiplicity of fracture points (a technique which did not in fact work very well until it was appreciated, some time after the Second World War, that the scoring had to be done on the inside surface of the casing, not the outside). Another technique for controlling fragmentation has been to construct the casing of helically-wound notched steel wire or rod. A technique for still greater control, developed during the 1950s, is to pre-fragment the casing into steel pellets, embedding them in a soft matrix. This is a modern twist in a line of development which stretches back through shrapnel shell to the earliest forms of artillery case shot (bullet-filled shell). In fact neither pre-fragmented nor scored casings are suitable for artillery munitions since they are too weak to withstand projection from a gun barrel: their use is limited to aircraft and mortar bombs, grenades, rocket warheads, and sub-munitions. Maximised fragmentation effects from artillery shell are currently obtained either by using shell casings made of special iron alloys whose crystal structure serves to narrow the fragment-size spectrum, or by using modern versions of case shot. These include the sub-munition-filled projectiles noted earlier and canister rounds having a payload of small metal missiles. The Beehive artillery ammunition provided to US forces in Indochina, largely on an experimental basis and mostly for direct-fire guns, is the latest manifestation of the latter: each round ejects some thousands of small fin-stabilised needles, known as 'flechettes'.[25] Quite large numbers of multiple-flechette projectiles were used during the Vietnam war, particularly as air-to-ground rocket warheads. Originally anti-personnel, multiple-flechette munitions are now being developed for armour-piercing uses as well.[26] Depleted uranium is a favoured material for making the flechettes.[27] Its density provides the necessary increase in weight, and it also has the chemical property of reacting exothermally with iron: the additional heat thus generated during impact with armour creates intense local overpressure which aids penetration, and pyrophoric fragments are strewn about which are capable of igniting fuel and the like.

Just as design techniques are available for maximising the fragmentation effects of explosive munitions, and for optimising the fragment-size spectrum for use against different hardnesses of target, so also may the blast effects be maximised (though at the expense of fragmentation) and optimised. The thinner the casing, the greater the blast. Light-case explosive munitions have been developed which range from the very small to the very large. At one extreme are the 'tea bag' anti-personnel minelets (such as the US Gravel minelet), consisting of a small fabric bag of pressure-sensitive explosive. About 25 grams (more than is contained in a Gravel minelet) of an appropriate explosive detonated at foot level is sufficient to amputate a man's leg. Mines of this type are designed to be scattered by the thousand over a wide area.[28] At the other extreme are such massive munitions as the $7\frac{1}{2}$-ton 'daisy cutter' bombs (BLU-82) employed in Vietnam for clearing helicopter landing-zones and as wide-area anti-personnel weapons.[29]

Optimisation of blast effects for particular targets is achieved by shaping the explosive charge so as to focus the blast or otherwise make it conform to the target. When hollow-charge munitions (also called HEAT or shaped-charge munitions) are used for armour penetration, a conical hollow is shaped into the impact end of the charge and lined with a thin layer of metal, usually copper. The detonating explosive vaporises the copper, and its directional effect squirts the metal forward in a thin jet capable of cutting through armour and injecting an intense pulse of thermal energy; the effects on people inside the tank are terrible. In the medical literature they have recently been characterised in terms of an 'anti-tank missile burn syndrome'.[30] Ten per cent of Israeli casualties during the 1973 Yom Kippur War displayed it: half of them had more than 20 per cent of their body surface burnt, and almost a third had third-degree burns, down to and through the subcutaneous tissue. In 'squash-head' (HESH) munitions, also used for the attack of tanks and other armoured vehicles, the explosive charge is adapted to flatten itself against the armour prior to detonation (only direct-fire weapons provide enough impact velocity for this flattening to take place). The blast wave transmitted through the metal breaks up the inside surface into a hail of high-velocity fragments, a phenomenon known as 'spalling'.[31] Fuel-air explosive munitions provide another means for optimising blast: the explosive charge—a detonatable cloud of fuel—is spread out like a gigantic pancake immediately above its intended area target.

Blast effects diminish more rapidly with distance (in air) than do fragmentation effects, but within the area over which they remain effective, their hit probability (so to speak) is essentially 100 per cent. Other types of casualty agent capable of entirely enveloping an area include fire initiated by incendiaries, and the toxic or infective aerosols of chemical/biological warfare. Weapons exploiting these kill mechanisms have a number of peculiar operational disadvantages, mostly stemming from uncertainties associated with the sensitivity of the kill probability to environmental factors; the uncertainties become translated into poor predictability of target effects and hazards to neighbouring friendly forces, meaning difficulty in calculating munitions requirements for specific operations. These and related technical problems perhaps serve to reinforce military inhibitions about using fire, poison, or disease as weapons, thus going some way towards explaining why chemical, biological, and incendiary warfare have remained on the periphery of military favour. This situation in the case of incendiary warfare has been changing since the Second World War; and there is a case for locating the reasons for the change in the rapid growth in understanding of how to create and direct fire. A similar process of technical advance may in due course come to increase the incidence of chemical warfare. As area weapons, chemical warfare munitions have strong attractions in the abstract, not least in economy of killing: decigrams or more of fragmentable metal in conjunction with a like weight of high explosive are needed to disable a person, but it may take less than a milligram of nerve gas to kill.

Kill mechanism trends during the Vietnam War

The US air-to-ground munitions procurement record provides evidence of the relative importance attached to the different kill mechanisms for indirect-fire munitions. Table 3.7, to which the same caveats attach as Table 3.4, categorises US Air Force annual procurements of air-to-ground munitions according to kill mechanism. Notable in it, once the procurement/use steady-state had been reached in 1967, is the remarkably consistent distribution of procurement between the three dominant classes of kill mechanism: general-purpose explosive, fragmentation-maximised explosive, and flame. The fluctuations, like the erratic procurements of other kill mechanisms, presumably stem from special military requirements in different phases of the war.

The procurement record also provides evidence of the extent to which the different categories of kill mechanism were exploited in the different categories of munition. It also displays time trends in their exploitation. Thus, as the Vietnam war progressed, three particular growth areas became prominent. The first was in incendiary cluster bombs (the M36/CBU-52 procurements). The second was in fuel-air explosive cluster bombs (the CBU-55 procurements). The third was the growth in the general area of fragmentation munitions and its increasing concentration in the anti-PAM rather than the anti-personnel or anti-materiel categories. These are trends which are worth exploring in more detail. Since fragmentation-munition design is already discussed rather fully in the open literature,[32] the remainder of this chapter will concentrate on new incendiary weapons and on fuel-air explosives.

Heat and flame: controlled fireballs

The trends of the 1960s and early 1970s in the exploitation of fire as a

TABLE 3.7 Relative importance of different categories of kill mechanism as indicated by annual US Air Force procurements of conventional air-to-ground munitions during fiscal years 1964–73

Percentage of total annual munitions procurement, by weight of munitions

Category of kill mechanism	1964	1965	1966	1967	1968	1969	1970	1971	1972	1973*	1964–73
Solid bullets	np	0.6	2.8	2.8	1.2	1.0	0.7	1.1	1.1	1.0	1.4
Explosive: general-purpose	1.3	31.4	62.1	79.0	90.5	85.8	81.6	83.8	89.9	89.3	82.8
Explosive: blast-maximised	np	np	..	0.2	0.1	np	0.2	0.3	0.1	0.5	0.2
Explosive: hollow-charge	5.2	1.2	..	..	np	..	np	0.6	0.2	0.9	0.2
Explosive: fragmentation-maximised	35.0	13.2	5.1	8.9	4.5	5.3	10.1	7.9	5.1	5.0	6.3
Napalm and other incendiaries	58.4	53.6	29.8	8.9	3.7	7.7	7.5	6.3	3.6	3.3	8.9
Chemical irritant (CS)	np	np	..	..	0.1	0.1	np	np	np	np	..

Conventions (np) no procurement; (..) less than 0.05%.

Note   * Programmed procurement as of 31 Dec 1972.

Source   As Table 3.4.

weapon show only faintly in the US procurement data. There are two main categories of fire weapon, though the distinction between them is not clear-cut: ones using flame munitions, with which the damage is mostly caused by direct contact with a burning flame agent; and ones using incendiary munitions, which damage not so much by direct contact as by initiating fires that then propagate through a target. Flame agents are broadcast; incendiary agents are used as intense point sources of fire.

Napalm, which is petrol gelled or otherwise thickened by means of additives, is an example of a flame agent; and many different varieties of it have been developed. The 1964–73 US Air Force and the US Navy procurement record indicates that, although napalm formed a high proportion of total US air-munitions procurement during the earlier part of the Vietnam war, the proportion declined as the war continued. Whether this reflects a similar decline in the use of air-dropped napalm during the war is not clear. The available data on the quantities of napalm dropped over Vietnam show that levels of use and of procurement paralleled each other during 1963–7, but with the latter so much above the former that large reserves would seem to have accumulated for later use. In contrast to napalm, incendiary procurement shows a rapid growth during the later period of the war. The growth was in large measure due to the effectiveness of incendiary cluster bombs in destroying vehicles during interdiction operations. When stocks of this type of munition—primarily the 750-lb M36 cluster of 182 magnesium/thermate 4-lb stick bomblets, dating back to the Korean war and suitable for carriage only in bombers or on the slower ground-attack tactical aircraft—had been depleted, in the spring of 1968, production lines were re-opened and development of newer versions hastened.[33] The chosen successor to the M36 was the CBU-52, which dispenses 254 BLU-61 2.2-lb spherical self-dispersing fragmentation bomblets incorporating metallic zirconium as an incendiary agent. This material was known, particularly from work on high explosive-incendiary (HEI) projectiles for aircraft cannon, to be an exceptionally potent incendiary, giving rise to long-burning pyrophoric fragments easily capable of setting fire to fuel tanks and the like.[34] Powders of zirconium, and of other reactive metals such as lithium, have also been under consideration, and perhaps also used, as a means for increasing the heat flux from burning napalm or other gelled-fuel flame agents.[35]

Incendiary cluster bombs were originally developed as a means for burning cities. In the tactical role, their new-found applications were not limited to anti-vehicle uses. In testimony before a Congressional committee, a US Air Force witness sought to justify the plans for increasing procurement of the CBU-52 during 1973 by citing increased military requirements both for anti-PAM weapons due to 'the introduction by the enemy of large ground formations into the Republic of

Vietnam' and for anti-aircraft defence suppression weapons due to 'the resumption of bombing in North Vietnam'.[36] Thus, heat as a kill mechanism, at least in conjunction with fragmentation, was evidently on the upsurge for air munitions. The same was apparently true for ground munitions. In its 1973 ordnance-research overview, the US Army Munitions Command wrote: 'Research studies have confirmed that rapid application of heat energy (heat flux) is the most effective method for destroying or damaging military targets'[37]—a judgement, it is to be noted, which refers to 'military targets' in general, regardless of their nature.

This is a remarkable appraisal. If justified, it can scarcely fail to be reflected in the munitions of the future. The performance of incendiary and flame munitions in Vietnam was no doubt part of the reason for it; but more important would seem to have been a particular laboratory development: a successful demonstration of what was called the 'controlled fireball concept'.

It is generally prudent to remain sceptical when, as in this instance, technologists claim a technological breakthrough. Yet on paper the development appears to be a major one. In particular, it looks as though those peculiarly awful weapons, the flamethrower and the napalm firebomb, may soon be outmoded; and that fire munitions will become increasingly popular for weapons to which at present they are poorly suited, such as artillery systems. The prospect thus seems to be a substantially upgraded status for incendiary warfare so that, in the years to come, fire, despite the repugnance which still attaches to its use as a kill mechanism, may be employed much more commonly in war than it has been so far.

The military allure of incendiaries and flame, if indeed it is growing, may explain the treatment they received at the Lucerne and Lugano conferences of government experts convened in 1974 and 1976 to explore the possibility of prohibiting particular conventional weapons. Burns were the one type of injury caused by conventional weapons which the medical experts present were prepared to regard as exceptional, which is the sort of validation that jurists need if the rule of international law is to be advanced in the field of weaponry. Yet despite the medical evidence, military experts produced a succession of reasons why it would be wrong to ban the use of even some types of fire weapon, let alone all of them. The fiercest opposition came, not from the US governmental experts (as might have been expected from recent US experiences with fire weapons), but from the West German ones. Possibly this reflected different modes of diplomacy; but it is also true that in preparing its defences against the forces of the Warsaw Treaty Organisation (WTO), the Federal Republic is in a somewhat different position from its NATO allies. Were there indeed to be an invasion of western Europe from the east, the initial onslaught would most likely be concentrated on West German territory. The nature of warfare demands that for success the attack must outnumber the defence, by perhaps as much as three to one. Should the WTO be able to muster and concentrate such a force, NATO would need to have some means at its disposal to compensate for localised numerical inferiorities. Area weapons are one possibility; but for the Federal Republic, possession of the most powerful of these—nuclear, biological, and chemical weapons— is forbidden under the 1954 revision of the Brussels Treaty. And in any event it would seem unlikely that a Federal government would willingly rest the Republic's security on an option to use on its own territory such cataclysmic categories of weapon. A definite stimulus therefore exists for the development and deployment of other area weapons; and in the Federal Republic there are indeed large investments in novel wide-area munitions, especially for indirect-fire weapons. Some of them, particularly fragmentation bomblet and minelet dispenser munitions, have been noted earlier; but there is also much West German activity in the development of novel flame and incendiary weapons.[38] In one part of the industrialised world, therefore, technological breakthroughs in incendiary warfare are likely to be exploited to the full.

These particularities are noted in order to illustrate a generality. Their purpose is not to assert that the controlled fireball concept is itself the most important new development in incendiary warfare, though it may well be. Neither are they intended to suggest that it is in the United States that such new developments are being sought the most avidly nor that it is in West Germany that they are being applied the most enthusiastically. The point is rather that, to an outside observer, there seems at present to be a ferment in the technology of incendiary warfare, and that real pressures exist for the rapid exploitation of whatever technical refinements may result. Were the open literature more extensive, one could probably provide additional illustrations from countries outside the Atlantic alliance. If true, one implication is obvious: by the time international agreement is reached, if it ever is, on specific incendiary-warfare constraints, the technology may well have developed far beyond the point where the constraints have much practical significance.

The most contentious aspect of incendiary warfare today is the tactical use of air-dropped napalm. Many people consider that the principal weapon used for this purpose, the napalm firebomb, is one of the most inhumane weapons ever invented, and one which by its very nature must act to subvert the ancient principle of the immunity of the non-combatant in time of war. This opinion has stemmed from three main considerations: first, the effects of napalm on the human body are judged to be extraordinarily horrible; second, the area of ground over which a single napalm firebomb may exert its effects is judged to be too great to permit discriminate use against enemy combatants in a region where there are also non-combatants, having regard also to the inaccuracy with which firebombs are commonly dropped; third, the inherent indiscriminacy of a weapon so readily available as the napalm firebomb is judged likely to encourage resort to indiscriminate modes of warfare. On each of these three matters, however, the opposite opinion has also been expressed strongly, particularly by military experts: first, all weapons can produce terrible injuries, and there is no hard evidence to show that napalm is any worse than, say, a fragmentation bomb; second, the latest types of napalm firebomb, if used with the latest techniques of fire control, are at least as accurate as any other form of indirect fire, and can actually be used with greater discrimination; third, except where demanded by military necessity, no principled military staff would ever resort to indiscriminate warfare.

These arguments *pro* and *contra* are set out in greater detail in the reports from the Lucerne and Lugano conferences, and it is not the intention here to traverse the same ground. Instead the purpose is to relate this flow of argument to new developments in incendiary-warfare technology, in particular the controlled fireball concept.

The firebomb originated with the US Army Air Force during the Pacific campaigns of the Second World War, subsequently being introduced into the European theatre as well.[39] At first no more than a field expedient comprising an auxiliary wing-mounted fuel drop-tank charged with some hundreds of litres of thickened aviation fuel, it was later developed into a regular inventory item, and is now a munition much like any other aircraft bomb. The results obtained with it during the Korean War, and during French operations against the Viet-Minh in Indochina, were sufficiently impressive for the firebomb subsequently to be adopted as standard air force armament by virtually all countries that possessed a significant air force. As such, the firebomb has been repeatedly used throughout the world: against guerrilla fighters in several South American, southern African, and Middle Eastern countries; in the border wars that have been, and are being fought in the horn of Africa; in the Arab–Israeli wars; in the Algerian war of independence; in Cyprus; in at least one of the Indo-Pakistan wars; in the Ussuri fighting of 1969; and so on. The most extensive, and certainly the most publicised, use has been during the last Indochina war, where it seems (from the US firebomb procurement data) that something in the order of a million and a half firebombs were dropped.

The popularity of the napalm firebomb in military circles has mainly resided in its flexibility: its apparent efficacy against many of the widely differing targets that strike aircraft may be called upon to attack, whether in ground-support or in interdiction. The French in Indochina and UN forces in Korea made much of its area anti-personnel role against concentrations of enemy troops; and for many years the firebomb continued to be one of the best weapons available for destroying tanks and weapon emplacements, and for reducing the simpler types of fortification. More recently, however, it is clear that some of the military attractions of the firebomb have declined. Techniques have been developed for lessening the vulnerability of important materiel, particularly tanks, towards napalm, and, at the same time, other more effective anti-materiel weapons have become available. Anti-personnel applications have thus come, increasingly, to dominate the uses to which the firebomb is put.

Such applications capitalise on the terror effects of napalm. The military manuals are quite explicit on this point. 'The psychological impact is probably one of the greatest effects of flame', says one, and explains how flame weapons may be 'used to demoralise troops and reduce positions that have resisted other forms of attack'.[40] On the regular battlefield, terror may thus secure immediate tactical gains; in irregular operations terror tactics can contribute and have contributed in several ways to counter-insurgency objectives, to such an extent that napalm has become a pre-eminent symbol of coercive warfare. A firebomb drop is an awesome sight. An area little smaller than a football pitch is suddenly smothered in a tide of orange fire, the flames reaching above treetop level, burning with enormous ferocity and billowing out dense black smoke. It seems impossible that anyone or anything could survive within the fireball, and those faced by it must feel that death of a most painful kind is upon them. Such fears can only be heightened in those who have seen the bodies of napalm victims.

Yet there is evidence to suggest that, setting aside their demoralising effects, napalm firebombs are not in fact very effective anti-personnel weapons. There is also evidence which suggests, to the contrary, that firebombs cause singularly high casualty rates, and that the mortality rate among the casualties is also high. It is perhaps surprising that, for a weapon so widely used, such fundamental disagreement should persist. But it has to be taken into account that weapon-effects data constitute valuable intelligence, and that it is in the nature of things that the side attacked with firebombs is generally in a position to deny the attacker quantitative data about the results of the attack. Under these circumstances, and in view of the sensitivity and responsiveness of public opinion regarding napalm, it could well be that the public literature on the subject has tended to over-estimate rather than under-estimate, the lethality of napalm.

As to case-fatality rates, estimates have been published—all of them during, or very soon after, the commitment of US forces to the Vietnam war—by Vietnamese, East German, Czech, and Soviet authorities.[41] The first three of these related to Vietnamese casualties, stating an average mortality rate of about one in three among people burnt by napalm. This referred to immediate mortality, i.e. within about half an hour. An additional, similarly large, proportion of casualties were said to have died subsequently. The Soviet authority, referring to Korean War cases, also wrote of a one-in-three immediate mortality rate but neither he, nor the other three authorities, provided estimates of the casualty rates within which this mortality was displayed. The Czech authority reported that more than one in four of the people struck by napalm during the types of napalm attack then current were likely to suffer burns over more than 25 per cent of their body surface, half of these burns being of the third degree. None of the four sources provide detailed substantiating data for the estimates, which, as regards evidence, are therefore left to be taken on trust or rejected on mistrust.

Conflicting data were presented by a US expert at the Lucerne conference, the data subsequently being expanded and amended at the Lugano conference, with the purpose of refuting the foregoing estimates. The new data related to seven accidental firebomb drops on US units in South Vietnam during 1968–9. Of the 51 people who had been caught within the fireballs, 48 suffered burns. There were no immediate deaths, but three later deaths, the first of them after seven days. One in four of those burnt had burns over more than 20 per cent of their body surface. Data were not presented on the depths of these particular burns, though one in five of the casualties was reported to have suffered third-degree burns over more than 10 per cent of their body surface.

These two contrasting sets of data are clearly incompatible as regards immediate mortality. As regards late mortality they are not necessarily incompatible, since it is to be supposed that the US casualties received medical aid far more rapidly than did the other casualties, and that medical aid was of a superior quality. Neither are the figures given on the extent of the individual burn injuries necessarily incompatible; and in the event of medical aid having been unavailable, high late-mortality rates would surely have been likely for burns of such severity. It must be said, however, that in both cases the information available is inadequate for reaching any firm, general conclusions about the quantitative casualty effects of napalm in comparison with better-known weapons. The US figures describe only a small sample, while for the other figures the size and circumstances of the samples on which, presumably, the estimates were based have not been given at all, despite the opportunity for doing so afforded by the Lucerne and Lugano meetings.

Subsequent studies may have clarified the situation, but, if they exist, they are to be found only in the secret literature. It may be noted that, by 1973, the US armed services had a 'Tri-Service Comprehensive Anti-Personnel Thermal Evaluation Program' under way; the 'Human Skin Burn and Pain Model' under development by the Radiation

Engineering Branch of the US Army's Ballistic Research Laboratories as an 'effectiveness measurement tool' presumably contributed to the programme.[42]

Among those who were privy to it, the US accident-data study, which was not completed until some four years after the accidents happened, is said to have had a profound effect on appraisals of the efficacy of napalm. For years it had been supposed that everyone caught within a napalm fireball was likely to be incinerated: an exceptionally high casualty and mortality rate was accepted without question: and who seeing the inferno created by a firebomb might think to doubt it? Yet it now seemed that the lethality was much the same as that of any other weapon. But more important from a military standpoint was the finding that every single one of the burn victims had remained capable of performing whatever physical activity was attempted during the period immediately after the napalm drop. Thus, not only did napalm fail to kill many of its victims but also, apparently, it did not even immediately incapacitate them. For US armed forces, the chief function remaining for the firebomb by that time was in close air support; and the primary requirement made of any close support weapon is that it should disable enemy troops fast. For the US, and for other industrialised countries which could afford better, napalm firebombs were already becoming outmoded as anti-materiel weapons; now there seemed to be little point in retaining them as anti-personnel weapons. With hindsight, therefore, one may cease to be surprised at the number of governments which, in a succession of public statements since 1973 aimed largely at humanitarian audiences, have announced that their armed forces are giving up napalm firebombs.[43]

It would undoubtedly be wrong to suppose that there is now a universal disparagement of napalm firebombs in military circles. This may be so for the advanced armed forces of the West, though even here napalm enthusiasts remain; and no doubt also for the Warsaw Pact. But in other parts of the world it is not the case that the chief remaining function of the firebomb is in close air support (a function which is in any case ruled out for all but the most sophisticated air forces). The armed forces of many countries are equipped with obsolete hand-me-downs from richer countries: tanks, for example, of a vintage still highly vulnerable to napalm. And the firebomb is still a terror weapon, valuable as such to military or counter-insurgency forces that see a need for such weapons.

Neither is it the case that the decline in anti-materiel utility of firebombs has been swift and clear-cut. Over the years the weapons technologists have contrived a succession of improvements in the composition of firebomb fills whereby anti-materiel efficacy has in some—though not all—cases kept pace with developing anti-flame counter-measures. For example, several 'loaded' napalms have been introduced in which special ingredients are incorporated in order to enhance the aggressive properties of the burning napalm against particular types of materiel.[44] This has of course meant an overall diminution of the variety of targets against which firebombs continue to remain cost-effective, but in some cases—and the special predicament of West Germany referred to earlier may be one such case—the loss of flexibility may be considered militarily acceptable. So far as may be judged from the limited information available in the open literature, the gains in anti-materiel efficiency obtained by 'loading' napalm are at the expense of anti-personnel efficiency: slag-forming additives, for example, decrease the area of ground over which the firebomb fill is spattered and therefore reduce the number of people placed at risk by each firebomb. Not all developments in napalm have been so specialised, however. The prime example of one which has not been is the development of 'Alectogel' or 'Napalm-B' in the mid-1960s. In composition, this new agent was a radical departure from earlier napalm, a viscous 50 per cent solution of a polystyrene in equal parts of benzene and gasoline, rather than gasoline or aviation fuel gelled with a few per cent of special soap. In performance, firebombs loaded with Napalm-B combined a doubled area-coverage with a substantially greater destructiveness of materiel, such as armoured personnel carriers. The latter property it owed to its increased propensity for starting secondary fires, stemming from its increased burning time. The results obtained with the new agent in Vietnam from 1966 onwards stimulated the development of new anti-materiel flame weapons, in particular napalm-B cluster munitions, as well as improved firebombs of the more traditional kind. Whether the new firebombs were more powerful than the old ones as anti-personnel weapons is not disclosed in the open literature, but such technical data as are available certainly suggest some increase in performance. It is not known whether the US accident data quoted above referred to napalm-B.

On the face of it, then, the introduction of napalm-B served to prolong military interest in air-delivered flame. This illustrates one characteristic feature of the history of this particular category of munition: that, over time, the properties for which the firebomb has been most valued have oscillated between anti-materiel and anti-personnel applications, the net result being the retention of firebombs in the operational inventory and hence their availability for use in either role. The process of technological evolution has, with each new technical change, carried the firebomb through the successive inflexions of its operational history. Thus, although the US accident-data report may at present seem to be ejecting the firebomb from the arsenals of the rich countries, technical change may still bring about a new upturn of military interest.

Application of the controlled fireball concept may very well prove to be that critical technical change. Not much has been openly published about the concept. It seems to have originated in a new weapon which the US Army was developing for use in Vietnam in place of the portable flamethrower. Most of the operational limitations of flamethrowers stem from the necessity of igniting the jet of fuel at the nozzle of the weapon, for much of the payload is thereby wasted en route to the target and the operator becomes highly conspicuous to enemy counter-fire. Hence the idea of using a flame agent which would ignite spontaneously in the air and of projecting it on to the target in frangible, rocket-propelled capsules rather than in a continuous jet. Many chemicals existed that had the necessary pyrophoricity, and some of them, notably the metal alkyls, had a heat of combustion per unit weight which exceeded even that of gasoline. They are extremely dangerous substances to manufacture and handle in bulk, since they can ignite with explosive violence in contact with air or water; but this was no great problem in a chemical industry capable of producing, for example, hypergolic rocket fuels. The necessary production and containment techniques were worked out, and a thickener was chosen which could hold the agent payload together so as to give a sufficiently dense and adhesive impact pattern on target. The new category of 'thickened pyrophoric agents' (TPA) thus came into being alongside the several other categories of flame and incendiary agent. The preferred TPA at that time was triethylaluminium (TEA) thickened with some six per cent of a polyisobutene (PIB). The new weapon was stand-ardised in 1972 as the M74 Rocket-clip/M202 launcher, a shoulder-fired, four-tubed system.[45]

During 1969–70, prior to standardisation, the US Army and the US Marine Corps between them procured nearly 600,000 of the rockets, together with 3200 of the re-usable launchers for them.[46] Despite the difficult manufacturing processes associated with the rockets, the price paid for them averaged out at $0.87 per kilogram—only about double that of the napalm firebomb, the cheapest of all munitions per unit weight. Much of the procurement was presumably used in Indochina.

It soon became apparent that the new weapon was remarkably powerful, even though each rocket is of a mere 66 mm calibre weighing no more than a kilogram and a half, and the total payload of flame agent in a four-rocket clip is about one-sixth of the napalm in current US portable flamethrowers. In May 1972, two North Vietnamese T54 tanks were destroyed with M74 rockets,[47] and tanks are not the sort of target against which portable flamethrowers are normally recom-mended for use.

Thickened TEA is inherently more destructive than napalm. It releases more heat per unit weight when it burns, and it tends to burn at a higher temperature, which means that a higher proportion of the heat which it gives out appears as thermal radiation. When napalm burns, some thermal radiation is of course emitted, but the dominant modes of heat transfer are conduction, through whatever material happens to be in contact with the burning agent, and convection, the creation of hot air currents. The hotter the air the faster it rises; this means, in effect, that the most destructive region of a napalm fireball is its outer surface: inside the fireball, except where there is direct contact with gobbets of burning napalm, the environment is not as hostile as it may appear to the onlooker. This came out clearly in the statements recorded by survivors in the US accident study. Radiant heat, in contrast, is omnidirectional (unless the emitter is shielded in a particular direction) and transmitted, so that radiation damage may be suffered even at a distance from the emitter without direct contact with it. The stronger the thermal radiation, the greater is the distance over which it may damage. Thus, in contrast to a napalm fireball, the internal environment of a TEA fireball is intensely destructive, the zone of destructiveness reaching out, moreover, to a distance considerably beyond the periphery of the fireball.

Further laboratory studies showed that TPA munitions could be made more powerful still. By reducing the proportion of PIB thickener, the heat pulse became so great that people inside a bunker would, it was calculated, receive third-degree burns over most of their body surface within a few seconds.[48] Experiments with pigs showed that this was indeed the case.[49] Materiel targets of various types were also found to be vulnerable if the composition of the formulation, and hence its combustion rate, was appropriately adjusted. From this it was but a short step to the idea of 'controlled' fireball: formulating the mixture so as to provide particular combustion rates from specific munitions, which would then be optimal for the destruction of particular types of target. The technologists involved reported, 'Predictive mathematical models indicate that this controlled fireball technique can be weaponised in an unlimited number of concepts since the flame agent can be tailored to specific operational requirements'.[50]

Orders were soon placed for other TPA munitions. The army wanted an 'encapsulated flame round' for its 152 mm tank armament, and also started work on a 'Directional Ground Flame Munition System', an emplaceable TPA device for perimeter defence and terrain denial.[51] The marine corps, already the chief customer for the M74/M202 system, wanted a 105 mm round. The air force wanted TEA bomblets for their aircraft dispenser munitions, and they started work also on TEA air-to-ground rocket warheads and TEA firebombs.[52] Stimulating results from field trials continued to be reported, particularly test firings against materiel targets including armoured vehicles. For the developmental 152 mm round, the results 'indicated that a near miss, 50 feet short in range, would still permit defeat of hard targets'.[53] A 1000-lb general-purpose HE bomb must fall within 10–15 metres of a tank even to stop it, let alone destroy it.[54] The 152 mm round could create a fireball 25 metres in diameter within which the temperature could reach above 1200°C and the peak flux 6 kilocal-sec/cm².[55] Here indeed was a fireball within which everyone caught unprotected was likely to be incinerated.

So far as public sources reveal, none of these new TPA munitions have yet emerged from the development laboratories; and it may be that technical problems have been encountered. One can certainly see grounds for hesitation on the part of the air force since there would be exceptional danger in carrying TEA inside or underneath an aircraft. But it seems that there is a way round this problem, for the army is now working on what it calls 'binary flame agents', a concept whose feasibility was, in 1974, said to have been confirmed, thereby making TEA 'a candidate agent for air-delivered flame weapons'.[56] The scheme is to mix the TEA with a volatile diluent, such as a hexane or heptane, so that spontaneous combustibility is lost, returning only when the diluent evaporates away after rupture of the munition on target. It seems that a large quantity of diluent is needed for this: the payload in the developmental 'Directional Ground Flame Munition System' noted above contains 35 per cent of heptane. But one would apparently be wrong to suppose that the need to devote limited payload space to diluent must substantially weaken the power of the munition: the army has found that if things are arranged properly the evaporating diluent will form itself into a cloud of vapour which explodes when the TEA ignites. As a result, a totally new type of munition seems to be emerging, one which combines intense wide-area incendiary effects with the area blast effects typical of the fuel-air explosive munitions described below. There is now talk of 'flameblast' munitions.[57]

Until a good deal more is published about flameblast experiments, one must remain sceptical both about the feasibility of flameblast munitions and about their military utility. Here is yet another instance, surely, of the internal momentum of weapons technology carrying it far beyond military requirements, though in time the requirements will no doubt adapt themselves so as to demand, as usual, whatever happens to be available.

Be that as it may, it is certainly remarkable how slight has been the attention given to TEA and other such late-model incendiary weapons at the conferences where possible incendiary-warfare constraints have been discussed. The talk has been primarily about napalm, as though napalm was, from the humanitarian point of view, the worst of the incendiaries. Indeed, the neglect of TEA—and it is but one of several varieties of novel incendiary agent under examination—appears very much to be a studied neglect.

Fuel-air explosives
The destructiveness of a munition is limited by its payload capacity:

only so much high explosive can be packed into a shell that is to be fired from a particular gun or into a bomb that is to be dropped from a particular bomb-rack. A search for increased destructiveness is thus in part a search for more efficient ways of using payload capacity. In this respect incendiary munitions offer the decided attraction that they need carry less than half the weight of what is needed to do damage: the remainder is drawn from the environment, in the form of the atmospheric oxygen that reacts with the incendiary agent to create fire, and also, in the case of some anti-materiel applications, from the target itself, in the form of additional fuel for the fire. It has long been recognised that a similar saving of payload capacity is in principle also possible with explosive munitions, since a chemical (as opposed to nuclear) explosion is nothing more than an extremely rapid combustion reaction, no less dependent upon an adequate supply of oxygen. Conventional chemical explosives carry the oxygen with them—in the nitro groups of TNT, for example. But there are many fuels which, if intimately mixed with air, can be made to explode rather than deflagrate. This is what happens in an internal-combustion engine. The phenomenon is now being exploited to an increasing extent in the novel class of munitions known as 'fuel-air explosives' (FAEs).

The basic problem in building an FAE munition is the mixing of the fuel with air: if there is too much or too little air, the mixture will not explode.[58] Volatile liquid hydrocarbons are the most amenable fuels. for it is relatively easy to suspend them in air as a vapour or aerosol cloud of the requisite dilution. Finely-powdered solids, such as coal dust, can also explode in air, as innumerable accidents have demonstrated; and there has been talk of using a metal-powder FAE in the propellant system of rapid-fire guns. The latter scheme would certainly present engineering problems of great complexity; even the problems in the design of a simple FAE bomb have only recently become manageable.

Antecedents of current FAE programmes can be found in Second World War work. Throughout the war the US Army Chemical Warfare Service was studying an FAE bomb that used butane as the fuel, but the technical difficulties proved insurmountable and the project was terminated.[59] Similar work was going on in Britain. So far as may be judged from the open literature, the Americans are now the leaders in this field. As for the Russians, open Western publications on Soviet FAE work are as schizophrenic as they are in reporting other areas of Soviet military technology: on the one hand there are claims that the Russians are extraordinarily interested in FAE and far advanced in exploiting it; on the other, there are claims that Soviet FAE devices are crude, their development running far behind current US programmes.[60]) The reawakening of US interest in FAE is said to have begun in a navy ordnance laboratory around 1960. Concerted navy FAE R&D did not, however, commence until 1966, the air force following in 1967, building upon the lead technology established by the navy.

The outside world began to hear about US fuel-air explosives from odd rumours and guarded allusions,[61] including a reference in 1967 to a mysterious new navy weapon called 'FAX' that was capable, so it was said, of shearing the landing gear off parked aircraft without at the same time cratering air-field runways.[62] No connection was made in the public statements between FAX and the devices which the US Marine Corps were then just beginning to use in Vietnam for clearing helicopter landing-zones of mines and booby traps, which were in fact ground-functioned experimental versions of the BLU-73 FAE bomb, then under development as payload for the CBU-55 cluster bomb, the navy's first FAE munition.[63] In autumn 1968 the US Air Force began to employ its own early experimental FAEs—the big BLU-72 and BLU-76 bombs being developed in a programme code-named Pave Pat—for interdiction in Indochina, though with no great success and virtually no publicity.[64] By October 1970 the CBU-55 was in fullscale production for operational evaluation in Indochina, and in March 1972 the navy told Congress: 'FAE is one of our newest and most successful conventional munitions. It was a rapid development for the S.E. Asia conflict.'[65] US Navy, and later US Air Force, procurements through 1973 comprised some 30,000 FAE cluster bombs, a large proportion for supply to the South Vietnamese air force. Other potential foreign customers for US FAE munitions have been less successful. At least one NATO country—Canada—has been denied them, under the Ford administration; and Israel's order for some $7 million worth of CBU-72 clusters (probably about 3000–4000 of them), accepted in October 1976, was subsequently denied by President Carter.

The Pentagon had started to release detailed information about the new weapons by the end of 1970,[66] but even though this information described uses to which FAEs could be put, FAEs for a long time received almost no mention in the war-reporting from Indochina. Then quite suddenly, during the battle for Xuan Loc in April 1975, immediately preceding the fall of Saigon, there were press reports of the South Vietnamese air force using a devastating new anti-personnel weapon, said to be a bomb that caused instant asphyxiation over a wide area. Government spokesmen hastened to explain that the 'asphyxiation bomb' was not a poison-gas weapon, but merely the CBU-55 FAE.[67]

It is surprising that use of so grossly spectacular an anti-personnel weapon should have remained unreported for as long as it did. Though the censorship and movement restrictions under which war correspondents have to operate may perhaps have contributed, this can surely not have been the only explanation. What seems more probable is that a weapon initially introduced for specialised anti-materiel applications finally came to be used, under desperate circumstances, against troop concentrations in the open.

An FAE munition is a pure blast weapon, lacking the fragmentation effect of conventional HE munitions. Most of the people killed by HE munitions die from fragments (shrapnel), though blast may contribute, and fragment injuries are immediately obvious for what they are. Blast causes internal damage to the human body, and the cause of death in blast victims may not at once be apparent. There were instances during the city air-raids of the Second World War in which underground air-raid shelters buried in bomb debris were later found to be occupied by rows of people seemingly frozen, and with no visible injury. They were dead from blast. Blast injuries are not, of course, always fatal, neither are blast deaths always quick. The effects of shock waves on the human body are complex and still not fully understood. The greatest harm seems to arise from the passage of the shock wave through the gas-filled cavities of the body.[68] Pulmonary damage is typical: the lungs are squeezed fiercely as the shock wave decelerates into the thoracic cavity. Bubbles of air may then be forced into the blood circulation by the collapsing lungs, causing that brain damage or rapid death characteristic of air embolism. There will usually also be damage to the abdominal organs. Swedish experiments with 30-kilogram ethylene oxide FAEs, reported at the Lucerne and Lugano conferences, indicate that the mortality rate among FAE blast casualties is likely to be about one in two.[69] The mortality rate would probably rise to 85–90 per cent for a single cluster of 30-kg ethylene oxide bomblets.[70] If this were so, FAE munitions would indeed be exceptionally lethal weapons, as the reports from Xuan Loc suggested. The US team of experts at Lugano denied this, however, and asserted (without supporting data) that the killed-to-wounded ratio among FAE casualties was not significantly greater than that among casualties from more conventional explosives.[71]

Wherever the truth may ultimately be found to lie in this matter, the salient operational feature of an FAE munition is that it can subject a wide area of ground to a blast impulse that is probably stronger, and certainly more uniform, than that from a comparable HE munition. This unique attribute has found several military applications. The most highly valued of these so far, and the one which has probably done most to stimulate FAE R&D, is the clearing of minefields, for an FAE shock wave can detonate all types of pressure-sensitive mine and damage other types of mine sufficiently to render them harmless; it can do this in rough terrain where some mines might be shielded from the blast from ground-burst HE.

US experiments with FAE warheads charged with 38.6 kg of propylene oxide fuel have shown a 100 per cent mine-killing area of effectiveness of 246 m^2 in the case of pressure-fused mines and of 2110 m^2 in the case of pull-fused tripwire mines.[72] The increasing prominence of mine warfare in military doctrine has been noted earlier; and FAE munitions represent the only major new mine-neutralising device since the Second World War. This factor alone will probably guarantee a place for FAE munitions in more and more military arsenals around the world; and the munitions will at the same time be available for any other applications to which they may lend themselves.

As to these other applications, the experience of the Vietnam war has already indicated some of the possibilities. Others are suggested by the different FAE R&D projects that have been under way in the United States: some of these are detailed in Table 3.8. In particular, US Army proving-ground test-firings of FAE devices are reported to have 'demonstrated the combat applications of FAE blast effects for ... inflicting casualties to personnel in foxholes, producing mobility kills on wheeled vehicles, and destroying artificial and natural camouflage.'[73] In one demonstration, a single FAE warhead denuded a 90-foot diameter area 590 m² of thick heavy underbrush, trees, and a tactically emplaced army camouflage net. In another demonstration, a $2\frac{1}{2}$-ton cargo truck was destroyed by an FAE warhead, being instantly set on fire, its engine and chassis severely damaged, and major parts blasted away; wooden targets in nearby foxholes were shattered. The effectiveness of FAE blast in killing or injuring people both in the open and inside structures into which the blast can penetrate is remarked in several sources.[74] Other US Army FAE developments noted in Table 3.8 include an FAE weapon intended for urban-warfare use and an FAE anti-ballistic missile warhead. The US Navy is reported to have a keen interest in FAE as a kill mechanism for anti-shipping weapons, including ship-launched cruise missiles.[75] In one trial, a simulated near-miss with a prototype FAE weapon against a destroyer caused such damage that the ship subsequently sank.[76]

Relatively small blast overpressures—on the order of 40kPa— can have great effects on ships, equipment such as masts, radar antennae, electronic-warfare devices, on-deck aircraft, and so forth being especially vulnerable. In these respects, areas of effectiveness on the order of 10–15 hectares are expected from the 1500-lb class of FAE antishipping warhead currently under study.

Further back in development are novel fuels and detonation mechanisms which promise an order-of-magnitude increase in FAE blast effects per unit weight of munitions. Thus peak overpressures exceeding 10 MPa are regarded as attainable within current programmes. Should such objectives in fact be attained, individual FAE weapons would then have the capacity for exerting blast damage over an area approaching that of a nuclear artillery shell. Of the many trends in munition design that are rooted in the Vietnam war, the fastening of interest on fuel-air explosives is perhaps the most threatening of all.

TABLE 3.8   Some US fuel-air explosive munitions and development projects

Munition or project	*Particulars*
750-lb FAE bomb, BLU-64	200 kg of hydrocarbon fuel. An early US Air Force development project, soon cancelled.[a]
2500-lb FAE bomb, BLU-72 (Pave Pat I)	US Air Force development, designated as a 'general purpose' bomb.[a] Basically a drogue-chute retarded commercial propane tank (450 kg propane) fitted with a burster and a 3–4 second time-delay cloud detonator. Used experimentally in air interdiction operations over Indochina from Autumn 1968, carried on low-performance aircraft (e.g. A-1E), but reported 'not very successful'.[b]
130-lb FAE bomb, BLU-73	US Navy development as payload for the CBU-55 FAE cluster bomb. Fuel is ethylene oxide (about 33 kg). Weighs 60 kg. Drogue-chute retardation; 4-foot probe for activating burster charge. Two 125-millisec time-delay cloud detonators ejected from wall.[c] Combat use from 1967 onwards.[d] Said to be capable of completely defoliating a 700 square-metre area even in thick forest.[e]
2500-lb FAE bomb, BLU-76 (Pave Pat II)	A streamlined version of the BLU-72, for high speed carriage (e.g. three per F-4) though not high speed delivery. Not used in combat before 1971.[b] Unit cost in 1972 was $5000. Two BLU-76 bombs are capable of stripping vegetation and blowing down trees over an area of 0.84 hectares.[f]
500-lb FAE cluster bomb, CBU-55	Navy/Honeywell development, entering full-scale production in October 1970. The first successful FAE weapon. For low-performance aircraft (e.g. 14 per A-1E or 2 per UH-1). Comprises an SUU-49 rear-ejection free-fall dispenser with three BLU-73 bombs.[c][d] Unit cost in 1972 was $1520.
500-lb FAE cluster bomb, CBU-72	Streamlined version of the CBU-55, for high speed (up to 450 knots) carriage; qualified for A-4 and A-7 aircraft.[d] Developed by 1971.[e] 'Designed to be an effective blast weapon against protected or concealed troops, land mines, booby traps and light material'. Unit cost in 1974 was $1770.[g]
Air-to-ground FAE rocket	For 4-tube launcher; studied in the early Air Force FAE work.[e]
500-lb high-speed FAE (?cluster) bomb	Being developed by the navy as a second-generation FAE weapon that can be delivered on target at high speeds, thus eliminating the delivery restrictions on the CBU-55/72.[d] In engineering development in 1972, but subsequently moved back into advanced development for further technology investigation rather than immediate weaponisation.[h] In July 1975 was scheduled to enter a joint navy/air force FAE-2 engineering development programme. Seems to use propylene oxide as the fuel.

Munition or project	Particulars	TABLE 3.8—*continued*

500-lb high-speed FAE bomb

In advanced development in 1973.[j] The air force contender for FAE-2. A version field-tested during 1974–5 had a 12-foot probe for the burster and trailed a cloud detonator on a 65-foot line, intended to function in the centre of the fuel-air cloud;[i] a 1975 air force patent application suggests that it uses propylene oxide (148 kg) as the fuel.[k] Other fuels under study by the air force include MAPP—a mixture of propyne, propadiene, propane and a trace of butane.[d l]

2000-lb high-speed FAE bomb

Also part of the air force FAE-2 project. In concept-formulation stage in mid-1974. May use a proximity fuse rather than a probe for the burster.[i] A 1975 patent application suggests a 725-kg propylene oxide payload.[k]

FAESHED (helicopter-delivered FAE system)

An army mine-clearing development undergoing DT-III testing in 1974–5. Comprises a CBU-55 munition attached to each side of a UH-1H helicopter plus aiming and release mechanisms. Type-classification as standard was scheduled for early 1976.[m] Unit procurement cost was estimated in in 1974 to be $8000–$9000.[n]

SLUFAE (surface-launched FAE unit)

Another army mine-clearing system in development at least since 1972 with completion scheduled for 1980.[j] Comprises a 30-tube armoured launcher mounted on an M548 5-ton tracked prime mover for single or ripple firing of modified navy Zuni 5-inch rockets, each with an oversize warhead containing 39 kg of propylene oxide and fitted with a foliage discriminating probe fuse. Maximum range approaches 1000 metres; can clear 8 × 100 metres of minefield per loading, either by detonating pressure-sensitive mines or by damaging them so that they can no longer function.[m] Successfully tested against mines fitted with complex, long-impulse and double-impulse fuses, including hydraulic long-impulse, seismic infra-red, electronic, and magnetic influence fuses.[o] The 1974 estimate of eventual procurement cost was $75,000–$100,000 each, including the launch vehicle; total R&D cost to completion estimated at $12.677 millions.[n]

MADFAE (mass air-delivery FAE system)

A marine corps development under way in 1973. Comprises a downward-ejection dispenser, weighing just under a tonne fully loaded, with twelve 60-kg FAE bombs, for sling-loading from helicopter cargo hooks, two per helicopter.[j]

LANDFAE (large-area nozzle delivery of fuel-air explosive)

Demonstrated feasibility reported in Spring 1976.[o] An army mine-clearing concept in which a M67A2 mechanized flame thrower with a modified (high pressure) nozzle is used to spray fuel over a minefield, the fuel-air cloud being detonable. Tests have shown that a traversible path 85 feet long can be cleared of mines with one spray; repeated sprayings could be done within seconds.

Munition or project	Particulars	TABLE 3.8—*continued*

Improved LANDFAE

In development in 1976: a high-pressure nozzle kit attached to an M60 tank enabling use of FAE 'in urban warfare and against other blast-sensitive targets requiring close-in attack by Army ground forces'.[p]

FAE warheads for space weapons or anti-ballistic missiles

In February 1973 it was reported that the navy was conducting detonation tests *in vacuo* of clouds from FAE munitions and that the results were 'expected to provide information leading toward perfecting a non-nuclear warhead for use in space'.[d] It seems that even under oxygen-sparse simulated high-altitude (10,000 metres) conditions FAE blast effects were significantly greater than those from comparable HE charges; this observation is said to have stimulated the army into evaluating the application of FAE to ABM systems.[e]

FAD/FAE follow-through hollow-charge warheads for 66 mm rockets

One of several SCIFT (shaped-charge incendiary follow-through) anti-armour munitions being developed by the army, this one for the M202A1 four-tube portable rocket launcher. Uses about 0.5 kg of liquid hydrocarbon fuel as follow-through for the hollow-charge jet: pentane, pentene, and propylene oxide have been studied. Larger calibre (80–90 mm) may be preferred. Stimulated by marine corps interest in more powerful portable weapons for use against bunker-type targets. In advanced development by 1975.[q]

FAE warheads for ship-launched cruise missiles

Navy development project, said to be under way in 1976.[e]

Shipborne FAE antimissile system

Early phase of a navy development project said to be under way in 1976.[e]

FAE warheads for antisubmarine torpedoes

Feasibility studies by the navy said to be under way in 1976.[e]

FAE warhead for Lance battlefield support guided missile

An army project apparently in concept-formulation stage in October 1976.[r]

Notes

[a] US Air Force Armament Laboratory, *Guide to non-nuclear munitions and associated equipment under the cognizance of AFATL* (1970).

[b] R. D. Anderson (Tactical Division, US Air Force Directorate of Operations), statement before a subcommittee of the Senate Armed Services Committee (19 Nov 1970). *Investigation into electronic battlefield program:* Hearings (Washington, D.C.: committee print, 1971), pp. 135–6.

[c] US Naval Air Systems Command, Technical Manual NAVAIR 11-5A-26, *Fuel-air explosive bomb cluster CBU-55/B.*

d C. A. Robinson, 'Fuel air explosives: Services ready joint development plan', *Aviation Week and Space Technology* (19 Feb 1973), pp. 42–6.

e G. Johannsohn, 'Fuel air explosives revolutionise conventional warfare', *International Defense Review* 9(6) (Dec 1976), pp. 992–6.

f Engineer Strategic Studies Group (Office of the Chief of Engineers, US Army), *Herbicides and military operations*, Vol 3 (Feb 1972).

g Admiral Gaddis, written response to the Chairman of the Senate Defense Appropriations Subcommittee, spring 1974: *Department of Defense appropriations for fiscal year 1975:* Hearings (Washington, D.C.: committee print, 1974).

h US Navy, justification statement in support of the 'Air-to-ground weapon technology (engineering)' FY 1973 RDT&E budget line-item submitted for the record of the Senate Defense Appropriations Subcommittee: *Department of Defense appropriations for fiscal year 1973*, Hearings (Washington, D.C.: committee print, 1972), Vol. 3, p. 1168.

i 'Armament lab verifies new technology', *Aviation Week and Space Technology* (15 July 1974), pp. 270–2.

j C. A. Robinson, 'Soviets begin fuel-air explosive tests', *Aviation Week and Space Technology* (22 Oct 1973).

k A. G. Bilek, assignor to the Secretary of the US Air Force, US patent no. 3 999 482 (app. 9 July 1975, iss. 28 Dec 1976), *High explosive launcher system*.

l G. A. Carlson, assignor to the US Energy Research & Development Administration, US patent no. 3 955 509 (app. 21 Mar 1969, iss. 11 May 1976), *Fuel-air munition and device*.

m J. A. Dennis, 'MERDC demonstrates fuel air explosive mine neutralization capabilities', *Army R&D Newsmagazine* 16(1) (Jan–Feb 1975), pp. 12–13.

n Office of the Assistant Secretary of the Army (R&D), written statement for the record of the House Defense Appropriations Subcommittee, in *Department of Defense Appropriations for 1975,* Hearings (Washington, D.C.: committee print, 1974), Vol. 4, p. 1231.

o Ibid. Vol. 4, p. 1233.

p 'LANDFAE feasibility shown: 6 nations send representatives', *Army R&D Newsmagazine* (May–June 1976), p. 13.

q US Army Munitions Command. Research, Development and Engineering Directorate, *Laboratory Posture Report FY-72* (1972) and *Laboratory posture report FY-73*, RCS AMCDL-101 (1973); and US Army Armament Command. Research Development and Engineering, *Laboratory posture report FY-74*, RCS AMCDL-101 (1974) and *Laboratory posture report FY-75* (1975); and R. E. Brown and G. E. Taylor, *HEAT follow-through warheads for improved lethality,* contract report from Shock Hydrodynamics Division, Whittaker Corporation, to US Army Edgewood Arsenal, report no. ED-CR-74001, Jan 1974.

r 'Latest US Army equipment on show', *International Defense Review* 10(1) (Feb 1977), pp. 101–8.

NOTES

1. T. N. Dupuy, 'Quantification of factors related to weapon lethality', annex III-H in R. Sunderland *et al., Historical Trends Related to Weapon Lethality,*

contract report for the Advanced Tactics Project of the US Army Combat Developments Command (Washington, D.C., 1964). See also 'Tactical nuclear combat', *Ordnance* (Nov-Dec, 1968) p. 292.

2. Ibid.
3. E. Prokosch, *The Simple Art of Murder: Antipersonnel Weapons and their Developers,* rev. ed. (Philadelphia, 1972); J. S. Tompkins, *The Weapons of World War III: The long road back from the bomb* (London, 1967).
4. F. Scott, 'To strike unseen', *Journal of the Royal United Services Institute* (June 1971) pp. 30–5.
5. M. Lumsden, *Antipersonnel Weapons* (Stockholm, SIPRI, forthcoming).
6. US Dept of Defense, Reports of programs for fiscal years 1964–73: 'Procurement of equipment and missiles, Army: Ammunition, P-4800'; 'Other procurement, Navy: Weapons and support equipment'; 'Procurement, Marine Corps: Budget activity 1: Ammunition'; and 'Other procurement, Air Force: Munitions and associated equipment' (30 June 1966–31 Dec 1972).
7. US Dept of Defense, Congressional testimony. Submission for the record of the House Defense Appropriations Subcommittee, Feb 1974.
8. For a partial listing see Table 5.12 in Lumsden, op. cit.
9. N. Thimmesch, 'War's Double Standard', *Philadelphia Bulletin* (20 Dec 1973).
10. US Dept of Defense, Report to the Congress by M. Laird (Secretary of Defense). Annual Defense Department Report FY 1973 (Washington, D.C., 1972).
11. US Dept of the Air Force, Congressional testimony, W. W. Snavely (Assistant Deputy Chief of Staff, Systems and Logistics), Statement before the Senate Defense Appropriations Subcommittee (18 Feb 1972).
12. C. A. Robinson, 'ADTC presses weapon studies', *Aviation Week and Space Technology* (15 July 1974) pp. 265–7, 269.
13. Weapon notes no. 12: BL-755 cluster bomb, *Flight International* (14 Feb 1974) pp. 221–3.
14. R. T. Pretty and D. H. Archer, *Jane's Weapon Systems 1976–77* (London, 1976).
15. S. Geisenheyner, 'Letter from Europe: Area weapons', *Air Force Magazine* (Feb 1971) pp. 19–21.
16. 'New weapons to counter land attack', *Aviation Week and Space Technology* (24 Apr 1972) p. 60.
17. Pretty and Archer, op. cit.
18. US Dept of the Army, Congressional testimony. Col. Whalen, statement before the Senate Armed Services Committee (9 Mar 1976); and 'Latest U.S. Army equipment on show', *International Defense Review* (Feb 1977) pp. 101–8.
19. See E. Prokosch, 'Antipersonnel weapons', *International Social Science Journal* (1976), Vol. 28, no. 2, pp. 241–358; and E. Prokosch, 'How large is your wound?', unpublished MS.
20. US Army Materiel Command, 'Program achievements 1962–1972' (23 Mar 1972).
21. US Dept of the Army, Congressional testimony, J. R. Deane, Statement before the House Armed Services Committee (21 Mar 1974).
22. US Army Materiel Command (n. 20, above).
23. S. Geisenheyner, op. cit.; and 'Tri-lateral RS 80 artillery rocket project', *International Defense Review* (Apr 1973) p. 147.

24. 'German mine-laying techniques', *International Defense Review* (Aug 1976) p. 648.
25. US Army Materiel Command, Historical Office, *Arsenal for the Brave: A History of the United States Army Materiel Command 1962–1968* (Sep 1969) pp. 155–7.
26. 'Flechette warhead for 2.75 in rockets', *International Defense Review* (1973) no. 3, p. 376.
27. 'Ballistics unit tests research concepts', *Aviation Week and Space Technology* (15 July 1974) p. 275; D. Dardick, S. Green, S. Rush and F. Fedowitz, 'Gun/ projectile systems', *Space/Aeronautics* (Mar 1967) pp. 92–9.
28. US Dept of the Air Force, Congressional testimony, R. D. Anderson, statement before a subcommittee of the Senate Armed Services Committee (19 Nov 1970).
29. A. H. Westing, 'The super bomb', *American Report* (New York, 8 Sep 1972) p. 3.
30. N. Ben-Hur and H. Soroff, 'Combat burns in the 1973 October war and the anti-tank missile burn syndrome', *Burns* (1975) no. 1, pp. 217–21.
31. US Army Materiel Command, *Research and development of materiel, engineering design handbook. Elements of armament engineering. Pt. 2: Ballistics* (Sep 1963).
32. J. Pearson, R. G. S. Sewell and R. T. Carlisle, assignors to the Secretary of the US Navy, US patent no. 3 566 794, *Controlled fragmentation of multi-walled warheads* (app. 26 Nov 1958, iss. 2 Mar 1971); P. Crevecoeur, 'Anti-personnel hand grenades—some recent European developments', *International Defense Review* (1973) no. 3, pp. 372–4; M. Held, 'Air target warheads', *International Defense Review* (1975) no. 5, pp. 719–24; E. Prokosch, "How large is your wound?', unpublished MS.
33. US Dept of the Air Force, Congressional testimony (*supra*, n. 28).
34. C. C. Balke and W. S. Graff, assignors to the Secretary of the US Army, US patent no. 2 801 590, *Pyrophoric element* (app. 14 June 1951, iss. 6 Aug 1957); G. H. Custard, assignor to the Secretary of the US Army, US patent no. 3 421 439, *Incendiary projectiles* (app. 29 Sep 1961, iss. 14 Jan 1969); T. Stevenson, assignor to the Secretary of the US Army, US patent no. 2 951 752, *Incendiary composition* (app. 21 May 1958, iss. 6 Sep 1960).
35. US Army Munitions Command, *Laboratory posture report FY-73* RCS AMCD1–101 (1973).
36. US Dept of the Air Force, Congressional testimony. W. W. Snavely, statement before the Senate Defense Appropriations Subcommittee (13 Sep 1972).
37. US Army Munitions Command (*supra*, n. 35).
38. G. Buck, British patent no. 1 061 631, *Incendiary compositions containing highly inflammable liquidcarbon compounds and a thickener and a process for the production of such compositions* (app. 12 Feb. 1964, pub. 15 Mar 1967); F. Hobart (ed.), *Jane's Infantry Weapons 1975* (London, 1974); R. T. Pretty and D. H. Archer, *Jane's Weapon Systems 1974–75* (London, 1974).
39. B. E. Kleber and D. E. Birdsell, *The Chemical Warfare Service: Chemicals in combat,* US Dept of the Army, Office of the Chief of Military History (Washington, D.C., 1966).
40. US Dept of the Army, *Combat Flame operations,* Field manual FM 20–33 (1970).
41. Do Xuan Hop 'Napalm-och fosforbomber', in J. Takman (ed.), *Napalm*

108 *The World Military Order*

(Stockholm, 1967); H. R. Gestewitz, 'Der Einsatz von Brandbomben (-granaten) der US-Fliegerkräfte gegen die Demokratische Republik Vietnam and ihre Wirkung unter besonderer Berücksichtigung von Napalm', *Zeitschrift für Militärmedizin* (1968) no. 5, pp. 275–80; J. Franek cited as a private communication in United Nations Secretary General, *Napalm and other incendiary weapons and all aspects of their possible use*, UN document A/8803/rev. 1 (New York, 1973) p. 33; V. A. Dolinin, 'Clinical picture, organisation and level of medical care for napalm casualties', *Voenno-Meditsinsky Zhurnal* (1975) no. 12, pp. 33–7.

42. US Army Armament Command, *Laboratory posture report FY 74*, RCS AMCDL-101 (1974) and *FY 75*, RCS AMCDL-101 (1975).
43. United Nations Secretary General, *Napalm and other incendiary weapons and all aspects of their possible use*, UN document A/9207 with Corr. 1 and Add. 1 (1973) and UN document A/10223 (1975).
44. *Napalm and other incendiary weapons (supra*, n. 41); and M. Lumsden, *Incendiary Weapons* (Stockholm, 1975).
45. US Army Munitions Command, *Laboratory posture report FY-72* (1972).
46. US Dept of Defense, Reports of programs for fiscal years 1964–73: 'Procurement of equipment and missiles, Army: Ammunition, P-4800', and 'Procurement, Marine Corps: Budget activity 1: Ammunition' (*supra*, n. 6).
47. US Army Munitions Command (supra, n. 45).
48. Ibid.
49. US Army Armament Command, FY 74 (*supra*, n. 42).
50. US Army Munitions Command (*supra*, n. 35).
51. US Army Armament Command (*supra*, n. 42).
52. 'Ballistics unit tests research concepts', *Aviation Week and Space Technology* (15 July 1974) p. 275.
53. US Army Munitions Command (*supra*, n. 35).
54. UK Royal Air Force, statement by A. W. Fraser at the First Session of the Conference of Government Experts on the use of Certain Conventional Weapons, Lucerne (9 Oct 1974).
55. US Army Armament Command, FY 74 (*supra*, n. 42).
56. Ibid.
57. US Army Munitions Command (*supra*, n. 35).
58. A. G. Bilek, assignor to the Secretary of the US Air Force, US patent no. 3 999 482, *High explosive launcher system* (app. 9 July 1975, iss. 28 Dec 1976); G. A. Carlson, assignor to the US Energy Research and Development Administration, US patent no. 3 955 509, *Fuel-air munition and device* (app. 21 Mar 1969, iss. 11 May 1976).
59. L. P. Brophy, W. D. Miles, and R. C. Cochrane, *The Chemical Warfare Service: From laboratory to field*, US Dept of the Army, Office of the Chief of Military History (Washington, D.C., 1959).
60. An appraisal of Soviet FAE work appears in a recent article by G. Johannsohn, a West German writer, who states that 'the USSR has probably had a very large arsenal of FAE weapons for several decades'. However, the article goes on to say that 'it can be concluded from the available test results that Soviet FAE weapon systems are comparable in type, size, and effect to those of the USA,' a conclusion that is based on a 1965 paper in a Soviet journal reporting rather unremarkable findings from an experiment in combustion kinetics at the level of basic research. The author of the article refers to this

experiment as 'the Kogarko tests' and then immediately quotes the Pentagon to the effect that 'the USSR continued testing in 1973 and thereafter.' He cites a published source for this; in fact it reads as follows: 'Soviet Union is in the early stages of testing fuel air explosives, but devices being used are somewhat crude in comparison to those in development in the US by navy and air force. In confirming the USSR's work in the area of FAE, Pentagon officials said the Soviets have made rapid progress during the past year (1972–3) but appear to be running far behind this country's development program.' It might be, of course, that the West German author had access to uncitable sources; but this is belied by the informedness of his article as regards other aspects of FAE, and by the extent to which it draws from recognisable prior publications. See G. Johannsohn, 'Fuel air explosives revolutionise conventional warfare', *International Defense Review* (Dec 1976), pp. 992–6. The published source which he cites is C. A. Robinson, 'Soviets begin fuel air explosive tests', *Aviation Week and Space Technology* (22 Oct 1973).

61. *The Reporter* (14 Sep 1961) p. 31.
62. Aviation Studies (International) Ltd, *Armament data sheets,* sect. 14, Novel weapons.
63. C. A. Robinson, 'Special report: Fuel air explosives: Services ready joint development plan', *Aviation Week and Space Technology* (19 Feb 1973) pp. 42–6.
64. Ibid., US Dept of the Air Force, Congressional testimony (*supra*, n. 28).
65. US Dept of the Navy, Congressional testimony, FY1973 RDT&E budget line-item submitted for the record of the Senate Defense Appropriations Subcommittee (8 Mar 1972).
66. US Dept of the Air Force, Congressional testimony (*supra*, n. 28).
67. 'Vietcong protest at new type of bomb', *The Times* (24 Apr 1975).
68. US Dept of the Army, Office of the Surgeon General, *Wound Ballistics* (Washington, D.C., 1962) esp. R. W. French and G. R. Callender, 'Ballistic characteristics of wounding agents', pp. 91–141.
69. Conference of Government experts on the use of certain conventional weapons, 2nd session, *Report* (Geneva, 1976).
70. Ibid.
71. Ibid.
72. US Dept of the Army, congressional testimony Office of the Assistant Secretary of the Army (R&D) written statement for the record of the House Defense Appropriations Subcommittee (Apr 1974).
73. J. R. Dennis, 'MERDC demonstrates fuel air explosive mine neutralization capabilities', *Army Research and Development Newsmagazine* (Jan–Feb 1975) pp. 12–13.
74. US Dept of Defense, Congressional testimony, M. Currie, prepared statement for the Senate Armed Services Committee (Mar 1975); 'Armament lab verifies new technology', *Aviation Week and Space Technology* (15 July 1974) pp. 270–2; 'Jungle flatteners', *Ordnance* (Sep–Oct 1971) p. 157; C. A. Robinson (*supra*, n. 60).
75. G. Johannsohn (*supra*, n. 60).
76. C. A. Robinson (*supra*, n. 63).

4 Counter-insurgency: the French War in Algeria*

Hartmut Elsenhans

Political scientists have shown an increasing concern with counter-insurgency in recent years, particularly after the heavy military involvement of the United States in Vietnam. In order to combat resistance movements during the Second World War, the German Army developed counter-insurgency doctrines.[1] The need to defeat popular anti-colonialist and anti-imperialist movements in colonies and newly independent countries has led to an elaboration of the doctrines and techniques used by the German Army. The French experience in Algeria from 1954 to 1962 provided important lessons in anti-subversive warfare which were different from the later lessons of American counter-insurgency in Vietnam.[2] While the American war in Vietnam could draw on huge financial and material resources, including sophisticated technology, the French war in Algeria was more labour-intensive. The French used military, economic, social and political means to create a new bridgehead in Algeria: one that was capable of self-defence against political 'contamination' and was thus equipped to defend itself eventually against what became an increasingly isolated liberation movement.

Within the limits of the foreign currency and budget restrictions imposed by France, modern arms technology was available to the colonial army in Algeria. But whereas in Vietnam technologically sophisticated weaponry was an important factor, in Algeria it was relatively unimportant, serving to make the army's police operations simply more effective, rather than having a decisive influence on the outcome. Indeed, it may have been the *absence* of advanced technology (moulded, as in Vietnam, by orthodox strategies and backed by industrial and scientific interests), that enabled the French army to adapt itself to successful counter-insurgency strategies. In Vietnam such strategies were ruled out by the untenable socio-economic position of the United States. In Algeria, where the French position was equally untenable, strategies such as internment and torture revealed deep-rooted social and political contradictions in a way that led to the

---

* This article draws on the author's doctoral thesis: 'Frankreichs Algerienkrieg 1954-1962: Entkolonisierungsversuch einer kapitalistischen Metropole. Zum Zusammenbruch der Kolonialreiche' (Munich, 1974). This is cited in the notes as Elsenhans (1974).

eventual sympathy of both 'neutral' Moslems and international opinion with the liberation. Ultimately, military victory led to political defeat, and the strategies through which victory was engineered had profound consequences for the politicisation of the French army and for France itself.

Origins of the Liberation Movement

The importance of Algeria to the French empire cannot be underestimated. Geographically the French bridgehead to Africa and the cornerstone of a bloc composed of the metropolis and its African possessions, Algeria represented the first stage in the construction of the second colonial empire. Algeria was occupied before the phase of growing real wages and the end of the population surplus occurred in France, and it became a settlement colony. By 1954 one million Europeans (called *pied noir*) lived among eight million Moslem Algerians.[3]

At the end of the nineteenth century, many Europeans who were originally settlers were entering Algerian services and professions. Colonial Algerian society was thus characterised by the political and economic predominance of a European minority composed of agrarian capitalists and great merchants, supported by a European middle class whose jobs were protected by racial discrimination against Moslems. The Moslem proletariat lived partly in Algeria and partly in France: the low level of industrialisation in Algeria meant that there were relatively few jobs available there. The needs of French industry led to the importation of Moslem workers to France, where they worked as manual labourers. Moslem intellectuals—who emerged from the 'assimilation' effort officially pursued by the colonial administration— could not find jobs appropriate to their qualifications.[4] Large numbers among the rural population had either had their land expropriated or lived in the rather barren land of the interior and the mountains.[5] Because of the rising population in the country, the annual yield of Algerian lands per capital decreased. At the same time the European agricultural sector demanded less native labour due to increased mechanisation. Modern Algerian nationalism began as an urban phenomenon, originating in early twentieth-century France. In the 1920s, the attempts of Moslem workers to organise themselves led to the emergence of the movement known as messalism. Taking its name from the leader, Messali Hadj, this movement was to become the radical wing of Algerian nationalism.

The movement in Algeria itself was primarily a reformist one. From the end of the 1920s onwards, the *Oulema*, doctors of Islamic law, had provided primary and secondary education, and had propagated the revival of Arabism and Islam. In the 1930s, francophile intellectuals in Algeria organised constitutionalist movements seeking equality through assimilation or through Algerian autonomy. It was only in 1936 that the messalistic parties of working-class origin began to organise in Algeria. Despite repression, they achieved predominance during the Second World War. However the long imprisonment of Messali Hadj provided an opportunity for Ferhat Abbas, the leader of the bourgeois nationalists, who were demanding autonomy within a federal French republic. Though post-war elections demonstrated the strength of the radical wing, due to intense political pressure from the *pied noir* the French administration was unable to implement the reforms they had voted for.[6]

The War

Political crises in the Messalist party, caused by growing reformist tendencies and by Messali's authoritarianism, discredited the party leadership in 1953–4 and increased the power of more radical groups in the movement's paramilitary organisation. These groups saw insurrection as a means of forcing a resolution to the internal political divisions within the party.[7]

A wave of attacks and bomb raids, organised by urban cadres, swept Algeria, demonstrating the national, rather than tribal, character of the movement and its potential effectiveness. A continuous climate of insecurity in the country, particularly after the summer of 1955, dispelled the belief that the colonial army was necessarily superior to the liberation movement. This enabled the liberation movement to mobilise the anti-colonialist sentiments of the rural population.

By 1956 the liberation army had set up an autonomous political and administrative organisation over at least two-thirds of Algeria, effectively destroying all French control in these areas.[8] In order both to extend and cement their power the liberation army created two national and constitutional bodies: an Algerian parliament appointed by the *maquis* (CNRA: Conseil National de la Révolution); and an Algerian government (CCE: Comité de Co-ordination et d'Exécution). Both were dominated by the activist groups of the liberation movement, whose leaders were unknown to the French. Consequently the influence of those leaders whom the French considered respectable declined.

The liberation movement began increasingly to carry out mass actions in urban areas. But as the French government was capable of repressing such actions (e.g. strikes), the activities of the movement became more and more terrorist in nature. French official literature has explained this terrorism as the last effort of a defeated movement,[9] overlooking the fact that such generalised terrorism was successful only because of massive support from the civilian population, who were forced to obey certain laws (such as avoiding certain cafés or other public sites).

Some generalisations can be made about the objectives of liberation movements. The unequal military potential of the interventionist and liberation armies makes military victory, in the conventional sense of the term (i.e. destruction of the enemy forces) a remote goal, and one not necessarily to be sought. The essential aim must be the mobilisation of the population against the colonial power in order to thwart any of its attempts to regain stability. The organisation of the masses forms a protective shield, maintaining a general climate of insecurity in which any claim of the colonial power to legitimate sovereignty is frustrated. In a period of decolonisation it becomes essential for the colonial power to maintain an appearance of legitimacy in order to avoid international interference. The first major proof of the nationwide effectiveness of the Algerian revolution was the successful destruction, by threat and persuasion, of French administrative penetration into Algeria. Police spies no longer furnished information; local notables ceased to co-operate; auxiliary policemen (*gardes champêtres*) and official representatives (the so-called *élus* of the colonial Algerian Assembly) either resigned or were killed. Meanwhile the new administrative organisation of the liberation army served as its logistical base, dealing with guides, arms, ammunition and food, as well as providing systematic intelligence on the movements of French troops. The population grew less dependent on the services of the colonial administration because alternative services were provided by the new one (for example, there was a considerable reduction in the number of civil law suits which were dealt with by the colonial administration as people turned to the legal bodies provided by the administration of the liberation army). It was expected that continued insecurity would finally lead to an untenable political position for France, which would have to retreat from the colony regardless of its military power to remain.

The liberation movement challenged the colonial power in a number of ways:

    through its military potential and its firepower, and therefore its capacity to maintain a climate of insecurity;

    through the non-cooperation of local people and thus the absence of intelligence for the French;

    through mass actions demonstrating the unpopularity of the colonial presence.

The colonial army had to:

    destroy the military potential of the liberation army;

    destroy the administrative and political organisation of the liberation army;

    control the population in order to use it for French purposes;

    control territory in order to minimise the possibilities of military success for the liberation army.

These objectives had to be attained by the colonial army within the specific configuration of politically admissible deterrence capabilities and intelligence levels. However, the development of an offensive counter-integration of the population deprived the colonial army of its intelligence, so that it no longer knew whom or where to strike.[10] Unable to isolate the individuals responsible for an action, it was forced to strike at entire villages. A village now became the smallest community to be held responsible for acts committed on its territory.

The liberation movement, on the other hand, was well informed: those who disobeyed its orders were easily identified, so that it knew whom to punish. They were thus able to undertake an effective policy of deterrence through the execution of a relatively small number of culprits. Similarly, the liberation army killed relatively few innocent people as compared to the numbers of innocent people who fell victim to the deterrence policy of the colonial army. In addition, it was possible for the liberation army to justify its killings of those who abstained from active solidarity, by saying that it was defending a just cause. The colonial army, on the other hand, was supposed to kill only armed rebels: if civilian deaths became known to the public, sympathy for the nationalists would intensify.

THE MILITARY BUILD-UP IN ALGERIA

The liberation army undertook military preparations long before the outbreak of war. By 1945, arms were being secretly cached by the OS (Special Organisation) of the messalist Mouvement pour le Triomphe des Libertés Démocratiques. The expatriation of Ben Bella in 1952 seems to have provided fresh impetus for the enlargement of military resources, particularly after 1953. The arms of the liberation movement included not only local stockpiles, but also arms captured from the French army, and imported weapons. The imports—financed by money from Arab countries and from Algerian workers in France—came mainly from the international arms traffic. After 1958, the East European countries agreed to supply the liberationists with arms; however, by this time the French army had effectively sealed off Algerian frontiers.

The documents on arms captured by the French army are the best sources of information on the armament of the liberation army.[11] In 1956, two-thirds of their weapons were hunting rifles. During 1957, this proportion declined as the relative importance of pistols grew. It was not until 1958 that the majority of the guerrillas had automatic pistols and military rifles; at that time there was one machine gun to every ten fighters. In the same year, serious groundfire against aircraft was reported, but this was found to come primarily from sanctuaries across the border in Tunisia. Though the military equipment and military infrastructure of the liberation movement were extremely primitive, by 1958 the guerrillas possessed 30,000 military weapons, and constituted an efficient underground military force which the French had great difficulty in detecting.[12]

One of the preconditions of any counter-insurgency is a military build-up. When the Algerian revolution entered its armed phase in 1954, the French colonial army was rather weak.[13] Many professional soldiers had been killed in the war in Indochina. From the very beginning of the Algerian war it was clear that France could not rely solely on its professional army, and draftees had to be speedily mobilised. By the end of 1955, there were 180,000 troops in Algeria: one year later the colonial forces reached their maximum metropolitan strength of 400,000 (army alone, excluding the air force and navy). From this time on, the colonial army could further strengthen itself only by upgrading troops or by mobilising local manpower from the Moslem population. The upgrading of troops posed problems of training and equipment, while local manpower could only be mobilised when the colonial army had succeeded in re-establishing its control, and this was not seen as a viable proposition in the early days of the war.

The mobilisation of draftees, trained and equipped for combat in Europe, meant the deployment of troops ill prepared for Algerian conditions. Officers of the reserves were often old and poorly trained for this type of warfare. Intensive training programmes were effective only from 1968 onwards: before that the French army was to a large degree confined to simple infantry missions.

There are physical limits to the movement of men on difficult terrain. Successful counter-insurgency depends on trucks and helicopters to assure the increased mobility of troops. But the French post-war military industry, oriented towards war in Europe, produced supersonic interceptors and similar aircraft (designed for use against the Red Army) rather than the slow-flying bombers, observation planes or helicopters which were capable of carrying combat troops. These aircraft had to be bought with scarce dollars on the world market, and initially against the wishes of the US. The US was afraid of jeopardising its good relations with pro-Western Arab governments, particularly those of Tunisia and Morocco; this was considered central to the policy of communist containment in the Mediterranean. The French army in Algeria was thus able to collect only a limited and heterogeneous air transport and observation system.[14] Most of their trucks were left over from the Second World War, taken from the French army in Europe, and kept going only by 'cannibalising' spare parts from the most worn-out ones. The supply of 26,000 trucks in 1956 actually increased the number of roadworthy vehicles from 40,000 to only 50,000.[15]

During this period the French economy could not compete success-fully on world markets, and dollars had to be reserved for essential raw materials and equipment for modernising the French productive apparatus. The mobilisation of men for Algeria was more acceptable than using up foreign currency reserves in order to purchase suitable modern military equipment.

Although there was intense debate between the advocates of a defensive strategy of territorial control and the propagators of offensive military operations, the tactics used by the French army in Algeria were determined by the quality of the troops engaged. From 1956 to 1958, Commander-in-Chief Salan gave priority to territorial control. His aim was to occupy every Algerian village with small detachments of soldiers, in order to control the population and to prevent contact between the liberation army and the population. Operations against the guerrillas were undertaken only with precise intelligence. Despite this policy, the liberation army was very strong in several parts of Algeria in 1958.

The new Commander-in-Chief, General Challe, appointed by de Gaulle in December 1958, was more interested in operational tactics than in territorial occupation. Challe considered that decentralised operations against guerrilla units were ineffective, because they were based on piecemeal knowledge often manipulated by the liberation movement, and the colonial troops would arrive only to find the guerrillas gone. The Challe offensive was launched in 1959 by forming reserves capable of 'treating' a given region. This meant the region was isolated from other parts of the country, so as to make it possible to identify secret arms caches in it, and crush the military potential of the liberation army in that region. New popular self-defence structures then carried on the work of the colonial army. The initial stages of the strategy consisted of 'treating' the least 'contaminated' regions (those in the west, which were furthest from the 'sanctuaries' of the Algerian Liberation Army) in order to enlarge the potential for directly 'chasing the rebel'. Small operational reserve units were sufficient at this juncture.

The backbone of this strategy was a helicopter fleet of some 250 aircraft, capable of taking combat troops close to the ground, so that time-wasting parachuting was no longer necessary. These combat groups were equipped with automatic pistols and machine guns, and, in the second wave, with mortars and other light artillery, as army infantry. With superior communications they could call on artillery and aircraft support. In 1959, Challe deployed some 30,000 troops and 250 helicopters in operations first in the Ouarsenis, then in the mountains south of Algiers, and at least in the two Kabylias, purging these regions of insurgents. He saw these tactics as a means of gaining the essential goal of organising the population politically.

There were two reasons why General Challe and others thought that an attempt to crush the liberation army could destroy the vital links between it and the population. Firstly, such a demonstration of colonial military efficiency would change public attitudes; people would no longer believe in the possibility of ultimate victory. Secondly, any diminution of the liberation army's striking capacity would mean less risk for collaborators and would undermine the frequent excuse that help was being offered to the liberation army only to escape reprisals.

FRANCE'S TECHNOLOGICAL SUPERIORITY TO ALGERIA

Throughout the war, superior weaponry was of very little importance to the colonial army, but superior communications and transport were vital. Napalm and heavy artillery were used, but they were more effective in minimising French losses than in actually eliminating guerrilla groups, which were too widely dispersed to be attacked with these weapons. Except for a short period during 1958, the liberation army was never organised in units of more than 200 men; this limited the effectiveness of heavy weaponry, and indeed the decision to keep the guerrilla groups small may have been made in order to forestall the French use of such equipment. Thus the colonial army depended more on mobility than on firepower. For road transport, France had the AMX13 and Panhard armoured carriers, although these were easily avoided by the guerrillas. It also made wide use of trucks to deploy troops with the aim of encircling FLN combat groups,[16] and undertook extensive road building.

In the first years of the war, there were efforts to increase air observation and air-ground fire capacity. Although France could produce the Broussard and Potez 75 aircraft, suitable for observation and air-ground combat missions, the cost of production was considered too high, and the French defence authorities preferred the American T6, which could apparently carry more bombs.

In August 1957 there were 370 observation and combat aircraft in Algeria, of which 303 were American produced. They were almost certainly purchased second-hand from the US. Because the war lasted longer than anticipated, they eventually purchased new aircraft (American T28s).

The build-up of a helicopter fleet began in 1955 and was speeded up in the following years. In March 1956, when French draftees were mobilised, there were 80 helicopters in Algeria (all US produced), of which 29 were suitable for troop transport. By 1958 the fleet had been trebled to 250, including 94 heavy helicopters. Only the Alouette light helicopter was French produced. By 1959, the fleet had been increased by a further 50 per cent; this was its maximum.

In addition to road and air transport, the colonial army relied heavily on modern communications systems. These were originally developed for use in Europe, and were transferred to Algeria without any change in technology. It is probable that the radio equipment available to the army during the early years of the war was insufficient: but it was definitely more than the FLN units had.

THE EMERGENCY RULE IN ALGERIA AND THE CREATION OF CAMPS

The French adopted military means for political purposes. They used the army to negotiate the creation of a more acceptable colonial system, and to isolate the liberation movement. Police repression complemented the army's political role. Existing punitive methods against the resistance movement were reinforced, as were French juridical sentences. The colonial regime's facade of legitimacy rapidly broke down under the stress of the military and political activity of the liberationists and their supporters. The crumbling of this facade was exacerbated by the public response to the increasingly harsh measures taken in French courts. Emergency legislation was passed in an effort to destroy communications in Algeria and to isolate the nuclei of resistance from the rest of the population. This allowed for various forms of repression: internment, torture and resettlement.

Internment

Under emergency law it was stipulated that the civilian authority could assign any person to a particular residence. People could be put under house arrest or interned in camps. When the first internment camps were established in 1955, their existence was officially denied. By March 1956, there were two types of camps, the Centres de Triage et de Transit (CTT), in which suspects were kept until a final decision was reached on their further treatment (e.g. trial, execution, internment camps of other types, release, etc.); and the *camps d'hébergement,* for lengthy imprisonment. The CTT, charged with uncovering intelligence in 'subversive' organisations, became the centres of torture. Other unofficial camps were set up, because every army unit had to guard prisoners and to extract intelligence.[17] Any Algerian suspect came under the arbitrary arm of the administration. Decision-making on internment was gradually decentralised and put into the hands of local army units. The army now became the supreme arbiter of the liberty of the people.

The number of people in camps remained relatively low, because internment was regarded as necessary only for the most dangerous elements, mainly of urban origin. In the central region of Algeria there was a maximum of 24,000 internees in 1957, and official figures for 1959 and 1960 indicate that there were fewer than 10,000. But the importance of the camps should not be underestimated, because they set the stage for the development of torture.

Torture

Torture is a necessary method of counter-insurgency against a politically aware population. Because acceptable methods of deterrence and intelligence gathering were no longer viable for the French, they had to resort to the torture of a silent population (who were protecting the liberation organisation) as the fundamental means of maintaining their colonial sovereignty. In Algeria, it was a new kind of torture, directed not at establishing guilt, but at extracting information on the members of the liberation movement. In a hierarchically organised chain of responsibility and subordination, each militant knew only a few others. The official policy of the government in 1957 became the destruction of the liberation organisation through a painstaking unravelling of these links. The operation was called *'Remonter la filière'*. Anyone taken into custody by the army had to be made to confess what they knew, by *any* means. This *'any'* was explicitly stated in official orders from the government.[18] The extraction of such information became crucially important to the French Army during the Battle of Algiers. In this confrontation the liberation army intensified its activities in the hope of demonstrating its effectiveness to international spectators. The French Army retaliated by arresting massive numbers of people and using torture extensively. It is worth mentioning that the French Army had used torture earlier, in Indochina, and that the colonial police in Algeria had practised it before the war.[19]

Certain officers protested against these methods, believing, in the abstract, in a code of honourable conduct. The practice of such a code, they argued, would pacify Algerian nationalists, and defuse the conflict.[20] This approach may well have brought a quicker end to the war. Respectable though it was, its evaluation of the political situation was unrealistic. Torture in Algeria was no longer dependent on the individual decisions of local commanders. Instead it had become a system of rules which the army believed to be sanctioned by the French government.

The systematisation of torture in Algeria destroyed conventional restrictions on army activity and created certain specialised institutions. Some officials in the French administration suggested that allowed procedures be limited to the use of 'pure torture'.[21] This is a form of torture which leaves no physical evidence, and which therefore makes it almost impossible to prove. Another way of preventing evidence of torture, which was used at certain times in the Algerian war, was the murder of torture victims. Where evidence of torture was either invisible or destroyed, the publicly stated goal of the French to limit sadism was unenforceable. Those officials who were opposed to torture probably avoided being personally involved in this practice, and left it to those who enjoyed it. The brutality of the war grew from this immodest beginning; prisoners were often refused surrender, or thrown out of moving aircraft.

For torture to have become the principal method of gathering intelligence, it had to be hierarchically organised. The first step was the order given in 1956 to different branches of the police to co-operate in the use of torture. Next, in 1957, the French Army organised a system of protection, the Dispositif de Protection Urbaine (DPU), which was a civilian paramilitary group taking as its base a hierarchy of locally responsible individuals (e.g. the chief of a building, street, town, district, etc.). In Algiers the central organisation of the DPU was the notoriously ruthless Organisation O of the major Aussaresse. The DPU was subordinate to the Centre de Coordination Interarmée (CCI), a central intelligence unit which at first had been only a coordinating staff unit. In the summer of 1957, regional divisions and the Détachement Operations et Protection, with their own camps, were created. Gradually all intelligence units in Algeria, both military and civilian, came under the exclusive control of the CCI, which was able to develop its own liaison with these units as it was not under the control of the General Command of the French Army.

Protected villages and resettlement camps
The practice of torture could have been extended to include the whole Algerian population, but to have done so through the medium of camps would have been impractical, since their maintenance required the provision of food and other elements of subsistence for non-productive residents. Moreover, the existence of well-filled camps would not create a social basis for the legitimisation of the French presence in Algeria. Something else was needed, and was found legally in the emergency regulations of 1955, which gave the administration the right to forbid transport and communication in specific areas, as well as the right to declare certain areas out-of-bounds. The first provision made it possible to isolate different villages; the second sanctioned the evacuation of whole populations from certain regions. Essentially, this meant that the rural population could be transformed into quasi-internees.

The control and isolation of villages was achieved by the tactics of quadrillage: here an intensive army occupation took place in all the villages in a particular area, in order to prevent communication between the villagers and the liberation army. Because of security controls at night, villagers had to stay within the area 'protected' by the French Army. Work in the fields during the day was governed by the army's supervisory capacity. There is little reliable information on the number of 'protected' villages, but reports indicate that this sort of quadrillage was not prevalent throughout Algeria, largely owing to a scarcity of manpower.[22]

An adaptation of the concept of 'protected' villages was carried out by *regroupements*, which were resettlement schemes. Initially the French army tried to clear those areas which they found difficult to control by ordering the population to leave their homes and by attacking the area with artillery fire or aerial bombardment. This led to considerable population displacement in random directions, rather than a systematic resettlement in pre-determined areas. With increasing territorial control by the nationalists, supporters of the colonial regime and nationalist infiltrators fled to the towns. As a consequence the administration tried to initiate resettlement schemes from September 1956. These schemes were expanded during 1957, when the army reoccupied the whole of Algeria and tried to enforce municipal reform in order to recreate local bridgeheads.

The army regarded the resettlement schemes as a great social success because facilities such as schools and dispensaries were more easily established. But a confidential report[23] made by the civilian administration in 1959 illustrated the extremely poor living conditions of the resettled groups. They were often deprived of their means of production because their cattle could not graze in the resettlement areas and had to be slaughtered. Sayad and Bourdieu have shown that a process of *dépaysannification* occurred in this period. It consisted of the destruction of the traditional peasant norms of economic foresight, time and consumption, and their replacement by a sub-proletarian way of life in these resettlement camps.[24] This resulted in an abnormally high mortality rate, particularly among children. Although de Gaulle's Governor-General in Algiers tried to prevent new resettlements, the resettled population rose from one million in 1959 to over two million (or one-third of the total rural population) in 1961.[25]

For the army, protected villages and resettlements had a considerable importance: they organised men who might have become involved in the liberation movement into units which were kept busy with responsibility for the subsistence of women and children. The army's political aim was to provide a local government which gave the appearance of 'normal' life. If a village refused to elect a municipal council, the army retaliated by reporting that it was 'encountering unforeseen and insurmountable difficulties' in providing food and supplies. Similarly, if ALN actions were reported, or if lambs or cattle were missing, the army could again cut off supplies. The liberation army was helpless in this situation and deterrence became possible. However, regroupment was just the first indication of the paradox that what was good militarily was bad politically: the suffering endured by people in resettlement areas turned their sympathies to the FLN. It also influenced international opinion, the 'neutral' Moslems, and liberals in France.

ADMINISTRATIVE PENETRATION AND THE ORGANISATION OF THE
POPULATION BY THE FRENCH ARMY

Like the old colonial regime, the new repressive system had its basis in the fear and apathy of the people, which served as protection for the activities of the liberation movement. The French Army knew that it had to maintain a high level of public fear of its military power, because it would be unable to contain a resistance movement which spread into mass activity. In order to isolate the revolutionary movement the French Army had to create its own organisations, following the doctrine of interlinking membership. The principal bases of organisation were territorial and functional.

Territorial administration
The Section Administrative Spécialisée (SAS) was the territorial organisation based on the village or, in some cases, on urban slums. Its principal agent was the Officer of Special Administration, whose job was to gain the trust and confidence(s) of the local people by assuring them of economic and social security. The SAS consisted of a doctor, a teacher, and a locally recruited armed force. It initiated economic programmes for the benefit of villagers, as well as employment programmes with no economic value, such as cutting down trees along roads in order to prevent ambushes. Some SAS officers showed real concern for the rural poor, but many did not. The army found it difficult to get sufficient numbers of good officers. In many cases officers lived as petty autocrats, oblivious to the needs of their subjects. Many did not know Arabic. Nor was the SAS strong enough to restrain the excesses of French operational troops passing through the area. Then again, the civil administration had promoted municipal reform in order to create a political élite which would be quite different from the personnel of the local councils, and they wished to oppose this élite to the national liberation movement. With the success of municipal reform (1960), competition in efficiency immediately surfaced, particularly when, as was often the case, these new élites were not anti-FLN. Finally, the Officer of Special Administration was not a philanthropic distributor of economic benefits: as a representative of the colonial power, he also gathered intelligence. The two functions were clearly not unconnected. Politically he had little to offer, and even economically material progress was made only through hard work. The liberation army, on the other hand, offered the same economic possibilities with concrete political advantages.

Even so, the SAS spread rapidly and were soon seen as a major threat by the FLN. Instituted initially as an emergency measure in April 1955, when the civilian administration in the Aurès mountains collapsed, by the end of 1955 there were 180 units, reaching a peak of 688 in 1961.

Functional organisation
Beyond doubt the SAS were the principal means by which the French maintained contact with the population. Functional organisations, the

second element of the doctrine of the organisation of the population, were less effective. The French did not attempt to organise workers: there was no army-controlled trade union and no association of landless peasants. The main functional organisations were of the nature of the Mouvement de Solidarité Féminine, the Diar-el-Askri, and Amitiés Africaines, as well as organisations for the professional development of young people.

The Mouvement de Solidarité Féminine was begun in 1958 and became known through its 'Operation Sewing Machine', which consisted of the collection of used sewing machines in France and their distribution in Algeria. The movement worked in collaboration with EMSI, Equipes Médico-Sociales Itinérantes, which went into villages to teach modern hygiene and child care.

The Diar-el-Askri and Amitiés Africaines were organisations for the veterans of the French Army, in which the Moslem population had to serve. These two organisations provided social aid, distributed useless distinctions and sometimes found jobs for its members. About 700,000 predominantly Moslem veterans of the French army lived in Algeria; some of them, especially those who had served in Vietnam, were the actual spearhead of Algerian nationalism (notably Ben Bella).

There were two youth organisations: a *moniteur* programme, and the Service de Formation des Jeunes en Algérie. After 1958 the latter was no longer controlled by the army and became politically neutral. The *moniteur* programme aimed at providing military and civil instruction to 200,000 *moniteurs*. This goal was not realised.

Despite their relative lack of success, these functional programmes show the strong connection between economic and social reform and counter-insurgency in Algeria during the war. From its inception, the French knew that it would not be sufficient to win the war militarily. To a certain extent administrative penetration had to serve the interests of the colonised people in order to win their support and to undermine their sympathy with the liberationists.

Aspects of economic reform

French social and economic policy in Algeria showed certain basic contradictions. If administrative penetration was to create a new social base for continued French sovereignty then each step had to be linked to a general theory of development. French economic policy aimed at rapid industrialisation capable of eventually absorbing underemployment in the countryside. The landless proletariat had to be transferred to industrial occupations because the French had failed to mobilise them in long-term expansion of the agricultural sector. Only the new middle classes, composed of well-to-do industrial workers, and the richer peasants were likely to support these colonial policies, and the SAS were left with the job of organising the masses. Though the SAS often saw themselves as protectors of the destitute, such contradictions in the overall strategy of the government made it impossible for them to offer effective social and economic reforms. In any case, the effects of economic reform were anticipated only after a considerable time, and meanwhile their initiation was hampered by the insecurity and resistance of the people, who did not believe in these promises of reform. Indications of the French ideal of a new French Algeria, *Algérie française et nouvelle*, such as promises of economic reform, became tools in the struggle between the liberation movement, which represented the deep aspirations of the people, and a colonial power making concessions to retain its sovereignty.

The officers in closest contact with the population (e.g. the OAS) often developed models of quasi-socialist growth, which were hostile to Algerian agrarian capitalism.[26] Politically these ideas were represented by 'Patrie et Progrès', which supported a Yugoslav model of society, although civilian officers were vehemently opposed to the idea of world communism. These officers were estranged both from the French left which weakly raised issues of decolonisation; and from the supporters of *Algérie française*, who protested strongly against the slightest moves towards equality.

Contradictions were vicious. It seemed that no amount of economic and social reform would suffice to win the loyalties of even the 'neutral' Moslems, let alone the nationalists. Moreover metropolitan interests continued to support the war effort, though as the ideology of *Algérie française et nouvelle* evolved, it became clear that the economic advantages to France were diminishing: Algeria would no longer supply its products at low prices and was no longer a protected market. These problems were exacerbated by the intransigent attitudes of the *pied noir*, who came to hate the intentions of the French government almost as much as the goals of the FLN. In addition to this, the army violently disagreed with the policies mooted by de Gaulle. These are some of the factors which necessitated the elaborate techniques of psychological warfare designed to contend with the many political, economic and emotional contradictions which were implied by the continued French control of Algeria.

Psychological warfare

The liberation movement represented a simple solution to the aspirations of the people: a solution which the French called the 'myth of independence'. They knew that neither their administrative presence, nor military defeat, nor the organisation of the people would explode this myth unless another myth was at hand to replace the old one. For French political, military and administrative measures to be effective, the myth of independence had to be discredited. Psychological warfare, a specialised branch of counter-insurgency, seeks to propound an ideal differing from the ideal of a liberation movement. 'Psychological war-fare is the planned use of propaganda and of all means capable of influencing opinions, passions, attitudes and behaviour of human groups (enemies, friends and neutrals), in order to help the realisation of national goals of the country'.[27]

Psychological warfare has to demonstrate its own resolution against the enemy in order to weaken his resolution. It tries to lead the enemy into tactical errors by disseminating inaccurate information about military operations or troops. The most notable operation of this kind in Algeria was the successful attempt to make the FLN believe that some of its own militants were traitors. Further confusion was created by the use of non-identifiable radio transmissions and leaflets, addressed to guerrillas living in poor conditions, about the privileged lives of their leaders. These activities were not particularly original: they had been used before in other wars with mass civilian participation.

The decisive new field of action in Algeria consisted of the so-called Moslem neutrals, a large section of the population whom the French wished to win over. The nature of this type of counter-insurgency was demonstrated by the army instructions of 1956,[28] which recommended that the neutral section should be taught to believe the following: a certainty that France should remain in the country; a certainty that the rebels were guilty; a certainty that the rebellion would be defeated. Further, the neutrals should be made to feel that economically the French solution was better because the French would remain in the country; and they should be made to wish for a return to a normal and balanced life, together with a realisation of France's ability to provide this return.

The importance of showing that the power relations were favourable to France cannot be explained solely in terms of the gravity of the military situation in 1956. Nor can it be explained as a consequence of the infancy of the reform programmes. An analysis of the leaflets distributed by the 10th military region (the High Command in Algeria) in 1958 and 1959 shows that 38 per cent of the leaflets attempted to depict France's international and military power; 38 per cent said that France represented economic progress while the FLN symbolised misery; and 14 per cent were related to the emancipation of women under the French.[29] It is significant that the leaflets demonstrating French power were printed in larger numbers than the others: there were 250,000 copies of de Gaulle's speech announcing the economic reforms contained in the Plan of Constantine (3 October 1958); there were 1,500,000 copies of a leaflet on the death of the FLN leader, Amirouche (1959); there were 500,000 copies of a leaflet dealing with the desertion of an FLN unit under Ali Hambli; and there were 1,000,000 copies of one announcing the successful conclusion of the 1959 parliamentary elections in Algeria (with 80 per cent of the population voting).

Propaganda continued to centre on French military supremacy but fundamental changes occurred between 1956 and 1959. The 1956 instructions seemed to suggest that the Moslem population was to be treated with force and with justice: the emphasis was on justice, paternalistic though it was. By 1959 the Moslems were being asked to evaluate their immediate interests in terms of higher incomes, and were given the impression that French Algeria could use all the resources of the metropolis for its economic development. The army, which had attempted to participate in the definition of the ultimate *political* goals to be pursued by the French in Algeria, resented the implications of this approach of appealing only to material advantages, which, however, were not granted. But apart from such statements of principle as 'France stays in Algeria and France makes reforms', the governments of the Fourth Republic could not define a French position. The French Army then stated its own position: integration. In Kabylia, in 1957, army propaganda focused on integration: 'You're as French as the people of Marseilles'. The army pictured a France sweeping from Dunquerque to Tamanrassett, divided by the Mediterranean just as Paris was divided by the Seine. However this view was unacceptable to French capitalism, as it would have required enormous transfers of income to underdeveloped Algeria, and this was not compatible with the level of development in France. The most conservative advocates of colonialism now proposed integration without economic equality. Other political groups, excluding the extreme left, called for some sort of internal autonomy in Algeria, with France acting as a referee between the two ethnic communities. After 1961, however, these groups accepted the idea of an independent Algeria which would maintain informal ties and a *de facto* economic and political dependence. The real appearance of the conflict occurred when General de Gaulle, approached by the army in order to gain Moslem acceptance of integration, refused to even use the word 'integration' in French propaganda.

This conflict was only one aspect of the problematic and hostile relationship between the army and the civil government. The army had been transformed into a political policy-making body by its use of psychological warfare. When the war in Algeria broke out, the morale of the soldiers and the officers was very low—they were not eager to lose another colonial war, burying their comrades for nothing, as they had done in Indochina. Thus the 'service for strengthening morale' in the French army had to intensify its activity in 1955–6. At the same time isolated groups of officers were elaborating theories of anti-subversive warfare. The two strands came together in Algiers, where in late 1955 a central service of psychological action was established. The SAPI, Service d'Action Psychologique Interarmée, became immensely important, both in France and in Algeria. To maintain morale it had to convince soldiers of the necessity of the war. It did this by spreading an ideology of anti-subversive war, providing pragmatic instruction on how to win it. At the same time, conscious of the morale problems of an army deeply frustrated by metropolitan criticism and the slow local implementation of its programme, SAPI had to represent the army's apprehensions to the political authority. As the central instrument for the dissemination of propaganda, SAPI was used by the French proponents of *Algérie française* as well. Since the SAPI hierarchy felt that the success of psychological warfare in Algeria depended on a firm French commitment to *Algérie française*, the service felt itself bound to support *Algérie française* groups. In 1957, the service boosted its image in France by nominating officers of anti-subversive warfare for all French regional staffs and chairs of psychological warfare in French military schools. In this way, psychological warfare attempted to transform the Algerian war into a civil war, or at least a civil struggle.

As the theory of anti-subversive war had a set of hypotheses sufficiently broad and coherent to explain all misfortunes (though it might do so primarily in terms of internal French developments), its proponents were unwilling to pay attention to contradictory evidence. Thus psychological warfare succeeded in producing a nucleus of people who would never accept the inevitability of decolonisation. Equally, as the use of torture necessitated a conviction of the justice of its cause, an intractable nucleus of people who could never allow the end of French Algeria was created: they could not face the realisation that they may have tortured unjustifiably, or in a lost cause. The two groups reinforced each other.

The success of psychological action, administrative penetration and organisation, as well as the resettlement areas and protected villages, meant that the population could participate in the destruction of the enemy. This realised the ultimate goal of counter-insurgency, which was the creation of an indigenous organisational network capable of defending itself in the interests of the interventionist nation. The use of local personnel in colonial wars is nearly as old as European expansion. In Algeria the Moslem population had been subjected to military service since 1912, though nationalists were rejected for 'medical reasons'. In 1955 and 1956, these troops had to be transferred to Europe because they deserted en masse—often in whole units—after killing European officers. However, after 1957, when the French army had stabilised its position, new recruitment was possible. Moslem troops were recalled from Europe to Algeria, and in 1962 there were 27,000 Moslem professional soldiers and 60,000 draftees in the French army in Algeria.

At the same time, supplementary forces were built up, and the local population was used militarily in various ways. For example, they were used to exploit internal rivalries in the liberation movement. There were five cases of French collaboration with nationalist anti-FLN guerrillas: the most famous of these was the messalist *maquis* of Bellounis, which fought for France under the flag of Algerian nationalism in 1957–8. However, army operations also failed. A spectacularly unsuccessful operation was the K Force, a supposed anti-FLN *maquis* armed by France, which in fact provided a way for Belkacem Krim to get arms and to gain control of Kabylia.

Local populations were also used in the GMPR (Groupement mobile de protection), a police force of relatively secure collaborateurs, which was established in 1955 and never exceeded 10,000 men. In 1957 it recruited FLN deserters and organised them into a police force operating in the Moslem quarters of Algiers. *Harkis* were supplementary forces of variable military quality who served for relatively high wages. At first they were only given inferior, easily controlled jobs, but from 1959 onwards some of them were formed into the *commandos de chasse*, the élite troops of the general reserves. In January 1957 they numbered 2200; in 1960 nearly 60,000. Local populations also participated in the SAS units of protection, the *maghzen*, which increased from 3400 in 1957 to 19,000 in 1960.

Moslem regular forces and Moslem supplementary forces each equalled some 90,000 men. Besides these military forces, self-defence units were built-up, composed of peasants defending their protected villages and resettlement camps. The intention had been that following the Challe offensives, resulting in the destruction of the liberation army, these self-defence units would be capable of defending their villages. In reality, the self-defence units and the FLN often connived with each other. If the peasants could not refuse the arms offered by the French, they could agree to play the game with the liberation movement; the strength of the liberation army in the last phases of the war lay less in its power to act in certain villages, than in its ability to maintain a climate of insecurity, and to continue its international mobilisation of sympathy.

The fact that these 240,000 Moslems (180,000 regular and supplementary forces, and some 60,000 self-defence members) did not play any role in the final decision-making in Algeria demonstrates both their isolation and their low level of commitment. Men very often served reluctantly, sometimes just for money in order to live, and it is interesting that no other Algerian group was treated with so much contempt by France after the war as the Moslem supplementary forces. They were abandoned to the mercy of the liberation army, who are said to have killed some 10,000 of them. Neither the regular nor the supplementary forces nor the self-defence groups provided any basis for the continued sovereignty of the French in Algeria. The attempt to draw these forces into common organisations with the European population, thwarted by Paris in 1959, would in any case have failed. The army's Algerian policy could be based on the European population alone, who accepted the army's precepts of counter-insurgency and built up viable, if somewhat over-zealous, organisations and secret commands in order to defend their rights to stay as French citizens in Algeria.

The military success and political failure of French counter-insurgency in Algeria

Any evaluation of the effectiveness of French counter-insurgency in Algeria must distinguish between the purely military and the political. From the military point of view, French counter-insurgency was fairly effective, considering the number of guerrilla troops, their firepower, their units of combat, and the number of their violent actions. The number of guerrilla troops increased rapidly until 1957. In mid-1955 French sources indicated that there were 3000 guerrillas; in spring 1956, there were between 15,000 and 20,000, and in 1958 there were 30,000 to 40,000 regular soldiers. There were considerably larger numbers of supplementary forces, which are difficult to estimate since a large majority of the population favoured the FLN. After 1958 the regular forces of the FLN decreased as a consequence of the Challe offensives. Official Algerian sources suggest that there were only 2,000 to 3,000 regular soldiers in 1962.

A similar trend can be noted in the development of the liberation army's firepower. An official report estimated the firepower of the liberation army as being up to 15,000 military arms in May 1957, and up to 7,500 military arms in June 1960. This was because after January 1958, when the French army sealed off the borders dividing Algeria from Morocco and Tunisia, supplies of arms could no longer reach Algeria. The French secret service also tried to intervene directly against freelance arms dealers selling to the FLN, and established firm naval and air control off the Algerian coast. There is no denying that the guerrillas of the interior faced serious difficulties in maintaining adequate firepower.

The decline in manpower and firepower was reflected in the size of the ALN combat units at different stages of the war. In 1958 the ALN began to organise itself into battalion units, but it had to give up this plan, and by 1960–1 it was acting in comparatively small units. By 1958 the ALN had abandoned its 1955 plan of creating a liberated zone where a national government could reside, because from 1958 onwards more and more of the so-called *zones interdites*, regions in which the French army had given up territorial control and which were being regularly bombed, were now effectively reoccupied by the French.

Any estimation of the numbers of military actions carried out by the

guerrillas is imprecise, because it does not differentiate between types
of actions. But a parallel evolution can be seen between the size of
combat groups and the number of actions. From a low level of 100–200
actions per month, the figure rose in October 1955 to 1000 and was
stabilised in autumn 1956 at around 2500–3000, reaching a height of
3900 in January 1957. This rise was accompanied by massive ALN
losses: in February 1956, 400 were killed; from April 1956 to the end of
the war in 1962, 1400–2000 were killed. French figures of ALN military
actions for the years 1958–9 indicate a fall from 1750 actions per month
to under 1000 by the end of 1959. Even the cessation of French offensive
operations, declared unilaterally at the opening of negotiations in 1961,
did not raise this number above the spring 1956 level.

The effective working of the resettlement schemes against the ALN is
illustrated by the 1959 report of an ALN official, who said: 'The
resettlement of the population has literally asphyxiated the rebels.
Any possibility of rebirth cannot be envisaged'.[30]

These findings do not diminish the extraordinary sacrifices and
successes of the Algerian people in their war of liberation. But, contrary
to the tenets of some romantics of revolutionary war, they demonstrate
that the revolutionary armed movement could be crushed militarily.
The questions now are why the French army was unable to exploit its
victory, and why the military decline of the liberation army did not
coincide with political defeat. The adherents of French Algeria said
that de Gaulle deserted Algeria at the very moment the French army
achieved success: that is, in September 1959, when he uttered the fateful
words, 'self-determination'. There is a certain limited truth in this,
since the French military victory did not alter the general feeling that
France would have to leave Algeria. The contention of French liberals
that Algeria gained nationhood and independence only through the
war has some explanatory value: in fact, French military success was
achieved at the cost of so many lives and such atrocities that it was
impossible to believe that Algerians could simply become French
citizens after the war, and all alternative solutions to the problem rested
upon acceptance of Algeria's right to independence. This implied a
takeover of power by the liberation movement. But the decisive factor
in this matter was the effect of the war on the 'neutral' Algerians; the
deepening of their self-consciousness and the awareness of decolonisation. Nobody believed that Algeria could be assimilated into France
after the war, even if generations of reform were undertaken. And
because nobody could think of a return from the situation, the majority
of Algerians behaved as if independence was at the door, thus depriving
France of a social base for its anti-FLN collaborators.

Moreover, the prospect of a military build-up of the French Army
in Algeria in the indefinite future was unacceptable to France. For one
thing, the Algerian war was proving more expensive than initially

anticipated when its heavy military build-up was undertaken. This occurred in a period of prosperity, under a social democratic cabinet which was introducing reforms in France. Later the costs of the war and rising real wages fostered inflation and hampered French competition on world markets. The conservative government under de Gaulle shifted the burden of the cost of the war to the working class and the peasants. The belief that de Gaulle would bring peace postponed open social conflict, but after the failure of de Gaulle's attempts to force the FLN into substantial concessions, in mid-1960, conflicts in France became more and more intense.

The principle of France's right to intervene in Algeria began to be increasingly contested in France. Undoubtedly French public opinion favoured the argument that Algeria was part of France. Algeria had been French longer than any other large colony; the administrative system, the schools, the way of life, seemed to be French. The great cities, Oran and Algiers, had for a long time been inhabited by the *pied noir*, who constituted the majority of their populations. However, French people, bred in the values of their civilisation, found the use of torture in Algeria shocking. A former defence minister, one of the individuals who were principally responsible for the military build-up in late 1955, publicly declared his opposition to torture;[31] and a commanding general, de Bollardière, chose imprisonment by refusing to transmit an order to torture.[32] This aversion to torture was one of the outcrops of a tradition which drew its strength from the experience of the Second World War, at which time France had felt proud of its opposition to the atrocities committed in Nazi Germany.

But the real shock of Algeria began to be felt as the prospect of a short war increasingly retreated. During the first two years of the war, public opinion in France found it impossible to envisage a protracted Algerian resistance. When draftees were sent to Algeria, the French government, ignoring warnings given by leading French officers, placated the French population by saying that more French troops in Algeria would mean a quicker end to the war.[33] As these promises came to be seen as ill-founded, public opinion in France split: one section protested vigorously against the methods of the war, while the other sheltered behind accusations against weak-kneed politicians, and foreign powers who thwarted French efforts in Algeria, such as the US and Britain.

Internationally, France became more and more isolated. The third world, including China, was willing to accept that France could not simply withdraw from Algeria, but they wished to see it take concrete steps towards Algerian independence. France lacked the military potential it required in order to maintain all its colonies; it had to accept independence in Africa south of the Sahara. The governments of these countries would not continue friendly relations indefinitely, without the prospect of an end to the massacres in Algeria. Equally, French capital realised that the maintenance of a colonial imperial economy was neither in its interest nor a viable proposition. Foreign capital had penetrated into the richest parts of black Africa, leaving the costs of the stabilisation of colonial sovereignty—and, later, of the politically independent regimes—to the French taxpayer. Efforts to modernise French industry were not primarily dependent on third-world markets; in fact, the continued underdevelopment of these countries made them unlikely customers for the fastest-growing economic sectors, such as automobiles, electronics, and aircraft.

Impossible in any case, integration was no longer even desirable, because it hampered capital accumulation for modernisation in France. It became vital to come to a settlement in which major French interests would be safeguarded, but there were three sets of obstacles in the way of such a settlement.

The first was whether such a shift could be realised in the French parliamentary context of the Fourth Republic. Though the process initiated in late 1957 and 1958 had culminated in a new understanding between the centre parties and the socialist party, this understanding was difficult to put into practice because of internal tensions within the parties. Anyway, a popular front coalition was impossible after Budapest. Eventually, only a prestigious conservative leader like de Gaulle would be able to ease the transition.

Secondly, by the time de Gaulle took power, there were powerful and well-established groups in the army and administration in Algeria, who had built up defences against intervention from Paris by cementing ties of solidarity with groups in France. Convinced that they could always repeat the *Algérie française* upheaval of May 1958 in order to dethrone de Gaulle, these groups actively opposed any change in French policies.

Thirdly, we can identify a specific configuration of conditions necessitating an end to revolutionary war by negotiation. The interventionist power's principal goal is to segregate the liberation movement from the population. Consequently the liberation movement had to be denied any legal existence. However it is impossible for the liberation movement to engage in negotiations without recognition of its legal status as a body representing the insurgent population. Such a recognition would leave the interventionist nation no bargaining power.

In a situation in which *dégagement* (a retreat without assuring the negotiated protection of interests) is not desired, the two parties have to agree to jointly create a transitional coalition government *before* embarking on negotiations. This is the inevitable consequence of a double-rule situation of the revolutionary war kind, in which the military strength of the interventionist army effectively nullifies the potential of its opponents to chase collaborators from office; while

the political strength of the liberation movement denies the interventionist power any further opportunity to exercise its sovereignty.
In this situation to come to terms is difficult. It was possible in the
decolonisation of Algeria because the primary decision to hand over
power to the FLN was achieved by negotiation.

The example of Algeria shows that counter-insurgency is not merely
a technology of war, but an instrument whose use is determined by the
historical moment at which genocide becomes impossible without
incurring unthinkable political costs. The truth of this can be seen in
countries with an anti-fascist history. Intervention in Algeria was
limited by the anti-fascist heritage of most of the powerful nations of
this time. French public opinion was a significant mediator in this game.
In an amalgam of repressive, manipulative and reformist measures,
new strategies had to be invented. These had to be located in the international context of decolonisation, determined by the crises caused by a
colonial decline in power and the growing resistance of the colonised.
Increased rivalry between the US and the USSR for political influence
in the third world, as well as the internationalisation of the capitalist
world economy, put French capitalism under specific pressure and
imposed a need for reductions in outlay which had to be met by cuts in
external commitments. In this international and democratic context,
colonial repression was bound to fail. But when it failed, the attempts
made to re-ground colonial sovereignty led to the creation of distinct
social groups, such as the terrorist Organisation Armée Secrète (OAS),
who were capable of considerably impeding strategies for an end to
colonial or imperialist power. The extent to which their resistance
could be broken determined the potential for an orderly take-over by
revolutionary forces. In the last stages of the Algerian war, the
prolonged struggle of the OAS made the transition almost as violent
as any stage during the war.

What succeeded militarily failed politically. The field was open to a
'peaceful' change, but this would only have been possible could the
leaders of the interventionist power have somehow neutralised the
effects of their strategy. And neither the French nor the new Algerian
government could neutralise years of atrocities and 'betrayals'. Their
disastrous delay in seeking a political solution meant that the French
had to concede all political and economic benefits. The most painful
of these was the situation of the estimated one million *pied noir* who had
no choice but to leave their homeland.

NOTES

1. Franklin Mark Osanka, *Modern Guerilla Warfare: Fighting Communist
   Guerillas 1941–1961* (New York, 1962) pp. 96ff.
2. Alberto Manual Garasino, 'Gobierno y contrasubversión', *Estrategia*
   (May–June 1970) p. 512.

3. Algerian history is analysed by Abdallah Laroui, *Histoire du Maghreb* (Paris, 1971); Charles-André Julien, *Histoire de l'Algérie contemporaine* (Paris, 1964); Yves Lacoste, André Nouschi and André Prenant, *L'Algérie, passé et présent* (Paris, 1960); Marcel Emerit, 'L'Etat intellectuel et moral de l'Algérie en 1830', *Revue d'histoire moderne et contemporaine* (1955) pp. 199–212; Jean-Claude Vatin 'L'Algérie en 1830', *Revue algérienne des sciences juridiques, économiques et politiques* (Dec 1970) pp. 977–1058.

4. In 1954 the white population included 17,000 independent farmers, including great landlords; 17,000 independent merchants of different sizes; 100,000 employees of whom 50 per cent were in the administration; and 100,000 workers. The Moslem population included 1 million peasants in the traditional sector; 500,000 seasonal workers in agriculture; 100,000 permanent workers in agriculture; 255,000 urban workers (of whom 39,000 were in 'large-scale' industry and services, such as railway and ports); and 250,000 workers in France. Elsenhans (1974), pp. 108–12.

5. One-quarter of Algerian land was in European hands; nearly one-half had been expropriated by the colonial government up to 1920. Elsenhans (1974) p. 91; Arthur Doucy and Francis Monheim, *Les révolutions algériennes* (Paris, 1972) p. 321.

6. Roger Le Tourneau, *Evolution politique de l'Afrique du Nord musulmane, 1920–1961* (Paris, 1962) pp. 358ff.

7. Charles-Henri Favrod, *La révolution algérienne* (Paris, 1959) pp. 91ff.

8. *L'Express* (30 Jan 1956 and 29 Feb 1956); *Demain* (11 Nov 1956).

9. For example, see Roger de Roquigny, 'Le térrorisme urbain', *Revue Militaire d'Information* (Feb 1958) pp. 77–83.

10. Passive counter-integration sticks to traditional norms in apathy; active counter-integration transforms the *potential* of defining oneself as different from the dominating system into actions. Elsenhans (1974) pp. 132–7.

11. Hartmut Elsenhans, *Materialien zum Algerienkrieg 1954–1962* (Berlin, 1974) pp. 58–74. In 1956 one-third of all guerrillas were equipped with arms, according to a confidential report of the French army.

12. Elsenhans (1974) pp. 380–1; Philippe Tripier, *Autopsie de la guerre d'Algérie* (Paris, 1972); *La semaine en Algérie* (8 Nov 1960) p. 17; Clostermann, parliamentary speech, *J.O.Assemblée Nationale, Débats Parlementaires* (13 May 1958) p. 2261.

13. The then defence minister (and lord mayor of Algiers), Jacques Chevallier, declared that only two-thirds of the budgetary allotment of 80,000 soldiers were in Algeria in mid-1954. Jacques Chevallier, *Nous Algériens* (Paris, 1958) pp. 117–23; and *France Observateur* (29 Dec 1955). The low level of morale was admitted by the minister for Algeria, Lacoste, in *Bulletin de Paris* (1 Mar 1956).

14. In March 1956 there were 80 helicopters in Algeria: 50 Bell 47 and 29 S55. It was planned to deliver 126 more by the end of 1956: 10 Bell 47, 20 Djinn, and 20 Alouette (light helicopters), 36 S55, 20 S58, and 20 Piasecki (carrying 20 soldiers). At the same time SNCASE (French state enterprise) was developing X316, a helicopter carrying 120 men. In 1958 there were 249 helicopters in Algeria, of eight different types. R. Lacroix, 'L'emploi des hélicoptères n'est-il justifié en Algérie?', *Revue de Défense Nationale* (May 1958) p. 844; see also June 1958, p. 1241. Also Günther Engelmann, *Die*

Streitkräfte Frankreichs (Berlin, 1961) p. 80; Robert G. Landa, *Natsional 'noe osvoboditel'noe dvizenije v Alzire 1939–1962* (Moscow, 1962) p. 234.

15. Elsenhans (1974) pp. 407–8, refers to data from a confidential report of the National Assembly's defence committee.
16. The FLN was the Front Libération National. Its military wing was the Armée de Libération Nationale (ALN).
17. *France Observateur* (16 June 1955); Patrick Kessel and Giovanni Pirelli, *Le peuple algérien dans la guerre* (Paris, 1958), pp. 25, 71ff: Jacques Vergès, Michel Zavrian, and Maurice Courrégé, *Les disparus. Le cahier vert* (Lausanne, 1959); Vidal-Naquet, *La Raison d'Etat* (Paris, 1962) pp. 104ff; Yves Courrière, *Les Temps des Léopards* (Paris, 1969) p. 532; Elsenhans (1974) pp. 434–9; Hafid Keramane, *La pacification* (Lausanne, 1960); Abdelhamid Benzine, *Le Camp* (Paris, 1961); *Le dossier Jean Muller* (Paris, 1957) p. 25.
18. Jacques Massu, *Le torrent et la digue* (Paris, 1972) p. vii.
19. Raphael Leygues, parliamentary speech, *J.O. Assemblée Nationale, Débats Parlementaires* (9 Nov 1961) p. 4157; and the Wuillaume report (1955) quoted in Vidal-Naquet, pp. 55ff.
20. This was especially the belief of General Paris de Bollardière, who commanded a sector in Algeria. Paris de Bollardière, *Bataille d'Alger, bataille de l'homme* (Bruges, 1972) pp. 83ff.
21. Wuillaume report, quoted in Vidal-Naquet, op. cit., pp. 55ff. See also *L'Echo d'Alger* (3 Mar 1958); *Le Monde* (20 Dec 1959); *Témoignage Chrétien* (16 Dec 1959); Jacques Massu, *La vraie bataille d'Alger* (Paris, 1971) p. 343.
22. Elsenhans (1974) pp. 440, 710–16.
23. The author, Rocard, was later Secretary-General of the PSU, the leftish socialist party. The report is printed in Vidal Naquet, op. cit., pp. 217ff.
24. Pierre Bourdieu and Abdelkader Sayad, *Le déracinement* (Paris, 1964) pp. 111–67.
25. *Le Monde* (14 and 18 Apr 1959; 26 May 1961).
26. See *La Semaine en Algérie* (11 Oct 1959).
27. Ministère de la Défense nationale, Etat Majeur Forces Armées, *Elements de guerre psychologique*. La compagnie des Hauts Parleurs et des Tracts. Notice provisoire d'emploi (Paris, 26 June 1956) p. 1.
28. This text is reprinted in Elsenhans, *Materialien*, pp. 78–83.
29. Elsenhans (1974) p. 491.
30. Ahmed Benchérif, *L'aurore des mechtas* (Algiers, 1962) p. 88.
31. *Le Monde* (11 Nov 1957).
32. *L'Exprès* (22 Mar 1957).
33. *Carrefour* (7 Mar 1956).

5 Military Technology and Conflict Dynamics: the Bangladesh Crisis of 1971

Javed Ansari and Mary Kaldor

Analysts of third-world conflicts place great emphasis on a Euro-centric concept of the balance of power, based on imported military technology. Journalists and academics anxiously count up numbers of tanks, ships, and aeroplanes, and the more ambitious modify their estimates with measures of technological sophistication, based on such criteria as speed or electronic complexity, which roughly correspond to the modernity of the weapons in question. Thus one Phantom aircraft is worth four Starfighter aircraft or one SAM-3 missile complex is worth two SAM-2 missile complexes. In this way, the capacity to wage war can be tallied while the inclination to do so can be neatly assessed on the basis of calculations about the existence of a possible 'imbalance'.

In this chapter, we argue that this concept of the balance of power is fictional, that the size and 'sophistication' of imported military technology has little or no bearing on the capacity of third-world armies to sustain a position by force (although it does affect numbers of casualties). This does not mean that the concept is empty or irrelevant; fiction can have important consequences. Imported military technology plays an important part in the development of conflict and the outbreak of wars through its influence on the structure and attitudes of the armed forces and on the perceptions of protagonists in conflict.

We elaborate this argument through examples taken from the Bangladesh crisis of 1971. This crisis can be said to date from the partition of the Indian subcontinent in 1947 and the division of Pakistan into two wings separated by thousands of miles of hostile Indian territory. The crisis began to erupt with the demonstrations, riots, and strikes which shook all of Pakistan in 1968–9 and forced the resignation of Ayub Khan, its President and virtual military dictator. His successor, Yahya Khan, promised free elections and these were held in December, 1970. They were won by the Awami League, a moderate Bengali nationalist party, led by Sheikh Mujib and committed to regional autonomy for the Eastern wing of Pakistan. But Awami League rule proved unacceptable to the politicians of the Western wing and the consequence was military crackdown by the Western-dominated army on 25 March, 1971. Nearly nine months later, after thousands had died and millions more been made refugees, Indian troops invaded East Pakistan and, after a fourteen-day war, the region became an independent nation, known as Bangladesh.

The effects of imported military technology on the crisis were indirect; Western-type weapons affected the political role of the Pakistani Army and hence the causes of the crisis, and they affected the judgement of Indian leaders and hence the decision to intervene in the crisis. However, the direct effects of imported military technology in determining the outcome of the fourteen-day war, were, contrary to conventional expectations, more or less unimportant.

The causes of the crisis

Pakistan inherited from the British a strong state apparatus. It consisted of an army and bureaucracy established to carry out imperial policy, and it was dominated by those sections of the Indian populace most loyal to the British Raj, notably the Punjabi landowning classes. Despite the appearance of an unrepresentative parliamentary democracy from 1947 to 1958, it was this state apparatus which ruled Pakistan throughout its short history.

The crisis of 1971 can be said to stem from this fact; for the rulers of Pakistan systematically pursued a development strategy which led to high rates of growth in the Punjab financed by the impoverishment of East Bengal. Until the mid-sixties this strategy was, at the most, tolerated—if only because the state apparatus could claim to be the defender of the common cause, Muslim Nationalism, against the common enemy, India. Military aid played an important role in strengthening the state apparatus. Financially, it insulated the army from the domestic political process. Technologically, it provided the visible signs of the regime's ideological determination and it helped to induce a set of 'modernising' attitudes which justified the regime's economic policies.

POLITICAL STRUCTURE OF PAKISTAN, 1947–70

At the time of independence East Bengal had a political and economic structure that was radically different from that of the West Pakistan provinces. The wealthiest strata of Pakistani society lived in West Pakistan; it was they who dominated the Muslim League (the Muslim Nationalist Movement), the army, and the bureaucracy. East Bengal had no industry and its landowners were almost entirely Hindu or British; the nationalist movement of East Bengal had been based on the demands of the Muslim peasantry. In contrast, it was the Punjabi landowning classes, who owed their positions to the British, and who feared the consequences of Hindu rule, who formed the basis for the nationalist movement in the West. Furthermore, West Pakistan possessed an industrial base which, although tiny, was able to absorb the Muslim businessmen who migrated from India at partition.

The parliamentary form of government established in Pakistan at independence did not last long. Indeed, it began to disintegrate as soon as the disparate elements of the Muslim League were pulled apart, as they were, after the death of Jinnah, leader of the League, in 1948. For the Muslim League had provided a mechanism through which the Punjabi élite could command mass support in the name of Muslim nationalism. After 1951, all presidents or governors-general of Pakistan were civil servants or soldiers. The power of the bureaucracy was the power of the president and, through the 1950s, it was demonstrated in the arbitrary dismissals and appointments of cabinets, and in the manipulation of bitter political disputes (over such issues as East–West parity and the proposal to integrate West Pakistan into one unit) which rendered the politicians totally ineffective.

The military *coup* which brought Ayub Khan to power in 1958 merely enabled the state apparatus to rule in name as well as in fact. It was followed by the abolition of political parties and elected bodies. Although a national assembly was reinstated in 1962, it never became more than a rubber stamp for improving the government's image. It was based on the system of 'Basic Democracy', an hierarchical system of government, in which the smallest unit was an elected village board. The Basic Democrats were the members of these boards and they constituted the electoral college for the national and provincial assemblies. They were, for the most part, local personages who owed their privileged positions to support from the central government, personified by the district officer or magistrate. It was a system which served to entrench the strength of the bureaucracy throughout the countryside yet further.

The significance of military–bureaucratic rule lay in the fact that it ensured the continued dominance of the wealthy landowning and urban families, who came mainly from Punjab. Over the period 1947–70, 54.2 per cent of the Pakistani population came from East Pakistan, yet among the Indian civil service officers inherited by Pakistan, only one came from Bengal; Bengali representation in the armed forces was also negligible. Although the 1956 and 1962 constitutions theoretically gave Bengalis parity in administrative and military recruitment, little was done to rectify the situation. By 1968, the Bengali share of administrative posts reached a peak of 36 per cent, while 90 per cent of the military manpower continued to be West Pakistani, mainly Punjabi and Pathan.[1] Further, the important posts were situated in West Pakistan. The Civil Service of Pakistan—the apex of Pakistani bureaucracy—contained an élite cadre of 300 men, three-quarters of whom served in West Pakistan. The bulk of the armed forces were situated in West Pakistan, mainly because of Kashmir, but also because they were equipped by the Americans to meet a Russian 'threat', which was expected in the north-west. East Pakistan units, in contrast, did not receive US military aid. By 1970, only one Bengali had reached the rank of Lieutenant-General in the army, and no Bengali had ever achieved equivalent status in the air force or navy.[2]

ECONOMIC STRUCTURE OF PAKISTAN, 1947–70

In these circumstances it was not surprising that the military–bureaucratic rulers should have pursued an economic policy that discriminated in favour of the Punjab. On paper, the policy was aimed at the fastest possible overall growth rates, particularly after the *coup* of 1958. Pakistan became a model 'success story' in the eyes of the economists of Harvard University, who had helped to prepare its economic plans and formulate its overall economic strategy. An average annual growth rate of 6 per cent was achieved in the Second Plan period, 1960–4, and, in 1967–8, the rate of growth of GNP soared to 8.3 per cent. Further, the structure of the economy underwent a significant change during this period; the share of agriculture in total output fell from 49 per cent to 32 per cent. Nevertheless, the production of cotton and wheat, predominantly in the Punjab and Sind, increased rapidly.

This rapid expansion was achieved largely through the substitution of imported consumer goods with domestically produced equivalents. It was financed by the easy availability of foreign aid and by a complicated system of indirect controls for channelling scarce resources from agriculture to industry. The planners deliberately ignored the costs of such a strategy. The system of import control, foreign exchange rationing, and tariff discrimination that was devised in order to accelerate industrialisation led to the emergence of highly inefficient and non-competitive industrial enterprises. Towards the end of the 1960s, it became evident that 'easy' import substitution was no longer feasible and that the economy was more than ever dependent on increased flows of foreign aid. But after the 1965 war with India, foreign aid was no longer freely available so that the economic structure could only be preserved through an increased squeeze on agriculture—something which proved politically untenable.

The transfer of resources from agriculture to industry involved the redistribution of income in favour of a rich 'saver class' and in favour of West Pakistan, at the expense of the Bengali peasantry. It was accomplished through reliance on the private investor; on a small entrepreneurial class which was reputed to have a high propensity to save. By the mid-1960s, the top 5 per cent of the population received more than 20 per cent of the total personal income.[3] The twenty leading families controlled 68 per cent of industrial assets, 70 per cent of insurance funds, and 80 per cent of banking assets.[4]

A far-sighted government might have seen that if initiative was left to the private sector, the 'logic of the market' would lead to an accentuation of regional disparities. This is, of course, what occurred. The Gross Provincial Product of East Pakistan was 86 per cent of the Gross Provincial Product of West Pakistan in 1949–50. By 1967–8, it was around 65 per cent.[5] The rate of growth of per capita income in East Pakistan was lower than in West Pakistan in every year of the period. In some years, the rate of growth in East Pakistan was negative. Furthermore, the structural change that took place in Pakistan was more pronounced in the Western wing. The patterns of saving, investment, and trade were also quite different in the two wings. Indeed, the figures indicate that the higher growth rates in West Pakistan were partly achieved by the ability of East Pakistan to provide finance and foreign exchange.

Savings

Statistics on investment and saving rates are somewhat shaky; they must be treated as broad approximations with substantial margins of error. Nevertheless, they provide general indications of the overall picture. Throughout the period, East Pakistan received only 32 per cent of total investment allocations; moreover, its share consistently declined. The ratio of saving to the Eastern Gross Provincial Product was higher than that of the Western wing.[6] In other words, the gap between savings and investment was much smaller in East Pakistan than in West Pakistan. Indeed, the figures would suggest that East Pakistan financed all of its provincial investment itself and even, perhaps, provided resources for investment in the Western wing.

The difference in investment rates in the two wings primarily reflects the unwillingness of the private sector to invest in East Bengal. During the first twenty years of Pakistan's existence, less than 25 per cent of total private investment occurred in the Eastern province. Moreover, the public sector has failed to fill the gap. Except in the Third Plan Period, public investment per capita in East Pakistan has been about one-third of that in West Pakistan. Moreover, only a small part of public investment was devoted to development purposes. Industry received only 8 per cent of total public investment funds,[7] while public investment in agriculture has been negligible. Hence the East Pakistani economy could not draw on public funds in lieu of private funds for rapid industrial or agricultural development.

Trade

The two regions that subsequently constituted Pakistan were areas which produced primary products for trade mainly with the rest of India. Trade with the outside world as well as between the two regions that composed Pakistan was very small.[8] In 1949 India devalued its currency and, subsequently, refused to trade with Pakistan at the new exchange rate. A considerable trade diversion occurred in both wings of

Pakistan. There is substantial evidence to suggest that this resulted in a commodity transfer of resources from East to West Pakistan. Over the period 1950–65, East Pakistan had a deficit on her account with West Pakistan and a surplus with the rest of the world. In contrast, West Pakistan had a large and growing deficit with the rest of the world and a surplus on her account with East Pakistan. Over the period as a whole, East Pakistan had an overall trade deficit of Rs4 crores (40m.) per annum compared with Rs70 crores per annum for West Pakistan; up to 1960, East Pakistan had a surplus on its overall trade balance. In fact, if a correction is made to reflect a higher and more realistic price of foreign exchange,[9] the East Pakistan deficit becomes a surplus which corresponds to the size of the West Pakistan deficit. In other words, earnings from East Pakistani exports to the rest of the world were spent on goods produced in West Pakistan, at a higher price than they would have fetched in the world markets. West Pakistan, in turn, was able to spend its earnings from exports to East Pakistan on imports from the rest of the world. Through this mechanism, foreign exchange earned in East Pakistan could be used to further the industrialisation of West Pakistan. East Pakistan's share in total Pakistani exports continued to rise but its share in imports tended to remain constant.

The government of Pakistan did little to check the growing regional disparity. Quite the contrary; its economic policy accentuated the disparity, mainly through the transfer of resources from agriculture to industry. The fixed exchange rate, combined with the policies of import control, ensured that the prices of agricultural commodities, which were influenced by the prices of exports, were maintained at a lower level than the prices of manufactured goods, which were raised because of the restrictions on imports of competitive goods. Not only did this adversely affect East Pakistan because of the greater share of agriculture in the economy of the Eastern region, but it can be shown that the squeeze on agriculture was greater in East than in West Pakistan. Farmers received more rupees for a dollar's worth of agricultural goods in West Pakistan than in East Pakistan, and they paid less for a dollar's worth of manufactured goods in the Western wing than in the East.[10] The differences in industrial prices were largely the consequence of the system of import licensing which favoured West Pakistan throughout the period.

THE EFFECT OF IMPORTED MILITARY TECHNOLOGY

Military aid was an important factor in underwriting the government's ability to carry out this economic strategy. First of all, it provided the state apparatus with an external, and hence independent, source of funds. From 1954, when Pakistan joined the Western military alliances CENTO (then the Baghdad Pact) and SEATO, the US provided

$1.3 billion in military aid, thus meeting two-thirds of Pakistani military requirements and enabling the Pakistan government to maintain a constant annual military expenditure at one-third the level of the Indian military budget. Secondly, the weapons provided by the US government enhanced domestic and foreign perceptions of Pakistani strength. They did not affect, for the most part, the army's domestic military position—relatively primitive weapons like lathis (big sticks) were sufficient for the suppression of riots. But they preserved the Western image of a military balance *vis-à-vis* India. Pakistan's manpower inferiority was claimed to be offset by its fire-power superiority. In conventional Western terms, its Patton tanks, its F-104 Starfighters armed with missiles, and its heavy artillery were thought to surpass anything possessed by India.[11] And this view was accepted in both India and Pakistan. Finally, military aid, together with economic aid, carried with it an aspiration towards the American model of development. Pakistan's firepower superiority was, after all, based on American technology and could be operated best in an institutional framework based on the American model. Pakistan's economic strategy was a textbook case for the American development theorists—indeed it was largely devised by Harvard economists. Their abstract justification removed the unpleasant necessity of explaining its inequitable and exploitative aspects.

The 1965 war destroyed the tenuous links that had held the two wings of Pakistan together. It destroyed the ideological appeal of the state apparatus. Pakistani firepower superiority failed to defeat the Indian army and, for the duration of the war, East Pakistan was left defenceless and without outside communication. It also destroyed the government's economic strategy because it led to the American decision to halt economic and military aid. This meant not merely a cut-back in imports and development expenditure, which in itself entirely undermined the third five-year plan, but also involved a considerable diversion of resources to pay for an increased military build-up, which might otherwise have been financed by the United States. Industrial workers, particularly in East Pakistan, who had received few or none of the benefits of bloated growth rates, experienced a rapid rise in prices, particularly of food, and dislocation of the industrial sector. They joined the students and professional groups in demonstration against government interference, demanding wage increases of 50 per cent or more. Agriculture was also squeezed, and discontent in the villages increased as attempts, inspired by the American economic advisers, to offset regional imbalance through rural aid programmes enhanced the wealth of Ayub Khan's Basic Democrats and petrified village social structures. In the wave of riots and strikes of March 1969, peasants forced the resignation of Basic Democrats and attacked or killed those who did not resign.

From 1965 onwards, the Bengali autonomy movement achieved a momentum of its own. In retrospect, it was inevitable that the Punjabi-dominated state apparatus should either cede its position to the Bengali nationalists or crack down on the autonomy movement as it did in March 1971. The removal of Ayub Khan in 1969, and the decision of his successor Yahya Khan to hold democratic elections was bound to lead to a break-up of Pakistan, so long as East Pakistan represented the majority. The reversal of that decision and the army's attempt to rule Bengal directly by force was only practicable in the long run if it was assumed that India would be content to stand aside.

The Indian intervention of December 1971
There were plenty of reasons why the Indian government should have favoured intervention in the Bangladesh crisis. But there were also obvious reasons why the Indian government might have preferred to avoid the costs and risks of war. It is possible to argue that it was the provision of Soviet military aid to India, combined with the arms embargoes on Pakistan, that, in the last resort, determined the decision to risk war.

MOTIVES FOR INDIAN INTERVENTION

The most important motive for Indian intervention was probably rooted in the long-standing conflict with Pakistan. Even without analysing the causes of that conflict, it is reasonable to assume that any move to weaken the central government of Pakistan was likely to be supported in India. East Pakistani politicians had always been less hostile to India than their West Pakistani colleagues and, from an early date, demands for regional autonomy had included demands to weaken the restrictions on trade with and travel to India. The Kashmir problem had often been regarded as a Punjabi problem and Sheikh Mujib himself had been one of the few Pakistani leaders to support the Tashkent Declaration of 1966. The Indian business community may also have seen an advantage in a future alliance with Bangladesh, creating, as it were, a new captive market.

But there were also motives which stemmed from the internal political situation in India. No Indian government could have viewed the prospect of a left-wing leadership in East Bengal with equanimity. The Bengali parties to the left of the Awami League had strong links with similar parties in West Bengal. Membership of NAP liaised with the Indian Communist Party—Marxist (CPI-M) and the Naxalites, while the West Bengal unit of the Indian Communist Party (CPI) was largely responsible for ensuring that the Communists of East Bengal continued to operate during the years 1954–71, when their party was banned.[12] Moreover, in March 1969 peasant unrest was particularly strong in areas adjacent to some of the Indian trouble spots; for example the Mizo area of West Bengal and South Assam. It was fairly clear that a left-wing Bangladesh could have provided a haven for revolutionaries operating in West Bengal. And it was also clear during 1971 that the longer India tolerated the situation in East Pakistan and resisted the temptation to intervene, the more likely were the left to gain ascendancy in the East Bengali mass movement. As it turned out, the rise of the Awami League and the subsequent Indian intervention enabled the Congress Party to eliminate its left-wing opponents in West Bengal. The process of elimination partly took the form of direct action. Naxalite leaders, for example, were rounded up and executed. But more importantly, the wave of euphoria which followed the Indian army's triumphant entry into Dacca was expressed in a resounding victory for Indira Gandhi in the West Bengali elections of 1972.

In addition, the Indian leaders shared with the Awami League leaders a similar outlook and perspective on the nature of their circumstances. It is likely that the Awami League drew much from the example and experience of the Congress Party. Both are middle-class parties with mass support based on a nationalist ideology and both are moderate parties with claims to radicalism. This common sympathy, combined with a common interest in confining left-wing activities in their respective spheres of influence, must have been a major factor in determining India's attitude to Bangladesh.

Finally, of course, the burden of supporting literally millions of refugees in a country whose own inhabitants are desperately poor was difficult to tolerate for long.

INDIAN POLICY DURING 1971

Nevertheless, from March 1971 until the summer, the Indian government exhibited all the signs of hesitation. India certainly provided material support for guerrillas attempting to resist the Pakistan Army. Indian troops were moved into West Bengal in early 1971 to maintain order during the elections. They remained there following the East Pakistan crisis. Some units may have crossed into East Pakistan during March or April but no serious clashes were reported between Pakistani and Indian troops during this period, although India did attempt to intercept Pakistani ships on the high seas. Contact between the Indian armed forces and the guerrilla units seems to have been established in late March and India seems to have promised arms as well as training facilities. In April 1971 government-backed committees to collect money for the purchase of arms and ammunition for the guerrillas were set up all over India. Recruiting centres were established to train the guerrillas. In June *The Times* reported the existence of a hundred such units in West Bengal.[13]

But about direct intervention by Indian troops, there was evidently no consensus among Indian leaders. On 30 March, Mrs Gandhi had called upon the United Nations to intervene in the East Pakistan crisis. Reportedly India had in early April persuaded President Podgorny of the USSR to put pressure on Yahya Khan; Yahya apparently believed that the Soviet Union was as yet not fully committed to India and he sent his version of the story to the USSR on 5 April. India exercised considerable restraint during April and May when Pakistani forces came into conflict with Indian units while securing East Pakistan's borders. Presumably, the Indian government hoped that the international community would influence the Yahya regime and force it to accept a political settlement with Sheikh Mujib. As late as May 1971 Mrs Gandhi asked 'the Great Powers to take the initiative in the East Pakistan crisis'. In that month President Yahya had initiated discussions with the East Bengali leader, Nur al Amin; and Tajuddin Ahman, the Prime Minister of the Bangladesh government in exile, had indicated that the Awami League was not unwilling to participate in a political dialogue. These attempts at negotiation clearly reflected India's unwillingness to embark on a full-scale war with Pakistan for which she was unprepared.

At the same time, all options were kept open. The India-based 'Bangladesh Radio' had from 25 March carried on propaganda against the Pakistan army highlighting its ferocity and barbarism. It urged the people to flee to India—for the Bangladesh guerrillas were convinced that it was in India alone that they could set up training and recruitment centres, especially after the Pakistan army had routed them so comprehensively. By the middle of June, India was claiming that there were 6 million East Pakistani refugees and was actively soliciting world sympathy for them. By June most Western countries and Western-backed international organisations, such as the World Bank, had cut off economic aid to Pakistan; but it was becoming increasingly clear that this was not enough to make Pakistan bend and the Western countries were not prepared to go any further. The Jana Sangh paper, *The Organizer*, had been advocating armed intervention since early March. (The Jana Sangh Party is a right-wing Hindu nationalist party which has taken a consistently anti-Pakistan position since 1947.) Sources closer to the Congress had also been putting forward this view. On 7 April 1971 Mr Subramaniam, Director of the Indian Institute of Defence Studies, stated 'What India must realize is the fact that the break up of Pakistan is in our interest and we have an opportunity the like of which will never come again.'[14] It is evident that by June Mrs Gandhi started taking such advice seriously. On 15 June Mrs Gandhi stated 'India would not for a moment countenance a political settlement which meant the death of Bangladesh.'[15] Jag Jivan Ram, the Indian Defence Minister, talked openly of war for the first time.

The Indian leaders' commitment to war might be traced to early June, for it was then that refugee relief and other operations on the East Pakistan border were placed under the direct control of New Delhi. The airlift of refugees to Madhaya Pradesh was stopped and gradually all foreign personnel—including those engaged in relief work—were removed from the border.[16] From July onwards, India consistently refused to station United Nations observers along the borders. Pakistan, on the other hand, was eager to station UN representatives—presumably because she had crushed the Mukti Bahini (the Awami League guerrillas) and the Liberation Army in East Pakistan and did not want an escalation of the conflict. In August India showed that she was prepared to sacrifice her traditional policy of non-alignment for the sake of unreserved Soviet support in the ensuing conflict. On 9 August, the Indo–Soviet Treaty of 'Peace, Friendship and Co-operation' was signed. This represented the first steps towards the development of an Asian Collective Security system, designed by the Soviet Union. India was prepared to put Brezhnev's plan into operation provided the Soviet Union was prepared to lose its influence in Islamabad; 'the main expectation', as an Indian analyst put it, 'from the Soviet Union, is what the Soviet Union could do *vis-à-vis* Pakistan.'[17] With the signing of the treaty one great power was finally committed against Pakistan.

India was also attempting to isolate Pakistan, through diplomatic means, from the West. This task was facilitated by international sympathy for India as a poverty-stricken nation doing everything possible for the refugees, a sympathy particularly aroused by the cholera epidemic which, according to Indian sources, was killing 2000 persons a day in the refugee camps. In July, the USSR and France announced a total ban on arms shipments to Pakistan. The same month, the Foreign Affairs Committee of the US House of Representatives voted to halt all aid to Pakistan. In August, Senator Edward Kennedy came out in open support of the Indian position. India was thus assured that it would be extremely difficult for President Nixon to resume large-scale military aid to Pakistan.

From September onwards, the guerrillas, operating within Bangladesh, appear to have become more active. A Consultation Committee to unite the Liberation Army (composed of the East Bengali regiments of the Pakistan army) and the various Bahinis (irregular guerrilla groups) was set up 'to direct the freedom struggle' and their activities were increasingly reported from various urban centres. On 14 October, the guerrillas assassinated a former governor of East Bengal. Nevertheless, the Indian Government apparently realised that the guerrillas could not be relied on to lead a swift and successful major offensive against East Pakistan. Indian shelling of Pakistan border posts increased drastically during October. On 17 October, Jag Jivan Ram stated that

India would not withdraw her troops from the border areas until the crisis was resolved. He hinted that India would not evacuate any territory occupied in the event of war, which suggests that India was considering the occupation of some areas within East Pakistan where an Awami League administration could be installed. On 22 October India called up army, navy and air force reserves and, on the 28th, Mrs Gandi departed on a tour of six Western capitals to seek support for and appreciation of India's position in the conflict.

The tour was successful. It succeeded in isolating Pakistan from her Western allies of SEATO and CENTO. On 8 November the US government revoked licences for arms to be shipped to Pakistan and on 17 November, Edward Heath, President Nixon and Chancellor Brandt sent a joint appeal to Yahya to launch a new political initiative in East Pakistan. It was clear that the Western powers would not intervene to protect Pakistan's existing political structure.

In early November Indian attacks on East Pakistan were camouflaged behind a rejuvenated Mukti Bahini. The guerrillas for the first time since April succeeded in penetrating deep into the heart of East Pakistan. Major attacks were however made on the border cities; for it was here alone that India was prepared to provide ground and air support. India did not commit itself irrevocably to the struggle until it was sure of Chinese reaction. On 8 November Mr Bhutto, the prime minister of West Pakistan, was advised in Peking by his Chinese hosts to search for a political settlement in East Pakistan. Undismayed, Bhutto reiterated Pakistan's intention to 'defend her integrity' and on 12 November stated that he 'would never tolerate an East Pakistan dominated government'. It became clear that Pakistan and China were in some disagreement and that China would provide little other than verbal and diplomatic support in case of war. On 12 November Mrs Gandhi admitted training and providing arms and ammunition for the guerrillas. She rejected UN intervention. On 21 November, Indian troops supported the Mukti attack on Jessore and on 23 November, the Indian army entered East Pakistan in a number of regions. Right up to the last moment Pakistan did not expect India to launch an all-out war. Pakistani army reserves were not called up until 24 November and air force reserves not until the 29th, more than a month after India had called up her reserves. Pakistan attacked on the western front only when the fall of a large number of towns in East Pakistan became imminent.

THE EFFECT OF IMPORTED MILITARY TECHNOLOGY

India's budgeted defence expenditure for 1971–2 was US $1700 million, this was 2.3 per cent less than the military expenditure incurred during the previous year. This provides evidence for the view that India was perhaps not expecting a major confrontation during this period. However, this statement is subject to a number of qualifications. First of all it has proved impossible to determine India's actual military expenditure during the period April 1971 to December 1971. Secondly the 2.3 per cent cut-back does not mean much in relative terms; for in the previous year Indian defence expenditure had soared by 12.8 per cent over the previous year, and a significant proportion of this expenditure was incurred after the crisis became imminent. Finally the cut in military expenditure may simply have reflected the greater availability of Soviet assistance.

During 1971 India procured the following major weapons:
  90 HAL MiG 21 M and HAL MiG-21FL fighters built in India with Soviet collaboration;
  50 Sukhoi SU-7 fighter bombers from the USSR;
  1 unit SA2 Guideline SA missile from the USSR;
  1 'Petya Class' frigate from the USSR;
  6 torpedo boats from the USSR;
  150 PT-76 amphibious tanks from the USSR;
  3 HAL Hs 748-7 transport aircraft built in India with UK co-operation;
  6 Canberra bombers from New Zealand;
  350 Vijayanta tanks built with UK co-operation;
  20 Alouette III helicopters from France;
  8 Canberra B(i)12 bombers from New Zealand.

The weapons were mainly procured for the naval and air forces, which were expected to be of immense importance in a war with Pakistan. Of significance for the army was the acquisition of additional PT-76 amphibious tanks which were clearly envisaged for use in a waterlogged environment like Bangladesh. Since the bulk of military spending was devoted to the army,[18] it seems evident that the major weapons were obtained through Soviet military assistance.

In the late 1960s India was experiencing difficulties in obtaining spare parts and equipment supplies from the Soviet Union for Mil Mi4 helicopters, MiG 21 fighter aircraft, heavy artillery, tanks and 100 and 130 mm guns. Reportedly the Soviet Union was intentionally withholding these spares and India had stocks sufficient for only 10 days combat.[19] In December 1970 India acquired 10 B(i)12 Canberra bombers from New Zealand (they were originally British), 8 more were given in 1971. In February India announced plans to manufacture submarines with Soviet collaboration. In June it was reported that the Indian navy procured some Harriers, and in July it is reported to have acquired 2 Westland Sea King ASW aircraft from the UK.

After the signing of the Indo–Soviet Treaty, it was reported that the USSR put considerable pressure on India to induce her to buy all military hardware in the USSR. Negotiation on this question is said to have delayed Soviet arms shipments to India. But it was not until

November that the Soviet Union began arms shipments to India in earnest. *The Times* reported that the USSR ferried arms, missiles, and instructors and also provided 10 loads of military spares in late October.[20] Three Soviet ships carrying about 5000 tons of hardware arrived in early November.[21] In November/December 1971 the USSR is reported to have sent advanced versions of Soviet SAM missiles as well as experts to operate them.[22]

It would thus appear that India's extraordinary arms procurement drive began to bear fruit somewhere in October; a month and a half after the signing of the Indo–Soviet treaty. If the foregoing analysis is right, then arms procurement would seem to be a crucial factor in the escalation of the crisis after April. India exercised considerable restraint and caution until August. It was only after the USSR definitely changed her policy *vis-à-vis* the subcontinent that India made plain her readiness to intervene in the crisis.

Crisis escalation was also affected by India's ability to stop the supply of arms to Pakistan. Pakistan's total military expenditure for 1971/72 was about 6 per cent higher than the previous year; but it was still only two-fifths of Indian military expenditure during that year. Pakistan's major weapons procured during 1970 included:

4 Cessna COIN trainers from the USA;
9 gunboats from China;
10 DHC2 Beaver STOL transport aircraft from China;
2 Alouette helicopters from Saudi Arabia.

Major arms procurement by Pakistan during this period was meagre compared with that of India. In November 1970 the US had promised to supply F-104s, B-57s, patrol aircraft and replacements and spares, but Pakistan did not hurry over the order and eventually it fell through. Following the crisis, one country after another imposed a ban on the shipment of arms to Pakistan. By June the United States, the USSR, France, and the UK had imposed such bans. According to Indian sources China did continue to supply some arms, and in June it promised to supply military equipment to raise two new divisions of 400,000 men for border security in East Pakistan. But it is doubtful whether China's assistance could have been of immediate value, in view both of China's own arms supply capabilities and of the Western orientation of the existing Pakistani military inventory. In July the United States airlifted $3.8 million worth of military equipment to Pakistan. These included spares for F-104s. In September the US is reported to have supplied spares for armoured carriers.[23]

India thus succeeded diplomatically in cutting off Pakistan's military assistance. She did not invade East Bengal until it was clear that, except for China, there was no country that would supply arms on a large scale to Pakistan. The US ban of November 1971 reassured India and the subsequent US policy of supplying arms during the war was viewed with great hostility. China's policy was foreseen and the extent of her support to Pakistan was accurately estimated by New Delhi. The Indian decision to attack in November 1971 was thus influenced by her success in procuring arms from the Soviet Union and her success in stopping the flow of arms to Pakistan.

The outcome of the conflict

Table 5.1 shows the deployment of forces on 3 December, when war broke out in the subcontinent. It shows that India had a clear two to one overall advantage. Its position in the East was vastly superior to that of Pakistan: it had seven infantry divisions, some independent brigades, and 400 combat aircraft on the Eastern front, while Pakistan had only three infantry divisions and a lone F-86 fighter squadron. In the West however there was a parity of forces; India and Pakistan had approximately equal numbers of infantry divisions and combat aircraft, although Pakistan had two tank divisions while India had only one. India's main tank force remained in central India and did not take part in the fighting.

During the war both China and the United States gave considerable aid to Pakistan. According to Indian reports, China sent arms and ammunition for tanks in the Western front.[24] It provided Pakistan with facilities to fly military planes to East Pakistan.[25] The United States provided military spares, and ten F-104 Starfighters sent to Jordan by the United States were transferred to Pakistan during the war.[26] Some planes were also said to have been provided by Iran, Turkey, Libya, and Saudi-Arabia.[27]

TABLE 5.1   Deployment of forces by India and Pakistan in December 1971

Fronts	India	Pakistan
East	7 infantry divisions 400 combat aircraft	3 infantry division 20 combat aircraft
China	6 infantry divisions	
West	1 tank division 12 infantry divisions 400 combat aircraft	2 tank divisions 11 + infantry divisions 360 combat aircraft

Notes: (a) India's main tank division remained uncommitted during the struggle.
(b) India's independent brigades were mostly in the East.
(c) Pakistan's military brigades were in the West.

Source: Sisir Gupta, 'Why India Won the Fourteen-day War', *Armed Forces Journal* (Apr 1972).

India was wholly dependent on the Soviet Union for supplies during the war. As noted earlier, the USSR started sending large quantities of arms and ammunition in November. During the war, according to Pakistani sources, it was responsible for operational maintenance.[28] The Soviet Union also transferred some of its planes from Egypt to India in December 1976.[29] According to the Pakistan Air Force Commander-in-Chief, the USSR provided the Indian Air Force with an airborne early-warning and combat aircraft thought to be either a Tupolev TU 114M 'Moss' with a Soviet operator crew or a specially equipped Canberra with Soviet radar and electronic counter-measures.[30] Defence production in India, particularly the production of the ordnance factories, also increased substantially during the war.

From the beginning of the war, Pakistan's firepower superiority was a thing of the past. In 1965, India had also had a two to one manpower advantage but the Pakistan Army was said to be better equipped and better trained than its Indian counterpart. The Pakistan Air Force (PAF) had missiles as well as a modern communications system. The Indian Air Force (IAF) had neither. In the interim period the Indian military increased in efficiency and co-ordination. By the early 1970s the planning that had been done in the wake of the 1962 Chinese misadventure was considered to have improved effectiveness.

The battle on the land seems to have begun in the West when one Pakistani corps with six infantry divisions, one tank division, and an independent artillery brigade attacked Chamb, the gateway to Indian-occupied Kashmir. The Indians defended their positions for 72 hours, but were then pushed back across the river Tavi. India had two infantry brigades and three tank regiments in the battle. The Pakistanis lost control of the river after nine days' struggle but fortified their position in Chamb, which is Indian territory. Despite heavy casualties (3000 men lost by Pakistan and about 2000 by India), Pakistan was not forced back into Azad Kashmir. This was Pakistan's only major gain on land during the war.

The Indians scored substantial gains in the Rajhasthan desert and near Shakargarh. In both these cases India was on the offensive. One of the important causes of India's victory on these fronts as well as its success in stopping Pakistan in Kashmir was the superior manoeuvrability of its troops. Indian generals were better tacticians and caught Pakistani units by surprise many times.

Tanks and heavy armour were infrequently used during the war. India was waiting till Pakistan committed its armour before committing its own. Both had strongly fortified areas where tank breakthroughs could be expected. Pakistan's armour was concentrated near the battle fronts and thus became involved in a number of minor Indian probes. India's main armour remained at its central Indian base. Their crack armoured division started to move towards the front days after the war had started only when it was feared that Pakistan might break through at Chamb. The main tank battle was near Shakargarh, where Pakistan is reported to have lost about 50 tanks. Pakistan's 1st armoured division was crippled in heavy woods by the IAF before it could really join the attack. The Indians were well on the way to effecting a major breakthrough when the ceasefire agreement was arrived at.

In East Pakistan, the Pakistan army simply did not fight. It had been estimated by Indian experts that in December 1971 East Pakistan could have held out for three to six months.[31] Moreover, despite obvious difficulties in establishing a supply line, China was firmly committed to providing facilities for military overflight.[32] But the ground forces in East Pakistan were never really committed to the struggle. By 7 December with the capture of Jessore (which held out for 15 days) and Shylhet all resistance to the Indian advance in East Pakistan seems to have come to an end. On 10 December Fauman Ali Khan was talking of the repatriation of troops and the second week of fighting in East Pakistan saw the Pakistan army in headlong flight towards Dacca which duly surrendered on 16 December.

In the air war the Pakistan Air Force claimed a spectacular victory. Towards the end of the war it was claiming that the IAF had lost 130 aircraft compared with only eight lost by Pakistan on the Western front. The start was certainly impressive when PAF planes in their pre-emptive strike on 3 December succeeded in penetrating a thousand miles into Indian territory. But the PAF itself admitted that these raids on IAF bases had resulted 'in the destruction of very few Indian aircraft, perhaps none at all'.[33] India was well prepared for air action. On 4 December, they launched counter-attacks on targets in East and West Pakistan and seem to have done much better. The air campaign was carried out by anti-airfield and close support strikes, by fighter aircraft on both sides during the day, and by night strikes using Pakistan B57 Martin Canberras and Indian BAC Canberras. The Pakistanis successfully used Sidewinder AAMs on MiG-17s to shoot down India SU-7s and MiG-21s. India used helicopters extensively in operations in support of the Mukti. The IAF also airlifted paratroopers to the suburbs of Dacca on 11 December. After the first week both India and Pakistan seemed to be conserving their air strength. The PAF was used sparingly to support Tikka Khan's units in Chamb and the F-86 squadron in the East fought bravely until the fall of Dacca. As many as eleven planes (out of a total of twenty) are said to have been destroyed by the PAF themselves on 16 December to prevent them from falling into Indian hands. The PAF may not have done as well as it claimed but it certainly did not do badly. The IAF claimed to have destroyed six of the PAF's 24 Mirages and nine Starfighters but immediately after the war the PAF was able to show 23 Mirages and four out of seven Starfighters that it possessed.[34] And although India admitted to losing only 30 aircraft in West Pakistan during the war the PAF had identified the wreckage of 32 IAF planes in its territory alone by the end of January and reports were still coming in. The SU-7s were most vulnerable to PAF attacks.

In naval operations, the Indian Navy was totally successful in blockading East and West Pakistan. It effectively established sea control over the Bay of Bengal and the Arabian Sea. The Indian Navy, though far larger than the Pakistani fleet, was by no means modern or even well equipped. Yet by the end of the operation it claimed two Pakistani submarines, two minesweepers, and about 16 gunboats for the loss of one frigate and a few patrol craft.[35] It attacked the Pakistani fleet at Karachi and destroyed East Pakistani ports and also carried out river operations in East Pakistan. Pakistani naval losses may be estimated from the fact that naval build-up was a top priority in the military budget subsequent to the war.

Estimates of losses vary: India admitted about 10,000 casualties and the loss of 80 tanks and 54 aircraft. It is probably more accurate to estimate about 20,000 casualties, over 100 tanks, and about 70 aircraft.[36] The IAF losses may have been considerably greater; even in peace times it is known to be very accident-prone.[37] Pakistan is said to have lost about 70 aircraft and about 200 tanks. In June 1972 one source reported that China had promised to give Pakistan 60 MiG-19s and about 100 T-54s and T-59 tanks to cover its war losses.[38] Pakistan also lost a large number of men in the action in the West theatre and in the East, 90,000 men were taken prisoner. Pakistan occupied a meagre 50 square miles of Indian territory near Chamb and lost 1200 square miles in Sindh and 830 square miles near Sialkolt.[39]

It is clear that factors other than military superiority were important in resolving the crisis of 1971 in the Indian subcontinent. It is indisputable that India possessed, according to conventional calculations, vastly superior military resources and her advantage, particularly in the East theatre, was overwhelming. However, Pakistan did not lose because it could not withstand the Indian attack. Isolated regiments in Jessore and Hilli showed that the Indian offensive could be contained for several days. The Indians themselves estimated that East Pakistan could have held out for three to six months, yet the Pakistan Army preferred to blow up vast quantities of its spares, ammunition, and equipment on its continuous retreat before the Indian Army. The truth is that Pakistan never expected the Indians to launch an all-out attack in the East and when the attack came the Pakistanis were utterly overwhelmed by the hopelessness of their situation. India became committed to total conquest only when it witnessed the Pakistani flight. Had the struggle been prolonged, India might have been quite content with 'liberating' a part of East Bengal for the Awami League.[40] But within a

week Pakistani leaders were talking of troop repatriation. They were
convinced that there was no point in staying on in East Bengal.

In the West, Pakistan's only attack came in the Chamb area. Despite
Tikka Khan's initiative, little or no reinforcements were made available
and once the Indians had contained his attack, Pakistan was on the
defensive all along the line. Superior Indian generalship may have out-
manoeuvred Pakistan, but the fact is that Pakistan's armour was never
committed to the struggle. The Indian advance into Shakargarh
succeeded largely because of Pakistan's inability to co-ordinate her
forces and to launch a counter-offensive. The Pakistanis lost in the
West primarily because they had no definite plans after the Chamb
initiative had failed; they were only fighting to contain the Indians.
It was the ceasefire which saved West Pakistan. The Indian victories
on the Western front could not be attributed to superior armament,
for the Indians and the Pakistanis were evenly matched.

The IAF was superior to the PAF in numbers of aircraft, technical
'sophistication', and support and maintenance (which was undertaken
largely by the Soviet Union). Yet the PAF acquitted itself creditably.
Despite its misadventure on 3 December, it quickly regained control.
In the West, Indian and Pakistani air forces were roughly equal.
However the PAF was soon on the defensive; unlike the IAF, it did not
participate heavily in the major land battles to provide air support for
the army. Most of the PAF losses were on the ground and the PAF
could manage only half as many sorties as the IAF. The Pakistan Navy
was also on the defensive and rendered ineffective by the Indian Navy.

Certainly, Pakistan's military inferiority was a factor in its defeat,
but far more important was the lack of political will. The discrepancy
between Pakistani and Indian military equipment was not so great that
Pakistan could not have held out valiantly and perhaps even won.

Conclusion
In this chapter we have put forward three hypotheses about the
Bangladesh crisis of 1971. First, we argued that the causes of the crisis
lay in the regional economic and political imbalance between East and
West Pakistan, and that imported military technology was a significant
factor in influencing this imbalance. The political domination of
Pakistan by a small Punjabi élite was made possible by the role of the
army, which, in turn, was strengthened ideologically by Western
military technology as a symbol of the commitment to defend Pakistan;
and politically by US military aid. The economic domination was built
up through a policy of unbalanced growth, justified by American-
inspired ideas about development, which are widespread among
recipients of American aid, who are forced to adapt to the attitudes
which accompany Western technology. Both economic and political
domination were financed by US aid. When this was partly withdrawn

after 1965 and when the war with India undermined the appearance of military might, the crisis came out into the open.

Secondly, we have argued that imported perceptions about the balance of power in the region played an important role in the escalation of the crisis. In particular, the 'Treaty of Friendship and Co-operation' signed between the Soviet Union and India in August 1971, which granted India virtually unlimited military aid, strengthened the Indian government's image of its own power and critically influenced the decision to liberate Bangladesh in December 1971.

Finally, we suggest that in the ensuing fourteen-day war of December 1971, India's overwhelming military superiority, by conventional Western measurements, was not the determining factor in the outcome of war. In the air war, it can be argued that victory went to Pakistan, despite inferior equipment. In the land war in the West, where Indian and Pakistani forces were deemed by experts to be evenly matched, and in the East, where Indian analysts estimated that the Pakistani Army could hold out for three to six months, it can be posited that the Pakistanis did not try. They held back some of their best equipment and failed to plan even the most elementary tactics to thwart the Indian advance.

This chapter does not deal with the role of Bengali guerrillas in the crisis. A fourth hypothesis might be put forward for future exploration; namely, that the success of the guerrillas, with limited arms and equipment, in liberating areas of Bangladesh prior to the Indian invasion bears testimony to the inadequacy of conventional estimates of military strength. At the same time, the postwar experience of Bangladesh suggests that the role of military technology continues to influence the mode of development. The conventional units of the Bangladesh Army, which were formerly part of the Pakistan Army and which continue to receive US military aid, are now the dominant political force in Bangladesh and the condition of the Bangladesh peasantry is not so different from, and perhaps worse than, before the liberation.[41]

NOTES

1. Mohammed Ayoob, *'Pakistan's Political Development, 1947–70:* "Bird's Eye View" ', *Economic and Political Weekly* (Bombay, Annual Number, 1971).
2. Anthony Mascarenhas, *The Rape of Bangladesh* (India, 1971).
3. Bergen, J., 'Personal Income Distribution and Personal Saving in Pakistan', *Pakistan Development Review* (Summer 1967).
4. M. ul-Haq, press report of speech in Karachi, 25 Apr 1968.
5. This is likely to be an underestimate, since the value of the Pakistani rupee in the hands of industrial workers had been shown to be 10–15 per cent higher in the Western wing of the country. See Bergen, op. cit.

6. *Plan Document of the Government of Pakistan.* A study, done for the years 1963–4, indicates that personal and private saving rates, both in urban and rural sectors, were greater in East Pakistan. See Bergen, op. cit.
7. Papenek, *Pakistan's Development, Social Goals and Private Incentives* (Cambridge, Mass., 1967).
8. M. Alehlap-W-Rahman, *Partition, Integration, Economic Growth and Regional Trade* (Karachi, 1963).
9. Nur-ul Islam, *An Estimation of the Extent of Over-Valuation of the Domestic Currency* (Karachi, 1963).
10. W. Lewis, 'Effects of Trade Policy on Domestic Relative Prices, Pakistan 1951–1964', *American Economic Review* (Mar 1968).
11. See SIPRI, *The Arms Trade with the Third World* (Stockholm, 1971) pp. 489–91.
12. *Asian Analysis* (Mar 1972).
13. *The Times* (London, 15 June 1971).
14. *Indian Express* (Bombay, 8 April 1971).
15. *Indian Express* (Bombay, 16 June 1971).
16. *The Observer* (London, 18 July 1971).
17. S. Gupta, 'The Soviet–Indian Treaty', *Survival* (London, Nov 1971).
18. *Milavnews* (Aviation Advisory Services Ltd., Stapleford Airfield, Essex, England, Apr 1971).
19. *Milavnews* (Sep 1970).
20. *The Times* (London, 6 Nov 1971).
21. *Daily Telegraph* (London, 11 Nov 1971).
22. *Milavnews* (Dec 1971).
23. *Milavnews* (Nov 1971).
24. *Hindustan Times* (Delhi, 7 Feb 1972).
25. *Milavnews* (Feb 1972).
26. *Milavnews* (Feb and Nov 1972).
27. *Milavnews* (Apr 1972).
28. Ibid.
29. Ibid.
30. *Milavnews* (Feb 1972).
31. Sisir Gupta, 'Why India Won the Fourteen-day War', *Armed Forces Journal* (Apr 1972).
32. Ibid.
33. *Jung* (Karachi, 6 May 1972).
34. *Milavnews* (Feb 1972).
35. Sisir Gupta, op. cit.
36. Ibid.
37. *Milavnews* (June 1972).
38. Ibid.
39. *Milavnews* (Feb 1972).
40. Jag Jivan Ram had hinted at this in October.
41. See Alan Lindquist, 'Military and Development in Bangladesh', *IDS Bulletin* (July 1977).

6 Militarised Sub-imperialism: the case of Iran

Ulrich Albrecht

Perhaps the most important characteristic of the recent history of Iran is the grotesque arms build-up. Iran's rise into the ranks of the big military powers appears to be based almost entirely on the enormous importance of oil in the Gulf States and on the oil confrontation since 1973. But Persian history and military development cannot be understood without taking into account European and later US interference; moreover, Iran used military means to gain a key position in the political development of the Middle East long before the discovery of oil.[1]

This chapter attempts to demonstrate the concrete relationship between arms, oil, and the historical competition between the great powers. This has established Iran as a sub-imperial power with dangerous implications for the whole Gulf area. It has also shaped the 'development' strategy, involving integration into the multinational economy, particularly through arms production; dependence, emiseration and repression of the mass of the population.

Background

At the beginning of the nineteenth century, when Napoleon sought to attack Great Britain in India with the help of Tsar Paul I of Russia, he sent political and military delegations to Fatali Shah, King of Persia. Britain countered by sending gifts to the Shah and promising to provide military and economic aid. The British–French conflict over Persia was soon replaced by a British–Russian rivalry, in which Persians were directly involved. A Cossack brigade, commanded by a Russian and financed through the Russian Banque d'Escompte with tariff revenues, was raised in Teheran in 1898. This brigade soon proved to be the most effective unit of the 'Persian' armed forces. The other troops were drawn, according to the military traditions of the Osman empire, from towns, big land holdings, and nomadic tribes; they were barely trained and received no pay. The Cossack brigade soon became the most important pillar of the ruling Qadshar dynasty and at times occupied parliament, so that for a time Teheran had a Russian officer as military governor. Together with Russian troops invading from the north, the Cossacks managed to subdue the uprising of 1905 to 1911 and to keep the Shah in power.

A similar situation arose from British attempts to safeguard their influence in the south of the country. The South Persian Rifles, a strike force with Indian NCOs, were recruited by the British from nomadic tribes, and had British officers. This contingent was deployed exclusively at British discretion, but the Persian government used it as an official constabulary. After the Russian Revolution, Britain also undertook the financing of the Cossack brigade operating in the north, which by this time had reached division strength. This unit was deployed against insurgents in 1919 and 1920 and as an expeditionary corps against the Red Army, but the British did not succeed in keeping control over this brigade or in displacing Russian officers. When the Persian authorities started to fill the Cossack division command structure with Persians, the British were in favour of dissolving the unit.

Central Persia, controlled neither by the Russians nor the British, was dominated by Turks and armed guerrilla volunteers trying to align themselves with the two great powers Germany and Turkey. Military co-operation between the German empire and Persia can be traced back to 1885. Given the rivalries between the leading powers, the Persian government expected a military alliance with the emerging German empire to yield political advantages, above all more autonomy. One advance made in 1885, to get military instructors of the Prussian army to Persia, was rejected by Bismarck. Consequently, two German officers were hired privately by the Persian government. Their activity became the basis for a long and at times close military co-operation between the countries, and was characteristic of later German military co-operation: a hesitant political leadership leaving it to private initiative to deliver weapons and military personnel to foreign countries.[2]

In the same year, the Persian embassy in Berlin acquired two small naval vessels. Persia's attempts to control its coasts and to acquire warships, considered at the time to be the decisive weapon, were eyed with apprehension by Russia and Great Britain. According to the Treaty of Turkmantchai of 1828, Persian warships could not sail the Caspian Sea, and so, publicly, the two new German ships were said to be for the prevention of smuggling. At Persian request one of the ships was delivered in parts and was assembled in Persia—another approach which was to remain characteristic of German naval deliveries.

Persia was trying to free itself from the control of big powers. This effort reached its peak immediately after the First World War, after the Soviets had annulled Tsarist Russia's contractual arrangements with Persia and had withdrawn all Russian troops. The German attempt to penetrate the Persian coast by extending the Baghdad railway ended with Germany's defeat in the war. Great Britain then seized the chance to expand its sphere of influence and occupied all of Persia in 1919.

In August 1919, the Persian government was offered a treaty whereby Great Britain reserved the right to control the country's army, economy, finances, and tariff policies. According to article 3 of this treaty, the

British government was to supply, at Persian expense, officers, munitions, and modern equipment. This had been declared necessary by a joint commission of British and Persian military experts. The long-standing British efforts to bring the whole Persian military apparatus under British control by creating a uniform Persian force culminated in the order to the joint military commission to raise and equip a troop of 80,000 men.

As a result of an adept policy of *rapprochement* towards the Soviet Union, and uprisings and protest demonstrations against the British decree, the Persian government succeeded in subverting British plans. Britain then decided to cease financing and to disband the South Persian Rifles. Munition supplies and military buildings were destroyed, horses and mules were shot, and there was extensive confiscation to redress supposedly outstanding claims of the retreating British.

But this by no means put an end to British involvement in Persia. On the contrary, Britain found a new role, based on control of the Arabian/Persian Gulf as well as the Suez Canal. This new role can best be understood in connection with oil, which was discovered in 1908 and which from then on determined the interests of foreign powers in Persia.

The Anglo-Iranian Oil Company, founded in 1909, is said to have put around £1 million into preparations for the *coup* which eventually overthrew the recalcitrant Persian government.[3] The so-called 'Iron Committee' which planned the *coup* was headed by Tabatai, a political journalist who had from the beginning argued in favour of accepting the unpopular British decree.

Under the leadership of Reza Khan, who rose from the ranks to officer status, parts of the Persian Cossack division stormed the capital in 1921 and brought the government down. Reza Khan was at first minister of war in the Tabatai cabinet, but was soon a key figure in the administration as well as the military. With the announcement of social reforms, he gained enough popularity to oust Tabatai in 1923, and took the post of prime minister for himself. Reza Kahn had made secret arrangements with the British. In 1923 there was ratification of a new oil treaty with Britain, containing details about expenditure for the Persian army and the formation of a new Pahlawi dynasty. Thus the fundamental principle of Persian politics for the next 50 years was established: oil and the army were the means to advance the Pahlawi dynasty; and thus the dynasty fostered the production of oil and a strong army. At the end of 1925, Reza Khan seized the crown; parliament ousted the Qadshar dynasty, proclaiming Reza Khan formally Reza Shah Pahlawi. The military dictatorship lasted until 1941, when the Allies occupied Persia.

After Reza Khan's takeover, the Persian military apparatus underwent thorough reform and was organised according to plans previously made by the British. The only posts left open to foreigners were those of riding instructors or technicians of the imperial arsenal. Military expenditure increased dramatically reaching almost 47 per cent of the central government's budget in 1922. The Persian Cossack division, the South Persian Rifles, the Gendarmerie (a militarised police contingent) and other military contingents became united in the armed forces. By 1924 Reza Khan commanded a well-ordered army of 80,000 men. A year earlier, Persian career officer students were for the first time sent to France for their training, and within a year 500 were being trained there. At the same time, Reza Khan vigorously pursued the project of arming his country with modern weapons. Warships were received, against British objections, from Italy. The establishment of a small fleet started with the delivery of a series of gunboats. Several hundred Persians were trained to operate these ships.

Reza Khan considered it of utmost importance to become independent of British and French arms supplies, by revitalising the old Osman tradition of producing weaponry within the country, especially in the imperial arsenal. These efforts coincided with the German desire to increase its arms production in foreign countries, because of the prohibitions on domestic production imposed by the Treaty of Versailles. Along with Japan and the new Soviet power, which were readily accepting German military and arms exports, Persia became an important testing-ground for German military technological experiments. Persia had placed orders for German arms as early as 1913–14, but the outbreak of war prevented delivery of a large part of the order via Russia, and it was not until 1923 that the Persian government managed to get Soviet approval for the delivery and transport of German weapons straight through the Soviet Union.

Persian–German military co-operation 1922–41
Persia's first large order from Germany, in 1922, was for military trucks. The German supplier was asked at the same time to build a repair workshop in Persia, to be managed by a German. In 1924, Germany was commissioned to install and modernise the Persian war arsenal.[4] Later Germans in key positions within the Persian military system provided a vital link for extensive transfers of army and aviation equipment. Once Germans had been put in charge of the Persian war arsenal, large numbers of rifles and machine guns, as well as equipment to build a munitions factory and an iron foundry, were bought in Germany. The *Gutehoffnungshütte* and the firm Wönckhaus were especially involved, the latter supplying the Shah with an armoured limousine. However, a bulk order for 100,000 Mauser rifles was prevented by the objections raised by the Belgian diplomatic delegation, despite attempts by the manufacturer, Steffen und Heyman, to have the German embassy in Teheran intervene in the affair. (The Belgians

offered the Mauser at a cheaper price.[5])

The establishment of an arms manufacturing capability made speedy headway. Apart from the iron foundry a gunpowder factory, linked to the arsenal and also under the management of German specialists, was built in Partchin. As the necessary raw materials for the manufacture of high-grade military equipment were available in Persia, construction of a brass rolling-mill was undertaken. Again, Germans prepared the plans. The Shah ordered all the equipment to be bought second-hand in Germany. The Germans drawing up the order were careful to exclude any German equipment which might be needed for production in a crisis; hence the only equipment available to the Shah was so outmoded as to be useless to Germany.

At this time co-operation between the Persian army and the Reichswehr was at its peak, and the Persian general staff proceeded to structure its training system according to the German pattern and to recruit German instructors. The Persian chief of staff asked von Schulenburg, the German ambassador, to provide copies of the programmes of German military academies and information about various weapons systems. In the mid-1920s, Persian officers were sent to Germany for their training, but this was regarded as unsatisfactory, and with the help of the 'Council for the training of students of the Imperial Persian Government', Persia turned to the artillery school in Jüterborg and the infantry school in Dresden. Germany, however, was not particularly interested in training Persian cadets, and introduced strict requirements: no more than five or six cadets were to be admitted, and they had to speak fluent German.

German–Persian military relationships improved during the National Socialist era. A Berlin firm, Fritz Werner, signed a contract in autumn 1933 for delivery of rifles worth two million Reichsmark. In addition, the firm was to appoint ten German specialists for the manufacture of arms in the imperial arsenal. Top names in the German arms sector, among them Krupp AG, Rheinmetall-Borsig AG, and Busching & Co, soon received lucrative orders. Krupp deliveries included diesel engines for several coast guard boats built by the Italian shipyard Cantieri Navali Riuniti in Palermo in 1935.

In 1937 Persia placed a large order for Japanese gunboats and cruisers, and even Czechoslovakia was able, in 1934, to sell more than a quarter of its weapons and munitions production to Persia.

Shah Reza tried to build up a small air force, again with German help, as the most modern military sector. Junkers tried to sell not only German military aircraft, against heavy international competition, but also civilian aircraft. The company was commissioned by the Persian war ministry, which also controlled civil aviation, to plan three airports and build and equip one school for pilots. Junkers delivered two W-33 planes, but then faced liquidity problems and had to pull out of its

Persian contracts. Nonetheless German pilots and the German aircraft factory played an important role in Persia's military system, as is shown in foreign office documents about bombardments with German planes.[6] German aircraft were also used by Shah Reza against insurgents.

Subsequently, the attempts to build up the air force proved over-ambitious. More and more aircraft were lost after only a short time.[7] The Green and Fricker air force handbook reports laconically, 'Several other aircraft were acquired in 1924, among them Spads, Breguets, and Potez biplanes from France. French pilots were hired to fly these planes from Buschire (a port in the south) and other places to Teheran, but only one arrived intact; one made a forced landing in Kazeron, one in Shiraz, two between Isfahan and Teheran, and the rest crashed in the Bakhtiari mountains.'[8] An attempt by Russian-trained pilots to fly a squadron of Russian R-1 reconnaissance planes (licensed type De Havilland DH9A) had the same result; only one arrived safely.

As a consequence of these losses, a more modest air support squadron for the army was built up, with Russian, French, and German military advisors. In autumn 1932 there was a modest expansion (compared with original plans), with Swedish instructors and eight newly acquired British De Havilland Tiger Moth training planes. Twelve Persian officers were sent to England for training.

The contract signed by the Shah in April 1933 for the exploitation of Persian petroleum was very favourable to the Anglo-Iranian Oil Company. This 60-year agreement was to serve long-term stabilisation of the Shah's politics, above all the financing of the costly armaments programme. But the Second World War and the Allies' desire to secure oil production in the Gulf for themselves disrupted any stabilising effects. The country was occupied by British and Soviet troops in 1941, the Shah was forced to resign in favour of his eldest son, and the large number of Germans living in the country were handed over to the Allies.

The American relationship 1942–67

The invasion of Allied troops signalled a new period in Iranian history. The Soviet Union and Britain initially controlled the country, but American influence soon became dominant. The presence of foreign troops was legalised in a treaty signed in 1942, according to which the Allies were allowed to station troops of all service branches to the extent deemed necessary. One American military contingent, which stayed on after the war had ended, was especially important in further military development. In 1942—at first without legal basis—Colonel Schwarzkopf started to reorganise the gendarmerie as a security troop for the Shah.[9] On the recommendation of the US State Department, Millspaugh was appointed general administrator of Iranian finances, with power of authority far beyond that of the Iranian cabinet. The motive for this direct appointment was stated quite succinctly in a report to President Roosevelt by a commission of experts: 'The future of big power oil no longer lies on the American continent. The centre of gravity is shifting more and more from the area of the Gulf of Mexico and the Caribbean sphere (Venezuela) to the area around the Persian Gulf. This development is to be expected to continue in the future and to lead to a final relocation.'[10]

At the end of the Second World War, Iran carried on its arms programme with massive American aid, and 'the Shah followed his father's tradition in relying on the army to strengthen the authority of his government.'[11] Iranian air force fighter squads at the end of the war consisted exclusively of British Hawker biplanes, more than ten years old, except for two Hurricane fighter bombers, handed over just prior to the occupation. Between 1945 and 1947, 34 British Hurricanes arrived.

The so-called Soviet Crisis in 1946 led to a massive wave of US aid. The Allies had agreed to withdraw their troops from Iran by 1946. Soviet occupation forces however stayed on until April 1946, when an Iranian–Soviet contract on oil supplies was signed. The Soviets also supported the attempt to establish an autonomous Kurdish state which was to include some Iranian territory. Nonetheless the Shah's decision to increase his acquisition of arms may have been based primarily on internal considerations. The Soviet Union had given support to secessionist movements in Iranian Azerbaijan and Kurdistan, but the Shah was involved in severe conflict with parliament about internal political issues. In contrast, the American decision to foster a massive arms programme in Iran was based on global strategic interests and the politics of the Cold War. The US wanted to prevent further Soviet access to Iranian oil, and wanted to cut off direct Soviet access to the Indian Ocean. In 1947, $51 million in credit was given to Iran for the purchase of weaponry, including associated expenditures. This military aid was to be repaid at a 25 per cent interest rate over 12 years.

In three years, the Iranian air force increased its fighting force fivefold. Republic F-47 D Thunderbolt fighter bombers and Douglas transport planes were bought. A large-scale training programme was established, and the first group of officers and NCOs in the Iranian air force left the country on 1 May 1948 to undertake special training in the US. Shortly thereafter, the Iranian air force opened its own Air Officers Training College for the education of maintenance engineers, a college for higher officers, and a college for non-commissioned officers. A significant number of Iranian pilots were trained in the US and the Bavarian Fürstenfeldbruck.

The army, too, was being modernised, receiving 15 Sherman tanks in 1951, and about 50 M-24 light tanks between 1954 and 1956. The navy, which had consisted only of coast guard ships of less than 100 tons water displacement, was also expanded. In 1949, a frigate (built in 1944) and a mine sweeper (built in 1941) were acquired, and a steady construction programme was introduced.[12]

Iran's formal association with the West, when it joined the Baghdad Pact in November 1955, created a renewed push for modernisation of the armed forces. The Shah received the first jet planes, long since requested, for his air force: in 1956, 24 Lockheed T-33 training and reconnaissance planes arrived; between 1956 and 1958 about 75 Republic F-84G Thunderjet fighter bombers were delivered. These aircraft were not as modern as the Shah had wished; both were of the first generation of American jet fighters, belonging technically to the pre-Korean era. Newly acquired Sherman tanks played a key role in the *coup* leading to the fall of Mossadeq. When the *coup* in Iraq toppled the monarchy, the Shah pointed to the 'dangerous' political developments in the neighbouring state, and then the Iranian air force acquired modern swept-wing planes: 70 sabre-jets, built under licence in Canada, were handed over in 1959. The army had by now trebled its tanks, having received about 200 Patton tanks in 1958. The navy no longer relied on second-hand Second World War equipment, but was supplied with recent designs. US military aid, which had amounted to $166 million in the five years between 1949 and 1953, increased from 1953 to 1960 to a total of $387 million.[13]

In the mid-1960s the Shah had to accept that although American arms supplies enabled him to control his country militarily, several neighbouring countries had more modern weaponry. There is no doubt that Iranian military strategy at this time was directed primarily towards internal control. With the propeller fighters on which it had to rely until 1956, the Iranian air force could have done little against the Soviet air force's jet fighters, and the Shah's relatively small force of tanks posed little threat to the Red Army. However, propeller aircraft were highly suitable for fighting insurgents, and there is a continuous record of their use in these operations. In 1954, for example, the military was involved in armed clashes between the trade unionist Tudeh Party and the conservative Party of the National Will led by Tabatai, in repression in the central regions, and in bloody confrontations during strikes in the oil fields. In 1946 the army was used against workers striking for freedom of association and soldiers were ordered to stand in for workers in the factories. Secessionist insurrections broke out in Azerbaijan and Khuzestan in September 1946, and one year later, the Iranian army moved into Kurdistan under the command of the American Schwarz-kopf. (This bloody campaign is said to have cost 20,000 lives.) The army's new Sherman tanks played a key role in the *coup* leading to the fall of Mossadeq. Gradually, the American-instructed army and the police auxiliary troops managed to suppress open resistance. Thus, the main task of the Iranian armed forces was internal security; strategically, it had only a small defence force.

And it was domestic politics rather than international strategy which caused a reorientation of the Shah's military policy. When serious unrest force a replacement of the cabinet, the Shah introduced a reform programme known as the White Revolution. A bill for land reform was passed in 1962, and a comprehensive reform programme was presented in 1963. One of the most important points in this reform programme gave the armed forces a central role in social change. Nearly 50,000 school leavers were sent through the country as an 'army of knowledge', to undertake literacy campaigns. Military service and this teaching under the aegis of the military thus involved a significant number of young men who might have become a political threat. The literacy teachers were also used to gather information about social conditions in various regions, and to keep the peasant population under surveillance. The 'army of health', founded in 1964, in a similar way fostered the development of the military control network. Physicians, dentists, pharmacists, medical assistants, and other medical personnel were drafted into this 'army'; after six years of this programme 40 per cent of Iran's 8400 doctors were serving in the army, constabulary, or police. The 'army of reconstruction and development', established in 1965, undertook tasks that are best compared with the 'civil action' of other armies.

Land reform and other internal measures for reform brought conservative powers into sharp opposition to the Shah. Despite the limitations of his reform measures, the Shah could no longer be sure of continued American support and he sought *rapprochement* with the Soviet Union on external and military policy. In 1967 a contract for 'non-sensitive' arms purchases was completed with the Soviet Union—the first time that the US had accepted arms procurement by a state militarily allied with it. The Iranian army received about 100 Soviet BTR-152 armoured personnel carriers, lorries, and small anti-aircraft guns. This purchase showed Iran's desire to achieve some sort of detente in foreign policy, as well as to prevent a one-sided dependence on the US. The Shah saw the deal as reinforcing Iran's independence. Immediately after the purchase, Iranian troops stationed on the Soviet border were moved to the Gulf coast.

Thus, the Shah freed both hands for a resolute policy of expansion in the Persian Gulf, considered necessary after the British decision of 1968 to withdraw from East of Suez. One requirement was control of the Straits of Hormuz, a channel through which access to the Gulf could be blocked by relatively simple military means. Iran also wanted to prevent another power, such as Iraq, from assuming hegemony or taking on the role of Gulf policeman which had been held by Britain until it withdrew from the area in January 1968. To secure the Gulf of Iran, the Shah needed arms—more modern and in greater numbers than had been supplied so far by the US.

Arms expansion 1967-77

Shortly after the delivery of Soviet armoured personnel carriers in November 1967, the US government declared that Iran had to be regarded as a developed country and was thus no longer in need of development aid. The immediate suspension of civilian aid was announced with details about military aid to follow later. Despite these statements, US foreign aid statistics for the following years show that civilian and military US aid to Iran decreased only slightly.[14] Iran continued to cover part of its growing food deficit out of American surplus, on preferential conditions laid down by the law P.L. 480.

Even without US financial aid, the rapidly increasing income from oil exports allowed the Shah to increase the volume of arms procurement without any particular difficulty. Until 1967, Iran had been almost completely dependent on the US for military technology. All armoured vehicles, nearly all the ships in the navy, and nearly all of the more recent aircraft (some built under licence in Canada) originated from the US. There existed a bilateral military agreement with the US, and Iran was further allied to the US through CENTO.[15] At the same time, the Shah came more and more into conflict with foreign firms about the conditions for exploiting Iranian oil resources. The most powerful of the firms using Iranian oil were based in the US. Hence, the obvious way for the Shah to increase his own bargaining position in the long run seemed to be the reduction of a one-sided military–technological dependence on the US.

The Shah first ordered more than 200 helicopters from Italy; these were manufactured under American licence. Four missile destroyers and four torpedo boats for military operations in the Persian Gulf were ordered from the British shipyard Vosper Thornycroft; not much later, the contract for the world's largest fleet of military hovercraft was signed with a British manufacturer. The French state-owned SNIAS provided Frelon-type helicopters, and the Shah later ordered a dozen rocket launchers, built in France under German licence. Matching supply ships were ordered from West Germany, and the West German navy assumed responsibility for training the crew. Further purchases included helicopters, transports, and 34 McDonnell-Douglas Phantom fighter bombers, delivered by the US to Iran even before NATO allies had been supplied with them. The licence for their export had been given by the US in September 1966, when Soviet–Iranian negotiations became public.

This description of the Shah's arms build-up in the late 1960s appears modest when compared with military equipment shipped to Iran in the 1970s. According to calculations made by the US Comptroller General, from 1946 to 1969 $1500 million worth of military goods went to Iran commercially or at preferential rates under military aid agreements; from 1970 to 1975 they amounted to $6900 million.[16] It is worth noting that in the period 1946–70 military aid to South Vietnam, excluding costs for US forces, was also $1500 million—the same as to Iran.[17]

By 1975, the Shah possessed almost all conventional weapons systems below the nuclear threshhold. The American arms industry secured for itself most of the procurement avalanche. The Iranian budget for 1975 allocated   10,000 million for arms, but this was by no means Iran's total military expenditure. Numerous ventures, such as the construction of a repair-dock in Bandar Abbas, the expanding central naval base, counted as civilian projects and did not appear in the military budget.

Iran's armament programme is, in its extent and technological level, without comparison in the third world.[18] In the mid-1970s it included procurement of nearly 2000 Chieftain heavy tanks, 400 Scorpion light tanks, and 300 Fox armoured carriers, all from Britain, to add to the army's 800 American M-47 and M-60 tanks. In aircraft procurement 50 C-130 transport planes were bought from Lockheed and a fleet of 700 army helicopters was ordered, plus 600 jet fighter aircraft: 196 McDonnell-Douglas Phantoms of various types, 169 F-5E Tiger II from Northrop, 80 F-14 Tomcats from Grumman, and 160 lightweight F-16s. Seven AWACS electronic surveillance aircraft were also ordered.

The most spectacular acquisitions were the Tomcats. At the time this was the latest western jet fighter, just being introduced into the US armed forces, and the value of this one sale was said to be $1850 million. This deal was vital for the survival of the Grumman Corporation. The sale of the Boeing AWACS to Iran created considerable controversy and was approved by the US Congress only after President Carter resubmitted his original proposal with assurances that Iran's possession of this system would not compromise US defence and security. Iran was the first foreign customer for this system; even NATO countries have been unwilling to buy it, because the cost is so high.

Further aircraft purchases—the Lockheed C-5 Galaxy (the world's largest military transporter), a dozen Boeing 747 Jumbos, six Lockheed Orion long-distance reconnaissance planes with anti-submarine devices, and seven Boeing KC-135 Stratotankers (in use with the US and France for inflight refuelling)—suggest, in no uncertain terms, that the Shah was seeking to extend his action-radius beyond the sub-region of the Persian/Arabian Gulf.

There was also considerable procurement of guided weapons. Short Brothers, a British firm, sold Seacat surface-to-air missiles to Iran in the late 1960s, and in the early 1970s Iran ordered their Tigercat surface-to-air missile system. After purchasing large numbers of British Aircraft Corporation Rapier towed surface-to-air missiles, Iran helped to fund development of a tracked version of the missile. From Hughes Aircraft

Industries in the US Iran purchased nearly 3000 TOW anti-tank missiles and Raytheon, also in the US, sold large numbers of an improved version of their Hawk surface-to-air missile system. The French SNIAS received orders for SS-12 tactical missiles as well as Exocet ship-to-ship missiles. In addition, SAM-7/9 missiles were included in a $414 million arms deal between Iran and the Soviet Union in November 1976, along with anti-aircraft guns and BMP personnel carriers.

The Iranian navy did not lag behind in procurement. Six destroyers, at $110 million each, were being built by Litton Industries in the mid-1970s, and it was thought that the Spruance-class destroyer under construction for Iran would have better electronic equipment and greater firepower than similar ships being built for the US navy. Despite the shallowness of the Persian/Arabian Gulf, which renders it unsuitable for submarine operations, the Shah was pursuing construction of his own submarine fleet. The strategic task of this fleet has to be seen in the context of Iran's claim to predominance in south-west Asia and large parts of the Indian Ocean. The US sold three older submarines, ostensibly for training purposes, to Iran. There was some Iranian interest in procuring nuclear-attack submarines from France, and it can only be a matter of time until Iran obtains nuclear submarines, despite initial French and American refusals to supply them. The importance of Iranian financial participation in French nuclear research, and the French desire for a large share of Iran's other weapons orders, means that France will probably agree to provide Iran with nuclear submarines. Weapon systems developed and tested during the Vietnam war, such as laser-guided bombs and assault helicopters with night-flight electronics, were included amongst Iran's acquisitions.

The extension of military infrastructures and logistic capabilities also represents large-scale arms expenditure but has received little attention. Fifty new airports, most of them for strategic purposes, were under construction in Iran in the mid-1970s. As in many developing countries, the construction of roads and railway systems was determined, to a large extent, by military considerations. Military needs also dictated the expenditure of $225 million on a high-powered electronic surveillance system to cover the whole Gulf area—although in this case, the Iranian military was reluctant to approve such an expensive system and had to be urged to accept it by American military advisors.[19] This Integrated National Telecommunication System will, when it is completed, enable contact to be made direct, via satellite, with all navy vessels operating in the Indian Ocean. There are reports of underground shelters for Phantom jet fighters at the Dezfoul airbase, and of more than 39 logistic bases around the Gulf and Indian Ocean coast. The annual running costs alone of the navy headquarters in Bandar Abbas, with its multitude of installations, are estimated at $200 million per year. The construction of a joint navy–air force base in Chabbahan, close to the border with Pakistan, is estimated to have cost $60–70 million.

These are primarily military infrastructures, but military considerations were important in determining investment in other projects in the civilian sector. The cost-benefit relationship here is almost certainly to the disadvantage of the civilian sector, and to the advantage of the military.

The Iranian arms avalanche influenced arms programmes in the US and elsewhere. Certain weapons systems only came into production with Iranian pressure and Iranian money. When, for example, financial considerations led to abandonment of further development of the television-guided Condor missile system, Iran stepped in, and the programme was not stopped. In 1975, the US Comptroller General even said in a report to Congress that the defence capability of the US had been endangered by the massive short-term assignment of military specialists to the planning and construction of the Iranian military apparatus.[20] In the context of arms deals in Iran and the Gulf states, the sums known to have been spent on bribes can be taken as an indication of the expansion of the American armaments complex.

The Federal Republic of Germany also played a role in the arms programme of the Shah during this period. In 1969, the German government refused to allow Iran to purchase the Leopard battle-tank, made by Flick. But later the German foreign office decided that Iran was not to be regarded as a conflict area, and the Chancellor publicly said that the 1971 laws on weapons exports were too restrictive. The arms lobby, which for a long time had been demanding freedom to export, became more persistent. When restrictions on arms deals are eased, as seems likely, Iran will almost certainly become a leading customer. In 1974, the former chief of the planning staff in the West German defence ministry was named ambassador to Iran. Industrial co-operation between Iranian and West German enterprises, including the most important arms manufacturers except for the aircraft industry, developed rapidly in the mid-1970s, and despite restrictions on arms exports various weapons systems manufactured in Germany found their way via France to Iran.[21]

It is extraordinarily difficult to estimate Iranian military potential. Even before the final British withdrawal from the Persian/Arabian Gulf in 1971, Iran occupied several islands in the Straits of Hormuz. After 1975 an expeditionary corps of 3000 men operated in the Sultanate of Oman, but British officers in Oman criticised the poor training standard of the Iranian units. There is no lack of international co-operation for the Shah's efforts at speeding up the transfer of technological and strategic know-how. The US, Britain, Italy, France, West Germany, Israel, and many private agents are involved in

Iranian military training. According to American sources, by 1974 11,000 Iranian officers and crew had been educated in the US.[22] This figure did not include the training of Iranian police officers in the US.[23] In addition, the US had arranged with Israel for the training of Iranian officers in the Israeli army.[24] The US military aid corps, stationed in Iran since the Second World War, had in 1974 reached a strength of about 1000 men, and there were over 2000 American military personnel, mostly Vietnam veterans, working as trainers for Iranian soldiers. The Pentagon took out contracts with several private companies, among them important arms manufacturers, for training in Iran. The most comprehensive of these was with Bell Helicopters for the training of helicopter pilots and repair engineers, at a cost of $255 million. Iran also negotiated an unknown number of training contracts directly with private American firms. Thus, the P-3F Orion long-distance reconnaissance plane was flown by crews from Lockheed, until completion of the training of Iranian personnel. In addition to the many Americans involved in training, one must also consider the specialists in Iran in connection with the building up of arms production capacity.[25] By early 1978 there were altogether 25,000 American military specialists of one sort or another living in Iran, and it is estimated that this number could reach 50,000 on the basis of existing contracts. Apart from the American advisors there were British instructors responsible for the education of the army and navy at several technical schools. All of the commanding officers in the Iranian navy up to the mid-1970s had been educated at naval academies in the US, Great Britain, or Italy.

According to official data, there were 30,000 men in the Iranian armed forces in 1977. This figure did not include foreign military personnel in Iranian service, nor the 30,000–60,000 members of SAVAK, the secret police. The imperial guard and guard of the so-called 'Immortals' together constituted an army of 7000 men, a highly mobile élite unit, including ranger and parachute units, built up and trained by Israeli and American advisors. If the Gendarmerie, a paramilitary force of 70,000 men using patrol boats, helicopters and light aircraft, is added, the number of men under arms ready to fight is well above the 400,000 mark.

Iran's role as Gulf policeman is combined with extremely brutal repression of political opposition within the country. Strikes for better wages or working conditions end not infrequently with the murder of the strike leaders. One of the Shah's officers co-ordinates the broad spying and surveillance system—which keeps watch not only on the general public but on the military. This special surveillance centre exerts direct influence in the transfer of high-ranking officers; rotation for 'political' security is frequent.

Another aspect of Iranian armament is its dubious deals involving surplus weaponry. In 1966, for instance, 90 obsolete West German aircraft went to Pakistan via Iran, and were soon used in the India–Pakistan war. When in 1972 the US Congress prohibited the further supply of arms to the Thieu government in South Vietnam, Iran sent F-5 fighters. Both Ethiopia and Jordan obtained discarded F-5 aircraft from Iran with US approval. (Jordan was then able to get rid of its older British fighters by selling them to South Africa, circumventing the UN arms embargo.) Iran is now said to be the greatest arms trader in second-hand arms in the third world.

Arms production in Iran

The Shah's ambitions were not restricted to rechannelling increased oil revenues into the pockets of foreign arms manufacturers. Substantial amounts were devoted to starting his own large-scale arms production. In the mid-1930s, there had been attempts to build military aircraft in Iran, when the Shah's father obtained a licence from the British firm Hawker to rebuild the Audax combat aircraft at the state-owned firm Shahbaz near Deshan-Tabbeh. But there was no actual production, and the firm's activity remained confined to the maintenance and repair of imported military aircraft. Not until more than 30 years later did Iran begin to prepare for the manufacture of modern air defence systems. In 1969 the Iranian Aircraft Industry was founded by the Iranian government and the American firm Northrop. Both partners control 49 per cent of the capital, the remaining 2 per cent being held by IMBDI Iranian Bank. Northrop plays the main part, controlling management organisation as well as the employment and training of Iranian personnel. Plans drawn up in 1973 foresaw the employment of 75,310 people. When 85 per cent of these were working, full-scale production of planes under licence could begin. This was seen as the first stage in the intended independent development of aircraft.

The American firm Hughes Tool, in co-operation with IAI, established an industrial complex for the manufacture of electronic devices, close to Shiraz, at a total cost of around $25 million; it was intended that high-grade components for electronic equipment would be built here for the American Litton Industries. This venture also included Iranian participation in the production of a television-guided missile which had been ordered in great numbers from Hughes. American producers are offered the opportunity to exploit extremely low wages in Iran for their own production, and at the same time to control a considerable proportion of the market. According to Western military experts, the 'rapid construction of a conspicuous arms industry' is geared towards 'the supply of many of the highly complex weapon systems with locally manufactured spare parts'.[26]

The founding in Teheran of a Grumman Corporation subsidiary illustrates the technological infrastructural bottlenecks that arose for Iran through importing the most modern weapons systems. Grumman

Iran Private Company Ltd. was established especially to maintain 80 F-14 fighters earmarked for delivery at the beginning of 1978. It was expected to employ 2000 people, with 1000 in Teheran, 600 in Isfahan, and 400 in Shiraz. It was hoped that the proportion of American specialists would be reduced to 40 per cent.

Further steps in the construction of an indigenous arms industry in Iran included the manufacture of rifles, machine guns, and munition under German licence; the making of grenades; and, with American instruction, the installation of a tank repair workshop. A factory for tank spare parts was planned in Shiraz, to begin production in 1980. The Shah even wanted to have a go at the introduction of the relatively demanding technology for large-calibre guns. This production seemed only a remote possibility, but Iran had already made firm financial commitments (mostly to research and development costs) to several arms programmes, with a view to later Iranian production: to the British Aircraft Corporation for Rapier missiles, to Vickers for the licenced manufacture of Chieftain tanks, and to Bell for helicopters. Iran's development of its arms industry was different from that of, say, India or South Africa, in that it involved the integration of weapons manufacture with the world-wide production of big American armaments firms. In India as well as in South Africa, on the other hand, arms production was aimed at self-sufficiency in supplies for the armed forces.

Senior General Katorijan, chief of the control bureau of the Iranian armed forces, told the directorate of the Iranian Central Bank in the mid-1960s that military expenditure provides an important impetus to the development process and, for that reason, should be given priority.[27] He went on to extol the modernising, educative, training, and nation-building functions of the military. In fact, the US took advantage of its observer status at CENTO to transfer its conception of economic development and the concurrent role of the military apparatus into countries belonging to the Pact—as it did in Latin America under the aegis of the Alliance for Progress—by organising hundreds of training seminars for the military of the member states, covering topics from air support in counter-insurgency to civic action and well-digging.

General Katorijan also emphasised the contribution to industrialisation made by the arms industry, and declared it a precondition of the industrialisation process in Iran. Ten years later, these statements were proving to be true. There were numerous indications that the evolution of an industrialisation pattern for arms production was of prime importance. The arms sector is traditionally directly subject to state control, so the expansion of arms production offered a particularly advantageous negotiation point for Iranian capital. The Iranian arms import market was of great importance for manufacturers in Europe and the US, and it was not difficult for local capital to interest leading foreign enterprises in shifting further arms production to Iran, in the form of joint ventures.

The interest of European and American arms producers in partial relocation of their production lies in securing markets and in wage cost advantages. The availability of extensive state-financed infrastructure is also important. In negotiations with foreign firms for joint ventures, Iran is in a good position because it represents at the same time a considerable market for the goods to be produced. The advantages work both ways; enquiries on behalf of the American Defense Department found that procurement costs for the US army could be reduced through planned integration of production with Iran.[28] The export-oriented expansion of industrial production as well as the rapid transfer of methods of production, competitive on the world market, are the advantages to Iran. But such advantages come at the price of dependence. The development of the arms sector is not a sufficient basis for the development of an independent complex industrial structure.

In addition to integration with foreign companies and its own growth as an arms exporter, it is to be expected that there will soon be demands for the greatest possible self-sufficiency in the supply of weaponry. Attempts to produce complex weaponry will affect the industrialisation pattern. It is too early to predict the pattern of Iranian industrialisation, either in arms production or in other sectors. At the present, all that can be stated is that a significant part of oil revenues will be spent on arms production capacities and that Iran will be integrated tightly into the international armaments dynamic no longer only as consumer but also as producer of weaponry.

Atomic weapons for the Shah
After the explosion of India's first atomic bomb in 1974, a fierce discussion started about which countries would in the near future have nuclear weapons. Few observers doubted that Iran was one of these countries.

The main difficulties in the independent manufacture of nuclear weapons are technological and economic. Many experts regard economic problems as decisive, since even countries with only a moderately developed industrial structure, such as India and South Africa, can solve the technological problems.[29] As a result of the oil crisis in 1973, energy provision in all industrial countries was questioned and nuclear energy was seen as the primary solution. The construction of reactors became an industrial growth sector, and the most important industrial countries began vigorously competing for exports. Potential buyers, including developing countries, can reach agreements that include far-reaching measures for technological co-operation. European and American universities have expanded their training capacities to meet the demands of potential clients.[30] West Germany's treaty to provide nuclear reactors to Brazil was preceded by several years co-operation, during which, for example, Brazilian specialists were trained in German nuclear research centres.

At the height of the so-called oil crisis, the Shah stated publicly that petroleum was in the long run too precious a source of energy and had to be conserved as a raw material for the chemical industry. His country thus had to produce nuclear energy as quickly as possible. The French agreed to co-operate in nuclear research and technology, including the delivery of two light water reactors, built by a Creusot Loire subsidiary under American licence. Start of operations is planned for 1982 and 1983. In addition Iran became a participant in the Eurodif project, constructing a large uranium enrichment plant using the gas centrifuge method under French leadership, with participation from the Benelux countries, Spain, and Italy. Planned Iranian participation includes the right to be supplied with enriched uranium, so that Iran may be able to obtain plutonium, necessary for the development of nuclear weapons, as soon as the Eurodif installation has started to operate fully. By participating in this project the Shah could secure quantities of plutonium more quickly than would have been possible with a self-reliant programme.

At the same time the Shah developed other sources of nuclear technology and expertise. These included the US, West Germany, and Britain. Advisory services were obtained through the former director of the Argentinian Atomic Energy Office. This step was important, as Argentina had for more than a decade been involved in its own nuclear research and the construction of reactors for energy supply. Argentinian experience could be useful for Iran in, for example, negotiations with producers of reactors for the development of its own research capacities.

With US support, a centre for nuclear research was founded at Teheran University in 1959; one research reactor has been operating since 1967. By the mid-1970s there were agreements with the US atomic energy office for the delivery of reactor fuel for two 1200 megawatt-reactors; a French firm had a contract for uranium prospecting in the country, and negotiations were under way for Iran to procure uranium directly from Australia; talks were taking place with the US about recycling plants; and the West German government agreed in December 1977 to sell four nuclear power plants to Iran worth around $8 million. There is no doubt that the Shah was attempting to acquire the equipment and expertise necessary to develop nuclear weapons. The fact that Iran has signed the Nuclear Non-Proliferation Treaty by no means ensures that nuclear weapons will not be built.

The general dilemma of nuclear technology is that civilian and military use are hardly distinguishable from each other in the required scientific and industrial infrastructure. It is thus a matter of political judgement whether the nuclear potential available to Iran by the 1980s will be used exclusively for peaceful purposes and the Non-Proliferation Treaty will be observed, or whether by that time nuclear weapons will have become standard equipment even in developing countries, irrespective of the availability of military support systems. Military observers point out that it can hardly be in Iran's interest to spread nuclear arms to developing countries, as crossing the atomic threshold would considerably decrease the Shah's enormous conventional potential. This may be one of the reasons why, unlike Brazil and India, Iran signed the Non-Proliferation Treaty. Nonetheless Iran's developing competition with India, which now possesses atomic weaponry, could develop into a regional nuclear arms race. When the Shah visited France in 1975 some statements gave rise to assumptions that Iran was working towards the possession of atomic weapons—but these statements were denied by the Iranian government office the following day and were described as misunderstandings.

Iran's role as a sub-imperialist power
In 1961, the temporary deployment of British troops in Kuwait was still sufficient to secure the territorial integrity of that desert state. By the end of the 1960s, such an intervention had become unthinkable. A takeover of the British position by the US would, according to American strategists, have given the Soviet Union a pretext for establishing a naval base in Iraq. The US thus preferred to secure oil supplies from the Persian/Arabian Gulf by militarily enforcing its 'task force' in the Indian Ocean ready to intervene in case of emergency, and otherwise to make use of Iran as the military guarantor of oil supplies. The consequent super-arming policy infected the Gulf states. A special 'Middle Eastern task group' for the co-ordination of this arms escalation was created by the Pentagon. In return for arms co-operation, the Shah left one island in the Gulf to the US for the installation of electronic interception devices, and the US obtained the right to install bases in Bahrain. There were ample indications by the US that it would not hesitate to intervene militarily, if it ever became necessary, to ensure oil supplies. But with the growing military capacity of the Gulf states, such an intervention, from a purely military viewpoint, could become increasingly risky.

The expansion of Iranian military power is carefully adapted to the strategic role of the US armed forces in securing oil supplies from the Persian/Arabian Gulf region. The increased establishment of US bases in the Indian Ocean is usually discussed in connection with the Soviet naval presence, but even without reference to the USSR it is strategically important, serving to demonstrate military superiority in the area. This is a necessary factor in US politics, which tend to view American influence in any area in terms of its military potential.

Because of the immense arms build-up in Iran, the country will probably not have the resources to create complex and developed industrial structures, and these will remain the monopoly of industrial nations which dominate the world market as well as some socialist states. Iran is seeking its fortune through adaptation to the world-wide strategies of multinational firms, and is thus surrendering its claim to independent development. The vision of the powerful consumer society with an American standard of living by 1985, so often reiterated by the Iranian government, is finally turning into clear propaganda, intended to mask the enrichment of a small minority and the simultaneous hopelessness of the accepted 'model of development' for the impoverished Iranian majority, because of the worsening price ratio between oil and industrial production goods. Weapons to be delivered within the next few years will require eventual expenditures, on spares and maintenance as well as training, far above the original purchase price. At the same time, the dependence of the military on foreign specialists will also increase.

The super-arming of Iran has triggered off intensive arming efforts in the Gulf region and at the moment is stimulating arms races in a far more extended region. Iran, Saudi Arabia and India feed, with their increasing competition, an arms dynamic around the Indian Ocean.[31] Many factors indicate that Iran will strengthen its influence in East Africa and other states in the area of the Indian Ocean by military co-operation, provision of weapons, and economic aid. Given India's special relationship with East African states, a competition in military 'aid' can be predicted for the near future. The Shah wants to keep the Indian Ocean sea routes under surveillance jointly with South Africa. Thus, the procurement of long-range surveillance ships for anti-submarine warfare, the purchase of Stratotankers (enabling Iranian fighter bombers to reach base targets in India or Saudi Arabia), the planned development of a submarine fleet, and the contractual arrangement for a supply base for the Iranian navy on Mauritius, 5000 kilometres removed in the Indian Ocean, become strategically important. The Indian intervention in Bangladesh or Iranian interference in Oman will certainly not remain the only manifestations of sub-imperialist claims which are only conditionally controllable by the big powers, but which can possibly turn into catalysts for global confrontation.

NOTES

1. The author is indebted for historical material to Manoochehr Heshmati, *The Role of the Military in 'Underdeveloped' Society—with Persia as Example* (Berlin, 1974) and to Ahmad Mahrad, 'German–Persian Relations 1918–33', Dissertation (Berlin, 1974).
2. For similar examples see Ernst L. Presseisen, *Before Aggression Europeans prepare a Japanese Army* (Tucson, 1965); George Pope Atkins and Larry V. Thompson, 'German Military Influence in Argentina 1921–1940', *Journal of*

Latin American Studies, IV, no. 2, pp. 257–74; Hans von Kiesling, *Soldat in Drei Weltteilen* (Leipzig, 1935); Jürgen Schäffer, *Deutsche Militärhilfe an Südamerika, Militär- und Rüstungsinteressen in Argentinien, Bolivien, Chile vor 1914* (Gutersloh, 1974).

3. H. Nazari, *Der ökonomische und politische Kampf um das Iranische Erdöl* (Cologne, 1971) p. 57.

4. A German called Hartmann became director of the arsenal, and Colonel Haase, who had been active within the Persian government unit before the world war, was put in charge of the machine gun section. Alexander Teherani, *Iran* (Berlin, 1943) pp. 97 ff., discusses the production of rifles and machine guns in the arsenal, constructed by Germans. He also mentions a factory for gas masks, supplied with German machinery, in Wanak.

5. Mahrad, op. cit., pp. 362 ff.

6. Ibid., pp. 97 ff.

7. Large-scale armament efforts in the third world were often marked by such losses. Thus Japanese naval units from England were lost because of inadequately trained crews. See Gustav Jensen, *Japans Seemacht—Der schnelle Aufstieg im Kampf um Selbstbehauptung und Gleichberechtigung in den Jahren 1853–1937* (Berlin, 1938).

8. William Green and John Fricker, *The Air Forces of the World* (London, 1958) p. 163.

9. American support for the Iranian gendarmerie, officially begun in 1942, has continued ever since. The American mission apparently has considerable influence on the development of police policies—for example anti-drug activities. See J. Croizat, 'Stability in the Persian Gulf', *Proceedings,* United States Naval Institute (July 1973) pp. 48–50.

10. *Der Spiegel*, no. 32 (1958).

11. SIPRI, *The Arms Trade with the Third World* (Stockholm, 1971) p. 574.

12. SIPRI, *The Arms Trade with the Third World,* has a full chronological register of all weapons transferred to Iran since 1950.

13. 'U.S. Overseas Loans and Grants and Assistance from International Organisations, 1945–1970', Special Report prepared by the House Foreign Affairs Committee, Agency for International Development (Washington, D.C., 1971) p. 63.

14. R. K. Ramazani, *The Persian Gulf, Iran's Role* (Charlottesville, N.C., 1972) pp. 108–9; *NACLA Newsletter* (North American Congress on Latin America), VII, no. 6, pp. 24–8. NACLA cites publications of the US Congress which give $359 million for fiscal year 1973 for military aid to Iran. In 1974, the American Eximbank (state-owned) made available $200 million credits at a favourable interest rate for Iran's purchase of American weapons. Eximbank had been prohibited by Congress in 1968 from granting credits to underdeveloped countries for buying American arms, but Iran had by 1974 been 'released' from the group of underdeveloped countries.

15. Although the US only has observer status within CENTO, there are many indications that it is the driving power of the alliance. It was responsible for organising and financing a great number of conferences, training courses, and other activities of the CENTO Pact. See Margaret Laurence (ed.), *Coordinating U.S. Economic Action for CENTO.*

16. 'Comptroller General's report to the Congress: Issues related to U.S.

Military Sales and Assistance to Iran', Department of Defense, Department of State B-133258 (Washington D.C., 1975) p. 1. Those arms already on order and to be delivered in 1976 or 1977 indicated a high rate of increase for the second half of the decade. It should also be kept in mind that these figures include only arms, and do not necessarily include non-military equipment intended for military use. There are no reliable estimates about such exports to Iran, but it is reasonable to assume that they are rising along with the increased complexity of weapons systems.

17. 'U.S. Overseas Loans and Grants and Assistance from International Organizations, 1945–70', Special Report prepared for the House Foreign Affairs Committee, Agency for International Development (Washington D.C., 1971) p. 63. *NACLA Handbook*, 'The U.S. Military Apparatus' (Berkeley, 1972) p. 80, calculates the 'aid' for Vietnam at $2100 million whereas the former source arrives at a total sum of $6300 million for all war financing.

18. This statement refers to the conventional arms sector. India in fact has the atomic bomb and a relatively developed arms industry, but so far has had considerable difficulties in procuring modern weapons systems or producing them under licence.

19. The system was whipped through by an international consortium of four companies, including Northrop and the German Siemens. Bribes were involved: for example, Prince Chahram Pahlavi, a relative of the Shah received $\frac{1}{2}$ per cent of the contract sum. This information was revealed in enquiries about Northrop before a US Senate committee. 'Documents relating to foreign sales and operations of the Northrop Corporation' (Washington D.C., 1975) mimeograph. According to this report the project was originally estimated at $130 million and rose subsequently to $225 million. See also *Le Monde* (3 June 1975) and 'USAF pushes Iran Air Defense System', *Aviation Week & Space Technology* (24 May 1975).

20. John Finney, 'U.S. Military Readiness Seen Harmed by Arms Sale to Iran', *International Herald Tribune* (1 May 1975).

21. Torpedo boats delivered to Iran by France were equipped with propelling aggregates from the German Maschinen und Turbinen Union (MTU). 'France to build six gunboats for Iran', *Financial Times* (28 Feb 1974).

22. Dale Tahtinen, 'Arms in the Persian Gulf', *Foreign Affairs Studies* (Washington D.C., 1974) p. 26.

23. US AID reports that between 1961 and 1971 more than 200 Iranian police officers were trained in the US. Nancy Stein and Mike Klare, 'Police Aid for Tyrants', in *The Trojan Horse,* ed. Steve Weissmann (San Francisco, 1974) p. 234.

24. Rainer Kriebl, 'Der Iran und seine militärpolitischen Probleme', *Wehrkunde* (Dec 1973) p. 633, includes details of Iranian co-operation with Israel in specific military and economic areas.

25. A US Senate staff study mentions that the helicopter firm Bell and the F-14 contractor Grumman each have 2,000 employees and dependants in Iran, and that the total number of Americans (including dependants) is estimated to reach 36,000 in 1980 if all arms contracts are met. DoD personnel, which ought to be added, numbered 3,400 (including dependants) in 1976. 'US Military Sales to Iran', a staff report to the Subcommittee on Foreign

Assistance of the Committee on Foreign Relations (US Senate, Washington, D.C., 1976) pp. 36–7.

26. Tahtinen, op. cit., p. 18.
27. *Teheran Economist*, no. 591–3 (1965).
28. Gregory A. Carter, *Directed Licensing: An Evaluation of a Proposed Technique for Reducing the Procurement Cost of Aircraft* (Santa Monica, Cal., 1974) R-1604-PR.
29. South African atomic research has made such big advances in the last years that one should reckon with the fact that this country will soon own her own uranium enrichment plant. The South African example makes it clear that the necessary know-how is relatively easily transferable through (partially kept secret) scientific co-operation and by recruiting foreign experts, and that financially the resources necessary are within reach of countries with a medium-sized industrial capacity. David Fishlock 'Jet Nozzle Enrichment—South Africa's Way With Uranium', *Financial Times* (29 May 1975).
30. The nuclear engineering department of Massachusetts Institute of Technology (MIT) doubled its places to accommodate, among others, students from Iran. Anne Hessing Cahn, 'Determinants of the Nuclear Option: The Case of Iran' (Cambridge, Mass., n.d.), mimeographed, p. 13.
31. A US Senate staff study ('US Military Sales to Iran', op. cit.) refers particularly to differences over Pakistan ('there is evidence of incipient military competition between Iran/Pakistan, on the one hand, and India on the other', p. xi) and foresees in general terms 'the possibility of conflict in the East involving Iran, Afghanistan, Pakistan and India' (p. 11).

7 South Africa: Repression and the Transfer of Arms and Arms Technology

Asbjørn Eide

Introduction

The South African military apparatus was never a defensive force. It developed as an instrument for conquest and repression, an instrument through which white settlers, and the imperial interests they served, established and maintained their political, economic, and social control over the majority of the population.

South African forces have, during this century, served an additional function. In both world wars they were drawn upon by Britain, and since the Second World War, efforts have been made to utilise the South African military apparatus as a resource for the West in the Cold War confrontation, and to prevent radical change in the third world. These two functions are mutually dependent, but they are not always mutually compatible. The South African military apparatus relies upon imported military technology, on arms and equipment which are designed or manufactured abroad. Technological superiority is the basis for continued white dominance. It was firearms that enabled the original Boers to conquer the Africans. And it is modern counter-insurgency weapons that enables the white minority to rule today.

The import of military technology, along with the import of industrial goods and of capital and the export of gold and other precious minerals, of oranges and other primary commodities, form part of a network of relationships which link the South African whites to the international system. It is a complex linkage which at once suppresses, and sets in motion contradictions which have long since developed out of the social conditions in South Africa—the overwhelming conflict between white and black, and the divisions within the white population between the internationalist or pro-imperialist mainly capitalist groups and the nationalist groups which generally comprise Afrikaans farmers and privileged white workers. In the past, the use of South African forces for imperial defence has caused strains among the white population, threatening the very domestic stability on which foreign economic penetration was based.

Today, the white population shares a common commitment to the idea that domestic military coercion is critical to maintain not only its own position but also South Africa's contribution to the world economic order. But this idea is increasingly undermined by the political victories of blacks throughout Africa and especially in Southern Africa. In particular, the more or less active encouragement of some Western powers for the use of South African armed forces in Angola was a catastrophe for Western co-operation with Africa as a whole. Subsequently, the events of Soweto, the death in detention of Black Consciousness leader Steve Biko and other Africans, and the banning of journalists and religious workers shocked even those Western governments which had previously supported, tacitly or explicitly, the South African government's use of force. People in Africa—and throughout the world—know the sources of helicopters, armoured cars, and other equipment used by the South African government during demonstrations and strikes. They know the sources not only of the imported weapons, but also of the technology and capital which helped to build an indigenous arms production programme in South Africa. So it is that the use of armed forces for internal repression, a necessary condition for South Africa's participation in the current international system, alienates world opinion and has resulted in a series of arms embargoes, culminating in the Security Council resolution of November 1977.

This chapter explores South Africa's ambiguous role in the international system through the medium of military relationships. It describes the historical development of the two functions of the South African military apparatus, internal repression and external participation in Western defence. And it looks at the ways in which both attract and repel external interests in South Africa.[1]

Conquest and repression in South Africa

HISTORICAL SURVEY

European imperialism began in South Africa in 1652 with the establishment of a small post at the Cape to supply ships of the Dutch East India Company. In the decades that followed, the Boers developed their typical commando system, a raider army of civilians who managed to push African ethnic groups into the interior. They achieved this mainly by their superior arms technology; primitive though firearms were the Boers had a monopoly on them.

The Boers' links with the Netherlands were never strong, and were broken with the assertion of British supremacy on the seas during the eighteenth century. The Boer community thus became a self-reliant group of settlers rather than an extended arm for imperial penetration by the Dutch. But it was a self-reliant community of a special nature: not only did it push the Africans off their land, but it also used forced labour in what was basically a subsistence economy. The raider army of the Boers was not a military force separated from the civilian population. It was simply the male civilian population which came together for armed conflict when this was found necessary. The commando tradition continued among the Boers after the British occupation in 1795.

The Boers moved eastwards into the interior, particularly during the great treks in the 1830s and 1840s, and confronted resistance en route from the Africans who were pushed off their land. This resulted in a number of wars, in which raider armies consisting of mounted farmers with firearms easily won. In one area, for example, 'the Xhosa tribes encountered carried no firearms, and, on the rare occasions when they could be cornered, could do nothing against the buckshot and bullets of the commandos. They were a constant menace to the frontier farmers, and were not seriously tackled until the British found the time and opportunity to spend money freely on the problem.'[2] Thus the commandos with their firearms—and sometimes with some help from the British—gained control over Africans for slave labour, and could increasingly use Africans for manual work on their farms. The Boers could then devote more time to armed expansion into the interior. Raider warfare also played a significant role in the formation of the Boer lifestyle, creating individualistic warriors who came to despise manual work which could be done by subjugated Africans. It would be highly inappropriate to consider the raider army, with its emphasis on expansion and exploitation, as somehow comparable to the guerrilla armies of today's liberation movements.

In the Boer commando tradition, there was little or no place for African participation in the armed forces. This is different from the British tradition.

BRITISH CONQUEST AND THE COLONIAL ARMY

The British conquest during the Napoleonic wars met with little resistance, but it accelerated Boer migration into the interior, with the resultant pillage and plunder of African land and property. The wars against the Xhosa people became more intense, and the British developed their colonial army to break the African resistance. The British and their English-speaking descendants in the Cape did not use the commando system, but established uniformed regiments of volunteers. The British also made extensive use of African levees, under white officers, although these were always fully integrated into the British forces, and their arms and ammunition were rationed in very small quantities. Of special importance are the Mfengu, who in the 1830s became hostile towards their former friends, the Xhosas, as a result of European expansion and the consequent reduction of African land. In several wars, the British skilfully manipulated this conflict so that the Mfengu fought on their side against the Xhosas: White South African military history describes the defeat of the Xhosas thus:

Both Fortescue and Theal have left detailed and lengthy accounts of these Kaffir wars of the Eastern frontier, which took much the same course, the problem being to drive the Xhosas out of the bush and mountains into the open rolling country further to the East, where their cattle could be captured and their food supplies cut. The possession of comparatively good firearms by the Kaffirs made each succeeding campaign more difficult, but the result was the same—the tribes gave in when their food stocks were exhausted, or their great chief killed.[3]

The Mfengu represented a great asset to the British in their wars against the Xhosas, but care was taken not to give them benefits which could make them uncontrollable later. In particular, a strict inventory was kept of the arms given to them. When the Xhosas were finally defeated, legislation was enacted to disarm all Cape Africans including the Mfengu. Thus, the African population as a whole was subdued, and neither the Xhosas nor the Mfengu posed any threat to white hegemony. Gradually they lost their land and whatever economic and social advancement they had achieved during the decades of collaboration with the British.[4]

THE BRITISH–BOER WAR

The confrontation which developed between the British and the Boers initially centred around the nature of exploitation of the Africans. Influenced by political developments inside Britain, the British sought to abolish slavery and to give the Africans some political rights. This was a challenge to the life-style of the *Herrenvolk* farmers. The great treks in the 1840s were to a large extent due to the undermining of the economic and social system of the Boers which resulted from the elimination of slavery and the political rights given to the African population in the Cape colony. Slavery was not formally established in the new territories opened up by the great treks, but the Boers utilised subjugated African labour in their otherwise rather simple subsistence agricultural production. The Boers' quest for self-determination was to a large extent predicated on the desire to maintain labour-repressive agricultural production. Britain's imperial drive was motivated not by humanitarian concern for the Africans, but by the desire to obtain control over rich mineral resources. For the first decades after the treks, the British were inclined to leave the Boers alone. The great turning point was the discovery of large deposits of diamonds and gold, particularly in the Transvaal in 1886. Skilfully manipulated by financial interests like those of Cecil Rhodes, a considerably more imperialistic sentiment developed in Britain and led to the Boer Wars.

The final confrontation took place from 1899 to 1902 between a colonial army which was quickly increased in manpower from Britain, and a Boer army which was a grander version of the raiders' army. In the beginning, the two sides were not too different in technology, but the Boers failed to obtain further support from Imperial Germany, and gradually the British got the upper hand and forced the Boers into a kind of guerrilla warfare. The British then resorted to tactics widely used since, including concentration camps and extensive burning of homesteads. In the end, this broke the armed resistance of the Boers. But this was not the only reason for the British victory. Of great importance, although very much under-rated in later accounts of the Boer War, was the position of the Africans.[5]

It is important to remember that this war was carried out between two white minorities, and that the vast majority of the South African population was not a party to the conflict. Both the British and the Boers used African manpower only to a very limited degree. A few African scouts were used, but the British and the Boers both claimed that this was foul play, and the overall policy was clearly not to employ Africans. Africans were, in effect, non-people in this conflict between British imperialism and the Boer effort to set up internal colonialism.

African sentiments were divided, partly because of the hostile attitudes and fears between different African ethnic groups. There was some tendency to favour the British, on the assumption that British policy towards Africans would be better than Boer policy. More importantly, towards the end of the Boer War Africans started to re-assert their own autonomy. The Boers, engaging in guerrilla warfare, had to spread their forces over a wide territory to tie down the British army. This meant that they became vulnerable in many areas which they had previously taken from the Africans. Several skirmishes between Boers and Africans resulted.

It is possible to argue that one of the reasons the Boers yielded to the British was to prevent the Africans from gaining ground in military terms. Unlike present-day liberation forces, the Boers could not possibly mobilise the majority of the population in their favour, since they were themselves oppressors of the majority of the population. It was therefore not only British counter-guerrilla warfare, but also the risk of stronger African resistance, which contributed to the Boer decision to stop the war. Although the British won the war in military terms, they gave substantial concessions to the Boers. The conciliation between victor and vanquished might be considered magnanimous were it not for the fact that it took place at the expense of the silent—and silenced— majority, the Africans. They became the real victims of the Boer War.

One direct and concrete outcome was that the Boers obtained more weapons when the war was finished, weapons which were then used to suppress Africans in Boer-controlled territories. The new Boer leadership which had emerged towards the end of the war was more inclined to join in British imperial ambitions, utilising South Africa as a source for raw material, and keeping a reservoir of very cheap labour. British–Boer differences were thus minimised. For the Africans, the outcome was widespread destitution. The British scorched-earth policy resulted in homelessness and malnutrition. Africans suffered at least as much as the Boers during the war, and after the war they had fewer opportunities to recuperate. Efforts were made to help the Boers re-establish themselves, but very little attention was paid to the Africans.

THE PRIORITY OF REPRESSION

The commitment of the South African armed forces to both internal control and defending British imperial interests—and the priority given to the former—was already becoming apparent at the Imperial Defence Conference in 1909. When the British demanded that the dominions develop their forces in order to participate in the wars of the empire, General Smuts (later to become prime minister of South Africa) pointed out the special situation in his country:

> In the matter of helping in a war, South Africa could not go as far as New Zealand and Australia: South Africa's defence had to look inwards as well as outwards; the native populations numbered five times more than the white, not to mention the rest of the African population to the North. In view of the past history of native wars, the contingency of a conflict, an elemental conflict between the two alien forces, the white people and the native people in South Africa, could not be ignored.[6]

When the first legal regulation of South Africa's military system was enacted in 1912, it represented an amalgamation of the Boer commando tradition and the British tradition of regular armed forces. A small, permanent force was set up, backed by an Active Citizens Force and a General Reserve. There was little in the bill which reflected any fear of external attack. In introducing the defence bill, Minister of Defence Smuts made it clear that the main priority for the new armed force was to knit the white population together in controlling the African majority:

> This measure, sir, is one of those, this is the first of its kind, which has only become possible in consequence of Union, and which could only be dealt with as a consequence of the union of the various colonies of South Africa. And as this measure has been necessitated and arises from Union, so the day may come when the Union will only continue in existence because of this measure.[7]

The paramilitary police, the Cape Mounted Rifles, remained a pillar of the new system:

> The C.M.R. is a police force primarily, and most of its duties are police duties, but it is also intended to be a striking force in time of need in the Native Territories, and has a battery of artillery attached to it to provide artillery training for some of its members.[8]

This pattern of using the police as the first line of repression against the 'natives', and equipping them with weapons far beyond those normally required for police functions, is a typical feature of South African society which has persisted until this day.

NEW TENSIONS AMONG THE WHITES

Two years later, the First World War began. The South African government stated that since South Africa was an integral part of the British Empire, it was automatically at war with the common enemy. The British government requested South Africa to undertake military operations against German-occupied South-west Africa, and the government of South Africa agreed to do so. Sentiments were different, however, among officers of the Union Defence Forces. A number of these, including Commander-in-Chief Christian Beyers, were of Boer descent and harboured strong nationalist sentiments. They had to decide whether to fight as part of the British empire or against it. Several generals refused to invade South-west Africa; some were in secret negotiations with Germany for the recognition of an independent South Africa. A provisional government was set up by these generals, and a proclamation was announced calling for armed liberation from the British Empire by white South Africans. But this was from the beginning a lost cause. The integration of the Boers and those of British descent had gone too far, and the rebellious generals soon found that they had very little support. After several months of skirmishes, during which at least 124 rebels and 19 soldiers from the government side were killed and about 1000 people wounded, the rebellion was brought to an end.

Fewer Boers than expected had taken up arms against the pro-British government, but this Boer rebellion increased nationalist sentiments. It was another step in the process leading to the Rand rebellion of 1922, to the Pact government of 1924, and, many years later, to the complete victory by the white nationalists in the election in 1948. Each of these steps brought about a successive worsening of the political and economic conditions of the African population.[9]

The Boer rebellion was the last effort to assert autonomy by the Boer *farmer* society. By 1922, when the Rand rebellion occurred, agricultural transformations and the resultant influx from the white rural areas to the towns were leading to unemployment. This unemployment was aggravated in the opinion of white workers, by the increased use of cheap African labour by the international companies which controlled the gold mines and other key areas of South African production. The white trade unions, who co-operated with the considerably weaker national capitalists, organised strikes which escalated into political mobilisation. On 6 March 1922, a general strike was proclaimed. Strikers armed with chains, old swords, broken bottles, and firearms drawn from their Rifle Association (the descendant of the Boer commando system) attacked those mines which were still working. Martial law was proclaimed, and the Prime Minister, General Smuts, called up the Active Citizens Force to suppress the strike. The newly formed air force was also mobilised, with six aircraft. By 10 March, some 7000 members of the armed forces were in action against the strike. In the conflict 78 strikers, 76 members of the government forces, and 62 civilians were killed.[10]

The rebellion was brought under control, but its political impact continued. The strike generated political mobilisation which spread even further as a consequence of the armed repression. At the next elections, in 1924, a combination of white labour and Boer nationalists brought in the Pact government. This political alignment later became the dominant feature of South African politics. The Pact government represented the victory of national capital over international capital, and most of all a victory for white labour which could from now on determine conditions for the employment of non-white workers: African labour should not be used until all white labour had been absorbed, Africans were to be given only inferior jobs, and whites were to be paid substantially higher wages than Africans. In this way, African workers subsidised the inflated wages which over time came to be given to white workers.

Thus, the use of force by the British in the Boer war, and by the government against white workers in the Rand rebellion, had results different from those intended. In both cases the outcome was increased political power for those who had been *defeated* through the use of weapons. Both of these confrontations originated in the conflict between external imperialist or capitalist groups, and South African white nationalist and labour groups. The latter were defeated militarily, but enhanced their political position in the further process of integration.

THE USE OF FORCE AGAINST AFRICANS: NO WHITE PROTEST

Other incidents in the period after the First World War were directed against Africans. In 1921, an African religious community with political overtones undertook a non-violent action of defiance against

South African racialist laws. They refused to move from the territory where they had their tribal land, refused registration, and refused to get involved in the white cash economy. Armed forces moved in and shot dead 163 Israelites, as they called themselves, wounding 129 more.

Smuts also took action against the Bondelzwarts, an Afrikaans-speaking Christian tribe, many of whose members had been driven out of South-west Africa by German settlers before the First World War. After the war the exiles tried to return to their former tribal territories without the permission of the authorities. Both they and the permanent residents also objected to a high dog tax which the government had imposed in the hope of turning them from a race of hunters into one of farmworkers, whose labour could be exploited to develop the territory. In the rebellion that followed in the summer of 1922, flocks and herds of the Bondelzwarts were bombed from the air, 115 tribesmen were killed in action, and many women and children were wounded.[11]

POST-WAR PLANNING: PRIORITY FOR REPRESSION

South African participation in the two World Wars had a strong impact on the organisation and equipment of the armed forces. As a result of the Second World War, there was a transformation from the low-technology armed forces of an agricultural society to an industrialised army—but priorities remained the same. After the white nationalist landslide election victory in 1948, the defence minister of Dr Malan's government said in the South African Assembly in May 1949,

> In general I may say that South Africa is preparing in the first place to make itself secure internally and to be able to defend itself. It is the government's policy that South Africa should look first to internal security; and subsequently, when difficulties may arise from out side, it can at that junction determine to what extent and in what way it should participate.[12]

General Smuts, the South African politician with the longest experience of military matters, wanted to ensure that South Africa retained its modern fighting force and remained able to co-operate with Western powers, and not return only to a low-technology force concentrating on internal repression. In the Assembly debate he pointed out that under the Boer-dominated pre-war government, the main emphasis had been on the commando forces which had reached the extremely high number of 150,000. These were not the forces that had played an active role during the Second World War, and after the war, the number of commando forces had been placed at 25,000. The new nationalist government intended to raise this figure to 80,000.[13]

This emphasis on internal repression, with the armed forces as a second line of coercion to assist the police, was reiterated in 1960 when

Defence Minister Fouché stated that the national defence policy was first of all to maintain 'internal security', i.e. to uphold apartheid against African resistance. Only secondly, the task was to protect maritime routes around the Cape, in co-operation with the British Navy. The army and the air force were to take action to maintain internal security when the police needed support; for this purpose, twelve infantry units were equipped with Saracen armoured cars. In addition to these units, commandos were organised to contribute to internal security.

On 29 April 1960, the leader of the opposition said in Parliament,

One of our charges has been that the government has failed to provide South Africa with defence against external aggression and have converted what was an efficient defence organization into what is in fact now a type of Home-Guard, mainly directed for use as a secondary police force in the preservation of internal security within South Africa. The minister himself has stated quite recently, since he assumed office, that the Army and the Air Force have been reorganized to enable them to quell riots. Commando units have also been reorganized to act more efficiently on internal security missions.[14]

But he made it clear that he was not at all opposed to this internal use of the armed forces; he merely wanted a stronger and better equipped force for external uses as well:

We believe that the policy should be to organize South Africa as a base for operations with an organization for ourselves and the friends that we hope to have with us; to see that our ports are equipped and capable of handling the heavy war-time load; . . . and to honour our agreement for naval seaward and anti-submarine defence along the Union coast and to completely eliminate politics from the defence organization. That in general is the very broad outline of this Party's policy.[15]

That was the year of the Sharpeville massacre, when the military and police joined forces against peaceful demonstrators opposing the hated pass-laws. When low-flying military aircraft failed to disperse the demonstrators, heavily armed police in armoured cars shot at them, killing 67 and wounding 187.

The Sharpeville massacre had three direct results. First, as a result of nationwide protests by Africans, including the burning of passes, a national state of emergency was declared, 20,000 opponents of the regime were detained, and nationalist movements were banned. Secondly, the government embarked on a massive programme to expand and strengthen the armed forces. Thirdly, on the international level, the massacre led to the first demands at the United Nations for an arms embargo against South Africa.

In 1963, the defence minister reiterated that the armed forces had to be prepared to combat internal subversion as well as aggression from outside, and had to be equipped for both purposes. Competent officers, he said, had been sent abroad to study and to buy equipment. No doubt these studies included counter-insurgency courses, so popular at that time in the United States and elsewhere in the West.

In 1973 the Government White Paper on Defence and Armament Production said that the main task of the forces was 'to ensure, within its capabilities and the terms of government policy, that the government will have the time and freedom of action needed to develop its internal and foreign policies.'[16] In an article in *Paratus,* the magazine of the South African forces, Commodore Edwards in June 1973 listed the tasks of the armed forces:

1. To assist the South African police in preserving internal order.
2. To deal promptly and effectively with any unconventional attack against any part of our territory.
3. To ensure that no conventional attack, whatever its origin, is undertaken lightly against the Republic of South Africa.
4. To discourage hostile states from rash attacks of aggression against the RSA or from allowing their territories to be used for such a purpose.

Throughout, the main priority for the armed forces has been to maintain control over the African population which has been excluded from political participation.

INTERVENTION: POLICING NEIGHBOURING STATES

In the mid-1970s, as the liberation struggles in southern Africa became more urgent, South Africa tried to become an interventionist power, policing neighbouring countries against regimes representing potential support for the liberation of Namibia and South Africa. South African forces assisted the Smith regime in Rhodesia in repressing the liberation movement, and used aircraft and infantry patrols for counter-insurgency operations in occupied Namibia.

During the Portuguese colonial warfare, there were also numerous cases of South African military interference in Angola. At first, only relatively small groups of South African volunteers were involved in Angola. This changed when the Portuguese colonial empire collapsed and the future of white supremacy in Angola was threatened. It is probable that South African forces entered Angolan territory as early as June 1975, they were certainly there by August. The involvement increased, and by 23 October a large invasion was under way consisting of 2000 mercenaries (voluntaries) with Panhard armoured cars produced in South Africa under French licence. Following them was the first group of 1000–1500 regular soldiers with light vehicles. According to a secret report which was released in *The Observer* (London) on 11 January 1976, a new regular unit, using French AMX-13 light tanks and US M-41 Walker Bulldog tanks, was sent on 15 November. At the peak of the invasion, there were at least 5000 South African soldiers in Angola.

By late October, South African forces had penetrated deeply into Angolan territory, heading towards the capital Luanda which was controlled by one of the liberation movements, the MPLA. The latter asked for help from Cuba; this was forthcoming at the end of October or possibly on 5 November, the date given by the Cuban government. Cuban contingents, carried on USSR transport planes, turned back the South African advance, and in March 1976, after several defeats, the South African force was finally withdrawn.

This South African aggression, which was launched from the illegally held territory of Namibia, was condemned in a resolution by the Security Council on 31 March 1976. Five countries (the US, the UK, France, Italy and Japan) abstained from voting, and China did not participate.

The South African military complex: size and composition of the forces
South African military expenditure has increased rapidly since 1960, when the South African army was small and equipped with relatively low-technology, inexpensive equipment. Military spending rose sharply in the years which immediately followed the Sharpeville massacre, and again after 1973 when it became clear that Portugal was facing defeat in Southern Africa. The increase in military spending is shown on Figure 7.1.

The armed forces of South Africa, known as the South African Defence Force, comprise a small Permanent Force, the Citizens Force, and a Commando Force. The origin of the Permanent Force is in the British colonial army; the Citizens Force grew out of the volunteer regiments created by the British among the English-speaking population; and the Commando Force is a direct continuation of the Boer commandos, the raider army of the first *Herrenvolk* settlers. The Permanent and Citizen Forces consist of army, air force, and navy units, and the Commandos have ground and air units, the latter made up of light private aircraft. Defence capability is based on rapid mobilisation of the highly trained reserves in the Citizen Force—that is, of all recruits who have completed their initial training.

The total strength of the South African Defence Force is around

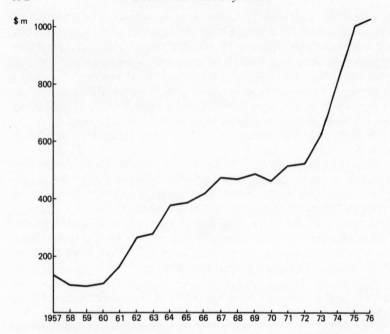

Source　World Armament and Disarmament, SIPRI Yearbook 1977 (MIT Press, 1977), p. 236.

FIGURE 7.1　South Africa's military spending, 1957–76 (US $m at 1973 prices and 1973 exchange rates)

310,000. In addition the 53,000 police form the core of the repressive force. Table 7.1 gives a breakdown of the strength of the armed forces and police as of 1976.

The army is organised into nine territorial commands, which have been given considerable autonomy in the planning and conduct of repressive (counter-insurgency) operations. The army relies heavily on armoured cars, most of them produced in France or in South Africa under French licence. On the fairly well-developed road system of South Africa, armoured cars are suitable for counter-guerrilla or repressive functions, whereas they would not be of such significance against an invader with advanced weaponry.

The air force has a large number of helicopters, most of them French made (Alouette III, Puma, and Super Frelon). In addition, there are 12 Wasp helicopters (British made) for naval purposes. There are also large numbers of light aircraft (145 Impala I, 22 Impala II, 25 Vampires). Recently there has also been substantial introduction of French jet fighter bombers and interceptors (Mirage III EZ, Mirage III DZ, Mirage F-1 AZ).

Even the local commando force units, which have always been low-technology, have been considerably upgraded, and in 1976 they had 250 light aircraft and large numbers of armoured cars.

The navy was largely equipped by the British under the terms of the Simonstown Agreement. Recently South Africa acquired submarines and corvettes armed with missiles. It is not unreasonable to suppose that these recent acquisitions are primarily intended for use against a possible naval blockade by black African or even international forces.

The South African police, although not part of the military, have been involved in counter-insurgency for many decades. Of 33,000 police in 1976, 3000 were serving in special counter-insurgency units. With reserves, the number of police could be increased to 53,000. The police administer the pass system which permits individualised control of the movements of all non-whites. Arrests are often used to keep severe discontent from erupting into demonstrations. When demonstrations do occur, the police are the first to fire on the demonstrators—as happened at Sharpeville in 1960, at Soweto in 1976, and in many lesser episodes. The police have 80 Saracen armoured cars, 430 riot trucks, and heavy infantry weapons.

The armed forces support the police when the latter fail to quell African unrest. In particular, the South African air force has been actively involved in fighting unarmed Africans; foreign-produced helicopters and fighter bombers were used in both Sharpeville and Soweto.

TABLE 7.1 Estimates of South African armed forces and police (1976)

| | Presently under weapons | | Citizens Force | |
	Regulars	Conscripts	(Reserve)	Total
Army	7,000	31,000	138,000	176,000
Navy	3,600	1,400	10,500	15,500
Air Force	5,500	3,000	25,000	33,500
Commando	90,000			90,000
Police	33,000		20,000*	53,000
Total	139,100	35,400	193,500	368,000

Note * Reserve of the police, *not* of the Citizens Force

Sources International Institute for Strategic Studies, *The Military Balance 1976/1977* (London, 1977); and South African Institute on Race Relations, *Survey of Race Relations 1976*.

THE RACIAL COMPOSITION

If the total number of men in the Commando Force and the police force is added to the number available for mobilisation in the armed forces, there were in 1976 more than 368,000 people trained and equipped to repress the political demands of the African majority. Very few of these are Africans; virtually all are drawn from the white minority. This has not always been the case; there have been periods when Africans were extensively used by the colonial or settler forces. Although the Boer tradition was rather hostile to the use of Africans from the very beginning, Africans served in the armed forces as unarmed labourers, bearers, etc. The British colonial army, and the volunteer regiments organised among the English-speaking community in the Cape province, relied for half a century on the aid of friendly African forces. When African resistance had been broken, the British also disarmed those ethnic groups which had assisted them. In this way, the whites secured an almost complete monopoly on firearms, a monopoly which has been very carefully maintained since.

During the First World War, a considerable number of non-white labourers were attached to the South African forces, but they were not armed. During the Second World War, for the first time since the Union (in 1910) there were efforts to use non-white soldiers; but the ruling white minority did not allow Africans, coloureds, or Asians within the normal organisation of the forces.[17] Only those who have lived in South Africa and know how intense is the feeling against any training of natives for military service, can realise the many difficulties encountered.

Basically, the same pattern has continued since the Second World War. Africans, coloureds and Asians have been enlisted on a voluntary basis as auxiliaries, but usually without significant arms. The Bantus have been prohibited by law from carrying arms. In 1963, the Coloured Corps was established, and was assigned jobs such as those of drivers, guards, stretcher-bearers, cooks, clerks, and storemen. Training in the use of weapons was limited to 'the handling of single-shot small arms for self-defence and the protection of Government property'. In May 1973, it was announced that an Indian service battalion, similar to the Coloured Corps, would be established in Durban, and in 1974, it was decided that black citizens of the 'Bantu homelands' would be trained to take part in 'the Republic's defence'. African personnel have been used as scouts and trackers, as well as service personnel, in the Caprivi strip. There are, therefore, a few non-white soldiers in the South African armed forces. They are practically all to be found on the lowest levels, although in May 1975 the first officers were commissioned in the Cape Coloured Corps. One member became a captain, and six others lieutenants.

This African participation in the armed forces is a marginal issue. Non-Europeans form an infinitesimal part of the armed forces. They are given the most unattractive tasks (such as acting as trackers in territory where liberation forces are operating), but they do not have arms, nor do they operate in numbers which could in any way represent a risk to the whites.

Of considerably greater significance is the development of counter-insurgency forces within the Bantustans. The Bantustans are intended to serve as labour reserves for the white-controlled South African economy. Since these areas have no prospects for sustaining their own populations, they serve only as locales for the rearing of new labourers and the discarding of exhausted labourers. Naturally, the social tensions in such a system are great. So the governments of the Bantustans—who operate under conditions determined by the South African regime—need counter-insurgency forces to repress their own populations. Nuclei of armed forces have already been established in Bantustans in South Africa and in Namibia. Tribal authorities set up by the South Africans in Ovamboland and Kavango are building up forces which are undergoing counter-insurgency training. It has been reported that some 190 of these took part in the South African invasion of Angola in the autumn of 1975.[18]

It is clear that equipment and training will be provided by South Africa, and that these forces will be an extension of the repressive South African forces. Even so, there is a fear among some South African politicians that independence might go too far. To avoid this, there have been demands that there should be a treaty between South Africa and the homelands, dealing with 'mutual self-defence, right of access, acceptance of responsibilities, and unified command'. For a long time to come, therefore, it must be expected that these tiny low-technology forces will serve the interests of the Republic of South Africa rather than the people of the homelands.

Within the police, a large proportion is non-white. Of the 33,000 members of the regular police, 50 per cent are white, 45 per cent African and 5 per cent Asian. The reserves (20,000) are all white. Control over the police is safely in the hands of the whites. There are 2145 white police officers, 26 African officers and 13 coloured. African policemen were not allowed to carry firearms until 1974 and still carry only small hand-weapons. The heavy infantry weapons, Saracen armoured cars, riot trucks and even aircraft of the police are all in the hands of the whites. An African constable starts at R65 per month, and can earn up to R175. A miner earns R19 on average, and in other areas the average income for Africans is around R50. The difference well explains the attraction that police jobs have, even though African police are used, on the lowest level, to maintain white control over the non-white majority.

POLITICAL CONSEQUENCES OF REPRESSION

It is not difficult to demonstrate the negative political consequences of
the use of the armed forces for repressive purposes in South Africa.
It prevents development towards participatory democracy, and serves
to intensify the perversion of the political system. The reliance on
coercion rather than democratic adaptation, brings to the fore
terrorism, torture, informers and secrecy, and continuously narrows
participation in decision-making.

What are probably the world's most comprehensive repressive
regulations, with the pass system at their core, have been enacted to
limit mobility and to provide wide-ranging control over individuals.
Capital punishment exists as a final sanction; the South African
criminal administration carries out the highest number of executions
in the world. The short-term political effects of this repression are
difficult to foresee. The entire white South African population—four
million people—benefits on a temporary and materialistic level from
the repression of the majority. There is some opposition to apartheid
in certain segments of the white population, but since material
privileges are so overwhelmingly on the side of white South Africans,
we can expect that they will continue to support armed repression,
even if casualties among whites become significantly higher. Nevertheless continued repression will lead to increased dissatisfaction, and
thereby also to further strangulation of democratic participation even
among the whites. This will come about as a consequence of police
actions against white dissidents, increased secrecy, censorship, and
other similar elements in such conflict escalations. The number of
bannings will be increased; the withdrawal of passports will become
more common for whites also, so that dissidents will be allowed only
no-return exits; the infringement of privacy inherent in police surveillance will affect large segments of the white population. How long
the minority can maintain control cannot be foreseen. In the meantime,
however, the policy of repression gradually reduces the possibility of
human self-realisation even for the privileged, white population. Apart
from the material benefits obtained by repressing the non-white
majority, they gain little and lose much: free choice in human contacts,
freedom of dissent, freedom to search for viable alternatives. All these
and other fundamental democratic rights disappear as the 'laager'
psychosis, the self-induced fear of being beleaguered, gains ground.

Humanitarian law in armed conflict, and the effect of repression
Basic human rights apply in armed conflicts, but more specific provisions, called 'Humanitarian law applicable in armed conflict', have
been developed in international law. These are found primarily in the
Geneva Conventions of 1949, and the two Protocols drawn up by the

Diplomatic Conference on Humanitarian Law Applicable in Armed Conflict in Geneva.

There is some difference in regulations concerning international and internal conflicts, but it would appear that the South African situation will be considered as an international, rather than an internal, conflict under the new Protocol I, which extends the Protocol and the Conventions to cover 'armed conflicts in which people are fighting against colonial domination and alien occupation and against racist regimes in the exercise of their right of self-determination, as enshrined in the Charter of the United Nations and the Declaration on "Principles of International Law Concerning Friendly Relations and Co-operation Among States in Accordance with the Charter of the United Nations".'

The basic principles of humanitarian law applicable in armed conflict are that action against combatants is limited only to what is necessary to put the combatant out of action; methods causing unnecessary suffering are prohibited; and—most importantly—civilian populations and individual civilians and civilian installations, are protected from the effects of armed action. Article 51 prohibits attacks against the civilian population and individual civilians, and prohibits actions intended to spread terror among the civilian population. Article 48 prohibits attacks on or destruction of objects indispensable to the survival of the civilian population, namely, foodstuffs and food-producing areas, crops, livestock, drinking water supplies, and irrigation works.

When armed forces are used for repression, this frequently leads to massive violation of such prohibitions. This has been extensively demonstrated in the Southern African conflict. Force has always been directed largely against the civilian population. The killing of livestock played a central role in the early Boer and British conquests of African-held land. At Sharpeville and Soweto, armed action was directed against non-armed, demonstrating civilians.

External links

From the very beginning, arms transfers to South Africa from Western countries served to establish and to maintain white dominance inside that country. The development of a labour-repressive system provided access to enormous natural resources—today it also helps to secure high profits for Western investment.

Arms transfers and technical co-operation from abroad have also enabled South Africa to develop a military capacity which has become a resource for the West in maintaining its historic dominance over the third world.[19] In the first half of this century, South African military resources were used by Britain in its conflicts with other imperial contenders. During the last decades, South Africa has in an informal way been made a military resource for the integrated Western military structure. The usefulness of South Africa has been severely questioned, however, in the wake of the withdrawal from Zimbabwe (Rhodesia) and the débàcle in Angola. That débàcle, which was more political than military, has shown the increasing political effect of the isolation of South Africa following the liberation of the former Portuguese colonies, and the inherent risks in co-ordinating military strategies with South Africa. This was one reason for the success of the Security Council Resolution 418 of November 1977 which

1. Determines, having regard to the policies and acts of the South African government, that the acquisition by South Africa of arms and related materiel constitutes a threat to the maintenance of international peace and security;
2. Decides that all states shall cease forthwith any provision to South Africa of arms and related materiel of all types, including the sale or transfer of weapons and ammunition, military vehicles and equipment, paramilitary police equipment, and spare parts for the aforementioned, and shall cease as well the provision of all types of equipment and supplies, and grants of licensing arrangements for the manufacture or maintenance of the aforementioned;
3. Calls on all states to review, having regard to the objectives of this resolution, all existing contractual arrangements with and licences granted to South Africa relating to the manufacture and maintenance of arms, ammunition of all types and military equipment and vehicles, with a view to terminating them;
4. Further decides that all states shall refrain from any co-operation with South Africa in the manufacture and development of nuclear weapons.

Over the last decades the South African military build-up has come to meet important economic and technological needs in other countries. The rapid increases in military procurement after Sharpeville opened up an important market for one of the most aggressive competitors in the international arms trade, namely France. The new South African market made it possible for France to undertake high-technology arms production. West Germany also benefits from South African military purchases. Its tradition of military trading was limited after the Second World War, but, partly through co-operation with France in producing weapons, and partly through direct technological co-operation with South Africa, it has been possible to circumvent these limitations.

These links help South Africa to expand its military capacity so that it can maintain the established repressive system, which allows a small minority to exploit the rich natural resources of the country and to use the black majority as a reservoir of cheap labour for extracting and processing those resources. A part of the profits obtained through this exploitation is then used to cover the expenses of armament procurement needed to continue the repression.

THE HISTORICAL CONTEXT

From the time of the Napoleonic wars until 1964, Britain was the main external link in the growth of the South African military forces. For Britain, as we have seen, South Africa was of military interest not only to maintain 'internal security' and thereby to safeguard investments, but also as a resource for participation in wars outside South Africa. South Africa took part in the First World War with some 10,000 officers and men. One of their main achievements was the war against Germany in South west Africa. German colonial rule was replaced by South African occupation, tolerated by the League of Nations which called it a mandate. South Africa has since maintained control to allow Western enterprises cheap access to the rich resources of what is now Namibia. Its illegal occupation is facilitated by arms supplies from the same countries which invest in Namibia under generous South African conditions.

During the First World War, South African forces also helped the British maintain their empire in East Africa, and they fought in France. Equipment for these actions was provided by the British. South Africans were actively involved in the formation of the Royal Air Force (General Smuts, a member of the British War Cabinet during the First World War, is frequently and with some justification described as 'the father of the RAF') and altogether 28 officers and 265 men from South Africa were enrolled in the joint air force, which was operative only in Europe. In 1920, the South African Air Force was established and received a gift of 100 aircraft (DH9, DH4, SE5, and Avro) from the United Kingdom as a token of gratitude for participation in 'imperial defence' during the First World War.

At the Imperial Defence conferences in 1923 and 1926, it was resolved that Commonwealth defence should be based on co-operation in the Joint Committee of Imperial Defence, similar systems of organisation and, so far as possible, similar equipment. Special attention was to be given to the 'air arm'. Each government was to take care of land defence for itself, and great emphasis was placed on the maintenance of harbours which formed 'vital links in the chain of imperial defence of maritime communications'. Out of this came the co-operation regarding Simonstown, as well as South Africa's almost exclusive reliance on British weapons (although it did import some aircraft from Germany). As a result of the Imperial Defence conference in 1926, it was decided that the SAAF should co-operate with the RAF in carrying out periodic flights on the Cape–Cairo air route. The object was to keep the route open and to maintain the mobility of the British and South African air forces. This co-operation played an important role during the Second World War and was carried on into the 1950s.

One reason for South Africa's willingness to accept this role in

British imperial defence was its total dependence on the British navy for external defence. The Simonstown agreement in fact dates back to the establishment of the Union. In 1921, the Imperial War Office of Great Britain undertook to transfer all its lands and buildings in South Africa to the Union Government, except for retaining the 'right of perpetual user' for the British Admiralty over land situated at the naval base of Simonstown. At the same time, the Union government undertook responsibility 'for the Cape Peninsula Land defences, including those of the naval dockyard at Simonstown', and would keep Simonstown 'in the necessary state of defence for Imperial purposes' so that 'it will at all times be able to discharge its functions as a naval link in the communications of the British Empire'.[20] South African naval forces were almost non-existent up to the time of the second Simonstown agreement in 1955.

The ground force of South Africa; dominated by the Boers and based to a large extent on the commando tradition, remained simple and low in technology until the Second World War. The white nationalists, whose political power increased during the inter-war years, saw no threat from the outside. Their main concern was to suppress the African population, for which the commando system maintained by the 1912 Defence Act was fully adequate. It became a major issue whether there was a duty to serve beyond South Africa, which was the geographical limit laid down by the Defence Act. Therefore, in the inter-war period, only small changes took place in the military forces.

The Minister of Defence during the last six years before the Second World War, Oswald Pirow, was not in favour of military co-operation with Britain. He was more inclined to lean in the direction of Hitler's Germany, but neutrality was the most that was politically possible. He considered the main role of the forces to be suppression of African rebellions, and for this purpose he believed in a 'bush-cart' conception of counter-insurgency warfare—a non-technological army moving lightly through the bush and living off the country. This was the old commando tradition of the Boers.

The Second World War brought about an acceleration in the mechanisation of the armed forces. There was again a conflict over whether to join Britain in the 'imperial defence' role, but General Smuts, once again Prime Minister, managed to isolate those Afrikaner nationalists who wanted either neutrality or co-operation with Hitler. In time South African participation in the war, although based solely on volunteers, became substantial. The air force was greatly strengthened, with deliveries of bombers and other aircraft, mainly from the United States; this laid the groundwork for future procurement from the US. Initially the South Africans fought with infantry and the air force in Africa. With the retreat of Rommel in 1942, South African forces went into hibernation for a period of substantial mechanisation.

Two South African divisions were converted to 'armour' and were provided with 400 tanks by the United Kingdom. These were used when South African forces participated in the invasion of Italy in 1943.[21]

The war also led to the development of domestic arms production, practically non-existent before that time. At the end of the war South Africa was able to produce its own anti-tank weapons, small arms ammunition, mortar bombs, grenades, howitzers and gun carriages, in addition to lorries and troop carriers. Thus, by the end of the Second World War, South Africa had reached an impressive level of military technology. For heavy arms and more sophisticated equipment it was dependent on Britain, but it was becoming self-sufficient in ammunition and small arms as well as many vehicles.[22]

SOUTH AFRICA A WESTERN ALLY IN THE EARLY COLD WAR?

In the first decade after the Second World War, British military relations with South Africa were heavily influenced by the emerging Western military integration during the formative stage of the Cold War. South Africa had been an important military resource during the war, and was expected to be so not only for the United Kingdom, but for the West as a whole. For the UK it was primarily a question of assistance in maintaining the rest of the empire, in particular the African colonies, preventing radical movements from obtaining control over the decolonisation process. For this purpose, South African air and land forces were considered as potential resources in conflicts in colonial Africa, and also in the Middle East. Additionally, South African naval bases were deemed essential for the defence of the West.

For both these reasons, efforts were made to integrate South Africa formally into Western alliances. Conferences exploring these possibilities were held in London in 1950 (between South Africa, the UK, Australia, and New Zealand), in Nairobi in 1951, and in Dakar in 1954 (on Pan-African 'defence', attended by Belgium, France, Italy, Portugal, Ethiopia, South Rhodesia, the UK, and South Africa, with the US as an Observer). The apartheid policy was already meeting such resistance internationally that these efforts at formally including South Africa in the Western military network had to be discontinued.[23]

Nonetheless, the process of expanding South Africa's value as a military resource for the West continued. Two destroyers and two seaward defence vessels were delivered by Britain between 1950 and 1955, and then came the Simonstown agreement in June 1955. In the memorandum accompanying this agreement, South Africa and the United Kingdom agreed to 'jointly sponsor a conference to integrate, forward and develop the planning already begun at the Nairobi

Conference' and 'to jointly endeavour, at this conference, to secure the setting up of a suitable machinery to pursue the aims of the conference on a continuous basis'.[24] The Nairobi conference of 1951, where no concrete and specific agreements had been obtained, had focused on co-operation in ground control over British Africa, with South African and Rhodesian participation. The intention was clearly to develop some form of a multilateral alliance to secure military control over Africa, with South Africa and Britain as the main partners. In 1955, the only specific agreements concerned two points: military control of the sea routes around Southern Africa, and the transfer to South Africa of the Simonstown base, which had previously belonged to Britain. The agreement declared that the two governments' intention was to ensure the safety, by the joint operations of their respective maritime forces, of the sea routes round Southern Africa. They further provided for the purchase by South Africa of six anti-submarine frigates, ten coastal minesweepers, and four seaward defence boats. This programme was to be completed by 1963. The agreement also expressed British willingness to hand over the administration and control of the Simonstown naval base to the South African government. The naval base would remain available to the Royal Navy and its allied navies 'in any war in which the United Kingdom is involved'. The agreement provided for the development by the South African government of additional facilities and the maintenance of Simonstown at least at the existing level of efficiency.

The Simonstown agreement stimulated South Africa to expand its military apparatus by developing a naval force to complement its ground and air forces—a policy of decentralisation pursued by the imperial power of a shrinking empire—and also stimulated it to develop a co-operation which could at some time be formalised into a regional military alliance. At the time of Simonstown it was expected that such an alliance would soon be forthcoming, but it did not materialise. In 1956, the Suez war severely weakened British standing in the third world, and in 1957 Ghana became the first of the British colonies to gain independence. A regional military alliance with South Africa as a partner, clearly aimed at opposing 'subversion'—which could mean national liberation—was politically impossible. But the naval vessels referred to in the Simonstown agreement were delivered, as were a number of aircraft mainly intended for naval action and thus related to the Simonstown agreement. These deliveries represented a substantial expansion of the South African air force.

POLITICAL OUTCAST, BUT TECHNOLOGICAL AND ECONOMIC PARTNER

The inclusion of newly independent Asian and African states in the Commonwealth strongly influenced British policies towards South

Africa. Commonwealth countries, alerted by the Sharpeville massacre in 1960, demanded an end to military ties with South Africa. The same demands were formulated by the UN in embargo resolutions, but there is no doubt that Commonwealth policies together with British public opinion had a greater impact on British policy.

When the Labour government took power in 1964, it declared its intention to abide by the Security Council embargo resolutions of 1962 and 1963, although allowing for completion of previously established contracts, and leaving several loopholes. These included continued deliveries of British-designed equipment produced either in South Africa or in a third country (the Rolls-Royce Bristol Viper engine for the Impala jet trainer), continuing deliveries of spare parts, and direct transfer of components essential to weapons systems, such as radar and other electronics.[25]

The Conservative Party was less influenced by Commonwealth demands and by anti-apartheid sentiments within Britain. When it came into power in 1970, it announced that it would re-open armament transfers. Very strong international opposition ensued, and only six Westland Wasp helicopters were delivered.[26] With the Labour Party's return to power in 1973, the embargo was again more strictly applied, despite numerous loopholes concerning components and electronic equipment.

But just as Britain was disengaging from South Africa, the process it had started—internationalising South Africa's military access—was taking effect. France soon stepped in to replace Britain. The more established arms suppliers felt obliged to abide—at least to some extent— by the embargos against Portugal and South Africa, but France felt no such need. Its military production and provision quickly expanded, apparently with no ethical considerations at all. Certainly it has been far and away the greatest violator of the embargo against South Africa, providing the most potent repressive armaments, such as helicopters and armoured cars.

A substantial part of the air force's strike capacity is equipped with French aircraft, and France has also led in supplying missiles. Most of the missiles of the South African armed forces are French, including AS20 and AS30 air-to-surface missiles, Matra R530 air-to-air missiles, and the joint French–German designed Milan anti-tank missiles. There is also a ground-to-air missile system developed in France with South African co-operation, known as Crotale in France and Cactus in South Africa. In the field of armoured vehicles, it is of interest to note that South Africa has not produced battle tanks, although its forces used such tanks during the Second World War and received further deliveries from Britain during the 1950s. Since then, procurement has been exclusively of light armoured vehicles, which are much more useful against technologically weak liberation movements. France has sold some of these to South Africa, and many more—perhaps as many as 800—Panhard AML60 and 90 have been produced under licence in South Africa. The naval forces have been supplied primarily, by Britain, but France is also encroaching here, and has delivered three Daphne submarines.[27]

Rolls-Royce Viper II turbojet engines produced in Italy under licence from Rolls-Royce, are used in Impala aircraft which are produced in South Africa under licence from Italy. The United Kingdom has not, even under the Labour government, been willing to prevent transfer of these engines to South Africa.

The Federal Republic of Germany has become one of South Africa's main partners in trade and other economic relations. It has also played an important role in arms transfer, by delivering components. German involvement in multilateral armament production has meant that German-produced components are found in several weapons sold by other countries to South Africa. For example the Transall transport aircraft delivered by France in 1969–70 were jointly produced with West Germany, and the Tyne engine used for this aircraft is produced co-operatively by German and French firms under licence from Rolls-Royce. The Milan missile delivered by France also contains components produced in Germany. The Mirage F-1 includes components produced by a firm registered in Belgium which belongs to the French Dassault and the German VFW-Fokker. This firm also provides components for the Puma helicopter, another French delivery to South Africa.

DOMESTIC ARMS PRODUCTION

Since South Africa has been unable to obtain the quantities of military equipment which it desires from foreign sources, it has developed a large-scale domestic arms programme. Today, it claims to be self-reliant in smaller and medium weapons and in ammunition, and it manufactures napalm bombs, aerial bombs, tear gas bombs, and the like. In the field of major weapons, the planning of Mirage F-1 production in South Africa from 1977 represents the peak of its domestic arms production efforts so far. South Africa also produces its own armoured cars. After initial deliveries by France, the Panhard AML-245 armoured car was redesigned to South African specification and is now produced in South Africa under the name of Eland. Increasingly, South Africa produces its own electronics, having obtained technical assistance and expertise from foreign firms, especially in the development of the navy's underground computer-control communications and operational centre at Silvermine, near Cape Town.

The development of productive capability for conventional weapons has usually started with the transfer of major weapons, followed by local assembly of weapons imported in parts, then local production of some of the parts and imports of others, and finally domestic production of the complete weapon under licence. The South African aerospace industry developed in this way. The Atlas Aircraft Factories were established in 1965 with advisory help from the French Sud-Aviation and with licences from Italy to produce the Aermacchi MB326M, a light attack plane called Impala in South Africa. British and Italian technicians and workers took part in early South African aircraft production. Since then the South African aerospace industry has become more sophisticated; it is now involved in licensed production of the French Mirage F-1. The capacity to produce armoured vehicles developed in a similar way, with France providing the licence for the Panhard armoured car, and South Africa adapting specifications. In the field of rockets and missiles, the Federal Republic of Germany established a rocket research centre in Tsumeb, Namibia, in 1963.

Even in the field of nuclear weapons, South Africa seems to have reached, or almost reached, the stage when it can produce its own bombs. On 6 August 1977, the Soviet Union informed the United States that South Africa was planning to carry out a test of a nuclear device in the Kalahari desert. This was corroborated by information collected by the US, and considerable international diplomatic activity ensued. It is still uncertain whether South Africa was in fact preparing to carry out such a test, but it became clear that South Africa now has the capacity to produce nuclear weapons.

Although South Africa has long had nuclear reactors, its recent acquisition of nuclear technology has been predominantly from West Germany and France, who have been the most active on the international nuclear market. Their concern is more commercial than strategic, and their desire to obtain a larger share of the international market has made them more aggressive and more willing to enter 'grey markets'—markets which are prohibited by embargo or which are in the twilight zone of endeavours to prevent proliferation of nuclear weapons. West Germany, which faces external and internal constraints on the transfer of weapons and which is also constrained in the field of nuclear weapons because of the adverse effects it would have on the relationship towards the Soviet Union, has been particularly eager to develop commercial export of nuclear technology.[28]

South Africa's military role: the 1970s and beyond
It has been noted that several attempts have been made to bring South Africa more centrally into Western military strategy. This has been encouraged by South Africa and by some political circles in the West. South Africa's potential role would be partly as a military resource to protect external economic interests in and around South Africa, and partly as a partner in the containment of Soviet and Chinese influence and expansion.

The two roles cannot be fully separated, nor can they be separated from the strategic interests of the South African white minority regime in controlling the surrounding African states and protecting its economic system from a blockade. Since co-operation with South Africa is morally and politically condemned, Western efforts to develop this co-operation have been full of setbacks and clouded in much secrecy. Nevertheless, the economic and technological attractions have been too great for some countries. According to South African government spokesmen, South African intervention in Angola was carried out with the full approval of several Western powers.[29] It is not surprising that these powers abstained from voting when the Security Council condemned this intervention on 31 March 1976.

Beyond encouraging the maintenance of the existing economic system in South Africa and Namibia, which allows for a cheap extraction of natural resources, and acquiescing in the policing by South Africa of the surrounding states, there is also a third level on which some political and military circles in the West would like to co-operate with South Africa: the naval arms race. Here, South African communications and naval bases are important assets.

In 1972, the Military Committee of the North Atlantic Assembly appointed a subcommittee to examine 'the Soviet maritime threat'. Patrick Wall, member of the British Parliament, presented as rapporteur a working paper in June 1972, and a final report of the subcommittee was presented to the North Atlantic Assembly in Bonn in November 1972. This committee asked for NATO defence planning and surveillance outside the NATO boundaries, for communications links from outside the region to IBERLANT (Iberian Atlantic Command) and SACLANT, (Supreme Allied Commander Atlantic region), and a permanent Western Presence in the Indian Ocean. A recommendation passed by the North Atlantic Assembly asked the North Atlantic Council to give SACLANT authority to plan for the protection of European shipping lines in the southern oceans. Since then, it has been ascertained that SACLANT has carried out contingency planning for military operations in the southern oceans, outside the established NATO boundaries.

In the development of the Silvermine communications centre near Simonstown, equipment has been provided by the US, Britain, West Germany, France, the Netherlands, and Denmark. The Advocaat communications system, consisting of computers, radar scanners, and communications equipment, collects and distributes information about naval and air movements in an area stretching from the South Pole to North Africa and from Latin America to Bangladesh. This information is provided by South Africa to the British Defence Ministry and to the US naval base in San Juan, Puerto Rico.

Through the West German firm AEG-Telefunken, which had large contracts to equip Silvermine, South Africa was provided with the NATO coding system for defence equipment. There is no reason to believe that NATO officials were involved in this, but it illustrates how co-operation between South Africa and one NATO state can provide access to the resources of the whole NATO system. That development would have been much more difficult if there was a firm NATO policy that individual NATO members should *not* co-operate in military affairs with South Africa. No such policy exists today; on the contrary, some prominent NATO officials are openly in favour of co-operation with South Africa.

The Chairman of NATO's military committee, the British Admiral Sir Peter Hill-Norton, in November 1975 suggested that the three or four NATO members with 'blue water' navies, including Britain, could combine in a group outside the alliance's framework to monitor what was going on in the Indian Ocean, where the Soviet naval presence in his opinion represented a serious threat to the West's lines of communication. In this way a NATO 'area of interest' could be established in addition to Europe. Implicit in his proposal was that an informal way should be found to extend NATO's concern and 'umbrella' to South Africa.

It is becoming clear, however, that in the future neither the West, nor the Soviet Union or others will be able unilaterally to police the so-called Cape route and the Indian ocean. Efforts by the West to restore and maintain its hegemony through military co-operation with colonial or racialist regimes have already proved to be counter-productive, and have led to increased, rather than decreased, Soviet influence. This will continue to be the case until the West foregoes the attempt to maintain an archaic international economic order through acquiescence and coercion. It will have to recognise and hopefully assist in the elimination of racial dominance and economic inequality. Increasingly, the fact that military methods cannot reverse political trends in Southern Africa has come to be recognised in the West. The necessity for change is a fundamental assumption underlying the policy of the new Carter Administration and the recent action in the United Nations.

NOTES

1. Further details about the South African military are available in Stockholm International Peace Research Institute (SIPRI), *Southern Africa: The Escalation of a Conflict* (Stockholm, 1976); J. E. Spence, *The Strategic Significance of Southern Africa* (London, 1970); J. E. Spence, *The Political and Military Framework*, Foreign Investment Study Project Paper no. 4 (London, 1975); Abdul Minty, *South Africa's Defence Strategy* (London, 1969); Abdul Minty, *Apartheid, A Threat to Peace* (London, 1976).

2. G. Tylden, *A Short Account of the Armed Forces of South Africa* (Johannesburg, 1954). This section is based to a large extent on Tylden's work.
3. Tylden, p. 4.
4. R. A. Moyer, 'The Mfengu Self-Defence and the Cape Frontier Wars', in C. Saunders and R. Derricourt (eds.), *Beyond the Cape Frontier* (London, 1974) pp. 101–26.
5. This is discussed more fully in D. Derbon, 'Participation in the "Boer War": People's War, People's Non-War, or Non-People's War?' in Bethwell A. Ogot (ed.), *War and Society in Africa* (London, 1972).
6. Duncan Hall, *Commonwealth: A History of the British Commonwealth of Nations* (London, 1971).
7. *House of Assembly Debates,* South Africa (1912) p. 619.
8. *House of Assembly Debates* (1912) p. 619.
9. Information on the Boer rebellion is based on John Fisher, *The Afrikaners* (London, 1969); Brian Bunting, *The Rise of the South African Reich,* rev. ed. (London, 1969); and M. Wilson and L. Johnson, *The Oxford History of South Africa* (London, 1971).
10. H. J. Simons and R. E. Simons, *Class and Colour in South Africa 1850–1950* (London, 1969).
11. An account of the killing of the Bondelzwarts is found in Peter Fraenkel, *The Namibians of South West Africa,* Minority Rights Group report no. 19 (London, 1974).
12. *Assembly Debates* (1949), col.5766.
13. *Assembly Debates* (1960) cols. 5752–60.
14. Ibid., p. 6401.
15. Ibid., p. 6402.
16. *White Paper on Defence and Armament Production* (1973) para. 8.
17. Tylden, op. cit., p. 29.
18. *Focus* (Mar 1976) p. 12.
19. Detailed information on the transfer of weapons to South Africa can be found in SIPRI, Arms Trade Registers: *The Arms Trade With the Third World* (London and Stockholm, 1974).
20. The various Simonstown agreements are discussed in G. G. Lawrie, 'The Simonstown Agreement: South Africa, Britain and the United Nations', *South African Law Journal,* LXXXV, pt. 2 (1968) pp. 142–77.
21. The participation of South African forces in the Second World War has been described in Wilson and Johnson, Bunting, and Fisher, op. cit.
22. See E. F. Lauppe, 'Rüstungswirtschaftliche Beziehungen der Bundesrepublik Deutschland zum Südlichen Afrika', Unpublished MS.
23. See Spence, op. cit. (1970 and 1975).
24. The Anglo–South African Correspondence of 1955, of which the Simonstown Agreement is the core, consists of several parts. The first is a Memorandum on the Need for International Discussions with Regard to Regional Defence, and the quotations above are from paragraphs 7 and 10 of that memorandum respectively. The document is found in (1956) 248 United Nations Treaty Series, No. 3945, and is discussed in detail by G. G. Lawrie in his article referred to in note 20 above.
25. Further information is found in Minty, op. cit. (1969), Spence op. cit. (1975), and SIPRI, op. cit. (1976).

26. M. Lipton, 'British Arms for South Africa', *The World Today* (Oct 1970) pp. 427–34.
27. For further information see SIPRI, op. cit. (1974, 1976).
28. For detailed information on the nuclear connection, see African National Congress (South Africa), *The Nuclear Conspiracy: FRG collaborates to strengthen apartheid* (Bonn, 1975).
29. See, for example, *The Star Weekly* (South Africa, 10 Apr 1976), where the South African ambassador to the US, Mr Botha, referred openly to the fact that the US stood beside South African in Angola.

8 The Economic Consequences of the Transfer of Military-oriented Technology

Peter Lock and Herbert Wulf

Historically, the militarisation of the third world has intensified during periods of capitalist crisis. In the First World War the colonised people of Africa and Asia were actively integrated into the British and French armies in Europe. In India, the incipient industrial base was expanded in order to support British war production, and raw materials and food were shipped to Europe to back up the war economy. More than a hundred thousand soldiers from African and Asian colonies, particularly soldiers from India, lost their lives in combat.[1]

After the First World War the politically independent countries of Latin America, China, Turkey (formerly the Osman Empire), and a small number of other states were drawn into the political and economic competition between the industrial powers of Europe, and to a lesser extent the United States and Japan.[2] One element in this competition was the provision of military missions for training, and the supply of arms and military equipment. At the same time, governments in the third world were becoming much more interventionist because their economies were forced to adapt to the slump in international trade. For these reasons the role of the military in political and economic affairs became more important. Even under colonial rule, the officer corps of the Indian Army were able to introduce an 'Indianisation' programme.

During the Second World War the colonies were again integrated into Allied war production. With US military assistance, arms production facilities and maintenance workshops were set up in India and other areas of British influence.[3] These later became the basis for all national arms production programmes in newly independent states. Territories occupied by the Japanese were also used for war production; just as the Allies built aircraft in India, so the Japanese produced aircraft in Manchuria and Korea.[4] The Latin American nations also initiated arms production during the war; a virtual embargo on industrial equipment (except for Brazil, after it sent an expeditionary corps to Italy), forced them to begin seeking self-reliant sources of supply for the armed forces.

210

These production capabilities were not converted for the purpose of industrialisation and development after the war; instead the colonial powers sought to revert as quickly as possible to the pre-war industrial situation in order to preserve the existing political and economic system. In India the dismantling of existing facilities was resisted, and some of these which were retained later became the base for the Indian arms industry. Argentina, in another strategy to resist the closure of facilities, initiated a vigorous attempt under Perón to industrialise the country within the context of a capitalist late-comer strategy of national development, with heavy emphasis on military technology and national arms production. This strategy was strongly opposed by the United States and failed.

In the post-war period, the United States provided millions of dollars worth of military 'aid' to the independent states of Latin America and Asia. Elsewhere, after the ending of colonial rule, the relative position of the military within the local political systems was strengthened. When, in the late 1950s political stability and alliance with the Western world were challenged in consequence of continued economic crisis and increased inequalities, liberation movements and rural guerrillas began to grow in importance and military doctrine became increasingly concerned with pre-emptive control of social conflicts. At the same time, new concepts of development were proposed, which assigned a key role to the military, if only temporarily. Especially in the United States, it was argued that the military were the most important modern, rational, and bureaucratically organised institution in traditional underdeveloped societies and were thus particularly well suited to speed up the development process and guide the political system accordingly.

The process of military encroachment into the political system in developing countries had as its corollary a huge influx of advanced military technology to the third world. When the United Nations declared the 1970s as second development decade, an unprecedented flow of modern arms was pouring into a large number of developing countries. Military aid from the United States was cut drastically, so that countries which wanted weapons had to purchase them. Worldwide shipments of sophisticated weapons increased and reached the value of $20,000 million in 1975.

Yet the transfer of arms, military advisors, and equipment to manufacture arms has been largely neglected in discussions about the transfer of technology; neither UNCTAD nor the renowned Club of Rome have dealt adequately with military transfers as an aspect of technological dependence. This chapter represents a first attempt to rectify this weakness. It puts forward the hypothesis that, in fact, military-oriented transfers of technology are of critical importance in structuring the whole system of technology transfer and, hence, the pattern of technological development in third-world countries.

The World Military Order

TABLE 8.1 *Imports of goods and imports of arms of the major third-world arms importers*

Country	Year	1 Total imports Cif in million US$	2 Imports of SITC no. 7‡ in million US$	3 Military imports in million US$	4 Military imports as % of total imports	5 Military imports as % of SITC no. 7
Egypt (UAR)*	1965	933	218	92	9.9	42.4
	1968	666	162	156	23.4	96.3
	1969	638	153	160	25.1	104.6
	1974	2949	565	583	19.8	103.2
India	1968	2507	704	168	6.7	23.9
	1970	2097	490	100	4.3	20.4
	1972	2230	604	205	9.2	33.9
	1973	3146	754	180	5.7	23.9
Iran	1964	669	221	26	3.9	11.8
	1968†	1407	580	135	9.6	23.3
	1972†	2593	1111	415	16.0	37.4
	1974†	6544	2072	870	13.3	42.0
Israel	1965	835	232	46	5.5	19.8
	1968	1089	278	55	5.1	19.8
	1970	1451	442	232	16.0	52.5
	1974	4237	1025	636	15.0	62.0
South Korea (Republic of)	1965	450	60	104	23.1	173.3
	1968	1468	533	323*	22.0	60.6
	1972	2522	762	510	20.2	66.9
	1974	6844	1849	114	1.7	6.2
Saudi Arabia	1968	562	189	79	14.1	41.8
	1971	806	248	19	2.4	47.7
	1974	3473	n.a.	393	11.3	
Turkey	1965	572	214	83	14.5	38.7
	1969	747	301	241	32.3	80.1
	1972	1508	677	327	21.7	48.3
	1973	2099	864	205	9.8	23.7
Vietnam N.	1963	n.a.	n.a.	365		
	1969	n.a.	n.a.	315		
	1974	n.a.	n.a.	400		
Vietnam S.	1965	357	70	243	68.1	347.1
	1968	466	130	726	155.8	558.5
	1970	325	76	917	282.2	1206.6
	1973	618	n.a.	665	107.6	

Sources United Nations, *Commodity Trade Statistics*, Statistical Papers, Series D; US Arms Control and Disarmament Agency, *World Military Expenditure and Arms Transfers, 1964–1973* (Washington D.C., 1974);UNCTAD, *Handbook of International Trade and Development Statistics* (New York, 1976).

Notes * Figures in Column 1 and 2 represent the imports of the former United Arab Republic. Military Imports in Column 3 are the combined figures for Egypt and Syria.
† Figures in Column 1 and 2 for financial year (March till March).
‡ SITC no. 7 = Machinery, Transport Equipment.

Absorption of import capacities

The capacity of developing countries to import what is needed for development and industrialisation is often drastically reduced by the import of military technologies.

On a global scale armaments constitute less than two per cent of commodities entering the world market. The recorded volume of arms transfers, however, represents but a fraction of imports for military use. Table 8.1 illustrates how the import statistics of developing countries, which do not report on arms, conceal military imports; in some cases the proportion of military imports reaches one third of total imports (Turkey in 1969) or one fourth (Korea in 1965, Egypt in 1969).

A more appropriate parameter for the measurement of the arms import burden would be the volume of those commodities essential for large-scale industrialisation as represented in the category no. 7 (machinery and transport equipment) of the Standard International Trade Classification. These imported capital goods can be taken as an index for the proportion of imported technology in total imports.[5] In many cases a substantial portion of imported technology is directly related to military activities,[6] as can be seen in column 5 of Table 8.1. In all of the major recipient countries the proportion of arms imports exceeds, at least for one year during the period observed, one third and often one half of foreign technology imports. Since armaments cannot contribute to the expansion of productive capacity, these figures are highly significant for development strategies.[7] A case in point is Iran which, in spite of considerable revenue from oil exports, could not balance its external account in 1976. The balance of payments deficit is, of course, related to huge deliveries of weaponry especially from the US,[8] but it also reflects the need to increase food imports and the consequence of sub-optimal allocation of resources in which priority has been given to military objectives.

The figures in Table 8.1 should be read with caution, since regular international statistics do not always account for armaments, and weapons could be included as transport equipment and the like. Furthermore the available sources on arms transfer differ substantially from each other, or cover only certain sectors of the arms trade.[9] The data collected for South Vietnam from 1965 to 1970 most clearly reveals the limitations of available sources. The volume of arms imports by South Vietnam, as recorded by the US Arms Control and Disarmament Agency, exceeds by a considerable margin the total commodity imports for this period, as reported by the South Vietnamese government to the United Nations. Despite these caveats the figures can be used to indicate the magnitudes involved.

As soon as a technologically advanced weapon system has been purchased for the armed services, a chain of supplementary import demands is induced. To remain operational, modern fighter aircraft, tanks, or naval units require an extensive network of support facilities such as a logistical system for the provision of spare parts. For an extended period foreign specialists are required and adequate residential areas must be provided for them. The chain of demands, generally with a high import content, seems endless. Precise data is not available of course, but a few examples can convey a general impression of the ramifications of arms imports. According to American estimates, it takes an inventory of 70,000 spare parts to keep a squadron of F-4 Phantoms operational under wartime conditions.[10] The Rand Corporation calculated the life cycle of the present generation of fighter aircraft as 15 years, and concluded that the acquisition price, which already includes a large number of spare parts, represents less than 50 per cent of the life cycle costs.[11] The introduction of jet-fighter aircraft in developing countries requires the construction of additional airports, the extension of existing runways and the installation of navigational and control systems; it also leads to the adoption of a costly air defence system, since the inventory of aircraft has to be protected while still on the ground. In other cases it is virtually impossible to distinguish between 'civil' and 'military' technology; for example imported 'civil' equipment such as computers and teleprinters have been crucial in making the South African military communications headquarters operational. From the limited evidence available it is clear that the militarily induced chain of supplementary imports primarily involves advanced, capital-intensive technologies.

Given the volume and the political priority of military activities in many developing countries, the complexity and expense of these imported commodities cannot but have profound repercussions on the general pattern of industrialisation. Unfortunately, it is statistically impossible to break down the debt services of developing countries into 'civil' and 'military' components. After the United States reduced the Military Assistance Programs,[12] the terms of the international arms trade have come closer to average commercial conditions and it seems reasonable to suppose that military imports fully absorb import capacity and increase the debt burden accordingly.[13] But military imports do not only absorb the import capacity at the time the transfer takes place; they constitute a claim on future and potential import capacity, since they do not contribute to the expansion of productive capacity and have high opportunity costs. Furthermore large proportions of future import bills must be prematurely allocated to keep the military imports operational, since the equipment cannot be serviced from the limited industrial base of a developing country without large imports of hardware as well as software.

Domestic arms production and industrial patterns

A survey of arms production carried out in 1976 reveals that 46 developing countries are engaged in domestic arms production or preparing to manufacture arms.[14] This figure includes five less industrial European countries and eight countries in Latin America, twelve in Africa, five in the Near and Middle East, and sixteen in Asia. The level

TABLE 8.2

	Fighter aircraft, jet trainers, engines	Light aircraft	Helicopters	Missiles, rockets	Large warships	Medium warships (up to 300 tons)	Small warships and others (below 100 tons)	Submarines	Tanks and armoured personnel carriers	Small arms and ammunition	Electronics and avionics
	1	2	3	4	5	6	7	8	9	10	11
Europe											
Greece	1								1[b]	1	1[a]
Spain	1	1			1	1	n	1	1	i 1	n
Portugal		1				n	1			1	
Turkey	1[a]	1[a]			1	1	i	n	1[a]	1	
Yugoslavia	i 1		i 1	1	1	1	n	n	n	n	1
Latin America											
Argentina	i	1		1	1	1	1	1		i 1	i 1
Brazil	i 1	i 1	1	i 1	1	i 1	i	n	i 1	i 1	n 1
Chile						n					
Columbia		1				n	1				
Dominican Republic						n				i 1	
Mexico	1[a]	1				n	1			1	
Peru	1[a]				1	i				1[a]	
Venezuela	n[b]								1	n	
Africa											
Algeria										n	
Congo										n	
Gabon						n	n				
Ghana										1	
Guinea										1	
Ivory Coast							n				
Malagasy Republic						1					
Nigeria	1[a]									1	
South Africa	1	1	1	1	1	1	n	n	1	1	n[a]
Sudan										1	
Zaire									?		
Morocco										1	
Near/Middle East											
Egypt	1		1	1		n			1	1	
Iran	1[b]		1	1[a]	1[a]	n				1	1
Israel	i 1[a]	i		i	1		1	i 1	i 1	i	i 1
Saudi Arabia										1	
Yemen (Aden)							?				
Asia											
Bangladesh							n				
Burma						n	1			1	
Hong Kong						n	n				
India	i 1		i 1	1	1	1	1	i	1	i 1	i 1
Indonesia	1	1	1			n				1	
Korea (North)	1[a]					n	n	n		1	
Korea (south)	1[a]		1[a]			n	n			n	1
Malaysia							1			1	
Nepal										n	
Pakistan	1[a]	i	1[a]	1	1		n			1	1
Philippines		1	1[a]	n			1			1	
Singapore						1	1			1	n
Sri Lanka										1	
Taiwan	1	1	1	n	n 1[b]		n			1	n
Thailand						n	1			n	
Vietnam		1								n	

i = indigenous design; 1 = licensed production and technical assistance; n = not known whether i or 1; a = planned; b = only refitting, repair etc.

Source P. Lock and H. Wulf, *Register of Arms Production in Developing Countries*, mimeo (Hamburg, Mar 1977).

of domestic arms production so far attained in these countries differs widely. Most produce only small arms or ammunition in relatively small quantities, or specialise in the construction of small naval craft. In some of the countries, however, domestic arms production is considerably advanced and diversified, and may even include production for export. These countries include Argentina, Brazil, India, Israel, South Africa, Spain, and possibly Taiwan, and Yugoslavia; Egypt, Iran, Pakistan, and Turkey are about to expand their domestic arms industries.

Of the 46 developing countries included in Table 8.2, 36 are involved in small arms production of some kind, although only a few of these have actually achieved self-sufficiency in the supply of light infantry weapons. Modern fighter aircraft, jet trainers, or aircraft engines are produced in twelve developing countries, generally under licence, and light aircraft are manufactured in fourteen of the countries. Helicopters are produced or assembled in eight of the countries, missiles and rockets in eleven, and military electronics and avionics in nine. The construction of hulls for small naval craft and fighting ships takes place in more than 30 developing countries, although engines, armament, and electronic equipment are normally imported. At least ten developing nations have constructed warships for their navies above 500 tons or plan to do so, while eight countries produce armoured personnel carriers or even tanks.

At present even more new projects than ever are envisaged, some of them quite ambitious. For example eight more countries are planning to produce modern fighter aircraft or jet trainers. Other countries, not included in this list, are certain to become involved in domestic arms production soon. Still others will expand and diversify their present productive capacity.

As can be seen from Table 8.2 in most of the projects and probably in all countries a licence for domestic arms production is granted by an industrialised country. Quite often the share of locally added value in the production of weapon systems is minimal.

From Table 8.2 it is evident that the present boom in the arms trade with the third world is associated with an equally rapid proliferation of industrial installations for the domestic manufacture of arms. There is considerable variation in the industrial strategies on which the establishment and expansion of domestic arms production is based, although two (overlapping) approaches can be discerned.

The first approach relies on sub-contracting and the production of components under licence, and/or the assembly of the final product in close co-operation with the company supplying the licence. Sometimes components are re-exported to the licensor. The control of the technologies involved remains to a considerable degree outside the country and only a very limited research and development capacity is created locally. The highly competitive situation in European and American arms industries has led to the widespread use of licensing. Manufacturers are prepared to accept co-operative schemes and to share some production with developing countries, since it allows them to penetrate into markets otherwise inaccessible. But sometimes companies are induced to transfer some production to developing countries with subsidies in the form of tax exemption or other low-cost production inputs. In some cases low labour costs alone may attract a company to manufacture certain labour-intensive components in a developing country; possibly the licensing company will even be able to increase its total sales to the developing country, since the re-export of locally produced components may attract the local government and hence offers the company relative advantages over competitors. The existence of export restrictions may also induce the transfer of production or assembly lines to developing countries.

The other approach to domestic arms production in developing countries is the attempt to achieve complete self-sufficiency in the procurement of arms in order to enhance national independence. This has been the proclaimed goal of countries like Argentina under Perón, India, Israel, and South Africa, all of which have large-scale investment programmes geared towards domestic arms production. Hundreds of foreign R&D personnel were contracted since top priority was given to the development of an indigenous research capacity and industrial base for the manufacture of modern weapon systems.[15] It is assumed that this approach will reduce the cost of military procurement in the long run; savings in foreign exchange are taken for granted. The economy as a whole is expected to benefit from this militarily oriented allocation of resources, since it is said to create new jobs, provide technological skills to the labour force, and enable indigenous research and development potential to provide an important 'spin-off' for non-military sectors of the economy.

Apart from the ambitious research and development programmes and the proclamation of the national goal of self-sufficient arms production, the two approaches have a number of common features. The distinction between them is, in fact, based largely on quantitative differences and reflects the economic potential, the level of industrialisation achieved so far, and the relative political autonomy of the countries involved. In the modes of technology import especially, the two approaches towards domestic arms production are broadly similar. The transfer of the necessary technology usually takes place step by step and follows a pattern well known in other sectors as well. Facilities for maintenance and overhaul of imported equipment are followed by assembly lines. In the next stage some components are ordered from local industries and the percentage of locally produced components is increased until full production under licence can be taken up.

The final stage would be domestic production of indigenously designed weapon systems without dependence on imported components, although no 'late-comer' has yet reached this stage. Even India and Israel, for example which have for more than a decade pursued a strict policy of import substitution in military procurement, have not approached self-sufficiency in the production of major weapon systems. All systems produced, whether under licence or of indigenous design, require the import of high technology components and quite often technical assistance (know-how). The licences or components are often accompanied by political constraints; in 1977 the US refused to allow Israel to export the Kfir fighter, which has an American engine, to Ecuador.[16] India's domestically designed HF-24 Maruta mach 2 fighter aircraft has never been completed since no appropriate power-plant could be purchased for the plane, and India was unable to manufacture an appropriate engine.[17]

Thus, the objective of domestic arms production, the import of technology in order to overcome dependence on foreign supply, has not been achieved. Even the People's Republic of China buys military technology abroad.[18] Other objectives implicit in all strategies of import substitution, such as savings in foreign currency, are particularly difficult to attain in the armaments sector. The experience of India is a good example. Several studies reveal that the costs of procurement have not been reduced, nor has the import bill been positively affected.[19]

The specific characteristics of arms production, in contrast to the production of 'civil' goods, explain why India and other 'late-comers' among the developing nations fared so badly. These characteristics include:
—steadily increasing R&D expenditure, which results in ever more complex weapon systems;
—a fast rate of product innovation, which leads to rapid technological obsolescence;
—steadily increasing requirements for specially adapted infrastructure in order to create the operational conditions for advanced weapon systems, which results in high indirect costs;
—fast increases of unit costs (as well as life cycle costs), which lead to shorter production runs;
—increasing complexity of weapon systems which reduces the possibility of 'copying' and which allows for effective control of the technology by the licenser over a considerable period of time.

Most underdeveloped countries have a limited home market for armaments and shortages of foreign exchange. Thus the export of arms becomes a necessary extension of a national strategy geared towards self-sufficiency; this means that arms developed and produced domestically must be competitive in the world market. For a country like India, which started with a relatively backward industrial base and an extremely small research and development capacity, the attempt to achieve a degree of technological competitiveness in armaments is bound to fail. The problems that arise from the interrelationship between exports and domestic production is best exemplified in the case of Israel. Domestic arms production was considerably intensified after the war in 1967 and self-reliance became the first priority after the French embargo. Today Israel is in a situation where the whole industrial base is tailored to meet the requirements of arms manufacture, and the economy's survival depends increasingly on the large-scale export of arms at almost any price.[20] Other countries, such as Brazil, Spain, Yugoslavia, and Taiwan, also try to economise on their domestic arms industry by promoting and subsidising the export of arms.[21] The total arms trade from one developing country to another is still quite small in volume and the technological level of weapons traded is low, but growth rates are high and the richer countries like Iran are involved in substantial sales of second-hand equipment.

A country which purchases a particular weapon system in large numbers can often acquire not only some share in the production, but also the right to service and overhaul the system for other users throughout the region.[22] The share in production often covers production for worldwide markets, thus providing the necessary economies of scale in the production of components. Non-sensitive and labour-intensive components are more likely to be subcontracted in this manner than others.[23]

Even with this type of production sharing, the supplying company retains ultimate control over the technologies involved. The focus of the whole production scheme remains in the licensing country, so that the emerging pattern might be described as vertical integration of production on an international scale. An exception can occur when the manufacturer converts his production lines to a new weapon system while there is still export demand for the old system; in this case licensed production abroad for re-export is likely.[24] Developing countries tend to view this type of production sharing as a contribution to a cumulative process of technology acquisition, which explains why subcontracted production is often subsidised to a considerable extent. But there are additional reasons for the collusion of interests behind the expansion and proliferation of arms producing facilities.[Producers in industrialised countries may seek to develop a 'worldwide' production network in order to by-pass export controls and bilateral embargoes.[25] Slowly a new pattern in the international arms transfer system is evolving, marked by an increased number of potential suppliers and by new associations of interest along North–South lines.]

The process of industrialisation in the third world tends to be dominated by the requirements of the arms industry whenever an ambitious programme is launched. In the absence of sufficient economies of scale and lack of potential civilian applications, a highly specialised and capital-intensive sub-optimal industrial agglomeration develops. Even in non-military industries, the choice of techniques is determined by the technological imperatives of arms production. Levels of capital investment, minimum scales of productivity, and standards of quality unnecessary or too expensive for civilian production are becoming increasingly important in defining industrial goals in these countries.

A few examples illustrate the pattern. The production of tanks requires the production of high quality steel and advanced foundry expertise. The minimum scale of production that is necessary for high quality steel may well exceed the demand of the country as a whole and it tends to be very difficult to export the surplus. Military production also requires special alloys which are very difficult to produce; some manufacturers have established a monopoly position, based on long experience, and this is the most difficult sector in which to catch up with the standards achieved in industrialised countries. Only simple weapons can be produced in enclave-like industrial units with limited links to other sectors of industry; hence, it seems reasonable to argue that decreased arms imports by underdeveloped countries are often accompanied by increased imports of industrial equipment, especially machine tools, and software such as patents and know-how.

Even the production of relatively simple weapons such as automatic guns and machine guns in developing countries involves a high level of imported inputs. Figures recently published by the US government indicate that imports account for 53 per cent to more than 80 per cent of the total cost of several programmes to develop factories for the production of American guns (M16). These figures include installation and production over a period of five years. All of the countries concerned, including Taiwan, South Korea and the Philippines, had at least an incipient industrial base when these new factories were introduced.[26]

As well as imports, other scarce factors of production—qualified technical labour, modern infrastructure, electricity—are also absorbed into military production, hampering the development of other industrial sectors.[27] And since the creation of an arms manufacturing capability is not an isolated process, it results in over-emphasis on capital-intensive technology, to the exclusion of alternative labour-intensive strategies for national development.

Alternatives in technology
[Weapons procurement in industrialised countries is characterised by ever-increasing costs.] A study prepared for the US Department of Defense, based on statistical extrapolation from present trends,

concluded that by the year 2036 procurement costs would have escalated so much that the US Air Force would be able to afford only one fighter aircraft.[28] The increased complexity of weapon systems requires highly qualified military personnel; this in turn results in drastically increased wage bills for modern armies. The high proportion of labour costs in military budgets only reinforces the escalation towards advanced technologies, because of the attempts to replace military labour whenever possible with capital-intensive complex weapon systems. The vision of an automated, high technology battle-field is the logical extension of present trends in the dynamics of armaments. Neither a proposed high–low mix of weapons systems, nor systematic efforts to 'modularise' the production of military equipment as much as possible, have so far succeeded in reversing these trends.[29]

Design and production techniques of advanced weapon systems reflect economic conditions and the political situation in industrialised countries. In the third world, however, the general situation is quite distinct; for example, labour costs are low so long as soldiers are employed, but increase drastically if foreign specialists have to be hired to operate or maintain advanced equipment. The economic dilemmas of military production in developing countries can be illustrated with a simplified production function, as shown in Figure 8.1.[30]

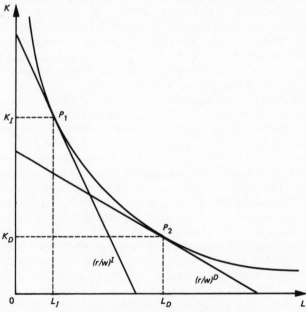

FIGURE 8.1 The hypothetical production function

The two-factor production function—with capital and labour as inputs
—can be given as

$$P = f(K,L)$$
where P = amount produced
K = amount of capital input
L = amount of labour input

Taking the cost of labour and the cost of capital into consideration the
algebraic equation is given us
$$Q = rK + wL$$
where Q = total cost of a given product
r = cost per unit of capital
w = cost per unit of labour

The points P_1 and P_2 are arbitrarily defined as the respective optimum
levels for industrialised and developing countries.

The slope represents a fixed level of output, a given level of military
activity for example. Each point on this isoquant identifies an alternative combination of capital and labour inputs needed to produce
a given output. In other words, the curvature measures the hypothetical
rate at which capital and labour can be substituted for each other,
assuming constant output. The two lines $(r/w)^I$ and $(r/w)^D$ represent
the capital–labour substitution ratios in industrialised and developing
countries respectively. The points P_1 and P_2 represent the optimal
combinations of capital and labour inputs for industrialised (P_2) and
developing countries (P_1). It can be seen that the optimal combination
in developing countries absorbs more labour than the optimal combination in industrialised countries, while the reverse holds for the
input of capital at the respective optimal points.

The simple two-factor production function draws attention to the
large differences in relative factor endowment between industrialised
countries and the third world in general. It does not reflect reality,
however, since the underlying assumptions do not correspond to actual
conditions of production or military activities. Neither unlimited
choices of technology nor homogeneity of labour can be expected in
reality. And the model fails to account for the time factor as well.

The relative disadvantage of developing countries in the field of arms
production—usually involving high technologies and rarely manufactured on mass scale—is further revealed if the simple two-factor
production function is converted into a three-dimensional function by
introducing a distinction between highly skilled and unskilled labour.
The production processes involved in the manufacture of complex
weapon systems absorb mainly highly skilled personnel and offer
relatively few jobs for unskilled labour—just the opposite of the
available labour force in developing countries.

The effects of capital-intensive modes of production on employment when introduced in a developing country can be illustrated further by Figure 8.2.

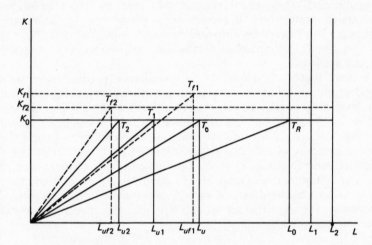

FIGURE 8.2 Impact of high-technology arms production on employment in developing country A

L_u = Labour employed
L_0 = Labour available at time 0
K_0 = Capital stock available at time 0
K_{f1} = Capital stock enlarged by foreign aid after period 1
K_{f2} = Capital stock reduced by debt services after period 2
T_0 = Capital/labour ratio of production at time 0
T_R = Capital/labour ratio necessary for full employment

Developing country A has a given industrial pattern or level of technology and a capital stock which remains constant in volume over time. T indicates the level of employment at a given time before a large-scale domestic arms production programme is started. T_1 and T_2 reflect the increased capital intensity of industry as a consequence of domestic arms production. Less labour is employed while the supply of L has increased to L_1 and L_2. In order to achieve full employment, entirely different choices of techniques would be necessary, as suggested by T_R. Only within the context of development strategies geared towards increased levels of self-reliance does it appear feasible to develop technologies or plan for a mix in technologies better adapted to the existing factor endowment of the third world. If one were to allow for the capital stock to be affected as well, then high technology arms production would be bound to reduce the country's capacity for accumulation, the only exception being production for export. But here again the huge sums spent in the leading industrial nations for military research and development suggest that even the most ambitious industrial strategy for domestic arms production in developing countries will always be outpaced by technological advances in the industrialised countries, and will thus have little opportunity to capture export markets.

Benoit[31] and others suggest that large military expenditures and arms production contribute to economic growth by improving political goodwill with respect to the availability of foreign aid and credits. Thus, in the short run, the accumulation fund might be increased through foreign credits and investments, which further enhance the capital intensity of industry as a whole (T_{f1} , K_{f1}). The foreign debts incurred tend to reduce (T_{f2} , K_{f2}) the potential for accumulation in the long run, since the investments related to domestic arms production have to be amortised out of surplus generated in other sectors of economy. The dotted lines would represent the change in capital stock and labour absorption.

The impact of military technology
The introduction of advanced military technology, particularly in developing countries is associated with changes in the consumption of energy and raw materials, in the labour market, in the infrastructure, and in the aggregate supply and demand. The imposition of an expanded military infrastructure, with sophisticated airports, road systems, transportation and communication networks, etc., is bound to disturb traditional sectors like subsistence agriculture, and does not provide alternative modes of living and production for the people affected.

These sophisticated installations are sub-optimal for the development processes, since they destroy existing traditional infrastructures and function as a superimposed network. They also serve as an incentive to introduce modern capital-intensive technologies into agricultural production, since the costs are not charged to the user. In the traditional system of agricultural production the infrastructure was part of the collective accumulation, best exemplified in the Asian mode of production, and hence the benefits of technological innovation were weighed against the costs incurred for additional infrastructure. The military infrastructure is paid for by the government and, hence, individual agricultural investors do not need to make any social cost-benefit calculation. Sharp increases in the consumption of commodities such as cement illustrate the magnitudes involved in the construction of militarily determined infrastructure.[32]

The relationship between changes in the infrastructure and fundamental changes in the structure of production is illustrated by the example of colonial India, where the construction of railways had devastating effects on the existing canal system. The penetration of the Mekong Delta by a network of military roads during the Vietnam war is yet another example. Suddenly the canal systems were no longer competitive for transportation, because the investment in the new infrastructure—in this case, the roads—was borne by the society as a whole and the users were not charged the true costs. The lorry—expensive imported equipment—dislocated traditional transport by water. The effects were lasting: the canal systems deteriorated, traditional employment opportunities such as the construction of river barges were destroyed, agricultural production suffered since the maintenance of rivers and dams was neglected.

Another factor is the allocation of scarce and valuable land for military operations, with subsequent dislocation of the population and negative effects on the civilian sectors. An extreme case in point is Singapore, where approximately 10 per cent of the territory is occupied by the army, while large-scale schemes to reclaim land from the sea are under way.[33]

South-East Asian countries in particular have been affected by the establishment of US military bases and the demand pattern deriving from American expenditures during the Vietnam war. The injection of foreign funds into local economies contributed to higher growth rates, including some multiplier effects. The 'war and base' boom altered the structure of demand, leading to a 'biassed' expansion of the secondary sector, particularly construction and maintenance, and to a virtual explosion in the tertiary sector, including entertainment. The inability of the parasitic services in the tertiary sector to support themselves in the long run became obvious in Thailand after the withdrawal of American troops.[34] After American withdrawal from Vietnam there were export crises in Thailand, South Korea, and Taiwan, when their support supplies for the war were no longer needed.[35] The wartime effects on the local economy had been so profound that it was not possible to change production structures very easily.

The transfer of military technology also leads to the absorption of scarce qualified manpower, especially in research and development; it further leads to the transfer of highly specialised personnel from industrialised countries, since the technical capacities of an underdeveloped country are too weak to service, maintain, use, or produce sophisticated weapons. In India the Defence Research and Development Organisation and related military research projects employ more scientists, engineers and technicians than private industry as a whole. Arms production absorbs 200,000 people, most of them highly qualified.[36] Although it is argued that the arms industry creates new employment opportunities most of the jobs created require a high investment of scarce capital, and it is legitimate to ask how many jobs could have been created, if the scarce funds had been invested else-where.[37] It is also argued that the arms industry improves the skill content of the labour force; but it is doubtful whether qualifications acquired in the arms industry are of great value for other civilian activities. Certainly a soldier who learns to drive a truck in the army can use his skill in civilian life, but it is not so easy to transfer specialised knowledge such as aerodynamics or missile propulsion technology, especially if capital is not available to fund R&D on civilian applications of such knowledge.

The mobility of labour has always been an important means for transferring military technology and know-how. In the past the transfer of qualified personnel in the arms production sector was usually limited to small design teams of a few scientists and engineers, but new dimensions are now being reached. By 1980 some 50,000 to 60,000 American specialists are expected to work in Iran, a majority of them employed to operate, service, overhaul, and produce military equip-ment. The growing demand for technical services which can no longer be provided by the US forces has resulted in the formation of a new corps of 'white collar mercenaries'. All of them will be paid out of the economic surplus of the recipient countries without contributing to a corresponding expansion in productive capacity.

Concluding remarks: military dissociation

Obviously the transfer of military technology and the militarisation process in the third world are closely related to the armaments dynamic in industrialised countries. The East–West conflict has been projected on to the third world and as a result of the economic crisis in some indus-trialised countries (balance-of-payment problems, unemployment, idle capacities), the export of arms has been dramatically increased. There are important economic and technological determinants in the intensification of the military transfer process, but it is primarily a political decision between supplier and recipient nations. These decisions might lead to some modification in the relations between industrialised and developing countries and within the third world, but the dominance and dependence pattern is not basically changed by the increased transfer of arms; if anything, it is reinforced.

The import of sophisticated capital-intensive technology and especially the establishment of complex arms production programmes increases the dependence on suppliers from industrialised countries and distorts the pattern of development. To put it more strongly, armaments should be treated as a determining factor in the continuation of uneven development and underdevelopment. Arms, and their application or the threat to apply them, may be necessary for the functioning of the production and accumulation process, but at the same time they represent a reduction of the available social surplus.[38] The cost of maintaining a certain mode of production and of controlling social frictions by force might well exceed the available surplus; this situation is already being approached in some third-world countries. The consequence is an increase in inequality which characterises the development process in almost every third-world country. The affluence of the few becomes ever more provocative to the poverty-stricken masses; in order to maintain the status quo the élites establish a system of social control guaranteeing economic apartheid of the majority outside the modern enclaves of booming industrialisation. The military, paramilitary, and police forces are continuously strengthened to secure the existing order, and public and private suppliers in industrialised countries are only too willing to transfer the necessary expertise and equipment. But in many cases the public security forces however large do not suffice to maintain the law and order of the few. Many private institutions are being set up in order to guarantee the uneven distribution of income and property. In this respect the trends in the industrialised countries and the third world are very much alike.[39]

An alternative to the prevailing conjunction of armaments and underdevelopment would be an entirely different model of development, i.e. the production of goods to meet the basic needs of the majority. Instead of relying on the import of sophisticated labour-saving technology and on production for the world market to earn the foreign exchange required for imports, priority would be given to production for mass consumption.[40] Instead of adapting the economy to the demands of industrialised countries, self-reliance would be favoured to dissociate the economy from the world market as far as possible. Optimal resource allocation and equal distribution would be emphasised instead of concentrating effort on the growth of isolated, export-oriented industrial sectors.

Given the legitimate right of any country to defend itself against outside aggression and given the fact that the level of armaments of a country is defined and legitimised by the potential aggressor, it might appear unrealistic to insist on an economic model of development based on alternative labour-intensive technologies and geared towards self-reliance. Indeed, the increasingly militarised élites in developing countries continually emphasise threats of aggression from within or outside the country, so that development strategies which do not give pre-eminence to the military are discredited. The perception of a potential aggression provides the ideological foundation for the initiation and continuation of an armament dynamic which generally leads to the adoption of modern weapon systems in virtually every country of significant size.

So long as third-world countries rely on military technology designed and mostly produced in industrial countries, and so long as developing countries adopt military doctrines which have been conceived in the industrialised countries and transferred/imposed via military aid and training, political independence and military self-reliance cannot be achieved in developing countries. But what alternatives exist? There is little empirical evidence to answer this question. Liberation movements have demonstrated some ingenuity in the indigenous production of implements of war. But there has been no serious study of these developments and the Vietnam war was, after all, fought with modern weapons on both sides. Pakistan is said to produce spare parts for foreign fighter aircraft in small workshops without foreign assistance.[41]

The pursuit of legitimate defence by alternative appropriate means corresponding to the available factor endowment of a developing country and compatible with a self-reliant development strategy requires an emancipation from existing military doctrines. Until now alternative doctrines developed during the struggles of liberation have been abandoned once political sovereignty was granted. The army was instituted along conventional patterns, thus introducing into society a structural variable which by its very nature impedes a self-reliant development strategy. No positive formula can be offered at this point, but it is worth drawing attention to the intrinsic contradiction which characterises current discussions about development. This is the contradiction between the proposals for autarkic strategies of development, oriented towards the fulfilment of basic needs, and the dominance of traditional military doctrines with all their technological, economic, and political ramifications.

NOTES

1. Chester A. Crocker, 'Military dependence: The colonial legacy in Africa', *Journal of Modern African Studies* (1974) no. 2, pp. 275ff.; Lorne J. Kavic, *India's Quest for Security* (Los Angeles, 1967).
2. This was partly a renewal of pre-1914 rivalries, particularly with respect to Chile, Argentina, and the Osman Empire.
3. U. Albrecht, D. Ernst, P. Lock, H. Wulf, *Rüstung und Unterentwicklung. Iran, Indien, Griechenland/Türkei: Die verschärfte Militarisierung* (Reinbek, 1976).
4. Katsu Kohri *et al., The Fifty Years of Japanese Aviation 1910–1960* (Tokyo, 1961).
5. Such an index is used for example by E. K. Y. Chen, 'The empirical relevance of the endogenous technical progress function', *Kyklos* (1976) no. 2, pp. 256–71, to measure the import of foreign technology.
6. The transfer of both civil and military technology to developing countries is a function of the level and complexity of the existing structure of production and the infra-structure in general. It appears safe to assume that military technology transfer contributing to an expansion of the productive capacity of the receiving country is trifling. The figures recorded include many ordinary 'non-technology' items, but can still serve as an approximation of military technology imported, because military technologies are extremely

demanding upon the existing level of production and infrastructure and are therefore associated with the acquisition of additional sophisticated technologies with high import content. Statistics of military transfers do not account for these additional military imports. The juxtaposition of military transfers and important groups of investment goods in import statistics in Table 8.1 should serve thus as a meaningful indication of the military drain on the investment capacity of developing countries.

7. See Michael Kidron, *Western Capitalism since the War* (London, 1968) esp. Ch. 3; P. Baran and P. M. Sweezy, *Monopoly capital: An Essay on the American Economic and Social Order* (New York, 1966).

8. According to the Pentagon's fiscal year 1977 presentation to Congress, over $8000 million worth of arms and services remain to be delivered in the period to 1982.

9. See the registers in the SIPRI Yearbooks, and the corresponding methodological remarks.

10. Michael Klare, 'Hoist with Our Own Pahlavi', *The Nation* (Jan 1976).

11. M. Fiorello, *Estimating Life-Cycle Cost: A Case Study of the A-7D*, Rand Corp, R-1518PR (Feb 1975). Estimated acquisition cost for one aircraft was $5.2 million (43.3 per cent), whereas the cost of ownership, such as depot costs, management personnel, maintenance and operations, training etc. amounted to $6.8 million (56.7 per cent).

12. From the record height of $5700 million in 1952 the Military Assistance Programme was reduced to $321 million in 1977. Total military sales for 1977 were expected to reach a record level of more than $12,000 million. Congressional Presentation, Fiscal Year 1977, Security Assistance Program, 1–2, 499/76, mimeo.

13. The recent order of two submarines by Indonesia worth more than $100 million is a good example. The supplier, a government-owned dockyard in West Germany, accepted the order only after the German government stepped in to guarantee the payment of the submarines by Indonesia, presently suffering from severe balance-of-payments difficulties.

14. P. Lock and H. Wulf, 'Register of Arms Production in Developing Countries', mimeo (Hamburg, 1977). It is likely that several additional countries also engage in some kind of domestic arms production.

15. Foreign experts are hired by virtually all third-world arms producers; Iran, Israel, South Africa, Brazil, and India are especially reliant on foreign expertise. During the 20 years after the Second World War displaced design teams from the German war industry spread over the whole world and helped to initiate the manufacture of arms in Argentina under Perón, Egypt under Nasser, India under Nehru, Spain under Franco, and other countries. See U. Albrecht *et al., op. cit.,* Ch. 2.

16. 'Israel arms exports spur concern', *Aviation Week and Space Technology* (13 Dec 1976) pp. 14–17.

17. For details see SIPRI, *The Arms Trade with the Third World* (Stockholm, 1971) pp. 745–8; more recent data in SIPRI yearbooks.

18. Advanced powerplants for military aircraft have been purchased by the People's Republic of China from Britain, and the Rolls-Royce Spey afterburning turbofan is to be produced under licence in China. The first 200 Chinese technicians have come already to Britain for training (*Milavnews,*

Dec 1976, p. 3). China is also considering purchasing British Hawker Siddeley Harrier jump jets. *The Times* (5 Nov 1977) p. 1.

19. SIPRI, *The Arms Trade with the Third World*, Ch. 22. See also the case study on India in U. Albrecht *et al.*, op. cit., Ch. 4; and D. Childs and M. Kidron, 'India, the USSR and the MiG Project', *Economic and Political Weekly* (1973) no. 38, pp. 1721–8.

20. Israel's arms exports amounted to US$500 million in 1976 and American sources predict a 100 per cent increase for 1977. See *Aviation Week and Space Technology* (13 Dec 1976) p. 14. The predicted figure for 1977 exceeds the 1974 non-diamond industrial exports by over 40 per cent. UNCTAD, *Handbook of International Trade and Development Statistics* (New York, 1976), p. 164.

21. For details see P. Lock and H. Wulf, op. cit. Virtually all capitalist industrialised countries pursue an export policy based on the same rationale, while the arms trade originating from socialist countries is based on a somewhat different rationale. The 'arms for oil' pattern has infected the third world; Brazil has entered a barter trade exchanging armoured vehicles for Libyan oil. See *Latin America* (1977) no. 9.

22. For example Pakistan is negotiating with Dassault for the right to service the French Mirage in Arab countries, and India services some of the British equipment in service with the Iraqi and Kuwaiti air forces. Singapore intends to establish its naval yards as a regional service and repair centre for foreign navies.

23. The term 'sensitive technology' refers to components and weapon systems embargoed by the administration for security reasons. The definition is political and is usually fairly flexible.

24. Italy's arms industry fits into this pattern. Italy has successfully pursued a policy of joining a large number of co-production schemes and has produced a wide range of aircraft and helicopters, some exclusively for export, under US licence. The ten largest aviation companies export about 50 per cent of output. M. Lambert and M. Hewish, 'Italy's aerospace industry', *Flight International* (4 July 1974) pp. 14–22. The licensed production of the Leopard tank for the Italian army by OTO-Melara is likely to be transformed into an export scheme as well. *Armies and Weapons* (July/Aug 1976) pp. 32–3.

25. The US embargo against Turkey in 1975 did not affect the sale to Turkey of Northrop spare parts produced in Taiwan. And despite the embargo, Northrop suggested going ahead with the manufacture of the F-5 aircraft in Turkey, starting with assembly and drawing upon Northrop subsidiaries in the Netherlands, Taiwan, or Spain for technical co-operation. *The Pulse* (a daily review of the Turkish press) (22 Dec 1975).

26. Michael T. Klare, 'Arms, technology and dependency—US military co-production abroad', *NACLA's Latin America and Empire Report* (Jan 1977) pp. 25–32.

27. There is some evidence that the lack of competitiveness of the British and French industries, particularly in the manufacture of machinery, is related to the heavy emphasis on the arms industry.

28. Norman R. Augustine, 'One plane, one tank, one ship: Trend for the future?', *Defense Management Journal* (Apr 1975) pp. 34–40.

29. A high–low mix of weapon systems—for example a small number of

advanced expensive fighter aircraft combined with a large number of simpler, cheaper fighter aircraft—has been proposed in the US for budgetary reasons. The concept of 'modularisation. is discussed in G. V. Gushaw, 'Research and development on the Soviet model: The case for the prototype', *Naval College Review* (July/Aug 1974) p. 74.

30. The literature on technological choice contains considerable controversy. Different methods of measuring labour-intensity or capital-intensity have been applied. The most common concepts are the labour coefficient (input of labour in relation to the ouput of a commodity), the share of wages in value added, the capital co-efficient (the input of capital in relation to a commodity), and the capital–labour ratio. For a discussion of these concepts and their limitations see A. S. Bhalla, *Technology and Employment in Industry: A case study approach* (Geneva, 1975) pp. 19–29. The production function as an analytical tool to optimise the allocation of military resources in the US is applied by Cooper and Roll, *The Allocation of Military Resources: Implications for Capital–labour Substitution*, Rand Corp., P-5036(1975).

31. Emile Benoit, *Defense and Economic Growth in Developing Countries* (Lexington, 1973).

32. In 1975 Nigerian harbours could not handle the huge orders of cement. The cement-boom and the subsequent bottle-necks were never explicitly linked to the fact that the Nigerian army was in the process of massive expansion including improvement of the infrastructure.

33. According to *Far Eastern Economic Review* (3 Sep 1976), Singapore troops are trained in Taiwan, since the 10 per cent of available space already occupied by the military is not sufficient for training the army (30,000) and the reserves (planned level 250,000).

34. George J. Viksnins, 'United States military spending and the economy of Thailand: 1967–1972', *Asian Survey* 5(1973) no. 5, pp. 441–57.

35. Seiji Naya, 'The Vietnam war and some aspects of its economic impact on Asian countries', *The Developing Economies*, Vol IX, 1(1971) no. 1, pp. 31–57, shows how the export pattern in South-East Asian countries was affected by war supplies.

36. Government of India, Ministry of Defence, Annual Report 1975–76 (New Delhi, 1975).

37. An economic study of US government expenditure, civil and military, argues that 'a high level of military expenditure creates unemployment', M. Anderson, *The empty port barrel, unemployment and the Pentagon budget*, Public Interest Research Group (Michigan, Apr 1975).

38. Mary Kaldor, 'The arms trade and society', *Economic and Political Weekly* (1976)n, nos. 5–7, pp. 293–301.

39. Sorrel Wildhorn, *Issues in private security*, Rand Corp. (Santa Monica, May 1975).

40. Many countries are forced to import basic food such as rice, maize, or wheat and export some 'un-nutritious' agricultural product like coffee.

41. SIPRI, *The Arms Trade with the Third World* (Stockholm, 1971), Ch. 22.

9 Militarism: Force, Class and International Conflict*

Robin Luckham

Introduction: the technology of force and the social and political conditions for its proliferation

International concern about the consequences of rapidly increasing military expenditures in the Third World is growing. The issue has been one of the dominant themes in United Nations discussions of disarmament,[1] including preparatory work for the 1978 Special Session, and it has been made the subject of numerous public pronouncements by world political leaders. Yet neither at the level of national policy nor at the level of international arms limitation discussion does it seem that this process of military expansion has responded to efforts to control it.

Militarism, moreover, is not confined to the acquisition of dangerous and sophisticated weapons, but in many developing countries has been associated with a militarisation of the political and social structure,† including expansion in the size and power of professional military establishments; a trend towards authoritarian regimes relying on military (and paramilitary) force as an instrument of governance; the persistence of conditions of either external or internal warfare; and the proliferation of ideologies which equate national independence with military power.

These developments raise fundamental questions about the role of military force in the accumulation and flow of economic surpluses, in the determination of patterns of underdevelopment, in the struggle between classes, in the organisation of state power and in the enforcement of international relations of dominance and dependence. In this paper an attempt is made to establish a framework for thinking about some of these interrelationships. The model in Table 9.1 is no more than the beginnings of such a framework. It is used as an *aide-mémoire* to indicate the range of relationships that would have to be considered rather than as a rigorous theoretical statement. It embodies five main propositions, namely:

1. The acquisition of arms by developing countries makes them

---

* This chapter is a revision of an earlier paper by Robin Luckham, 'Militarism: Force, Class and International Conflict', *IDS Bulletin*, 1977, Vol. 9, no. 1.

† It is in this very broad sense that the word militarism is used here, rather than in its classical meaning of the pursuit of national glory and territorial expansion by military means.

232

TABLE 9.1

	Nation state	Military organisation	Region	International system
Technology	Effects of importing technology of force on the economy, social structure, and conflict of the recipient countries	Effects on the military hierarchy of changes in technology of force	Distribution of technology of force (and of capacity to export/re-export it) among the countries of the region	Dependence on the technology of force and technological progress of the advanced industrial powers
Economy	Relationship between armaments and the pattern of accumulation (or under-development)	Transformation of economic surpluses into armaments	Linkage between international flow of resources and regional arms races	Linkage to world economy (and to accumulation in arms-producing countries) through international arms purchases
Class structure and conflict	Role of military in class formation and conflict; and in the conflict arising from uneven development between regions, ethnic groups etc.	Positions in military hierarchy as basis for structuring class and corporate commitments of soldiers	Effects on intra-regional stratification and conflict of variations in military professionalism and effectiveness	Transnationalisation of class structure via professionalisation of third-world military establishments
Political structure	Use of military force to uphold or replace dominant classes and groups, as an instrument of domestic repression	Maintenance (or strengthening) of military hierarchy and its capacity to coerce	Effects of variations in military power (and external military support) on regional power conflict	Exposure to great power intervention and attempts to influence composition and stability of third-world ruling groups and classes

depend on the technology of force of the advanced industrial powers. The latters' technological progress and military R&D tends thereby to have far reaching effects on the military organisation, economy, social structure, and national and regional conflict patterns of the former.

2. The accumulation of armaments in developing countries is directly linked – through international arms purchases – to the accumulation of capital in the industrial countries, with profound effects on arms races, resources distribution, and patterns of development or underdeverlopment in the third world.

3. Professional training and transfers of models of military organisation represent in certain respects a transnationalisation of the class structures of industrial countries to the third world, with consequences for the structuring of military roles and for the way that military force is used (and by whom) in situations of conflict.

4. Global conflict between the major powers encourages them either to intervene directly in the third world in pursuit of their competing interests or (increasingly) to seek to influence or stabilise national ruling classes through military and other links. The latter can sometimes use such links to strengthen their state structures, improve their military capabilities, or sustain ideologies of national power. Yet the fact that they are so often able to do so only because they have foreign support has profound implications for the way power is distributed nationally, for the nature of armed conflict, and for the international relations engaged in by the ruling classes.

5. Analysis cannot, however, be confined to any one of these four levels alone, but rather must take into account the way they interpenetrate. National or regional power struggles cannot be discussed, for example, without considering the effects on them of transfers of military technology and the working of the international market in arms. Nor can the military's role in economic development be understood without analysing the class commitments entered into by the armed forces or their role in repressing the social discontent which may arise from particular strategies of national development.

Insofar as one may say that the dynamism of the armament process in the third world arises from technical progress and the accumulation of capital in the advanced industrial countries, the causal direction of the relationships set forth in Table 9.1 is from right to left (from core to periphery of the international system) and from top to bottom (from technical progress and accumulation to class formation and political relations). In reality, however, a far more complex set of interactions would have to be built into such a model, for it is certainly not correct to view the third world as merely the passive recipient of flows of trade, capital, arms military missions, and political directives from the major powers. In reality there is a chain of reciprocal causation, not least because uneven development and international inequality have tended to provoke resistance in the third world itself to its penetration by the production and power of the centre.

Nor can one proceed as if technological or economic factors are always causally privileged. Nationalism, for example, tends to remain a powerful factor in the behaviour of ruling classes and military élites in the third world. And the Cold War and balance of power politics shape (via international and regional arms races) both the character and rate of accumulation and technical progress in the advanced countries and the nature of development and underdevelopment in the third world. (Nevertheless in no way would this remove the need to inquire beyond international action–reaction sequences and regional and national power balances, into the technology transfers and the international arms economy by which they are fuelled.)

In this chapter the main attention is given to the role of military force in the class structures, states and international relations of third-world countries: that is, to the relationships set forth in the third and fourth lines of Table 9.1, rather than those in the first and second lines.[2] This is partly because the direct effects of technology and the international arms economy are discussed at length in other chapters of this volume. And it is partly to emphasise that technology is in no sense socially or politically neutral. Military technology has a special place in third-world societies, not because it is 'modern' or technologically advanced, but because it is a particular kind of technology, that of force. And force is never used in the abstract, but in the struggle between different classes and groups. The functions of military force are different where it is used by an imperial power to secure its interests at the periphery directly (as by Britain or France in nineteenth-century Africa, the USA in Vietnam) or indirectly (as by US supplies of counter-insurgency technology to Latin American governments); in situations of revolutionary change (as in Cuba, Mozambique, or China); of broad social reform imposed by the military and other élite groups from above (as in Peru between 1968 and 1975 or Nasser's Egypt); yet again where it is used mainly to reproduce the existing regime and class structure (as in Iran); to change the regime in the interests of local or international economically dominant classes (as in Chile); or merely to secure (as in Uganda) the dominance of a parasitic military establishment.

The arguments put forward below are based on the contention that the social and political forces which proliferate military technology can only be dealt with if they are accurately understood. Peace, in other words, is a realistic programme only if it is sought through an understanding of the factors which create struggles for domination. The military is a crucial instrument in such struggles: both as an agent of internal repression and international domination; and (on the whole less frequently) of radical social change and national liberation.

There are two ways of approaching such issues. The first is more cautious and incremental: how, given *existing* forms of force, of class conflict, of state and international organisation, can conflict be averted, arms races be kept under control and the human and material costs of international conflict be minimised? The second looks at things more comprehensively: what transformations in class structure, military, state and international organisation would be required to assure conditions of lasting peace, both nationally and internationally?

The arguments of this chapter suggest that the patterns of accumulation which prevail in the world economy, the existing forms of force and the present organisation of the international system of nation-states, severely limit the scope for international agreement on arms control and conflict resolution of the first (incremental) kind. In addition, the present international system is based on a distribution of economic resources and of political and military power that systematic-ally disadvantages the third world and which the people of the latter will not for long be able to accept.

Military professionalism, class and uneven development

Class struggle is endemic in development. But the form and direction it takes is deflected by the major fractures within and between social formations created by uneven development. The expansion of capital from the capitalist core to the periphery disrupted the entire social fabric of the latter. Not only did it destroy old modes of production and replace them by new international forms of exploitation, but it also triggered off a series of political upheavals: war, colonial conquest, nationalism, inter-communal conflict and revolution.

At a national level these conflicts encompass the struggles between class and class but extend well beyond them. At international level conflict is inherent in the existence side by side of states dominated by different classes and modes of production, though as the Sino–Soviet split reminds us this is not the only way international differences arise. Nationalism is a phenomenon one ignores at one's peril. Yet it is profoundly contradictory in its nature. On the one hand it was itself internationalised by the expansion of the core capitalist countries into the periphery, providing the ideological charter of the nation-state, the political form of bourgeois society *par excellence*. On the other hand, nations also demark major fractures in the international system. Nationalism was the rallying cry for the dismantling of colonial empires. In most third-world countries it symbolises the revolt of the periphery against the international centre. It is sustained by an international stratification between nations in terms of the power, status and economic resources they command. And the major revolutions which have taken place in the third world—China, Vietnam, Cuba, Mozambique, etc.— were not only social but also national, this being a major ingredient in their success.

The military has a particular role in all this because of the functions of organised force in carrying out (and repressing) internal conflict, in international stratification and in international war and peace-making. Its institutional format reflects the contradictions inherent in the international system. On the one hand it is the most international of professions. The similarities between military élites, the brotherhood of arms, the multiple inter-connections between them created by training and service abroad might seem to suggest that they are an important element in a new international class structure. Yet armies are the instruments of individual states, have national rather than international command structures and often develop strong nationalist ideologies. Their interstitial position between the nation-state and the international system is critical in reproducing both.

The existing literature on the military in the third world fails almost completely, however, to establish the connections between the military's position in the class structure, its institutional characteristics and its international dimensions. Insofar as it deals with the subject of class at all it does so in terms of the alleged consequences of the recruitment and social origins of the officer corps. Officers are either said to be conservative because they originate from the upper levels of the class structure—an argument that was popular in the past with radical critics of the military—or they are said to be part of the 'new middle class', which brings about modernisation.

A sophisticated attempt by Huntington to synthesise these arguments in terms of different stages in modernisation postulates that when middle-class groups begin to challenge traditional landed oligarchies, the military plays a progressive role in dislodging the latter; but when lower-class groups begin to organise, the military increasingly plays a repressive role in defence of established class interests.[3] The military supports bourgeois revolutions but opposes socialist ones, although one could not expect a conservative American academic to say so in so many words.

No really convincing explanation, however, is given why the military should be located at some fixed 'middle point' in the class structure. Empirical studies of the class origins of army officers in the third world on the whole confirm that officers are neither recruited from the ruling or upper classes—even in countries like Brazil where the class structure is relatively well developed—nor are many of them sons of peasants and workers. Few of these studies demonstrate, however, that class origins have a significant effect on political behaviour. The important differences between the military juntas of Brazil and of Peru, would for example, be impossible to predict from their class origins, which are strikingly similar.[4]

Something akin to a process of class formation occurs in military organisations themselves and is visible in their tendency to fissure along the gradations of the military hierarchy. Coups are often the product of particular officer peer groups with similar rank, training, career experience and sources of grievance, such as the Free Officers who brought the military into power in Egypt; the Eighth Graduating Class prominent in the Korean coup of 1961; the majors and captains and lieutenants who staged coup and countercoup in Nigeria in 1966; the lieutenants who belonged to the *Tenentismo* movement in Brazil in the 1920s and 1930s; and the captains and majors who organised the Portuguese and Ethiopian military revolutions of 1974. Such fissures tend to occur precisely because military organisations are at the same time hierarchies in which rank and career create shared interest and experience between officers of similar rank; and power structures in which the tension between upper and lower levels of command is difficult to contain.

Most armies reproduce the two class division of capitalist societies in the cleavage between officers and the men over whom they exercise command. Again there are numerous examples of military revolts from the ranks, some with momentous political consequences: the sergeants' revolt and naval mutiny which precipitated the assumption of power by the officer corps in Brazil in 1964; the East African mutinies of 1964 which almost (but for British intervention) destroyed the newly independent regimes in Kenya, Tanzania and Uganda and contributed directly to the rise to power in Uganda of Amin; the coup of July 1966 in Nigeria which was as much a revolt of NCOs against the military command as it was a coup of Northerners against Ibo control of army and state; the revolt by ordinary soldiers in Sierra Leone who in 1968 locked up their entire officer corps and handed power back to civilians; and the Portuguese and Ethiopian military revolutions of 1974 the organisers of which acted under strong pressure from their own rank and file (in Ethiopia ordinary soldiers even put their officers under guard until they agreed to act on their behalf).

 Military structures, in sum, generate cleavages that resemble class conflict in that they are generated in a systematic way through the social relations of force;[5] by the way men are fitted together in large-scale organisations around a weapons system designed to produce a certain 'output' of violence.

Such cleavages make it impossible to assume that the military is a monolithic institution or that its role is always conservative. Groups of middle-level and junior officers have sometimes developed radical political programmes (the *Tenentismo* movement in Brazil in the 1920s, the Free Officers in Egypt in the 1950s, the Armed Forces Movement in Portugal and the Derg in Ethiopia in the 1970s).

Revolts from the ranks can be still more revolutionary in their potential than peer group interventions. The turning point in the Russian Revolution of 1917 was when the ordinary soldiers refused to turn their guns on the striking workers and joined them. The movements initiated by the Derg in Ethiopia and the Armed Forces Movement in Portugal would probably have been less sweeping without the active pressure and participation of the military rank and file.

Yet military revolts also tend to provoke reaction by the hierarchy. Both Nigerian coups of 1966 though initiated from below, were taken over in the one case by the military Supreme Commander and in the other by the most senior Northern officers. Among the reasons for the Brazilian coup of 1964 was the officers' alarm that the government had failed to deal firmly with mutinies which could have threatened the military institution itself. And what above all persuaded the army officers finally to divert Portugal from its revolutionary course in late 1975 was fear of the consequences of growing indiscipline among the rank and file. As the then Chief of Staff of the Portuguese armed forces, General Fabiao, put it in October 1975, when commenting on the rank and file organisation, Soldiers United Will Win (SUV), 'the SUV has a certain strength. But I have reservations, because it is a horizontal organisation and in the army we have a vertical organisation'.[6]

Although the social relations of violence themselves thus generate impetus both for military radicalism and for military reaction they are by no means a sufficient condition of either. The Russian Revolution was a revolution because soldiers joined the workers and peasants they were brought out to suppress and not the other way round. In some circumstances army revolt may amount to little more than narrow trades unionism: being easily suppressed because of the absence of wide social support or, like the East African Mutinies of 1964, as a result of external intervention; bought off by better pay and conditions of service; or (if successful) turning the army into a machine for the extortion of tribute by the new lumpen-militariat as in Amin's Uganda or Batista's Cuba. For soldiers and officers who rebel against the hierarchy always have the option of expropriating the latter for their own benefit rather than seeking to transform society. They are unlikely to choose (or indeed think of) the latter unless external class forces also impel them to do so.

Just as the military is not, because of its institutional distinctiveness, purely and simply the armoured fist of the ruling class; so on the other hand military upheavals cannot by themselves bring about class transformation unless they are associated with mass struggle outside the narrow confines of the military bureaucracy itself. Military revolutions are often little more than revolutions from above, enhancing the role of the State rather than transforming society. The natural heirs of the *Tenentismo* movement, for example, are the Brazilian generals of the 1970s. In Egypt the social transformation achieved under Nasser was in the final analysis rather limited and is now being reversed under Sadat.

Up to this point the conflicts of community, tribe, religion, culture, language and nation (or sub-nation) which are often also associated with military upheavals have been omitted. These are in part the residue of pre-capitalist social formations. But in their present form they are as much the product of the uneven development of capitalism and of the state, which characteristically incorporates some groups more fully than others and sets in motion struggles for scarce state-allocated resources—be they jobs, power, development expenditures or military recruitment and promotions.

Nowhere—because of the lack of fit between imposed state super-structures and pre-capitalist formations—are such conflicts more evident than in sub-Saharan Africa. Yet in few parts of the third world can they be completely ignored. Religion—Christian versus Moslem as in the Lebanon, Ethiopia and the Philippines, different Moslem sects as in Syria or the Sudan—race or tribe— for example, military recruit-ment as a basis of Malay hegemony in Malaysia, Tutsi repression in Burundi or Bedouin dominance in Jordan—and region—as in the conflict between sierra and coast in Ecuador or the regional balancing of power in the Brazilian army—have all been major factors in military struggles.

Such cleavages do not obliterate military and class relations, but interact with them. In a case study of the Nigerian military it was shown, for example, that one of the most extreme examples of ethnic and regional fragmentation in the military could also be accounted for in terms of the army's organisational cleavages, the social relations of force.[7] The distribution of power in the military hierarchy overlapped with regional and ethnic differences in such a way that ethnicity became a symbolic master key that unlocked the contradictions of both army and society at the same time in the two coups which took place in 1966. Depending on the recruitment base of the military, the demographic structure and geo-politics of the country and the nature of uneven development, several other variations in the interaction of primordial and military conflicts might be theoretically possible.

The military is also riven by the contradictions between those forces which hold together the national class structure and those which link classes together internationally. Armies are kept in operation by the international arms trade. Yet the surpluses with which arms are purchased are appropriated nationally. Soldiers fight external wars or at the very least keep themselves in a state of preparation for them. Yet they are also the agents of internal repression; indeed in some countries that is virtually their only function. Professionalism is an international ideology disseminated by the military assistance pro-grammes of the advanced countries. Yet army officers play out their careers in national military establishments and are not as internationally mobile as the managers of multinational corporations.

Military training makes army officers peculiarly susceptible to international influences. They often attend courses abroad at some stage in their military career: Latin American officers for the most part in the USA or in US-sponsored institutes such as the inter-American counter-insurgency school in Panama; English speaking African officers in Britain and other countries of the Commonwealth like Canada, Australia, India or Pakistan, but also in the USA: French speaking Africans in France. Military academies and training schools are often modelled on the metropolis, sometimes indirectly as in Nigeria, where the Military Academy was set up with Indian advice and technical assistance, thus passing on British professional values and modes of military organisation at second remove. The socialist countries have likewise recognised the importance of military training for transmitting their international influence; not only in countries where it supports an on-going transition to socialism (Chinese assistance in the reorganisation of the Tanzanian military or Cuban training missions in Angola) but also in countries where such a transition is more remote (Russian assistance to Uganda and Chinese to the Angolan FNLA).

The implications of military training and assistance programmes for external dependence are easy to see. They train soldiers in the use of the technologies of the donor countries. They give sustenance to the social relations of force around which the professional armies of both metropolis and periphery are organised. They create networks of professional contacts both with metropolitan military institutions and among course-mates in different peripheral countries. And they are often explicitly intended, like US counter-insurgency courses (or indeed Chinese guerrilla instruction), to promote the political philosophy and interests of the country which provides the training.

They also transmit into the third world elements of the major class contradictions of the advanced capitalist societies. On the one hand military professionalism means mastery of a range of skills—of management, of using, maintaining and controlling weapons, of technology, communication and transport—developed in parallel with the expansion of capitalism. At the same time these technical and managerial elements of professionalism are in tension with its heroic elements. The latter are a residue of feudalism, but continue to play a critical role in modern armies because they legitimise the military hierarchy.[8] Thus even these feudal elements are transmitted into the third world. Pomp and circumstance and the notion that 'officers are gentlemen' seem to be universal aspects of military culture be it in Thailand, Zambia or El Salvador.

The officer and gentlemen ethic is often used to create a special niche for the military in the national class structure. In Nigeria, for example, it is used to assert a distinctive military sphere of values in which social status is not allocated in accordance with the criterion of educational achievement which prevails among other élites (and according to which army officers measure up poorly).[9] The officer corps is thus set apart from the class structure as a whole, yet articulated with it, corresponding with the military's interstitial position both as the armoured fist of the dominant class or classes and as that part of the state superstructure which holds a national society together in periods of class conflict or international crisis.

The effects of international military links can sometimes, however, be quite the opposite of that intended by their sponsors. For example, in the counter-insurgency training organised by Western powers military intellectuals read and transmit to their colleagues the doctrine of the 'enemy'—Mao, Guevara, Giap or Fanon. When the military role is redefined in the direction of domestic repression rather than external security the contradictions to which these authors call attention begin to emerge. Doctrines of 'revolutionary war' politicise officers both in the direction of the radical right and of the radical left.

Putting down strikes, demonstrations and guerrilla uprisings acquaints army officers with the grim realities of poverty and strife in their own country's rural areas and urban slums. These are not perceived, however, in the abstract but from a particular vantage point in the military hierarchy and class structure, creating a deep ambi-valence. On the one hand it is feared that the disorder will get out of hand, and suspected that it is manipulated by international Communist subversion; and tough-minded new doctrines of 'national security' develop. On the other, radicalisation of some sectors of the officer corps occurs, based on the feeling that domestic repression is not the job of the army and threatens to destroy it by bringing it into contact with class conflict. The majors who staged the January 1966 coup in Nigeria and the officers of the Derg in Ethiopia were alienated by their experience in putting down strikes; the Peruvian military leaders espoused a programme of reform partly in order to deal with the real social problems they saw as responsible for guerrilla uprisings and to keep the military institution free of the taint of domestic repression.

The contradiction between the two variants of professionalism—that of conventional warfare and that of counter-insurgency—corresponds to an important tension in the class structure of a dependent social formation. On the one hand the techniques and organisational blueprints of advanced countries are transferred to the third world, interlinked with arms sales and industrialisation. On the other the armies and class structures of peripheral countries do not just become those of the advanced countries writ small, as they have been profoundly distorted by their contact with the latter.

Domination at the periphery requires different relations of force from those in use in the metropolis. Yet this sometimes conflicts with the vested interests of professional soldiers in more conventional military functions. Thus the Peruvian junta which took power in 1968 at the same time that it increased national control over the economy also reasserted the military's role in external defence by buying foreign military hardware of a kind which the civilian regime (under US government pressure) had denied the soldiers.

One may, in conclusion, see two contrapuntal themes in military professionalism in the third world: on the one hand, military nationalism directed towards the creation of an internationally effective nation-state supported by a well developed conventional army, increasingly linked through its arms purchases to the international economy; on the other, international pressure for political 'stability' at the periphery, requiring an internally powerful state machinery and enlisting military commitment to doctrines of 'national security' legitimising its role in internal repression. These themes are interlinked and contradictory. Both are present in military ideology and tend to be associated with conflict between opposed groups of army officers.

Military hierarchy, repression and international clientage

Power grows out of the barrel of the gun

<blockquote>
the gun on the tank

the warhead on the missile
</blockquote>

but also out of   the shout of the sergeant-major

<blockquote>
the *pronunciamento* of the junta

the whisper in the Pentagon
</blockquote>

Weapons are mute unless organised in a framework of social relations which determine how they are used and against whom, social relations which can be analysed at at least three levels: the system of command established within military organisations themselves; the system of domination established through the state apparatus; and the struggle for international power and spheres of influence between nation-states.

In the third world both army and state were in a real sense created or restructured by the expansion of the central capitalist powers. Their military hierarchies are based on imposed organisational blueprints. The state machinery as a whole is weak, narrowly based and as much the artefact of international as of national domination. And to shore up its fragile structure the military function is inverted: the armed forces being more often used to repress internal dissent than to maintain international security.

There is no more eloquent testimony to the internationalisation of the relations of domination than the uniformity of certain characteristics of professional armies: the hierarchy of ranks, the exclusiveness of the military brotherhood, the emphasis on rituals and emblems of rank, the codes of honour, the class distinctions between officers and other ranks. Part of this can be accounted for by the fact that a small number of models—basically British, French, German and American—have been consciously transplanted in the third world. But where other transplants like the ill-fated 'Westminster model' of parliamentary democracy did not take root, military organisations flourished. Organised force is essential for the reproduction of modern nation-states, voting is not.

Nevertheless armies are seldom monolithic institutions on which members of ruling classes can always rely. The use of military force to repress opponents of the regime or to settle struggles for political power often moves the conflict into the armed forces themselves, accentuating their internal contradictions and precipitating coups, mutinies and power struggles.

The majority of the countries of Africa, Asia, the Middle East and Latin America are under military rule. Still more of them have experienced military intervention or periods of military rule at some point or other during the past 30 years. And if one adopts broader criteria there are scarcely any where organised military force has *not* been used to keep in office or to change the regime or ruling class during the past three decades. Against this background most of the things social scientists have to say seem exceedingly banal. Much of the existing literature takes as its starting point the problem of assuring 'civilian control' over the military establishment: which can be looked at over a whole continuum of military participation in politics, ranging from gentlemanly bargaining over strategy or appropriations, outright blackmail of the regime, participation in the reshuffling of ruling élites right through to direct military control of all the major political institutions of a society.[10]

The absence of civilian control is only a 'problem', however, when contrasted with an idealised view of the relationship between soldiers and governments in the advanced bourgeois democracies. It is not an especially useful way of looking at the political institutions of Africa, Asia, the Middle East and Latin America, where military participation rather than civilian control might be viewed as the 'normal' state of affairs. Nor does the idea of a continuum from civilian to military take us very far. To be sure, the difference between a military establishment which intervenes as a 'moderating power' to resolve conflicts between civilian factions as in Brazil before 1964 and one which attempts permanently to substitute itself for parts of the state superstructure to become the State as it were, as in the same country after 1967, is important. Yet to view this as just a change from less to more military participation in political life is superficial, for the military's formal participation in politics is less important than the question of how far the state superstructure is or is not held together by organised coercion. To what extent do those who control that superstructure rely on repressive rather than ideological mechanisms to establish their hegemony?

The distinction between civilian and military regimes may well be less important than the similarities in the way they govern. Take a country like the Philippines where, under a civilian regime, civil liberties have been curtailed, the media browbeaten, trade unions deprived of the right to strike, opponents of the regime repressed. There is intensive surveillance by the police and military intelligence networks, internal warfare is waged against dissident Moslem minority groups, the military is frequently consulted about major government decisions, martial law is in operation and political offences are tried before military rather than civilian tribunals. The extent of repression and its methods differ only in detail from that practised in other third-world countries such as South Korea, Indonesia, Taiwan, or Pakistan; Brazil, Argentina, Peru or Uruguay; Iran, Iraq, Egypt, Syria or Jordan; Senegal, Ghana, Zaire or Ethiopia; be they formally under civilian governments or under the military and whether the regime is of a conservative or progressive political tendency.

Coups and military regimes are, to be sure, the prevailing trend in the third world, and this is hardly surprising. For when organised coercion is the main basis of state power, coups are to be expected merely because more 'democratic' methods of transferring power between different factions of the ruling classes cease to operate. But struggles to gain or to remain in power can also be waged by assassination, mob violence, surveillance and terror by the secret police, bribery and the skilful dispensation of political patronage. Frequent coups *may* betoken instability in the framework of the state—but not necessarily more so than votes of no confidence, reshufflings of cabinets and frequent elections in bourgeois democracies. Like the latter they speed the circulation of élites and the realignment of factions of the ruling classes more often than they bring about fundamental change in the organisation of state power and its allocation between (rather than within) social classes.

In Karl Marx's classic analysis of Bonapartism it was recognised that in periods of acute crisis or of historical transition between modes of production members of the ruling class would often be prepared to accept authoritarian government by a state machine over which it had relatively little direct control: the bourgeoisie would sometimes sacrifice its own class rule in order to secure the political stability on which the smooth functioning of a capitalist economy and its own class interests depend.[11]

Bonapartism, however is not a magical category into which the analysis of the military can be hammered. The historical circumstances of the present-day third world bring together a different combination of elements from that which prevailed in nineteenth-century France. The crisis of hegemony suffered by ruling classes is permanent and endemic rather than temporary and exceptional. Uneven development superimposes all the contradictions between centre and periphery, capitalist and pre-capitalist social formations, class and tribe, region, religion and nation; and makes it all the more difficult for any single ruling class or fraction thereof to establish its ideological claims to rule.

Add to this the effects of a colonial situation in which an alien ruling class had to rely on state repression to secure its domination. And a process of decolonisation from which there emerged a disjuncture between the national ruling class on the one hand and the economically dominant class with its commanding heights in the boardrooms of international firms on the other. This gives the crisis of hegemony a peculiar neocolonial twist. For it has retarded the formation of home-grown bourgeoisies and made it more difficult for the latter to function as effective ruling classes able through their policies to exert control over the national economy. But at the same time it creates a problem for the representatives of international capital who have to find ways of influencing policy and the political structure in peripheral countries, despite their inability to act directly as a faction of the ruling class.

On the face of it the military seems to meet the political requirements of international capital under these troubled circumstances almost better than any other institution. A powerful, relatively autonomous state-apparatus—buttressed by military coercion—provides a frame-work of stability and predictability within which it is relatively easy for multinational capital to operate. Further, the fact that the military usually depends for its weapons purchases on international purchasing power earned in the world market and appropriated through the state tends to cement the alliance with international capital. In the same measure that external penetration weakens the class structure, it increases—through arms supplies, military assistance, and political support—the military establishment's size, claims on productive resources and autonomy relative to other fractions of the ruling class.

Yet to postulate in these general terms that the military appears to fit the political requirements of international capital—stability and a solution to the problems created by international capital's inability to act directly as a ruling class—does not mean that in any given country it will in fact carry out these functions; or do so in a uniform way from one country to another. To begin with, the military and military regimes are hardly ever in a simple sense the political servants of international capital or of great power governments. It would be quite grotesque to label Colonel Gaddafy of Libya, Lt. Colonel Mengistu of Ethiopia, the members of the Peruvian junta or indeed General Idi Amin as the agents of imperialism. Even the most reactionary Latin American regimes have a degree of autonomy: witness for example the edifying spectacle of the governments of Argentina, Brazil, Chile, El Salvador and Uruguay threatening to turn elsewhere for arms and military assistance if President Carter continues to cut back aid to countries with a record of violation of human rights.

Indeed, the military's *own* institutional and material interests lie in the direction of a strong nation-state with control over the surpluses generated in the national economy. This determines the *class project* carried out by the military in two main ways. First, through the compact established between the state and international capital in which the military has a direct interest as a state institution and an indirect interest through its linkages with the international arms economy. Second, through the role of organised force in resolving— or rather in repressing the symptoms of—the crises generated under different conditions of dependent capitalist development.

Accordingly, in Table 9.2, an attempt is made to show how different patterns of incorporation in the world economy shape the varying class projects of the military establishment. The first two patterns set forth in the table arise in economies which are based on the production of raw materials for the world market, though it makes a considerable difference whether these are produced (like many agricultural commodities) by numerous indigenous petty producers; or are extracted (like most minerals) through large investments of foreign capital. The third and fourth patterns are determined by the nature of a country's process of industrialisation—whether by import-substitution or by the export of cheap manufactures produced by low-cost labour.

Armies and military regimes are seldom *directly* subservient to foreign capital. Even in countries whose economies are based on primary products extracted and sold abroad by foreign corporations, they often take up natural resource ideologies;[12] and favour state expropriation of foreign capital to the extent this can be achieved (as by the oil producers) without serious damage to the economy's international earning power. In industrialising countries the same factors incline the military towards state investment and regulation of the economy. Such regulation need not interfere with the compact established with international capital and may indeed create a new, more organic symbiosis between the state and multinational corporations. Even when the major means of production are no longer in foreign hands militarism and state capitalism together may still reinforce the integration of the national economy and its class structure in the circuits of the international economy: because foreign exchange still has to be earned to pay for armaments, technology and the expansion of the state and military bureaucracy.

Few countries fit fair and square into any one of the categories in the table. Indeed, the military often plays a critical role in the transition from one pattern to another. The crisis which led first to the rise to power of the Allende regime in Chile and then to its overthrow by the soldiers in 1973 was, for example, brought on by the exhaustion of the process of import-substitution and the international forces set in

TABLE 9.2 Variations in military

Structure of Economy	Nature of State Project
1. Petty capitalist commodity production Agricultural and natural resource based commodities produced for export and/or local sale by indigenous producers under petty capitalist or pre-capitalist relations of production. Examples: most countries of sub-Saharan Africa, Bangladesh.	1. Minimum conditions of law and ord 2. Mediation between petty producer world market, either (i) via foreign chant capital, or (ii) directly via marketing monopolies. 3. Extraction of surplus from export–i trade and conversion into (i) increa size, power and military spending of apparatus or (ii) industrialisation grammes.
2. Enclave commodity production Agricultural commodities produced or natural resources extracted on large-scale (a) by international capital or (b) by state capital incorporated in circuits of international capital through export of commodities and imports of technology. Examples: most oil-producing (OPEC) countries and copper-producing (CIPEC) countries.	1. Minimum conditions of law and ore 2. Mediation between capital and lab enclave enterprises; ensuring stabili quiescence of labour, in the last rese physical repression. 3. Either (a) State is directly coopt foreign capital and serves its int (e.g. Gabon. Central American bana publics) *Or* (b) State expropriates f capital. The latter reorganises itsel appropriates its share of mineral re sales of technology, management ments, military sales etc. 4. (Where State not mouthpiece of f capital) promotion of natural res ideologies; maximisation of mineral and of state's share therein; convers state's share therein; conversion of surpluses into expansion of state app and/or industrialisation.
3. Import-substituting industrialisation Development of industrial base through either (a) foreign investment or (b) state investment or both, replacing goods previously imported. Examples: Brazil, Mexico, Argentina, Philippines and (combined with 2, above) Indonesia, Iran, Venezuela, Chile and Nigeria.	1. Maintenance of political stability to smooth process of industrialisation a prevent flight of foreign capital. 2. Mediation between capital and la repression of latter to subsidise inves by the former. 3. State promotion of industrialis bringing about symbiosis of state, and international capital. Variatic extent of penetration by interna capital, in the mechanisms (e.g. investment versus sales of technolog which it is achieved and in extent o control over the process.
4. Export-promoting industrialisation Examples: South Korea, Taiwan, Singapore and (combined with 3, above) Philippines.	As above except foreign capital (a) footloose because not tied to do resources or markets (b) tends to ar greater extent to be vertically inte production and markets in central tries. For these reasons (a) po stability (and organised physical r sion) are even more vital, and (b bargaining power of the State is w relative to that of international capi

ects in dependent capitalist countries

Nature of Crises	Nature of Military Project
Political crises brought on by reinvigoration of re-capitalist formations and loyalties (tribe, religion, languages, region etc.) in response to competition for state power, jobs, economic resources and benefits.	1. (a) Holding fragile nation-state together and/or (b) using state machinery to establish hegemony of the particular tribal, religious, linguistic or regional groups who happen to control the military hierarchy.
Instability induced by fluctuations in commodity prices in world market, undermining regimes and their long-term economic plans.	2. Intervention to secure changes of regime in response to externally-induced economic and political crises.
	3. Reinforcement (through arms purchases) of pressure to earn foreign exchange in world market or to save it by engaging in import-substituting industrialisation.
Conflicts between central regions/groups/ towns sharing the benefits of economic activity and employment created by enclave and peripheral regions/groups/rural areas.	1. Establishment of physical control by centre over peripheral regions.
Conflicts between capital and labour in enclave.	2. Intervention in conflicts between foreign or state capital and labour.
(a) Instability induced by fluctuations in commodity prices in world market, undermining regimes and their long-term plans, precipitating conflict between states and foreign capitalists *except* (b) when associations of producers (especially OPEC) exercise monopoly control in world market, minimising direct effect of externally induced crises on state machinery.	3. (a) Direct physical repression on behalf of foreign capital, particularly in times of economic and political crisis (e.g. Chile) or (b) intervention against foreign capital on behalf of nationalist projects to assure state control over natural resources (or support for such interventions by other groups or governments).
	4. Reinforcement (through arms purchases) of pressures to maximise natural resource rents and to participate in international arms economy.
Conflicts between industrial/urban centres and rural/agricultural peripheries, intensified to extent that the latter subsidise process of industrialisation.	1. Establishment of physical control by centre over periphery. Repression of peasant movements, rural guerrillas etc.
Conflicts between capital and labour in industrial sector, intensified to the extent that profits and investment subsidised by low wages.	2. Intervention in conflict between foreign or state capital and labour, usually to repress the latter on behalf of the former, but not always (e.g. the Peronist alliance between the military and unions in Argentina).
Marginalisation, creation of 'reserve army of unemployed' by industrialisation/urbanisation processes.	3. Establishment of physical 'security' in restive urban areas. Repression of crime, squatters, demonstrations, urban guerrillas etc.
Crises created by exhaustion of process of import-substitution. Cycle of foreign exchange shortages, inflation, unrest, repression, military spending and more shortages, inflation etc.	4. Reinforcement (through arms purchases and sometimes arms manufacture) of import-substitution and of the crises induced by it.
As above except (a) low wages often essential to attract foreign capital and hence greater repression of labour force (b) vulnerability to crises in international markets for manufactures rather than to constraints of narrowness of domestic market.	As above, except military involved to an even greater extent in establishment of physical security (particularly in urban centres), repression and counter-revolution.

motion by the government's expropriation of the foreign copper monopolies. In response to these external forces the military government has adopted economic policies—economic liberalisation, sale of state enterprises, the curtailment of import-substitution, withdrawal from the Andean Pact—which virtually amount to a reassertion of its traditional position in the international division of labour as a raw material producer.

Further, it is not necessary to assume that the class project the military finally takes up is necessarily agreed in advance or even understood by the officer corps, still less their men, nor that it will be stable. Periods of crisis bring major shifts in the way the military interposes itself in class conflict, which are usually accompanied by violent internal struggles. The social origins of the soldiers who win such struggles, their civilian allies and their original intentions will have some influence on the class project the military undertakes, but may be distorted by the circumstances with which they have to cope once they take power. Examples are not difficult to find: the Nigerian army intervened to establish national unity in 1966 but broke up into tribal and regional factions six months later; the Chilean military seized power with the active support of the national bourgeoisie in order to halt what was perceived as a process of national disintegration, and ended up restoring the dominance of foreign monopoly capital; the soldiers who took power in Brazil in 1964 quickly dropped their programme of economic and political liberalisation in favour of state-sponsored industrialisation under an authoritarian regime.

Although the crises of dependent capitalist development provoke military repression, this repression does not necessarily establish political order. Sometimes the military's weapons have simply turned conflict into more bloody conflict: witness, for example, the effects of military violence in Uruguay, in Bangladesh just before its war of liberation from Pakistan or indeed in Northern Ireland. Or the military itself has become deeply divided—as in Nigeria and the Lebanon before and during their respective civil wars—and thus unable to stand above the conflict. Nevertheless the fact that military force settles things in the last resort is critical, particularly in societies in permanent crisis, where the last resort is always close at hand.

Nor can one automatically assume that the military will intervene in these crises as the compliant ally of the dominant classes. Its internal fissures, as we have already seen, may create radical as well as reactionary tendencies both in the officer corps and among ordinary soldiers. On a number of occasions the military establishment has sided with the periphery against the centre—as in some African states where the recruitment base of the army has traditionally been in the less developed parts of the country—or with labour in its struggles with capital—as in the alliance between sections of the army and organised labour in Peronist Argentina in the 1940s.

Yet although particular factions of the military élite may intervene on behalf of peripheral or excluded classes and groups in times of crisis, the military establishment *as a whole* has a vested interest in what military ideologists call 'national security' and what its opponents call state and class domination. The natural response of professional soldiers is to suppress class struggle when it appears because it divides the nation, undermines the international economic standing of the economy—causing flights of foreign capital—and imposes certain real costs—casualties, disruption of routine, threats to its structure and its monopoly of organised force—upon the military establishment itself.

Let us turn, therefore to the interrelation between the international system and armed force. This can be analysed at a number of levels. In the first place a world in which conflict is endemic and force governs the relations between nation states enhances the influence of military organisations. More than 30 years ago Harold Lasswell suggested that growing international conflict would increasingly turn the world powers into 'garrison states' in which the influence of military managers of violence would predominate:[13] though he omitted to say that this conflict can sometimes itself be the consequence of the influence of these military managers in whose interests it is to exaggerate threats to security.

International insecurity contributes equally to military influence at the periphery. The armed forces are large and influential in most countries at the edge of the Cold War, like Greece, Turkey, Iran, Thailand and South Korea; and also in countries at the nodes of regional conflict as in the Middle East and the Horn of Africa. Military coups have frequently swept aside civilian governments which have failed (in the soldiers' view) to provide adequately for their country's security: for example the overthrow of the Egyptian monarchy by the Free Officers after humiliating defeats suffered at the hands of Israel; or the 1969 coup in Somalia which swept aside a civilian government which had pursued the border conflict with Ethiopia with less enthusiasm than the soldiers desired. Soldiers are also quick to react to the international aspects of internal struggles. For example the contagion effects between military coups, such as those which swept through west and central Africa in 1965–6. Or the spread of military garrison states in Latin America in the 1960s and 1970s; responding on the one hand to the establishment of socialism in Cuba and the spread of revolutionary movements across national boundaries; and on the other to the transnationalisation of American counter-insurgency training and doctrine.

As with military intervention in the internal politics of a country, so too there is a whole continuum of external intervention: from diplomatic pressure, economic aid and military assistance programmes;

various forms of blackmail such as threats to withdraw economic and military assistance; covert subversion and the destabilisation of regimes in the style of the CIA or KGB; reassurance of recognition and support to coup-makers if successful; actual material support for a coup, or alternatively support in putting one down; military assistance and advice in counter-revolutionary operations; taking direct part in such operations (the US in the early stages of the Vietnam conflict); direct participation in a revolutionary war (the Chinese in Korea or the Cubans in Angola); through to actual invasion by troops in the intervening power (the US in the Dominican Republic and in Vietnam, or France and Britain in the Suez crisis).

Yet one cannot measure the effect of external pressures on the military, the class structure or the political system as a whole solely by the level to which overt foreign interference has *actually* been pushed. In some countries, like Chile, intervention may have taken place precisely because the contradictions are sharper than elsewhere and the hegemony of imperialist powers less secure. In others the class structure and internal political forces may be self-sustaining and direct intervention unnecessary. The arms trade and discreet military assistance programmes are often all that is required to keep the professional military establishment in operation and the stability of the political system within tolerable limits. And in others again, like Iran, Indonesia or Zaire, external penetration may be massive but multi-faceted, so that to take one aspect alone such as support for a coup, covert CIA activities, foreign aid and investment, military assistance, or diplomatic pressure, may give an incomplete picture of foreign influence because all are important together.

Conversely, however, direct intervention has sometimes created more contradictions than those it represses. The Suez crisis, the American intervention in Vietnam and the South African invasion of Angola are perhaps the most glaring examples, but there are several others. Failure to examine abortive as well as successful interventions might lead one to underestimate the *limits* imperialism faces, the contradictions it creates for itself and the strength of the forces opposed to it on the periphery. These limits arise at a number of different levels.

First, the strength and disposition of anti-imperialist forces themselves: in Vietnam for example, the military effectiveness of the liberation armies and the presence of the Russian nuclear deterrent to discourage escalation of the conflict by the Americans; in Angola the extremely prompt and effective assistance provided by the Cubans and Russians and the reluctance of the USA to risk a diplomatic showdown in Africa by openly intervening.

Second, differences among the major Western powers, as during the Suez crisis, when the disapproval of the Americans and their refusal to support British borrowing from the IMF to halt the run on the pound caused by the crisis, brought the Anglo-French invasion of Egypt to a grinding halt.

Third, the internal contradictions by which imperialist powers are sometimes weakened: the bitter opposition to the Suez invasion by the Labour party; or the economic burden of arms spending by the US government in Vietnam and the gathering strength of the anti-war movement. There are strong pressures impelling the major capitalist powers to intervene in their interests at the periphery. But it would be a mistake to regard them as monolithic and to underestimate the constraints according to which they operate.

Intervention, furthermore, is not exclusive to capitalist powers but has also been an integral part of the struggle against them. External support has been a crucial element in most contemporary revolutions: Russian support (however grudging) for the Chinese revolution; Russian and Chinese assistance in Vietnam; Arab and communist bloc help to the Algerians in their war of national liberation from France; the assistance of the Russians and Chinese and of neighbouring African countries to the armed struggle in Guinea-Bissau, Angola and Mozambique.

Nevertheless such assistance is not without its own contradictions. External aid cannot overcome unfavourable objective conditions; witness, for example, the failure of Che Guevara to bring revolution to Bolivia. It all too easily triggers off nationalist responses and accusations of 'social imperialism' against the donor: visible already, for instance, in the ambivalence of the Angolans about the continued presence in their country of their Cuban and Russian liberators. Recipients of socialist assistance—however worthy according to revolutionary criteria— are vulnerable to changes in the interests of the donors. The revolutions in Laos and Cambodia were delayed because the Vietnamese gave and withdrew assistance in accordance with the progress of their own struggle. Socialist rivalries—for example Chinese support for the FNLA and Cuban and Soviet for the MPLA in Angola—have sometimes helped to create divisions in liberation movements.

In a very real sense the intervention of socialist countries is also limited and shaped by the constraints of balance-of-power politics. In several Latin American countries the Moscow-controlled communist parties have been ambivalent towards armed struggle: fluctuating between support for insurrection and for more 'legitimate' activity in accord with the turns and swings of international politics. The support of socialist countries for the revolutions in former Portuguese Africa was covert and limited in quantity until the international political conjuncture became favourable to larger-scale involvement after the invasion of Angola by South Africa.

Despite the expansion of capital on a world scale there is little semblance of an international superstructure, comparable to the national state. There are instead only *partial* international super-structures; some based on region (the EEC, ASEAN etc); some constituting military alliances between states (NATO, the Warsaw Pact and the moribund SEATO and CENTO); and some with specialised functions (the UN agencies, IMF, World Bank etc.). These do relatively little to bind the world system together. Indeed military alliances and regional pacts on the whole deepen the main fractures between blocs. Rather than superstructure it might be more apposite to talk of a superstruggle': but for the integrating mechanisms both of the international economy, which incorporates enterprises and states alike in the circuit of capital, and of balance of power politics which (at least for the time being) prevents the war of all against all.

Although most statesmen and military leaders subscribe to the concept of a balance of power—and thus make it take on the character of self-fulfilling prophecy—it is thoroughly ambiguous. The nature of the nuclear means of mass destruction on which the balance between the central world powers is based is such that balances computed merely in terms of the numbers of missiles, aircraft and nuclear warheads available to each side make little sense. Further, the very ability to participate depends on a very advanced technology and industrial base. The balance thus expresses the competing interests of the ruling classes of advanced industrial countries and the clientage of those of the third world.

Furthermore, a balance between societies with diverse modes of production is by no means a balance of equivalents. For its equilibrium is constantly disturbed by the contradictory pressures of capitalist and of socialist expansion towards the periphery. Such an international system does not even succeed in providing a political basis for the orderly expansion of capital on an international level; the tools of international economic management having proved woefully inadequate to deal with the current international economic crisis. Balance of power politics provides only temporary and largely inadequate solutions to the international pressures which beset the third world. Typically, it is devoted to stabilising the *existing* situation without getting to grips with the substantive issues, the very real contradictions which underlie conflicts such as the Middle East crisis or the wars of national liberation in Southern Africa.

The very severity of the present international crisis in some ways, however, provides favourable opportunities for the modification or destruction of existing relations of international domination: a nuclear stalemate in which great powers can be played off against each other; internal dissent within the large capitalist powers which makes it more difficult for their governments to pursue expansionist foreign policies; economic crisis which fuels this discontent inside capitalist countries, and, further, makes it difficult for them to finance external military ventures or to subsidise arms sales in order to gain political influence. The same crisis is also bringing things to a head in the periphery, concentrating economic grievances and mobilising popular forces (but also increasing the repression by dominant classes).

To the extent that attempts to stabilise the existing pattern of international arrangements merely buy time, in which lines of conflict harden and the international production and diffusion of destructive weapons continues, they may actually increase the ultimate danger. Weapons and military organisations—the means of force—are in the international domain, in that their deployment and or use is a matter of common danger and common social concern for all mankind. Yet they are still appropriated and controlled by national ruling classes which use or threaten to use them to reproduce their national power and international interests. This makes social control over their use and conditions of lasting peace almost impossible to bring about without major transformation in the structures of international production, power and force. But the risks of the struggle to bring about such transformation impose heavy responsibilities on those who undertake it.

NOTES

1. United Nations, *Economic and Social Consequences of the Arms Race and of Military Expenditures,* Report of the Secretary-General (New York: UN, 1972); and United Nations, *Economic and Social Consequences of the Armaments Race and its Extremely Harmful Effects on World Peace and Security,* Report of the Secretary-General (New York: UN, 1977).
2. For a further discussion of technology and the arms economy, see Robin Luckham, 'Militarism: Arms and the Internationalisation of Capital', *IDS Bulletin,* 1977, Vol. 8, no. 3, reprinted in R. Jolly (ed.), *World Armaments or World Development?* (Oxford: Pergamon Press, 1978).
3. Samual P. Huntington, *Political Order in Changing Societies* (New Haven: Yale U.P., 1968) Ch. 4.
4. Alfred Stepan (ed.), *Authoritarian Brazil* (New Haven: Yale U.P., 1973) Ch. 2.
5. They do not, however, strictly speaking arise from the exploitation of soldiers as a workforce from which surplus value is extracted; but from their domination in a hierarchy of power relationships controlled by their superiors.
6. *Economist* (18 Oct 1975).
7. Robin Luckham, *The Nigerian Military: A Case Study in Authority and Revolt 1960–67* (African Studies Series 4, Cambridge U.P., 1971).
8. For a perceptive analysis of this contradiction within the mainstream of bourgeois military thought see Morris Janowitz, *The Professional Soldier* (New York: Free Press, 1960).
9. Robin Luckham, *The Nigerian Military,* Ch. 4.
10. S. E. Finer, *The Man on Horseback* (London: Pall Mall Press, 1962).

11. Karl Marx 'The Eighteenth Brumaire of Louis Bonaparte' in Karl Marx and Frederick Engels, *Selected Works* (Moscow: Foreign Languages Publishing House, 1958) Vol. 1, pp. 243–344.
12. Carlos Fortin, 'The State and Multinational Corporations in Latin American Natural Resources', *IDS Bulletin*, 1977, Vol. 9, no. 1.
13. Harold Lasswell, 'The garrison State', *American Journal of Sociology*, XLVI, Jan 1941.

Conclusion

Asbjørn Eide and Mary Kaldor

The implications of the world military order which emerge from this book are difficult to comprehend, such is their magnitude. The use of new military technologies in the third world has already caused untold misery. Their transfer to local élites has provided the sophisticated wherewithal for repression and has served to mould patterns of development in such a way as to cause massive economic and social dislocation and to produce the necessity for authoritarian and militaristic forms of rule. The acceleration in the development of new military technologies and in the pace of military transfers from rich to poor countries can only result in more of the same and worse.

From an international perspective, the case for constraints on the development and transfer of military technology is self-evident. Yet when viewed from a national perspective, the world military order now prevailing appears to be a reason for increased armament. The development or acquisition of new military technology by a potentially hostile country is seen as a threat to security. The development or acquisition of new military technology by a friendly nation is seen as a political challenge, part of the competition for status within the international system. In particular, third-world governments frequently argue that attempts to control the transfer of military technology without controlling development and production amounts to discrimination; third-world nations must arm at a faster rate than advanced industrial nations if they are to reduce military inequality and increase political power. So it is that the international interest in disarmament is counterpoised against the national interest in armament in much the same way that the economic nationalism of the 1930s seemed an insuperable barrier to the creation of a liberal world economy.

In this book, we have tried to demonstrate that the assumptions on which this kind of thinking is based are largely false. The contradiction between international and national interest is based on a view of the international system in which the currency of international exchange is armaments. The fact that sophisticated military technology does *not* necessarily ensure military superiority, even when used by the military organisations for which it was designed, and that military power does *not* necessarily contribute to political power implies that there are ways of controlling military technology that do not conflict with national interests. Indeed, one might go further and argue that the notion of military inequality is not only different but may actually contradict the notion of political and economic inequality. The idea that, militarily, third-world countries can 'keep up' with advanced industrial countries is an element in the ideology of the world military order which actually

257

serves to maintain the current hierarchy of unequal political and economic relationships.

Indeed, it may be argued that, owing to the increasing destructiveness of weapons, military means for resolving conflicts have become increasingly counterproductive. For various reasons, new developments in military technology have given rise to forms of warfare which hardly distinguish between combatants and civilians. Indiscriminate destruction tends to intensify popular resistance so that the notion that control over hostile populations can be indefinitely maintained through superior military technology is compromised.

In thinking about the kind of constraints on the transfer of military technology that might reconcile the international interest in disarmament with national concerns about security, it is useful to distinguish between the two forms of technology transfer that have been described in this book. One is the direct use of military technology by advanced industrial nations when they intervene in third-world conflicts, for example the US in Vietnam or the French in Algeria. It is evident that proposals for arms limitation as regards the rich countries must needs be based on an analysis of the armament process in those countries and of the momentum behind the development of military technology: this has largely been outside the scope of the book. But there is one area of possible constraint which should be considered here. This lies in the further development of international law, which if carried forward in the particular field of military affairs, would parallel, and could therefore draw from, the more general trend towards international co-operation as an alternative to the dangerously anarchic pursuit of national self-interest. If nations can agree to co-operate in protecting themselves by international legislation against, for example, environmental pollution or a purblind exploitation of marine resources, why should they not also seek to legislate against the excesses of military technology? The aim would be to formalise and strengthen an alternative ideology about the international system, based on respect for the sovereign equality of nation-states. If carried forward, the notion of military inequality would be rendered meaningless since the use of armed forces would become limited (as in principle they are already) to defence against external attack. And even if so grand an ambition remains unfulfilled, there are valuable intermediate goals. Some of them, particularly the development of the international law of armed conflict to proscribe the use of especially abhorrent weapons, are discussed below (on pp. 260–3).

The second form of technology transfer is the supply of arms, related equipment and skilled personnel to third-world nations. Constraints on this form of transfer are currently a major issue in international arms control circles and the subject of bilateral talks between the Soviet Union and the United States. It is very difficult to be optimistic about these efforts precisely because they are based on orthodox concepts of what constitute military power and, hence, tend to focus on minute differences in the perceived military power of nations based on what we have shown to be largely irrelevant military–technical criteria. The past history of attempts to control military technology and the possibility of new approaches based on alternative ways of thinking about the international systems are also considered below (on pp. 263–75).

The application of international law

There are three main ways in which international law might be extended or applied more rigorously in order to constrain the use of military technology. One is the emerging *jus contra bellum*; the second is the developing international system for the protection of human rights; and the third and currently most important is the further development of humanitarian law applicable in armed conflict.

Jus contra bellum is that branch of international law which limits the right to use force. The rise of the European nation-state coincided with the development of the concept of absolute sovereignty which justified the use of force against other states. During the twentieth century, this concept has been gradually eroded. A series of treaties, declarations, etc., have sought to draw a distinction between defensive and aggressive uses of force and have outlawed the latter. These include the adoption of the Covenant of the League of Nations, the Briand-Kellogg Pact, the Charter of the United Nations, the Declaration on Decolonisation, the Declaration on Principles of International Law Concerning Friendly Relations and Co-operation Among States, and the declaration in 1974 on the prohibition of aggression.

Essentially, they have transformed the notion of sovereignty, since the illegality of aggression implies an obligation to abide by the co-existence of other sovereign units. Thus, at a normative level, the legal scope of action for the most powerful states has been limited and the sovereignty of smaller and weaker states is consequently strengthened. An important dimension of the *jus contra bellum* is the principle of self-determination and the prohibition of what has sometimes been called 'permanent aggression', the coercive repression of self-determination, which may originate far back in history. In the future, an extension of this branch of international law might lead to constraints on the production, stockpiling and deployment of offensive weapons and the elimination of interventionist military capacity.

A closely related basis for constraints can be found in the developing international system for the protection of human rights. The system gives rise to a specific definition of national security. Originally, sovereignty was understood to emanate from 'the sovereign'—the monarch, prince or whomever else held political command. The later development of human rights, first in domestic law and gradually also in international law, transformed the notion of sovereignty to mean popular sovereignty, i.e. one in which government must be based on consent by and participation of the people. Thus legally, national security can be taken to mean the security of the people, not the security of the central power structure. On this basis, constraints could be constructed against those technological developments which support a centralised and hierarchical system and which, by implication, make it difficult to realise the ideal of popular sovereignty.

International humanitarian law is in the process of a major advance in the field of armed conflict, representing another possibility for new constraints. In December 1977, after several years of intergovernmental negotiations initiated by the International Committee of the Red Cross (the ICRC, a private Swiss organisation), two additional Protocols to the 1949 Geneva Conventions were opened for signature. They are designed to provide further protection to non-combatants caught up in war. The question arose during the negotiations of whether to include within the Protocols prohibitions on the use of particular weapons that were inherently likely to endanger non-combatants. This was, of course, a highly delicate matter, not least for those countries that possess nuclear weapons. It was ultimately agreed to treat weaponry only in the most general terms, referring the matter for detailed consideration to conferences outside the main framework of the Protocol negotiations. The ICRC duly convened a private working group of weaponry experts, which met at Geneva during 1973, and then a conference of governmental experts, which met first at Lucerne in 1974 and then at Lugano in 1976. The three gatherings produced reports which (a) reviewed the relevant principles of international law bearing upon weapons choice, including those from which such specific rules as the prohibition of Dum-Dum bullets had been derived in the past; and (b) described the properties of representative modern weapons (other than nuclear, chemical, or biological weapons) insofar as they related to those principles. The purpose was to work towards international consensus on new prohibitions; but by the time the negotiations on the Protocols had been completed—at the fourth session of what became known as the Geneva Diplomatic Conference (the CDDH)—no significant consensus was in sight. The length and complicated structure of the report from Lugano reflect the general obfuscation of issues as the matter of specific bans moved nearer the diplomatic arena, thus attracting wider political considerations. The CDDH did, however, resolve that a full-blown Conference of Governments should be held on weaponry no later than 1979; and a preparatory meeting for such a conference was held in Geneva during September 1978. Thus, though it remains doubtful whether important new weapons-restrictions will emerge, an institutional framework for their negotiation has at least been created.

As things stand at present, this enterprise is being treated primarily as an attempt to update the Hague component of the laws of war so as to parallel the developments in the Geneva component. The prospects which it affords for securing constraints on military-technology transfer are not necessarily insignificant, for intergovernmental agreement on new weapons-prohibitions necessarily entails intra-governmental concurrence; and once a bureaucracy has formally committed itself to an agreement, its own operating procedures impose a powerful inertia on activities that might violate the agreement.[1] Prohibitions of weapons-uses would then become transmitted backwards down the weapons-supply chain, thereby dampening the momentum of particular lines of weapons development. The requirement therefore is that the efforts to negotiate new prohibitions should be directed at those categories of weaponry whose exclusion from military-technology transfer is most to be desired.

Viewed in this perspective, however, one may seriously doubt whether negotiations confined within the framework of the laws of war will have any substantial value, for that framework has two fundamental inadequacies. The existing criteria of illegality in weapons—indiscriminateness, perfidiousness, and propensity towards superfluous injury or unnecessary suffering—are at once too general and too particular to relate to those qualities of modern weapons that render their prohibition especially fitting. And the concepts of military necessity and proportionality which are built into the framework are inherently inimical to qualitative arms limitation. The tacit understanding that has grown up over the years that nuclear weapons are exempt from the Hague-law restrictions compounds the problem, for what respect can there be for a body of law that proscribes only minor means of carnage, implicitly condoning major means; and therefore what assurance can it provide? Considerations of national security, transposed into the language of military necessity, thus quite rightly found stronger expression at Lucerne and Lugano than purely humanitarian considerations.

But in fact it is not at all obvious that national security, even when considered within the current orthodoxies of military strength, would benefit from an absence of restriction on some of the new types of conventional weapon, such as those described in Chapter 3. Exactly the opposite possibility exists; and for this reason the 1979 conference offers an opportunity which the imposition of unduly narrow terms of reference should not be allowed to destroy. The other institutional frameworks available for negotiating qualitative conventional-weapons limitations are the ones given over to arms control. But, in the first place, they are already fully occupied with other matters; and, in the second place, the precepts of arms control are in many ways no more suited to the necessary negotiations than those of the laws of war.

Above all, it has been humanitarian concern, acting through public opinion, that has forced governments to the negotiating table on the laws of war. Likewise, the outcry that is now being raised against the neutron bomb (illogical though it may be in its concentration on only one of the present nuclear horrors) is pre-eminently an expression of moral outrage: a gut-reaction to the gross obscenity of antipersonnel area weapons. Arms control precepts are essentially a means for excluding such emotiveness from inter-governmental negotiations on weapons. No doubt it is important that issues of national security should be deliberated as dispassionately as possible; but the cost of dehumanising negotiations in this way is at best procrastination.

At worst the cost is not only failure but also, because of that failure, a poisoning of the ground for future efforts. This is precisely what is likely to happen if the present dichotomy is maintained: if the laws-of-war negotiations are not loosened by admitting the subtle approaches to security politics that arms-control theory can provide, or if the arms-control negotiations are not invigorated by admitting humanitarian precepts. The problem therefore is one of finding internationally-acceptable concepts that can be applied so as to expand the two negotiating traditions to the point where they overlap.[2]

More is at stake here than the development of constraints on military-technology transfer. The current emphasis on military strength as the major determinant of security finds its most extreme expression in the doctrines of nuclear deterrence that the most advanced countries have adopted. This reversion to the medieval precedent of taking hostages as security is seen to be the only form of protection against a rampant military technology; and the hostages can be retained only by fostering the technology so as to preserve deterrence. Over the past four decades the potential physical and social destructiveness of war has been raised to the point where victory may no longer be distinguishable from defeat: war between states each possessing the most advanced weapons is now likely to end, not in the capitulation of one belligerent or another, but in a final suicidal invocation of 'mutual assured destruction'. Yet a capacity for waging war, if only in defence of the homeland, is still regarded as a necessary appurtenance of state: hence the search, conducted primarily through arms-control negotiation and the elaboration of strategies of flexible controlled escalation, for ways of preserving war as a non-suicidal policy option. But it is a search that is continually compromised by the burgeoning of the technology. The pattern has been one of weapons developments outpacing arms-control negotiations and providing for ever finer, and therefore less easily controllable, gradations of escalation. The real case for any form of arms limitation—whether via arms control or the laws of war—therefore lies in the extent to which that limitation can check the momentum of the technology, releasing states from the insecurity into which they are locked by its vicious circle, and removing the great burden of resource and opportunity costs which it imposes. Since the mainspring of military technology is provided, not by the apparatus of nuclear warfare, but by the industrial structures and military doctrines built up around conventional weapons, it is through conventional arms limitation that this vicious circle may most effectively be broken.

Constraints on the international transfer of arms

The conclusions of this book give rise to an interesting paradox. It is widely held that attempts to control the transfer of arms are discriminatory since they do not preclude production or stockpiling by producing states. They are thus said to maintain the dominance of producer countries and to reinforce existing inequalities in the international system. The new US–Soviet talks can be viewed in this light; they are designed to preserve superpower hegemony and to prevent the proliferation of destabilising technologies which might challenge the status quo. And yet, if we are correct in the view that arms transfers lead to political dependence and increased economic inequality, control over arms transfers might have the opposite effect—increasing the independence of recipients and removing some of the barriers to economic development. The solution to the paradox lies in the form of arms transfer control. Given the appropriate economic, social and political conditions, technology clearly does contribute to military power, for example in North Vietnam; the contention of the book is merely that its importance is overemphasised and depends on the conjunction of other phenomena. It is certainly true that past attempts to control the transfer of arms have been attempts to preserve a monopoly of effective military technology and to prevent the acquisition of certain kinds of military technology by 'undesirable' recipients who might make use of armaments for 'subversive' purposes. On the other hand, there *are* approaches to arms transfer control which might contribute to the creation of an alternative international system in which a major goal is comprehensive disarmament. One such approach would be the use of arms embargoes to reinforce an alternative international ideology. The refusal to supply arms to repressive, racist or colonialist regimes would be one such example. Indeed, the chapter on South Africa illustrates the conflict of international ideologies—the interest in the South African contribution to the world military order versus the repugnance towards the use of arms to underwrite apartheid. Another such approach would be unilateral or regional limitations in which recipients refuse to acquire arms which would increase dependence, divert resources from development, promote capital-intensive industrialisation or encourage repression and aggression.

1. THE HISTORICAL CONTEXT

International efforts to regulate transfers of weapons to what is now
called the third world, came at a late stage in the history of imperialism.
During the first centuries of European conquest, it was not uncommon
for selected local groups to be provided with weapons in order to
facilitate conquest or to increase armed manpower against competing
imperialists. Skilful manipulation of ethnic conflicts in Africa, Asia,
and the Americas, providing arms to some groups and thereby
increasing dependence, was a common approach in the seventeenth and
eighteenth centuries. Similarly, local groups were armed to take part
in the wars waged between French and British colonial armies on the
Indian subcontinent and in North America. In India, this gradually
led to the integration of Indian soldiers into the British colonial army.
To a lesser extent, this also happened elsewhere. The imperial powers
did not hesitate to transfer weapons to their colonial forces, and this
kind of proliferation was not included when at a later stage the first
international efforts were made to seek restraints.

In parts of the world where large-scale white settlement took place,
there soon developed a pressure on the colonial power to arm white
settlers and to prevent transfer of weapons to the surrounding non-white
ethnic groups. This demand was gradually accepted, and contributed
significantly to the establishment of racial domination. In other colonial
areas, the transfer of weapons gradually came to an end as the colonial
power gained the upper hand and no longer needed to co-operate with
formerly independent local groups.

When the imperial powers reached saturation point and settled down
to agree among themselves on the distribution of their possessions,
there was no more need to transfer weapons to local groups in order to
extend one's own empire. Significantly, the first serious efforts at international regulation of transfers came some few years after the Berlin
conference of 1884, at which Africa was finally divided. Of particular
interest is the Brussels Act adopted by an international conference in
1890, regulating export of arms to Africa. The prohibitions are found
in article VIII of the Act:[3]

> The experience of all nations that have intercourse with Africa having
> shown the pernicious and preponderating part played by firearms in
> operations connected with the slave trade as well as internal wars
> between the native tribes; and this same experience having clearly
> proved that the preservation of the African population whose
> existence it is the express wish of the powers to protect, is a radical
> impossibility, if measures restricting the trade in firearms and
> ammunition are not adopted, the powers decide, so far as the present
> state of their frontiers permit, that the importation of firearms, and
> especially of rifles and improved weapons, as well as of powder, ball

and cartridges, is except in the cases and under the conditions provided for in the following Article, prohibited in the territories comprised between the 20th parallel of North latitudes and the 22nd parallel of South latitude, and extending westward to the Atlantic Ocean and eastwards to the Indian Ocean and its dependencies, including the islands adjacent to the coast within 100 nautical miles from the shore.

The hypocrisy of this justification is not difficult to detect.

The St Germain convention of 1920 extended the prohibited zone beyond African territories to include non-African areas, where efforts to break out of established structures of dependence were under way. Included in the prohibited zone were Iran, the Arabian peninsula and the Gulf of Aden. Areas firmly under white settler control, particularly the Union of South Africa, were not included. The purpose of the St Germain convention was not to prevent transfers altogether, but only to require a licence from the government of the supplier nation. It was also decided that the signatories of the convention should not allow any armament export, even outside the prohibited area, unless the recipient was a government which had accepted the convention. One of the implications of this was that only governments could obtain weapons. This had previously been much less clear in international law. This new approach reinforced the coercive power of governments over their domestic opponents. It did not prevent the transfer of weapons for repression, but it excluded transfers for liberation, secession, or social revolution.

The St Germain convention had little impact since only a few arms-producing countries of significance accepted it. The US did not sign, for various reasons particularly the possibility of selling weapons to Latin American countries which had not signed. The US was also interested in providing weapons to opposition groups in Latin America under certain circumstances; this had been demonstrated in the tumultous events in Mexico during the preceding years.

Besides the governmental export-licence requirement, the other main point of the convention was that there should be publicity about arms transfers through the publication of the licences in the Yearbook of the League of Nations. It was therefore not a non-proliferation agreement but simply an effort to prevent the private arms industry from operating independently in the sale of weapons. Thus, again, it meant increased influence—for better or for worse—by governments over the transfer of weapons, but it did not mean international regulation, apart from the prohibited zones. The governments were free to set their own criteria for the granting of licences. From the areas defined as prohibited zones, there was little or no representation, and there was therefore not much protest. For governments of non-producing countries outside those

266

zones, the main concern was the inequity which resulted from the
provision on publicity. Some delegates objected because publicity, in
their view, reduced their security. But the majority of opponents were
ready to accept publicity if it was also applied to arms production, thus
placing producers and non-producers on the same footing. Provisions
for publicity of transfers alone were adopted, but the convention
never entered into force.

The main concern of the European countries taking part in the
efforts before the Second World War was to bring private arms sales
under governmental control. A commission set up by the League of
Nations concluded among other things that private armament firms had
   —been active in fomenting war scares and in persuading their own
       countries to adopt war-like policies and to increase their arma-
       ments;
   —attempted to bribe government officials both at home and abroad;
   —disseminated false reports concerning the military and naval
       programmes of various countries in order to stimulate armament
       expenditure;
   —sought to influence public opinion through the control of news-
       papers in their own and foreign countries;
   —organised international armament rings, through which the
       armament race had been accentuated by playing off one country
       against another.

Basically, it was assumed that the private arms producers, uncon-
trolled, were stirring up tensions and creating an artificial demand for
armaments. It was also feared that they would sell arms to their own
country's allies. There is no doubt that these fears were well founded.
But what was the alternative to private arms production? The prevailing
notion was that most of the problems could be solved by licensing of
arms sales by the government of the supplier country, or better still,
by production of arms in government-owned firms. The assumption
was that government-controlled production or sale would not lead to
the same abuses. This assumption now seems naïve. Governments
might not be as unsophisticated as private arms dealers were after the
First World War—but their approaches to arms transfers are not so
very different. The military-industrial complex has created a class of
scientists and publicists whose analysis and reporting serves to
motivate governments to buy weapons. The theory of 'modernisation',
according to which the armed forces have a beneficial role in the
transformation of society, has provided an important justification for
the active salesmanship of arms. Even more important has been the
utilisation of third-world countries by the major industrialised states for
their own strategic purposes. As part of the policy of containment, for
example, a number of countries were defined as 'forward defence areas'
and saturated with weapons. Governments have greater control over

arms producers than they did immediately after the First World War, but even so arms transfers are now proceeding on a scale not conceivable at the time when the League of Nations was combating the private arms industry. The assumption that governments could prevent weapons from being used against their interests has also turned out to be wrong. Weapons delivered by the Soviet Union were used by Indonesia from 1965 to suppress Indonesian communists and other radicals. Weapons transferred by the United States to Ethiopia have been used by the self-proclaimed marxist government there. British supplies to Uganda have been used by Amin partly to eliminate British interests in the area.

In addition to the control of arms transfer to prohibited zones and the control of private arms exports, the interwar period also witnessed the use of arms embargoes to buttress international opinion, as in the Chaco War in Latin America and the Italian invasion of Abyssinia. In neither case were the embargoes particularly effective but the embargo on Italy did enshrine a principle which remains important, that of international opposition to the use of arms for aggression.

2. SUPPLIER CONSTRAINTS ON ARMS TRANSFERS

The control of arms exports by governments implies an arms supply policy, whether or not this is explicit. All forms of arms supply imply some form of discrimination. Thus even a policy of sales to all buyers, as applies now with some East European arms trading companies or applied to private manufacturers before the Second World War, implies discrimination in favour of those who can afford to pay.

In general, most supplying countries follow explicit policies of discrimination. Western countries do not supply arms to communist countries and, in general, favour members of Western alliances. The Soviet Union does not, generally, supply arms to members of active Western alliances and tends to restrict the supply of arms to friendly socialistic regimes. There have been some coordinated attempts at control. In the early 1950s, the Western countries constrained arms supplies to the Middle East.[4] That they made exception for members of Western military alliances merely demonstrates that this form of constraint was in keeping with traditional forms of constraint under colonialism in which arms supplies were used selectively for political purposes. American attempts at controlling the supply of sophisticated military technology to Latin America, a protected sphere of influence, which broke down as a consequence of European competition in the mid-1960s, can be interpreted in a similar way.[5]

Smaller supplying countries like Sweden, West Germany or Japan adhere to the principle that arms should not be supplied to countries in conflict. Such a policy discriminates implicitly in favour of the stronger party to the conflict. Recognition that all supply policies are, by their nature, discriminatory has led to the explicit enunciation of international principles for discrimination. One such principle is the refusal to supply arms to repressive regimes that violate human rights. This principle underlay the international embargoes on South Africa and Portugal, which are discussed below, and has been adopted unilaterally by several small supplying countries. Most recently, the principle was enunciated by President Carter, although the selective application of the principle—to Marxist Ethiopia and not to conservative Iran—merely results in additional justification for the use of arms transfer as an instrument in the pursuit of self-interest. One proposal, which is rather unlikely to be accepted, which would expose the nature of discriminatory principles would be a prohibition on arms *sales*. As gifts, arms transfers would need much more serious justification.

In the United States in recent years, there has been considerable pressure to control the supply of arms in the interests of disarmament as well as humanitarianism. This pressure was consolidated by the exposure of the Lockheed and Northrop bribery scandals and the 1976 Humphrey bill which was intended to increase the constraints on arms exports. President Carter has expressed a sincere intention to pursue such a policy. The Presidential Review Memorandum of May 1977 and the new US–Soviet bilateral talks announced in November 1977 apparently confirm this intention. And yet the content of the Carter policy so far, belies the interest in disarmament and humanitarianism.[6] In the control over sophisticated technology and the selective control over the destination of weapons, the policy seems to be merely a reassertion of American political interests—after the bonanza of the Nixon period—in the tradition of all attempts to control the arms trade. The genuineness of Carter's intention to control conventional weapons could only be proved by measures which affected US products as well as trade.

3. NON-PROLIFERATION BY TYPE OF WEAPON: THE CASE OF THE NUCLEAR NON-PROLIFERATION TREATY, 1968

One multilateral approach to non-proliferation is to prohibit the transfer of certain types of weapons to all possible recipients. If recipients are to be parties to an agreement of this kind, there must be some special reason, such as the nature of the weapon in question, why they should accept such a discriminatory arrangement. There is in existence only one such arrangement, the Nuclear Non-Proliferation Treaty of 1968. The treaty was negotiated between the United States and the Soviet Union, but it had been discussed and recommended by the disarmament conference in Geneva, and endorsed by the United Nations General Assembly. It was later ratified by many states, although there have been a number of notable exceptions. We are concerned here mainly with the principle contained in this arrangement.

A treaty of this kind is clearly discriminatory in that it allows some states to maintain nuclear weapons and seeks to prevent others from obtaining them. There must be some justification for the nuclear weapon countries (NWC) not to abolish that weapon which they consider too dangerous for others to acquire. The only justification likely to be accepted is that the NWCs were caught in a 'security fix' from which they were, in the short run, unable to escape. The non-proliferation arrangement could then have two purposes: to prevent other countries from reaching the same situation, and to allow the NWC to extricate themselves from this security fix.

The security fix has arisen during the past decades, as the most heavily militarised states have come to rely on technological deterrence. The purpose of this deterrence is not to defend borders, but to threaten the other side with punishment. As technological capacity increases, a neurotic concern with this threat of punishment develops, and the continued control of the most advanced means of punishment becomes an obsession. Since, in our technological age, there is no limit to qualitative improvements, this obsession feeds on itself. Nuclear weapons represent, for the NWCs themselves, the most frightening component of this neurosis-forming process. But they can extricate themselves from this situation only through patient negotiation. The validity and universal acceptance of an arrangement such as the Nuclear Non-Proliferation Treaty then depends on the steps taken by the 'haves' to divest themselves of those weapons. This is also why Article VI of the Treaty reads: 'Each of the Parties to the Treaty undertakes to pursue negotiations in good faith on effective measures relating to cessation of the nuclear arms race at an early date and to nuclear disarmament, and on a treaty on general and complete disarmament under strict and effective international control.'

It was demonstrated during the review conference in 1975, that the superpowers had in fact done little in this regard. There certainly had been no nuclear disarmament among the NWCs, nor even a cessation of the nuclear arms race. Indeed, the NWCs had continued and intensified the nuclear arms race. The partial measures never touched the core of the problem, and served mainly to mystify critics. They imposed restrictions where the military value was low, and created loopholes where there was a potential for continued military development. As Alva Myrdal pointed out, the restrictions were purely cosmetic.[7] A good example of these cosmetic restrictions is the 1963 Partial Test Ban Treaty, which prohibited tests in the atmosphere, in outer space, and under water. But the NWCs maintained freedom to continue testing underground and *increased* the number of tests after the adoption of the Treaty, so that nuclear weapon development accelerated while the Partial Test Ban Treaty served to satisfy public demands for constraints. In 1974, the United States and the Soviet Union agreed not to carry out underground nuclear weapons tests having a yield exceeding 150 kilotons. Even this imposes no real restraint, since only a fraction of previous tests had been above this limit. Moreover, developments in the nuclear field now concentrate on quality rather than quantity, and there is a trend towards smaller bombs.

This process of mystification has become increasingly clear, and has weakened respect for the Non-Proliferation Treaty. The US–Soviet Strategic Arms Limitation Talks (SALT), which have been in progress now for almost a decade, do, in principle, provide an opportunity for nuclear disarmament, as promised in Article VI of the Non-Proliferation Treaty. But results have been negligible, and it seems that a primary purpose of SALT is to create the illusion that serious efforts are being made.

The SALT negotiations by definition exclude tactical nuclear weapons. The accumulation and spread of these weapons—artillery shells, atomic demolition devices, bombs, missiles to be fired from ships and submarines, air-to-air missiles, and surface-to-air missiles—have increased enormously. In addition, the US has deployed these tactical weapons around the world—in South Korea, in the Philippines, and 2,500 of them on the high seas. The US has made it clear that it is ready to use its tactical nuclear weapons even without being attacked by such weapons. This implies that the US would be prepared to use nuclear weapons in a conflict with a non-nuclear state. This might happen in the third world, and North Korea has frequently been suggested as a possible target.

The probable truth is that some of the nuclear states, including at least one and probably both of the superpowers, are unwilling under any circumstance to give up nuclear weapons. They feel that they have to maintain their perceived technological advantage, and want to retain the option of utilising this advantage despite the consequences. So long as this remains the case, the Non-Proliferation Treaty can slow down the rate of nuclear proliferation but can never prevent it altogether. The atomic explosion in India in 1974 bears testimony to its inherent weakness.

4. PROHIBITION OF TRANSFERS TO REPRESSIVE REGIMES

During recent years, the international community *has* been concerned about arms transfers to one area: South Africa. Until 1974, there were attempts to limit arms transfers to Portugal as well. The United Nations regulations concerning armament transfers to Southern Africa is based on the (partial) prohibition on transfers to repressive regimes, and on the legitimisation of transfers to liberation movements. This is in clear distinction to the previous efforts at limitation, which aimed more at securing dominance than at eliminating it. These embargoes are thus worthy of attention, even if they have been less than effective.

In August 1963 the UN Security Council demanded that all states should immediately stop the sale and transfer of arms and munition of all types, and military vehicles, to South Africa. The Security Council at this time rejected a proposed paragraph 3 which would have prohibited 'export of strategic material', i.e. material which could be utilised in domestic arms production in South Africa, but this was included later in Security Council resolution S/194, adopted on 18 June 1964 and covering equipment and material destined for the manufacture or maintenance of arms and munitions. In 1969, the General Assembly resolution A/2506(XXIV) demanded that there should be no provision of technical or other assistance which could help the South African government to produce arms, munitions, and military vehicles.

With regard to Portugal, the Security Council on 31 July 1963 (S/180) demanded that all states should immediately stop any support to the Portuguese government which would allow Portugal to continue its repressive policy against the colonial population. All measures were to be taken to prevent the sale and delivery of arms and military equipment to the Portuguese government. Except for Norway, which voted in favour, all NATO members abstained from this resolution, and this opposition to a comprehensive embargo continued during the following years and made it necessary for the General Assembly to take over the formulation of international regulation. In its resolution A/2270 (XXII) of 17 November 1967, the General Assembly demanded all states, and specifically NATO countries, to take the following measures:

—to immediately stop the provision of any assistance to the Portuguese government, including the training of military personnel;
—to prevent all sale or delivery of arms and military equipment to the Portuguese government;
—to stop the sale or other delivery to the Portuguese government of equipment and material which was destined for the manufacture or maintenance of arms and munition.

The General Assembly continued to deplore the aid which the government of Portugal received from its allies in NATO. In 1972, the Security Council again took action, and in resolution S/312 deplored the policies of certain states which continued to provide Portugal with military assistance. It also expressly demanded an end to all assistance which allowed the continuation of repression, and the taking of necessary measures to prohibit the sale and delivery of arms and military equipment, including also equipment and material which could be used for the manufacture and maintenance of arms and munition. This resolution was adopted by the Security Council only because the

NATO members—the US, France, and Britain—abstained, rather than voting against it.

It can be seen that the United Nations has adopted comprehensive embargoes not only on direct arms transfers, but also on participation in the development of domestic arms production in South Africa and in Portugal. But the same countries which have either prevented the Security Council from making decisions or have abstained in the voting, have found a number of excuses for not fully and effectively implementing the embargoes.

The United Kingdom, which had been the traditional arms supplier to South Africa, did to a very large extent opt out of this market, although some arms continued to be transferred through loopholes in the embargo regulations. The US also effected an almost complete embargo on major weapons to Portugal and South Africa. France, the Federal Republic of Germany, and Italy, however, stepped up their involvement in Southern Africa, and it has become a major outlet for their own arms production and development of military technology. These countries argued that the Security Council resolution on South Africa was not binding; since there was no threat to peace, they claimed, the Security Council could not make a mandatory decision, and states were therefore free to decide the scope of the embargo. They further claimed that the embargo applied only to weapons which could be used for repression. This is an interesting interpretation, and has been made by the US, the UK, and France, in differing ways. The United States prohibited the transfer of all major weapons, Britain allowed only weapons utilised in connection with naval defence, and France provided a wide range of weapons including helicopters for landward use. This approach does not, as is obvious, deprive South Africa of weapons to be used for repression, nor does it take into account the sub-imperial position of South Africa, in which internal repression and external interventionism are combined, and where therefore the whole range of armoury can be—and is—utilised for illegal purposes. This applies to the illegal occupation of Namibia, the intervention in Angola, and the repressive policies inside South Africa itself.

Other excuses were also given. The first Security Council embargo resolutions were adopted only in 1963, although they had been discussed since 1961. Western powers thus had ample time to enter into contracts during the intervals, and these 'pre-existing contracts' were held by the supplier countries to fall outside the scope of the embargo. Another excuse was the proviso, made by the US and the UK in 1963, that exceptions to the embargo could be made in the future if collective self-defence so required. Since then, several Western countries have in fact shown an interest in developing closer working alliances with South Africa. There is little doubt that the US State Department encouraged South African interventions in Angola, and there is also reason to believe that it came as a shock, not only to the State Department but also to South Africa, that the US Congress prohibited the transfer of weapons to the South African-supported UNITA and the Zaire-supported FNLA movements in Angola. This represented an important reversal in the increasingly close co-operation between South Africa and certain external powers.

Several efforts have later been made to obtain a mandatory and comprehensive arms embargo by a resolution of the Security Council. This would require a finding that there existed a threat to international peace under Chapter VII of the UN Charter. On several occasions these efforts were stalled by Western vetoes, but in November 1977 the Security Council adopted resolution SC418/1977 which does determine that the acquisition of arms and related material by South Africa constitutes a threat to the maintenance of international peace and security. Following this resolution, all Western powers seem to have halted overt deliveries of arms to South Africa, and abandoned attempts to distinguish between defensive and repressive weapons.

With regard to Portugal, the excuses were different. In this case, it was accepted that Portuguese colonialism was a threat to the peace and security of the independent African states. The main excuse, therefore, by those Western powers who continued to deliver weapons, was that there was a distinction between weapons destined for repression in Africa, on the one hand, and those weapons which allowed Portugal to fulfil its obligations as a member of NATO, on the other. The initial Security Council resolution is ambiguous on this point, but this ambiguity was eliminated by later resolutions, and the General Assembly made it clear that the embargo included *all* deliveries of arms and equipment to the Portuguese government. In practical terms it proved impossible to maintain the distinction between weapons for NATO use and weapons for repression. Several NATO powers considered it satisfactory to obtain a promise by the Portuguese government that the arms would not be used outside the NATO area. However, the Portuguese government made its position very clear by stating that the weapons would not be utilised except for defensive purposes inside Portuguese territory, which, according to Portugal, included Angola, Mozambique and Guinea Bissau. After the Portuguese *coup* in 1974, abundant evidence was obtained showing that a substantial part of the arms transferred from 1963 onwards were in fact utilised in the colonies.

One might easily conclude that the United Nations embargoes have been a failure. But this is too hasty a judgement. It would be more accurate to say that the approach was creative and adequate, but that *the implementation* failed because of the insincerity of certain major states, and because of the lack of vigilant public opinion inside those countries which could more actively push governments towards compliance with the UN regulations.

5. ALTERNATIVE APPROACHES

The Non-Proliferation Treaty and the embargoes on South Africa and Portugal are the main post-war international agreements to control the transfer of military technology. The subject has come up in international negotiating fora on a number of occasions. In general, proposals have centred around increased publicity for the arms trade either through some form of international register or through an inter-governmental study. Even these limited proposals have been strenuously opposed by third-world countries, particularly the so-called sub-imperial nations—Iran, Brazil, India, etc.—on the grounds that they are essentially discriminatory. This is, of course, true but the relevance of discrimination depends on the extent to which a register, or even some form of mild constraint on arms transfer, exposes or accentuates *actual* military inequalities. The problem about this kind of multi-national proposal is precisely the fact that it draws attention to *perceived* military inequalities—of particular importance for sub-imperial nations maintaining a position in the middle of the international hierarchy. The more that public investigation and international diplomacy is diverted into the statistics of the arms trade and the minutiae of calculations about military-technical capabilities, the more difficult it becomes to pursue meaningful disarmament policies and the more likely it is that well-intentioned politicians, peace researchers or dis-armament lobbyists will be caught up in the prevailing ideology of military technology.

An alternative approach would recognise the limited value of most types of sophisticated technology in the third-world context and would seek alternative approaches to defence based on alternative forms of force more appropriate to the prevailing social relations. The kind of thing that might be envisaged would be a citizen's army, perhaps on the model of Switzerland or China, organised around territorial defence. This would not necessarily involve the rejection of all arms imports. It might prove more cost-effective in terms of both economics and defence to import some kinds of weapons, which could be operated and maintained efficiently by relatively unskilled armies but which would be excessively costly to produce. An example might be a simple man-portable missile for defence against aircraft or tanks. The point would be—to use the terminology of the Introduction—to organise relations of force around indigenous social conditions, combined with a development strategy aimed at the fulfilment of basic needs rather than the rapid achievement of industrialisation; for, as we have seen, the relations of force that characterise the industrial army are inimical to those objectives. Hence the techniques of force would be those appropriate for the relations of force and those techniques based on the weapon system concept, which are only compatible with an industrial army, would be unsuitable. It might be possible to go further and consider alternatives to the use of force even for defence, i.e. non-violent defence, civil disobedience, etc. But this is a subject for further research.

An approach of this kind would evidently have global repercussions, not only by example. Dependence is not one-sided, and it seems that the function of arms sales in financing the industrial capacity to produce arms, in paying for essential raw materials like oil, and in opening up new markets for commercial products is becoming more important. In the absence of a planned policy for conversion, a major reduction in the volume of arms transfers could accentuate economic difficulties in advanced industrial nations and cause a major crisis in the defence industries. Hence the argument about political power and military technology could be turned on its head. By *not* buying arms, third-world nations could greatly increase their economic and political bargaining power in world affairs.

In effect, this is a proposal for unilateral or possibly regional initiatives. It is a proposal that is most likely to come into effect as a result of major political and social transformation in third-world countries; for at present there are many military regimes with a vested interest in the current global military structure. Nevertheless, there are indications that this approach may become increasingly acceptable. A limited form of sub-regional constraint is exercised by the Andean States of Latin America as a consequence of the Declaration of Ayachuco. In the General Assembly debate in 1976, several nations protested about exploitation through arms sales. The ambassador from Trinidad argued that the flow of arms was a form of subsidy to industrial nations. The foreign minister of Singapore, in a widely quoted statement,[8] said that:

> The massive flow of arms to the third world confronts it with a new danger. It is first of all a drain on their economies. But even more important, is the fact that it creates a new form of dependence on the great powers who can exploit the third world's dependence on them for arms, to manipulate them, to engineer conflicts between them, and to use them as proxies in their competition for influence.

This growing concern about the proliferation of armaments, by recipients as well as suppliers, is the impulse behind the decision to hold a Special Session of the United Nations General Assembly in May 1978 on the subject of Disarmament. It is also the impulse behind the Nordic initiative, which was approved by the 1978 Special Session, for an in-depth study of Disarmament and Development.

These are the platforms which could be utilised to transform current thinking about the world military order and to expose the myths about military technology and military power. Respect for unilateralism would perhaps be the most important and radical concept that could be propagated by an international body.

NOTES

1. On this point see, in particular, A. Chayes, 'An inquiry into the workings of arms control agreements', *Harvard Law Review* 85(5) (1972) 905–69.
2. Precisely what these concepts might be is a matter for detailed inquiry. Professor Bert Röling (in, for example, his *The Law of War and Dubious Weapons*, SIPRI, 1976) has offered important guidelines, most notably in his 'threshold principle'.
3. Brussels Act, 1890.
4. See SIPRI, *Arms Trade with the Third World* (Stockholm: Almquist & Wicksell, 1971) Ch. 17.
5. Ibid., Ch. 21.
6. The contradiction in Carter's policy was discussed by Emma Rothschild, 'Carter and Arms Sales', *New York Review of Books*, 15 Sep 1977.
7. Alva Myrdal, *The Game of Disarmament: How the United States and Russia Run the Arms Race* (New York: Pantheon Books, 1976).
8. 31st Session of the United Nations General Assembly, 29 Sep 1976.

Selected Bibliography

Military periodicals and journals

a. *Official or semi-official military journals, discussing strategic and military-industrial topics*
    Allgemeine Schweizerische Militärzeitschrift (monthly, Switzerland)
    Defense Management Journal (quarterly, USA)
    Military Review (monthly, USA)
    Défense Nationale (monthly, France)
    Journal of the Royal United Services Institute (quarterly, UK)
    Nato's Fifteen Nations (bi-monthly, Brussels)
    Osterreichische Militärzeitschrift (monthly, Austria)
    Soviet Military Review (monthly, Soviet Union)
    Militärwesen (monthly, GDR)
    Wehrkunde (monthly, FRG)

b. *Arms technology journals, discussing weapons development, technology and military-industrial topics*
    Aerospace International (bi-monthly, FRG)
    Armies and Weapons (bi-monthly, Switzerland)
    Aviation Week and Space Technology (weekly, USA)
    Flight International (bi-weekly, USA)
    Interavia (monthly, FRG)
    Wehrtechnik (monthly, FRG)

c. *Private information services, giving detailed information for arms producers*
    Defense Market Survey (monthly, USA)
    International Defense Business (weekly, USA)
    Milavnews (monthly, UK)
    Wehrdienst (weekly, FRG)

d. *Publications of different armed forces in the USA*
    Air Force (monthly)
    Armed Forces Journal International (monthly)
    Marine Corps Gazette (monthly)
    Navy International (monthly)
    US Naval Institute Proceedings (monthly)

e. *Military and strategic journals published in developing countries or regions*
    Asian Defence Journal (quarterly, Malaysia)
    Estrategia (bi-monthly, Argentina)
    Institute of Defence Studies Analyses Journal (quarterly, India)
    Pakistan Army Journal (monthly, Pakistan)
    Paratus (bi-monthly, Republic of South Africa)
    Revista Maritima Brasileira (quarterly, Brazil)
    United Services Institute Journal (bi-monthly, India)

f. *Journals, independent of the military establishment*
    Adelphi Papers (IISS) (bi-weekly, UK)
    Antimilitärismusinformationen (monthly, FRG)
    Armed Forces and Society (quarterly, US)
    Arms Control Today (monthly, USA)
    Bulletin of Atomic Scientists (monthly, USA)
    Campaign Against Arms Trade Newsletter (irregular, UK)
    Defense Monitor (monthly, USA)
    North American Congress on Latin America Empire Report (monthly, USA)
    Survival (IISS) (monthly, UK)

g. *Relevant peace research journals*
    Bulletin of Peace Proposals (quarterly, Oslo)
    Etudes Polémologiques (quarterly, Paris)
    Instant Research on Peace and Violence (quarterly, Tampere, Finland)
    Journal of Conflict Resolution (quarterly, New Haven, Connecticut, USA)
    Journal of Peace Research (quarterly, Oslo)
    New Perspectives (quarterly, Helsinki)
    Peace and Change (quarterly, Rohnert Park, California, USA)
    Peace Research in Japan (yearbook, Tokyo)
    Peace Research Reviews (six issues in a volume, Oakville, Canada)
    Pugwash Newsletter (four issues a year, London)

Reference books

Albrecht, G., *Weyers Flottentaschenbuch* (Munich, annual; English version published by the United States Naval Institute)
Archer, D. H. R., *Jane's Infantry Weapons* (London, annual)
International Institute for Strategic Studies (IISS), *The Military Balance* (London, annual)
Labayle-Couhat, J., *Flottes de combat* (Paris, bi-annual)
Moore, J., *Jane's Fighting Ships* (London, annual)
Moulton, J. L., *Brassey's Annual: Defense and the Armed Forces* (London, annual)
Owen, J. I. H., *Brassey's Infantry Weapons of the World* (annual)
Pretty, R. T., *Jane's Weapon Systems* (London, annual)
Senger and Etterlin, *Taschenbuch der Panzer* (Munich, several revised eds.)
Sivard, R., *World Military and Social Expenditures* (Institute for World Order) (New York, annual)
Stockholm International Peace Research Institute (SIPRI), *Yearbook of World Armaments and Disarmament* (Stockholm, annual)
Taylor, J. W. R., *Jane's All the World's Aircraft* (London, annual)
The Chanakya Defence Annual (Allahabad, India, annual)
US Arms Control and Disarmament Agency, *World Military Expenditures and Arms Transfers* (Washington, annual)
Wiener, F., *Die Armeen der NATO-Staaten* (Vienna, several revised eds.)

Selected General Works on Armaments and the Military

1. GENERAL

Albrecht, Ulrich, *Der Handel mit Waffen* (Munich, 1971)

—— 'Armaments and Inflation', *Instant Research on Peace and Violence*, Vol. IV (1974) no. 3

—— 'Transnationale Rüstungskonzerne in Westeuropa', *Leviathan, Zeitschrift für Sozialwissenschaft*, 1 (1974) 81–105

—— Lock, P. and Wulf, H., *Arbeitsplätze durch Rüstung?* (Reinbek, 1978)

Allison, G. T. and Morris, F. A., 'Armaments and Arms Control: Exploring the Determinants of Military Weapons', *Daedalus* (Boston, Mass., Summer 1975)

Andexel, Ruth, *Imperialismus—Staatsfinanzen, Krieg. Probleme der Rüstungsfinanzierung des deutschen Imperialismus* (Berlin, 1968)

Aspaturian, Vernon V., 'The Soviet Military—Industrial Complex—Does it Exist?', *Journal of International Affairs*, Vol. 26, no. 1 (1972) 1–28

Baran, P. and Sweezy, P., *Monopoly Capital* (London, 1968)

Barnet, Richard, J., *The Economy of Death* (New York, 1969)

Bredow, W. von (ed.), *Economic and Social Aspects of Disarmament* (BPP Publications, Nov 1973)

Cahn, A. H., Kruzel, J. J., Dawkins, P. M., and Huntzinger, J., *Controlling Future Arms Trade* (New York, 1977)

Carlton, David and Schaerf, Carlo (eds.), *The Dynamics of the Arms Race* (London, 1975)

Centre d'Information et de Coordination Pour l'Action Non Violente: François Maspero, *Les Trafics d'Armes de la France* (Paris, 1978)

—— (eds.), *Arms Control and Technological Innovation* (London, 1977)

Curnow, R., *et al.*, 'General and Complete Disarmament: a Systems-Analysis Approach', *Futures* (Guildford, Oct 1976)

Disarmament Study Group of the International Peace Research Association, 'Between Peace and War: The Quest for Disarmament', *Bulletin of Peace Proposals*, Vol. 6 (Oslo, Bergen, Tromsö, 1975)

Dumas, Lloyd J., 'Thirty Years of the Arms Race: deterioration of economic strength and military security', *Peace and Change*, Vol. 4, no. 2 (1977)

Engelhardt, Klaus and Heise, Karl-Heinz, 'Militär-Industrie-Komplex im staatsmonopolistischen Herrschaftssystem', *Institut für Internationale Politik und Wirtschaft* (Berlin: Staatsverlag der Deutschen Demokratischen Republik, 1974)

Feld, Bernhard T., 'The Charade of Piecemeal Arms Limitation', *Bulletin of the Atomic Scientists*, Vol. XXXI (1975) no. 1

Galbraith, John Kenneth, *How to Control the Military* (New York, 1969)

Galloway, Jonathan F., 'The Military-Industrial Linkages of US-based Multinational Corporation', *International Studies Quarterly*, Vol. 16, no. 4 (Dec 1972) 491–3

Gantzel, Klaus Jürgen, *System und Akteur. Beiträge zur vergleichenden Kriegsursachenforschung* (Düsseldorf, 1972)

Haftendorn, Helga, *Militärhilfe und Rüstungsexporte der BRD* (Düsseldorf, 1971)

Harkavy, Robert E., *The Arms Trade and International Systems* (Cambridge, Mass., 1975)

Huntington, Samuel, *The Soldier and the State* (Cambridge, Mass., 1957)

Janowitz, M., *The Professional Soldier* (New York, 1960)

Jolly, R. (ed.), *Disarmament and World Development* (London, 1978)

Kaldor, M., 'European Defence Industries; National and International Implications', Institute for the Study of International Organisations (Brighton, 1972)

—— and Cockburn, A., 'The Defense Confidence Game' *The New York Review of Books*, Vol. XXI (June 1974) no. 10, 24–32

—— and Robinson, J. P., 'War' in Freeman, C. and Jahoda, M., *World Futures: The Great Debate* (London, 1978)

Kidron, Michael, *Western Capitalism Since the War* (London, 1967)

Kurth, James R., 'The Political Economy of Weapons Procurement: The Follow-on Imperative', *American Economic Review*, Vol. 62 (1972) no. 2, 304–11

Lee, William T., 'The Politico-Military-Industrial Complex of the USSR', *Journal of International Affairs*, Vol. 26 (1972) no. 1, 73–86

Leitenberg, Milton, 'The Dynamics of Military Technology Today', *International Social Science Journal*, Vol. XXV (1973) no. 3

Leontief, Wassily, *et al.,* 'The Economic Impact—Industrial and Regional—of an Arms Cut', *Input–Output Economics*, ed. Wassily Leontief (New York, 1966)

Lumsden, Malvern, 'New Military Technology and the Erosion of International Law: The Case of the Dum-Dum Bullets Today', *Instant Research on Peace Violence*, Vol. 4 (1974) no. 1, 15–9

—— 'Incendiary Weapons', SIPRI Monograph (Stockholm, 1975)

Lydenberg, Steven, *Weapons for the World* (Update. The U.S. Corporate Role in International Arms Transfers) (New York, 1977)

Melman, Seymour, *Pentagon Capitalism. The Political Economy of War* (New York/San Francisco/St Louis/Toronto, 1970)

—— *The Permanent War Economy: American Capitalism in Decline* (New York, 1974)

Mischke, Ferdinand Otto, *Rüstungswettlauf, Ursachen und Auswirkungen,* (Stuttgart, 1972)

Müller, Wolfgang and Oelschläger, Rudolf, *Streitkräfte im Klassenkampf unserer Zeit* (Berlin, Militärverlag der Deutschen Demokratischen Republik, 1972) 9–151

Myrdal, A., *The Game of Disarmament* (New York, 1976)

Rilling, Rainer, 'Zur Analyse des "militärisch-industriellen Komplexes" in der BRD', *Internationaler Dialog* (1971) 360–8.

Robinson, Perry, 'The Special Case of Chemical and Biological Weapons', *Bulletin of the Atomic Scientists*, Vol. XXXI (May 1975) no. 5

Rosen, Steven (ed.), *Testing the Theory of the Military-Industrial Complex* (Lexington, 1973)

Schumann, F., *The Logic of World Power* (New York: Pantheon, 1974)

Senghaas, Dieter, *Rüstung und Militärismus* (Frankfurt, 1972)

Thayer, Georg, *War Business* (*Geschäfte mit Waffen und Krieg*) (Hamburg, 1970)

Trebilcock, Clive, 'British Armaments and European Industrialization, 1890–1914', *Economic History Review*, Second Series, Vol. 26 (1973) 254–72

—— ' "Spin-off" in British Economic History: Armaments and Industry, 1760–1914', *Economic History Review*, Second Series, Vol. 26 (1973) 254–72

United Nations, *Economic and Social Consequences of the Arms Race and of Military Expenditures,* Report of the Secretary-General (New York, United Nations, 1972)

—— *Economic and Social Consequences of the Armaments Race and its Extremely*

Harmful Effects on World Peace and Security, Report of the Secretary-General, A/32/88, (New York, United Nations, Aug 1977)
—— *Disarmament and Development*, Report of the Group of Experts on the Economic and Social Consequences of Disarmaments (New York: United Nations, 1972)
Vagts, Alfred, *A History of Militarism* (New York, 1959)
Vereinigung Deutscher Wissenschaftler, *Eine andere Verteidigung?* (Munich, 1973)
Vincineau, Michael, *La belgique et le commerce des armes* (Brussels, 1974)
von Weizsäcker, Carl Friedrich (ed.), *Kriegsfolgen und Kriegsverhütung* (Munich, 1971)

2. MILITARY AND ARMAMENTS IN PERIPHERAL COUNTRIES

Albrecht, Ulrich and Sommer, Birgit A., *Deutsche Waffen für die Dritte Welt. Militärhilfe und Entwicklungspolitik* (Reinbek, 1972)
Albrecht, Ulrich, Ernst, Dieter, Lock, Peter and Wulf, Herbert, 'Militarization, Arms Transfer and Arms Production in Peripheral Countries', *Journal of Peace Research*, Vol. XII (1975) no. 3
—— 'Armaments and Underdevelopment', *Bulletin of Peace Proposals*, Vol. 5 (1974) 173–85
—— *Rüstung und Unterentwicklung, Die verschärfte Militärisierung: Iran, Indien, Griechenland/Türkei* (Reinbek, 1976)
—— 'Arms Trade and Transfer of Military Technology', *Bulletin of Peace Proposals*, Vol. 8 (1977) no. 2 (special issue)
Barrett, Raymond, 'Arms Dilemma for the Developing World', *Military Review* (Apr 1970) 29–35
Be'eri, Elizier, *Army Officers in Arab Politics and Society* (New York and London, Pall Mall, 1970)
Benoit, Emile, *Defense and Economic Growth in Developing Countries* (Massachusetts/Toronto/London, 1973)
Bienen, Henry, 'The Background to Contemporary Studies of Militaries and Modernization', Henry Bienen (ed.), *The Military and Modernization* (Chicago, 1971)
The Comptroller General of the United States, *Foreign Military Sales. A Growing Concern*, Report to the Congress (Washington, June 1976)
Darling, Roger, 'Analyzing Insurgency', *Military Review* (Feb 1974) 27–37
Deutsches Institut für Wirtschaftsforschung (ed.), 'Verteidigungsausgaben und Rüstungsimporte der Entwicklungsländer 1961 bis 1970', *Deutsches Institut für Wirtschaftsforschung, Wochenbericht* 50/73 (Berlin, 13 Dec 1973)
van Doorn, Jacques, *Military Profession and Military Regimes* (Mouton/The Hague/Paris, 1969)
Duchêne, François, 'The Proliferation of Arms: Motives, Magnitude and Consequences', *Adelphi Papers*, no. 133, 14–23
Eide, Asbjørn, 'The Transfer of Arms to Third World Countries and their Internal Uses', *International Social Science Journal*, Vol. XXVIII, no. 2 (1976) 307–25
Ernst, Dieter, Lock, Peter and Wulf, Herbert, 'Die "Dritte Welt" rüstet', *Forum E*, no. 3/4 (1974) 71–6

Fairbairn, Geoffrey, 'Revolutionary Guerrilla Warfare: The Counterside Version' (RUSI, Dec 1974 and Pelican Books)

Feit, Edward, 'Pen, Sword, and People: Military Regimes in the Formation of Political Institutions', *World Politics*, Vol. xxi (Jan 1973) no. 2, 251–73

Finer, Samuel E., *The Man on Horseback. The Role of the Military in Politics* (New York, 1963)

Gardan, Eric, *Dossier A . . . comme armes* (Paris, 1975)

Glick, Edward Bernhard, *The Non-Military Use of the Military: Peaceful Conflict* (Harrisburg, Pa., 1967)

Gutteridge, William, *Military Institutions and Power in the New States* (New York, 1965)

Hanning, Hugh, *The Peaceful Uses of Military Forces* (New York/Washington/London, 1967)

Hoadley, Stephen, 'Social Complexity, Economic Development, and Military Coups d'Etat in Latin America and Asia', *Journal of Peace Research*, no. 1/2 (1973) 119–20

Huntington, Samuel P., 'Praetorianism and Political Decay', in *Political Order in Changing Societies* (New Haven/London, 1969) 2nd ed., 192–263

Internationale Forschungsgruppe über die politische Rolle der Militärs in den Entwicklungsländern, 'Wem dient die Armee?', *Probleme des Friedens und des Sozialismus*, no. 4 (1974) 478–95

Jackman, R. W., 'Politicians in Uniform', *American Political Science Review* (Sep 1976)

Janowitz, Morris, *The Military in the Development of New Nations. An Essay in Comparative Analysis* (Chicago/London, 1964)

Jenkins, Brian Michael, *High Technology Terrorism and Surrogate War: The Impact of New Technology on Low-Level Violence* (Santa Monica, Jan 1975)

Joenniemi, Pertti, 'Two Models of Mercenarism. Historical and Contemporary', *Instant Research on Peace and Violence*, no. 3/4 (1977) 184–96

Johnson, James R., 'People's War and Conventional Armies', *Military Review* (Jan 1974) 24–33

Johnson, John (ed.), *The Role of the Military in Underdeveloped Countries* (Princeton, N.J., 1962)

Joshua, Wynfred and Gibert, Stephen P., *Arms for the Third World* (Baltimore/London, 1969)

Joxe, Alain, 'Maitrise des Armements dans les Pays Sous-Developpés', *International Political Science Association, IXth World Congress* (Montreal, 19–25 Aug 1973)

Kaldor, Mary, 'The Arms Trade and Society', *Economic and Political Weekly*, Vol. xi, nos. 5/7 (1976) 293–301

—— 'The Military in Development', *World Development*, Vol. 4, no. 6 (1976) 459–82

Kemp, Geoffrey, 'Classification of Weapons Systems and Force Designs', *Less Developed Country Environments*, Arms Control Project (Cambridge, Mass.: Center for International Studies, Massachusetts Institute of Technology, Feb 1970)

Kende, Istvan, *Local Wars in Asia, Africa and Latin America 1945–1969* (Budapest, 1972)

Kennedy, Gavin, *The Military in the Third World* (London, 1974)

Klare, Michael T., *War without End. American Planning for the Next Vietnams* (New York, 1972)
—— 'The Pentagon Bleeds the Third World', *The Progressive*, Vol. 38 (June 1974) no. 6, 21–5
—— 'Dealing Arms in the Third World', *Latin America and Empire Report, North American Congress on Latin America*, Vol. VIII (Jan 1974) no. 1
Lock, Peter and Wulf, Herbert, *Register of Arms Production in Developing Countries* (Hamburg, Mar 1977) (mimeo)
Luckham, Robin, 'Militarism: Arms and the Internationalization of Capital', *IDS Bulletin*, Vol. 8, no. 3 (1977) 38–50
Luttwak, Edward, *Der Coup d'État oder wie inszeniert man einen Staatsstreich* (Reinbek, 1969)
Mack, Andrew, 'Sharpening the Contradictions: Guerilla Strategy in Imperialist Wars', *Race and Class*, Vol. XVII (1975) no. 2, 161–78
Miller, Martin J., 'Israel's Quest for Military Self-Sufficiency, *Military Review* (Mar 1971) 68–73
Nordlinger, E. A., 'Soldiers in Mufti: The Impact of Military Rule Upon Economic and Social Change in the Non-Western States', *American Political Science Review*, 64 (Dec 1970) 1131–48
Øberg, Jan, 'Arms Trade with the Third World as an Aspect of Imperialism', *Journal of Peace Research*, Vol. XII (1975) no. 3
Pauker, Guy J., *et al., In Search of Self-Reliance: U.S. Security Assistance to the Third World under the Nixon Doctrine* (Santa Monica, June 1973)
Pierson, Earl F., 'The United States' Role in Counterinsurgency', *Naval War College Review* (Jan–Feb 1973) 88–90
Price, Robert M., 'A Theoretical Approach to Military Rule in New States', *World Politics*, Vol. 23 (Apr 1971) no. 3, 399–430
Pye, Lucian W., 'Armies in the Process of Political Modernization', in John J. Johnson (ed.), *The Role of the Military in Underdeveloped Countries* (Princeton, 1962)
Rosenberg, Mark B. and Stupak, R. J., 'Military Professionalism and Political Intervention', *Society* (May/June 1975)
Rothschild, Emma, 'The Arms Boom and How to Stop it', *New York Review of Books* (20 Jan 1977) 24–30
Saunders, John, 'Impact and Consequences of the Military Transfer of Technology to Developing Countries', *Australian and New Zealand Journal of Sociology*, Vol. 12, no. 3 (1976) 204–12
SIPRI, *Arms Trade Register: The Arms Trade with the Third World* (Cambridge. Mass./London/Stockholm, 1975)
—— *The Arms Trade with the Third World* (Stockholm, 1971)
—— *Oil and Security* (Stockholm, 1974) monograph
The Soviet Military Aid Program as a Reflection of Soviet Objectives, submitted to Air Force Office of Scientific Research, Washington, D.C., June 1965, Contract no. AF 49(638)-1412
Staar, Richard F., 'Soviet Weapons for the Third World', *Allgemeine Schweizerische Militärzeitschrift*, no. 1 (Jan 1974) 14–17
Stanley, J. and Pearton, M., *The International Trade in Arms* (New York/Washington, 1972)
Tibi, Bassam, *Militär und Sozialismus in der Dritten Welt* (Frankfurt, 1973)

Wolf, Eric R., *Peasant Wars of the Twentieth Century* (New York, 1969)
Wolpin, Miles D., *Military Aid and Counterrevolution in the Third World* (Lexington, 1973)

3. MILITARY AND ARMAMENTS IN AFRICA

Antola, Esko, 'The Roots of Domestic Military Interventions in Black Africa', *Instant Research on Peace and Violence*, Vol. 5, no. 4 (1975) 207–21
Baumann, Herbert and Nimschowski, Helmut, 'Zur Rolle der Armee im Prozess der nichtkapitalistischen Entwicklung Algeriens', *Militärwesen*, no. 14 (1970) 1113–23
Booth, R., 'The Armed Forces of African States, 1970', *Adelphi Papers*, no. 67 (1970)
Crocker, Chester A., 'Military Dependence: The Colonial Legacy in Africa', *Journal of Modern African Studies*, Vol. 12 (1974) no. 2, 246–86
Davidson, *The Liberation of Guinée* (London, 1969)
—— *The Eye of the Storm* (London, 1975)
Decalo, Samuel, *Coups and Military Rule in Africa* (New Haven, 1976)
Edwards, R. A., 'Security Problems in Southern Africa', *Paratus* (June 1973)
Eleazu, Uma O., 'The Role of the Army in African Politics. A Reconsideration of Existing Theories and Practices', *Journal of Developing Areas*, no. 7 (Jan 1973) 265–86
First, Ruth, *The Barrel of a Gun: Political Power in Africa and the Coup d'État* (2nd ed.) (Harmondsworth, 1972)
Gutteridge, William, 'Foreign Military Assistance and Political Attitudes in Developing African Countries', *Bulletin of the Institute of Development Studies*, Vol. 4 (Sep 1972) no. 4, 24–33
Johns, Sheridan, 'Obstacles to Guerilla Warfare—A South African Case Study', *Journal of Modern African Studies*, Vol. 11 (1973) no. 2
Kemp, Geoffrey, 'South Africa's Defence Programme', *Survival*, Vol. XIV (July/Aug, 1972) no. 4, 158–60
Luckham, Robin, *The Nigerian Military. A Sociological Analysis of Authority and Revolt 1960–67* (Cambridge University Press, n.d.)
Marakis, John and Ayele, Nega, *Class and Revolution in Ethiopia* (1978)
Martin, Michele, *L'armée et la société en Afrique: essai de synthèses et d'investigation bibliographique*, Centre d'Etude Afrique Noire (Bordeaux, 1975)
Matthies, Volker, 'Militär, Gesellschaft und Gewalt in Äthiopien', *Vierteljahresberichte, no. 54* (Dec 1973) 355–78
Mazrui, Ali A., *Soldiers and Kinsmen in Uganda, The Making of a Military Ethnocracy* (London, 1975)
Miners, N. J., *The Nigerian Army 1956–1966*, Studies in African History (London, 1971)
Quandt, William B., *Algerian Military Development: The Professionalization of a Guerilla Army* (Santa Monica, Mar 1972)
Raeburn, Michael, *Black Fire! Accounts of the Guerrilla War in Rhodesia* (London, 1978)
Shremlau, John J., *The International Politics of the Nigerian Civil War, 1967–70* (Princeton, N.J., 1977)

Tibi, Bassam, 'Zur Rolle der Armee in Marokko. Hintergründe der Putsch-versuche', *Blätter für Deutsche und Internationale Politik*, no. 7 (1973) 941–59
Welch, Claude E., 'Military Intervention in Tropical Africa', *Military Review* (May 1970) 33–46
—— 'Praetorianism in Commonwealth West Africa', *Journal of Modern African Studies*, Vol. 10 (1972) no. 2, 203–21
—— (ed.), *Soldier and State in Africa* (Evanston, Ill., 1970)
White Paper on Defence and Armament Production, 1973, Republic of South Africa, Department of Defence
Zolberg, Aristide R., 'The Military Decade in Africa', *World Politics*, Vol. xxv (Jan, 1973) no. 2, 309–31

4. MILITARY AND ARMAMENTS IN ASIA

Abdel-Malek, Anow, *Egypt—A Military Society* (New York, 1968)
Ahmad, E., 'American and Russia in South Asia: Conflict or Collusion?', *Bulletin of Concerned Asian Scholars*, Vol. 6 (Jan–Mar 1974) no. 1
Anand, J. P., 'British Military Presence East of Suez', *Institute for Defence Studies and Analyses Journal*, Vol. 4 (Oct 1971) no. 2, 257–80
Ayoob, Mohammed, 'Iran in South-West Asia. The Local Gendarme?', *Economic and Political Weekly*, 31–3 (Aug 1973) 1415–16
Barang, Marcel, 'L'Iran—Renaissance d'un empire', *Le Monde Diplomatique* (20 May 1975)
—— 'Stratégie anticommuniste et pillage économique. La façade démo-cratique, l'ordre dictatorial et les conditions du profit', *Le Monde Diplomatique*, Sonderheft. *Les Militaires et le Pouvoir dans l'Asie des confrontations* (Feb 1975)
Baranwal, S. P. (ed.), *Military Yearbook 1973* (New Delhi, 1973)
Barber, Noel, *The War of the Running Dogs—How Malaya Defeated the Communist Guerillas 1948–60* (London, 1971)
Bix, Herbert P., 'Japan: The Roots of Militarism', in Marc Selden (ed.), *Remaking Asia, Essays on the American Uses of Power* (New York, 1974) pp. 305–62
Blood, Archer K., 'Nuclear Proliferation and the Indian Explosion', *Parameters*. Vol. 5 (1975) no. 1, 46–50
Bopegamage, A., 'The Military as a Modernizing Agent in India', *Economic Development and Cultural Change*, Vol. 20 (Oct 1971) no. 1
Boulding, Kenneth and Gleason, Alan H., 'War as an Investment: The Strange Case of Japan', in Kenneth Boulding et al., *Economic Imperialism* (University of Michigan Press, 1972)
Braun, Dieter, 'Der Indische Ozean in der sicherheitspolitischen Diskussion', *Europa Archiv*, 18 (1971) 645–58
Braun, Ursula, 'Iran als Führungsmacht im Mittleren Osten', *Europa Archiv*, 11 (10 June 1974) 373–82
Caldwell, Malcolm, et al., *Ten Years Military Terror in Indonesia* (Nottingham, 1975)
Chandrasekhara, Rao, 'Proliferation and the Indian Test', *Survival* (Sep/Oct 1974) 210–52.
Childs, Dennis and Kidron, Michael, 'India, the USSR and the MiG Project',

Economic and Political Weekly, Vol. VIII (Sep 1973) no. 38, 1721–8

Chopra, P. N., 'India and the MiG-21', *Air Enthusiast* (July 1973)

Cohen, Stephen, *The Indian Army, its Contribution to the Development of a Nation* (Berkeley/Los Angeles/London, 1971)

Cotrell, Alvin J., 'British Withdrawal from the Persian Gulf', *Military Review* (June 1970) 15–21

Croizat, Victor J., 'Stability in the Persian Gulf', *United States Naval Institute* (July 1973) 49–59

Crouch, Harold, 'Military Politics Under Indonesia's New Order', *Pacific Affairs*, Vol. 45 (1972) no. 2, 206–20

Dupuy d'Angeac, B., 'Le Japon et son Armée', *Défense nationale* (Apr 1973) 74–88

Fischer, Georges, 'L'Inde et la Bombe', *Politique étrangère*, 39, no. 3 (1974) 307–29

Furlong, R. D. M., 'Iran—eine Macht, mit der zu rechnen ist', *Internationale Wehrrevue*, no. 6 (1973) 719–29

Gandhi, Ved P., 'India's Self-Inflicted Defence Burden', *Economic and Political Weekly*, Vol. IX (Aug 1974), no. 35, 1485–94

Ghebhardt, Alexander O., 'The Soviet System of Collective Security in Asia', *Asian Survey*, Vol. XIII (Dec 1973) no. 12, 1075–91

Ghosh, S. K., 'Military Capability of China', *Institute for Defence Studies and Analyses Journal*, Vol. 4 (Apr 1972) no. 4, 480–95

Gough, Kathleen and Sharma, Hari (eds.), *Imperialism and Revolution in South Asia* (New York, 1973)

Government of India, Defence Services Estimates (New Delhi: Government of India Press, annual)

Government of India, Report of the Ministry of Defence (annual)

Gurtov, Melvin, 'The Nixon Doctrine and Southeast Asia', *Pacific Community*, Vol. 4 (Oct 1972) no. 1, 19–29

Halliday, Fred, *Arabia Without Sultans* (London, 1974)

Horelick, Arnold L., *The Soviet Union's 'Asian Collective Security' Proposal: A Club in Search of Members* (Santa Monica, 1974)

Hunter, Robert E., 'The Soviet Dilemma in the Middle East, Part II: Oil and the Persian Gulf', *Adelphi Papers*, no. 60 (Oct 1969)

Hurewitz, J. C., *Middle East Politics: The Military Dimension* (London, 1969)

Kapur, Ashok, 'India and the Atom', *Bulletin of the Atomic Scientists* (Sep 1974) 27–9

Katsu, Kohri et al., *The Fifty Years of Japanese Aviation 1910–1960* (Tokyo, 1961)

Kavic, Lorne J., *India's Quest for Security* (Los Angeles, 1967)

Klare, Michael T., 'The American Empire at Bay', *Society* (Sep/Oct 1974) 41–9

Komer, R. W., *The Malayan Emergency in Retrospect: Organization of a Successful Counterinsurgency Effort* (Santa Monica, Feb 1972)

Kraar, Louis, 'The Shah Drives to Build a New Persian Empire', *Fortune* (Oct 1974)

Kriebel, Rainer, 'Der Iran und seine militärischen Probleme', *Wehrkunde*, no. 12 (1973)

Kudryavtsev, V., 'Problems of Collective Security in Asia', *International Affairs* (Moscow, 1973) no. 12, 94–8

Lamballe, Alain, 'L'Inde et les Situations Belligènes (Étude Prospective 1974–1990)', *Etudes Polémologiques,* no. 12 (Apr 1974) 25–60

Lissak, Moshe, *Military Roles in Modernization: Civil–Military Roles in Thailand and Burma* (London, 1975)

Maxwell, Neville, *India's China War* (London, 1970)

McLean, D. B. G., 'The Soviet Navy in the Indian Ocean', *Royal United Services Institute,* Vol. 118 (1973) no. 4, 59–65

Moore, John E., 'The Persian Gulf and its Navies', *Navy International* (Sep 1973) 11–3

Naya, Seija, 'The Vietnam War and some Aspects of its Economic Impact on Asian Countries, *The Developing World,* Vol. IX (Mar 1971) no. 2, 32–57

Peltz, Steve, 'A Half-Decade and Air Defence', *Air Enthusiast* (Oct 1973)

Pfau, Richard, 'The Legal Status of American Forces in Iran', *Middle East Journal,* Vol. XXVIII (1974) no. 2

Quester, George H., 'Taiwan and Nuclear Proliferation', *Orbis,* Vol. XVIII (1974) no. 1, 140–50

Rangarao, B. V., 'Defence: A Socio-Economic Problem', *Economic and Political Weekly,* Vol. VI (Nov 1971) no. 48, 2407–11

Schneider, Eberhard, 'Das sowjetische kollektive Sicherheitssystem für Asien', *Internationales Asienforum,* Vol. 4 (1973) 615–31

Selden, Mark (ed.), *Remaking Asia. Essays on the American Uses of Power* (New York, 1971)

A Seminar Report, Indian Defence Budget 1972–73, *Institute for Defence Studies and Analyses Journal,* Vol. 4 (Apr 1972) no. 4, 425–46

Sethi, J. D., 'Military Aid and Foreign Intervention in the Indian Subcontinent,' *Institute for Defence Studies and Analyses Journal,* Vol. V (Oct 1972) no. 2, 225–47

Sielaff, Rüdiger, 'Die gesellschaftspolitischen Vorstellungen des Militärs und die Veränderung politischer Strukturen in Indonesien', *Vierteljahresberichte,* no. 48 (June 1972) 121–40

Sien-Chong, Niu, 'New Strategic Outlook of the Indian Subcontinent', *NATO's Fifteen Nations,* Vol. 19 (Oct/Nov 1974) no. 5, 9–69

Singh, Lalita Prasad, 'Indien und der Kernwaffen-Sperrvertrag', *Europa Archiv,* Series 12 (1970) 424–30

Subrahmanyam, K., 'Nehru's Concept of Indian Defence', *Institute for Defence Studies and Analyses Journal,* Vol. V (Oct 1972) no. 2, 196–211

——, 'Indian Nuclear Force in the Eighties?', *Institute for Defence Studies and Analyses Journal,* Vol. V (Apr 1973) no. 4, 457–71

——, 'Indian Defence Expenditure in Global Perspective', *Economic and Political Weekly* (New Delhi, June 1973) 1155–8

——, *Our National Security* (Economic and Scientific Research Foundation, Federation House, New Delhi, 1972)

Swadesh, R. de Roy, 'Prospects for Militarism in Japan, Pacific Community', *Asian Quarterly Review,* Vol. 5 (Jan 1974) no. 2.

Thee, Mark, 'War and Peace in Indochina, US, Asian and Pacific Policies', *Journal of Peace Research,* no. 1–2 (1973) 51–69

Weinstein, Martin E., 'Is Japan Changing Its Defense Policy?', *Pacific Community* (Tokyo, Jan 1973) Vol. 4, no. 2, 179–94

Wilcox, Wayne, 'Japanese and Indian National Security Strategies in the Asia

288   *The World Military Order*

of the 1970s: The Prospect for Nuclear Proliferation', *Adelphi Papers*, no. 92
(International Institute for Strategic Studies, London, 1972)

5. MILITARY AND ARMAMENTS IN LATIN AMERICA

'Arms Sales to Latin America. The State Department's Evaluation of the Basis of
U.S. Policy in Latin America, as of June 1971', *Inter-American Economic
Affairs*, Vol. xxv (1971) no. 2, 76–84, Government Documents

Bailey, Norman A., 'The Role of Military Forces in Latin America', *Military
Review* (Feb 1971) 67–73

Baines, John M., 'U.S. Military Assistance to Latin America', *Journal of Inter-
american Studies in World Affairs*, Vol. 14 (Nov 1972) no. 4, 469–86

Ballester, Horacio P., 'Conferencias de comandantes en jefe de fuerzas armadas
americanas', *Estrategia*, Vol. 5, no. 24 (Cordoba/Buenos Aires, 1973) 8–19

Burr, Robert N., *By Reason of Force, Chile and the Balancing of Power in South
America, 1830–1905* (Berkeley/Los Angeles, 1967)

Cannabrave Filho, Paulo, *Militarismo e Imperialismo en Brasil* (Buenos Aires,
1970)

Clinton, Richard Leo, 'The Modernizing Military: The Case of Peru', *Inter-
american Economic Affairs*, Vol. xxiv (1971) no. 4, 43–66

Codo, Enrique Martinez, 'Communist Revolutionary War in Latin America',
Military Review (Aug 1963) 3–20

Connolly, Stephen, 'A Systematic Analysis of the United States Military in Latin
America', *Journal of Contemporary Revolutions* (The International Relations
Center, San Francisco State College, special edition, 1970)

Cotter, J. and Fagen, R. R., *Latin America and the United States: Changing
Political Realities* (Stanford, 1974)

Drury, Bruce, 'Civil–Military Relations and Military Rule: Brazil Since 1964',
Journal of Political and Military Sociology, Vol. 2 (1974) no. 2, 191–204

Einaudi, Luigi R., *Beyond Cuba: Latin America Takes Charge of Its Future*
(New York, 1974)

——, 'Conflict and Cooperation among Latin American States' in L. R. Einaudi
(ed.) *Latin America in the 1970s* (Santa Monica) pp. 148–57

——, 'U.S. Relations with the Peruvian Military', in D. A. Sharp (ed.), *U.S.
Foreign Policy and Peru* (Austin/London: University of Texas Press, 1972)
pp. 15–56

—— et al., *Arms Transfers to Latin America: Toward a Policy of Mutual Respect*
(Santa Monica, June 1973)

Evans, Peter B., 'The Military, the Multinationals, and the "Miracle": The
Political Economy of the "Brazilian Model" of Development', *Studies in
Comparative International Development*, Vol. ix (1974) no. 3, 26–45

Evers, Tilman Toennies, *Militärregierung in Argentinien. Das Politische System
der 'Argentinischen Revolution'* (Hamburg/Frankfurt, 1972)

Fernández-Saxe, John, 'Ciencia Social y Contrarevolución Preventiva en
Latino-américa', *Aportes*, no. 26 (Oct 1972) 97–135

——, *Proyecciones Hemisféricas de la Pax Americano* (Lima, 1971)

Gonzalez, Heliodoro, 'Public Safety in Latin America: "State of Siege" ',
Inter-American Economic Affairs, Vol. xxvii (1973) no. 3, 87–96

Guglialmelli, Juan E., 'Fuerzos Armadas para la Liberación Nacional', *Estrategia*, no. 23 (1973) 7–30

Heare, Gertrude E., *Trends in Latin American Military Expenditures 1940–1970/ Argentina, Brazil, Chile, Colombia, Peru and Venezuela* (Office of External Research Bureau of Intelligence and Research, Dec 1971)

Joxe, Alain, 'L'armée chilienne et les avatars de la transition', *Les Temps Modernes*, 29, no. 323 (June 1973)

—— *Las Fuerzas Armadas en el Sistema Político de Chile* (Santiago, Chile, 1970)

—— 'Où vont les Militaires Chiliens?', *Politique Étrangère*, no. 1 (1974) 55–71

—— and Cadena, Cecilia, 'Armamentismo Dependiente: Caso Latinoamericano', *Estudios Internacionales*, Vol. IV (July–Sep 1970) no. 14

Klare, Michael T., 'How to Trigger an Arms Race—Latin American Weapons Market', *The Nation* (Aug 1975)

Körner, E., 'Die historische Entwicklung der Chilenischen Wehrkraft', Supplement to von Frobel (ed.), *Militär-Wochenblatt* (Berlin, 1910) no. 5

Kossok, Manfred, *Armee und Politik in Lateinamerika. Die nationale Befreiungsbewegung 1965. Bilanz, Berichte, Chronik* (Leipzig, 1966) pp. 135–62

——, 'Potencialidades y limitaciones del cambio en la función politica y social de las F. F. A. A. de los países en desarrollo: el caso de América Latina', *Revista Latinoamericana de Sociologia*, Vol. VII (1971) no. 2–3, 193–205

Kübler, Jürgen, 'Vom "Big Stick" zur "Good Neighborship". Vier Jahrzehnte Kontinuität und Wandel der USA-Militärpolitik gegenüber Lateinamerika', *Zeitschrift für Militärgeschichte* (1971) 645–59

Lieuwen, Edward, *The Latin American Military*, Report incorporated into U.S. Senate, Committee on Foreign Relations (Washington, 1969)

—— *Armies and Politics in Latin America* (Rev. ed., 1961)

Lowenthal, Abraham F. (ed.), *The Peruvian Experiment: Continuity and Change Under Military Rule* (Princeton, N.J., 1975)

Maullin, R. L., *Soldiers, Guerillas and Politics in Colombia* (Lexington, Mass., 1973)

Max, Alphonse, 'Arms in Latin America', *Review of the River Plate* (Mar 1974)

'Military Equipment for Brazil', *Interamerican Economic Affairs*, Vol. 28 (1974) no. 2, 84–94

Mires, Fernando, *Die Militärs und die Macht* (Berlin, 1975)

Nun, José, 'The Middle-Class Military Coup', in Claudio, Veliz (ed.), *The Politics of Conformity in Latin America* (London, 1967)

Nunn, Frederick M., 'Emil Körner and the Prussianization of the Chilean Army: Origins, Process, and Consequences, 1885–1920', *Hispanic American Historical Review*, Vol. 50 (Durham/North Carolina, 1970)

Ogelsby, John C. M., 'Argentinien zwischen Militärherrschaft und Peronismus', *Europa Archiv*, 28, Series 15 (Aug 1973) 525–34

Pinto, L. A. Costa, 'Nacionalismo y Militarismo', *Colección Minima*, 29 (Mexico, 1969)

Quartim, Joào, *Dictatorship and Arms Struggle in Brazil* (London, 1971)

Ronfeldt, David F., 'Patterns of Civil–Military Rule', in L. R. Einaudi (ed.), *Latin America in the 1970s* (Santa Monica, Dec 1972) pp. 74–97

—— and Einaudi, Luigi R., 'Prospects for Violence', in L. R. Einaudi (ed.), *Latin America in the 1970s* (Santa Monica, Dec 1972)

Rosenbaum, H. Jon and Tyler, William G., 'Zehn Jahre Militärherrschaft in Brasilien. Die politische und wirtschaftliche Entwicklung', *Europa Archiv*, Series 24 (1974) 863–76

Schmitter, Ph. C., 'Intervención militar, competencia politica y politica pública en América Latina 1950–1967', *Revista latinoamericano de ciencia política*, Vol. 2, no 3 (Santiago, Chile, 1971) 476–549

—— (ed.), *Military Rule in Latin America* (London, 1973)

Sepúlveda, Alberto, 'El Militarismo Desarrollista en América Latina', *Foro International*, no. 49, Vol. XIII, no. 1 (Mexico, July–Sep 1972) 45–65

Sotelo, Ignacio, 'Los Militares en el Peru: Continuidad y Cambio de Su Función Politica', *Papers, Revista de Sociologia*, published for the Universidad Autónoma de Barcelona (Barcelona, 1974)

——, Esser, K. and Moltmann, B., *Die bewaffneten Technokraten, Militär und Politik in Lateinamerika* (Hanover, 1975)

Steiner, Henry J., and Trubek, David M., 'Brazil—all Power to the Generals', *Foreign Affairs*, Vol. 49 (Apr 1971) no. 3, 464–79

Stepan, Alfred, *The Military in Politics. Changing Patterns in Brazil* (Princeton, N.J., 1971)

US House of Representatives, Committee on Foreign Affairs, Subcommittee on National Security Policy and Scientific Developments, Special Study Mission to Latin America on Military Assistance Training, Report 91st Congress, 2nd Session (Washington, D.C.: US Government Printing Office, 1970) pp. 27

Villanueva, Victor, *Nueva Mentalidad Militar en Peru* (Buenos Aires, 1969)

Waldmann, Peter, 'Gesellschaft und Militär in Argentinien', *Vierteljahresberichte*, no. 43 (Mar 1971) 30–50

Index

Abbas, Bandar, 167, 168
Abbas, Ferhat, 112
Abrams, C., 27
Abyssinia, 267
AEG Telefunken, 207
Afghanistan, 179
Africa, 12, 16, 131–2, 240, 264
  autonomy of, 184, 187–8
  East Africa, 176
  sub-Saharan, 240, 248
Ahman, Tajuddin, 145
aircraft
  bombers
    B-52, 31–41 *passim,* 47, 54, 61,
      76, 77
    B-57 Canberra, 148–52
  civil aircraft
    747 jumbo jet, 167
    W-33, 161
  electronic surveillance, 167
  fighters
    A-1 Skyraider, 45, 50
    A-1E, 102
    A-4 Skyhawk, 102
    A-7, 102
    Audax, 171
    F-4 Phantoms, 7, 31, 57, 136,
      166, 167, 168
    F-5 Freedom Fighter, 171, 230
    F-5E Tiger II, 167
    F-14 Tomcats, 167, 172
    F-15 Eagle, 6
    F-16, 167
    F-47D Thunderbolt, 163
    F-84 Thunderjet, 164
    F-86 Sabre Jet, 149, 150, 152,
      164
    F-104 Starfighter, 79, 136, 142,
      149, 150, 152–3
    HF-24 Maruta mach 2, 218
    Harrier 'jump jets', 148, 229
    Hurricane, 163
    Kfir, 218
    MiG-17, 152
    MiG-19, 153

MiG-21, 38, 152
Mirage, 152–3, 193, 204, 205, 230
P-3F Orion, 170
SE5, 199
SU-7, 148, 152–3
Tornado, 79
Vampire, 192
  ground support, 70
  reconnaisance, 25, 162, 164, 167
  side firing systems
    C-130, 38
    CHC-119, 38
    Puff the Magic Dragon, 26, 38
  trainers
    A-37 COIN trainer, 149
    Impala I, 192, 203, 204, 205
    Impala II, 192
    Potez 75, 117, 162
    T-6, 117
    T-28 Trojan, 45, 50, 117
    T-33, 164
    Tiger Moth, 162
  transport
    C-5 Galaxy, 167
    C-7 Caribou, 45
    C-47, 26, 45, 163
    C-123 Provider, 23, 45
    C-130 Hercules, 24, 25, 167
    DHC 2 Beaver STOL, 149
    DH4, 199
    DH9, 199
    HS 748, 148
aircraft carriers, 4
Albrecht, U., 228, 230
Alehlap-W-Rahman, M., 156
Algeria, 2, 8, 90, 110–35, 253, 258
  arms production, 215
  economic development, 110, 111,
    122, 123, 126
  pied noir, 111, 112, 124, 131, 133
  war with France
    Algérie Française, 124, 127, 130
      132
    Armée Libération Nationale
      (ALN), 112, 114, 118, 121,

Algeria *contd.*
129, 135
Challe offensive, 116, 128, 129
cost of, 130–1
Front Libération National
(FLN), 112–13, 116, 121, 122,
125–7, 129, 131, 135
Organisation Armée Secrète
(OAS), 133
police repression, 118–21
Section Administrative Specialisée
(SAS), 122–4
social effects of, 121–4
weapons employed in, 114, 116,
117, 129
see also France, Moslems
Algiers, 131
Battle of, 121
Ali Hambli, 125
Allende, S., 247
Alliance for Progress, 172
Allman, T. D., 47
American Friends Service Committee,
44
Amin, Idi, 238, 246, 267
Amin, Nur al, 145
Amirouche, 125
Andean Pact, 250
Anderson, M., 231
Anderson, R. D., 104n., 107
Anglo-Iranian Oil Company, 159, 162
Angola, 2, 181, 190, 191, 195, 198,
204, 209, 241, 252, 253, 272–3
Movimento Popular de Liberação de
Angola (MPLA), 191, 253
Frente Nacional de Liberação de
Angola (FLNA), 241, 253, 273
apartheid, 189, 201, 263
opposition to, 197
pass laws, 189, 193, 197
Ap Bac, 18
Arab-Israeli War, 7
Arabian Persian Gulf, 159, 168, 169,
175
Archer, D. H., 106, 107
Argentina, 13, 174, 211, 215, 216, 217,
228, 229, 245–50 *passim*
Argentinian Atomic Energy Office,
174

armed forces, 1, 10–12, 235–51 *passim*
citizens' army, 274
draftees, 115, 127
international army, 193
mercenaries, 9, 115
paramilitary, 112, 133, 171, 227, 232
revolts in, 238–9, 250
salaries, 221
third-world armies, 2, 8, 12, 136,
228, 236
training of, 18, 160–3, 166, 190,
210, 237, 241
see also individual countries
Armed Forces Movement (Portugal),
238–9
Armée Libération Nationale (ALN),
see Algeria
armoured cars, 167, 168, 181, 192,
193, 195, 203
AMX-13, 117, 191
Panhard AML-245, 117, 191, 204,
205
Saracen, 189, 193, 195
arms limitation, 232, 236, 257–75
Berlin conference, 264
Brussels Act, 89, 264, 276
Lucerne and Lugano conferences,
88, 90, 92, 100, 108, 260, 261
Nuclear Non-Proliferation Treaty
(NPT), 174–5, 268–9, 274
Partial Test Ban Treaty, 269–70
St Germaine convention, 265
Strategic Arms Limitation Talks
(SALT), 270
see also Disarmament
arms trade
aid, 4, 141–2, 251–2, 268
and civil technology, 169, 214, 217,
219–20, 226, 235
and co-production, 5
and employment, 6, 12, 13, 170,
171, 187, 217, 220, 222–5, 247,
250
and human needs, 13, 213, 227–8,
274
imports, 213, 219, 220, 247, 274
and industrialisation, 5, 6, 10, 13,
77, 79, 80, 114, 129, 136, 172–3,
211–20 *passim,* 235, 247, 258,

arms trade *contd.*
   263, 266, 274
  inflation, 39
  licensed arms production, 5, 8, 19,
     99, 164, 166, 181, 198, 204, 210,
     214–16, 219, 224–7
    infrastructure, 3, 50, 168, 170, 174
    labour, 171, 173, 217, 219–22
    R&D experts, 176, 217, 221
    self-sufficiency, 172, 173, 218
    political limitations, 5, 219, 267–8
    private dealers, 6, 169, 265–7
    in second-hand and spare parts,
     171, 198, 214, 219
  see also Militarism
Armstrong, O. K., 44
ASEAN, 254
Asian Collective Security, 146
Atkins, G. Pope, 176
Augustine, N. R., 230
Australia, 79, 201
Avro, 199
Awami League (Mukti Bahini), 136,
   143–7, 153
Ayachuco, Declaration of, 275
Ayoob, M., 155

balance of payments, 5, 39, 213, 226
balance of power, 136, 154, 235, 253,
   254
Balke, C., 107
Bangladesh, 8, 14, 15, 16, 136–56, 215,
   248, 250
  Bengali nationalists, 137, 143, 144
  communist party, 143
  guerrillas, 144–6
  and 1965 Indo-Pakistan war, 142
Bantus, 194–5
Bao Dai, 17
Baran, P., 229
Bay of Pigs, 18
Belgium, 80, 160–1, 174, 201, 204
Bell Helicopters, 170, 172, 178
Ben Bella, 114, 123
Bencherif, A., 135
Ben-Hur, N., 107
Benoit, E., 13, 16, 224, 231
Benzine, A., 135
Bergen, J., 155, 156

Berghahn, V. R., 11, 16
Berlin, 158
Berlin Conference, 264
Berlin Crisis, 18
Beyers, C., 186
Bhalla, A. S., 231
Bhutto, Z., 147
Bien Hao, 26
Bienen, H., 16
Biko, S., 181
Bilek, A. G., 105, 108
Bihn Duong, 32
Bihn Yugen, 18
biological warfare, 22, 70, 84, 85, 88,
   260
Birdsell, D., 107
Bismarck, 158
Boers, 180–3, 194, 196, 200
  nationalism, 200
  raider warfare, 191, 200
  war with British, 183–5, 187
Bolivia, 253
bombs and mines
  bomb live unit (BLU), *see* cluster
   munitions
  Claymore, 56
  fragmentation, 83, 85, 90
  free fall, 70
  Gator anti-personnel mine, 78
  Grasshopper anti-vehicle mine, 78
  guided bombs, 72, 82
  high explosive (HE), 68, 80, 97, 100
  Piranha anti-tank mine, 78
  scatter mines, 82
    Dragontooth, 33
    MSM/W, 80
  smart bombs, 62
  see also cluster munitions
Bondelzwarts, 188
Boris, H. D., 16
Botha, P., 209
Bourdieu, P., 121, 135
Brandt, W., 147
Brazil, 6, 13, 14, 16, 174, 175, 215,
   216, 219, 229–30, 237–50 *passim*,
   255, 274
Breguet, 162
Brezhnev, L., 146
Briand–Kellogg Pact, 259

British Aircraft Corporation (BAC), 167, 172
Brophy, I. P., 108
Broussard, 117
Brown & Root, 46
Brown, R. E., 105
Browne, M. W., 48
Brussels Act, 264, 276
Brussels Treaty, 89
Buck, G., 107
Budapest, 132
Bühl, H., 15
Bundy, M., 53
Bunting, B., 208
Burma, 16, 215
Burundi, 240
Busching & Co., 161
Buschire, 162

Cahn, A., 179
Callendar, G. R., 109
Cambodia, 6, 21, 22, 33, 34, 36, 37, 45, 253
Canada, 99, 164, 166
Cantieri Navali Riuniti, 161
Cao Dai, 18
capital punishment, 197
Cardosa, A., 16
Carlisle, R. T., 107
Carlson, G. A., 105, 108
Carter, G. A., 179
Carter, J., 99, 167, 207, 246, 268, 276
Caspian Sea, 158
casualties, non-combatant, 114, 187, 188, 197, 258, 260
Caterpillar tractors (Rome ploughs), 32
CENTO (Central Treaty Organization, formerly Baghdad Pact), 141, 147, 165, 166, 172, 177
Central Intelligence Agency (CIA), 21, 27, 32, 38, 252
Chabbahan, 169
Chaco War, 267
Chahram Pahlavi, 178
Challe, Gen., 116
Chamb, 151–4 *passim*
Chayes, A., 276

chemical biological warfare (CBW), 84
chemical warfare, 22, 32, 45, 67, 70, 82, 85, 86, 88, 98, 260
Chen, E. K. Y., 228
Chevallier, J., 134
Childs, D., 230
Chile, 215, 228, 235, 246, 247, 248, 250, 252
China, 4, 42, 210, 229, 235, 241, 252
    and Algeria, 131
    arms imports, 218
    arms production, 5, 58
    and Bangladesh, 147–53 *passim*
    citizens' army, 274
    revolution in, 253
    Sino–Soviet split, 236
    and United Nations, 191
    and Vietnam, 25, 38, 39, 253
Chobham armour, 6
CIPEC (Conseil Intergouvernemental de Pays Exporteurs de Cuivre), 249
civil dissent, 8, 9, 14, 18, 49, 61, 77, 97, 99, 110, 136, 142, 143–4, 159, 164, 170, 181, 187, 189, 193, 234, 242, 249, 254, 258, 262, 273; *see also* repression
    against Algeria, 111, 114, 118, 121, 130–3
    against Vietnam, 29, 36, 262, 272
    non-violent, 41, 187, 275
Clapp, A. J., 45
Clostermann, 134
Club of Rome, 211, 212
cluster munitions (minelets and bomblets)
    AK-2, 76
    AT-II, 81
    Beehive artillery ammunition, 83
    bomb live unit (BLU), 56, 77, 79, 85, 87, 99, 102
    cluster bomb unit (CBU), 57–62, 72–4, 76, 80, 85, 87, 94, 99, 102, 103
        CBU-2, 57
        CBU-24 ('guava'), 57–61
        CBU-28/37 (Dragontooth), 76
        CBU-33, 76
        CBU-34/42 (WAAPM), 76

cluster munitions *contd.*
   CBU-38, 76
   CBU-52, 62, 85, 87
   CBU-55, 85, 99, 102, 103
   CBU-58, 62
   CBU-59, 62, 102
   CBU-71, 62
   CBU-72, 62, 102
   cluster bombs/controlled firebombs,
      2, 49, 56–62, 63, 69, 70, 106
   DEDM, 80
   Dragon Seed bomblet, 79–80
   Giboulée (REDM), 76, 79, 81
   Gravel minelet, 84
   'guavas', 57–61
   M36/CBU-52, 85, 87
   M251 warhead, 79
   M453, 80
   Medusa, 79, 80
   Pandora, 78, 80
   REDM, 76, 79
   Sadeye and Rockeye, 77, 78
   Streuwaffen, 79
   SUU-24 Hayes Dispenser, 76, 77
   SUU-41 Gravel, 76, 84
   SUU-49, 102
   SUU-54, 78
Coctirane, R. C., 108
Cold War, 201, 235, 251
Columbia, 25
conflict theory, 236
Congo, 215
conventional weapons, 2, 7, 52, 54, 59,
      60, 64–7, 77, 80, 81, 104, 166,
      178, 261–4, 268
   Lucerne and Lugano conferences,
      88, 90, 92, 100, 108, 260, 261
Cornell University, 44
counter-insurgency, 6, 7, 12, 14, 17,
      19–24, 31, 34, 90, 91, 93, 110–35,
      142, 158, 162, 164, 180, 190, 195,
      200, 242
   internment, 110, 118, 184
   political prisoners, 41
   technology of, 193–5, 203
   torture, 110, 118–20, 127, 131, 196
   training for, 241, 251
   see also Psychological warfare;
      Repression

Courrégé, M., 135
Courrière, Y., 135
Creusot Loire, 174
Crevecoeur, P., 107
Crocker, C. A., 228
Croizat, J., 177
Cuba, 18, 191, 235, 236, 239, 241, 251,
      252, 253
Currie, M., 109
Custard, G. H., 107
Cyprus, 90
Czechoslovakia, 38, 91, 92, 161

Dacca, 152
Da Nang, 17, 26, 29, 42
Dardick, D., 107
Dassault, 204, 230
Deane, J. R., 106
de Bollardière, P., 130, 135
de Gaulle, C., 116, 121, 124, 125, 126,
      129–32 *passim*
Democratic Republic of Vietnam, 5,
      17, 25, 30, 33, 39, 40, 42, 212,
      263; *see also* Vietnam War
Denmark, 206
Dennis, J., 105n., 109
Derbon, D., 208
Derg, 238–9
de Roquigny, R., 134
Derricourt, R., 208
destroyers, 166, 201
   Petya class frigate, 148
   Spruance class, 168
diamonds, 183
Diem, Ngo Dihn, 17, 18, 50
Dienbienphu, 17
disarmament, 263, 268–9, 274, 275;
      see also arms limitation
Dolinin, V. A., 108
Dominican Republic, 215, 252
Doucy, A., 134
Dow Chemical, 49
Do Xuan Hop, 107
Dresden, 89
Duffett, J., 63
Duncanson, D. J., 44
Dunn, C. H., 46, 48
Dupuy, T. N., 65n., 105
Dutch East India Company, 181

Eastern Europe, 114, 267
East African Mutinies, 238–9
East Bengal, *see* Bangladesh
East Pakistan, *see* Bangladesh
Ecuador, 218, 240
Edwards, Comm., 190
Egypt (formerly United Arab
    Republic), 5, 13, 151, 212, 213,
    215, 216, 229, 235, 238, 245,
    251–3
Eisenhower, D. D., 19
electronic counter measures (ECM), 40
electronic warfare, 35; *see also*
    weapons technology
El Salvador, 241, 246
embargoes, arms, 8, 143, 146, 149, 181,
    190, 197, 203, 205, 210, 219,
    263, 270–3
Emerit, M., 134
Engelmann, G., 134
Engels, F., 256
Ernst, D., 228
Esso, 29
Ethiopia, 171, 201, 238–9, 240, 242,
    245, 246, 251, 267, 268
Eurodif project, 174
European Economic Community
    (EEC), 254
Eximbank, 177
Exocet, *see* missiles, surface to air

Fabiao, Gen., 239
Fatali Shah, 157
Favrod, C. H., 134
Federal Democratic Republic of Ger-
    many, 4, 5, 11, 78, 88–9, 94,
    166, 169, 170, 172–4, 198, 204,
    205, 206, 229, 267, 272
    Strebo programme, 79–81
Fedowitz, F., 107
Finer, S. E., 255
Finney, J., 178
Fiorello, M., 229
First World War, 11, 158, 180, 186,
    194, 199, 210, 266, 267
Fisher, J., 208
Fishlock, D., 179
Flechettes, 69, 83
Flick, 169

Flood, D., 41
Ford, G., 42
Fortescue, 183
Fortin, C., 256
Fouché, J. J., 189
Fraenkel, P., 208
France, 2, 4, 5, 79, 80, 81, 90, 112, 157,
    160, 162, 192–3, 198, 201, 203–4,
    206, 210, 235, 243, 252, 264, 272
    and Algeria, 8, 9, 110–35, 258
    economic relationship with, 112,
        115, 124, 126, 132
    political position, 113, 118, 120,
        126, 128, 130–3
    strategies in war, 113–14, 116, 122,
        125, 127
    armed forces, 123, 126–31
    and Iran, 166–9 *passim*
    and Israel, 219
    nuclear energy, 174
    and Pakistan, 146, 148, 149
    and United Nations, 191
Franek, J., 108
Freeman, C., 16
Free Officers (Egypt), 238–9
French, R. W., 109
Frente Nacional Liberacão de Angola
    (FNLA), 241, 253, 273
Fricker, J., 177
Front Libération National (FLN), *see*
    Algeria
fuel air explosives (FAE or FAX), 22,
    45, 69, 85, 98, 99, 103–4, 108
    M67A2, 103
    Pave Pat, 99

Gabon, 215
Gaddafy, Col., 246
Gaddis, Adm., 105n.
Galbraith, J. K., 44
Gallup Poll, 48
Gandhi, Mrs I., 144, 145, 147
Garasino, A. M., 133
Geisenheyner, S., 106
Gelb, L., 16
General Dynamics, 45
Geneva Accords (1954), 18, 51, 52, 196
Geneva Conventions (1949), 260

Geneva Diplomatic Conference, 260, 268
Geneva Protocols, 196, 260
German Democratic Republic, 24, 38, 91
Germany, 9, 11, 49, 110, 157, 162
  armed forces, 243
  in Boer War, 184
  and South-west Africa, 186, 188, 199
Gestewitz, H. R., 108
Ghana, 202, 215, 245
Giap, Vo Nguyen, 19, 46, 242
Gilbert, G., 49n.
glide bomb unit (GBU), 70, 79
Gliedman, J., 46
Glover, W. P., 47
gold, 16, 180, 183, 187
Graff, W. S., 107
Great Britain, 2, 4, 5, 11, 32, 79, 81, 185, 191, 199, 200, 201, 210, 229, 235, 243, 264, 267, 271–2
  and Algeria, 131
  armed forces, 108, 189, 199, 200, 202
  Conservative Party, 203
  and Iran, 157–76
  Labour Party, 203, 204, 253
  and Pakistan, 137, 148, 149
  and South Africa, 180–5, 193–9
  and Suez, 202, 252–3
Greece, 215, 251
Green, S., 107
Green, W., 177
Green & Fricker Air Force Handbook, 162
Grumman Corp., 171, 178, 242
Grumman Iran Private Company, 172
Guam, 34
guavas, *see* cluster munitions
guerrilla warfare, *see* counter-insurgency; liberation movements
Guevara, C., 242, 253
guided munitions, 37, 62, 73; *see also* missiles
Guinea, 215
Guinea-Bissau, 253, 273
Gulf of Aden, 265
Gupta, S., 155, 156
Gushaw, G. V., 231
Gutehoffnungschütte, 160

Gyaman, 16

Haase, Col., 177
Hague Laws, 261
Haiphong, 40, 48, 61
Hall, D., 208
Hamburg, 49
Hamlin, R. E., 45
Hanoi, 40, 48, 61
Hao Hao, 18
Hartmann, 177
Harvard University, 139, 142
Hawker Siddeley, 171, 230
Heath, E., 147
Heiman, G., 47
Held, M., 107
helicopters, 24, 25, 42, 43, 45, 70, 84, 99, 116, 117, 134, 148, 166, 167, 170, 172, 181, 193, 216, 272
  Alouette, 117, 134, 148, 149, 192
  Frelon, 166, 192
  Mil Mi4, 148
  night flight electronic, 168
  Puma, 192, 204
  Shawnee, 23
  UH-1 Huey, 102, 103
  Wasp, 192, 203
herbicides, 55, 60; *see also* chemical warfare
Heshmati, M., 176
Hewish, M., 230
Hill-Norton, P., 207
Hilsman, R., 20
Hindus, 137, 145
Hobart, F., 107
Holtz, R., 47
Honeywell, 102
Hong Kong, 215
Hormuz, Straits of, 169
Horn of Africa, 90, 251
hovercraft. 166
Hue Quang Ngai, 42
Hughes Industries, 167, 171
Huk movement, 21
human rights, 183, 245, 247, 259, 268; *see also* international law
Humphrey bill, 268
Huntington, S. P., 237, 255

Ibo, 238
ideology, 3, 7, 9, 14, 15, 19, 20, 43, 154,
    185, 232, 236, 240, 244–6, 257,
    258, 263, 274
IMBDI Iranian Bank, 171, 172
incendiary and flame weapons, 32, 49,
    63, 67, 84–8, 95–7
  controlled fireballs, 85, 87–9, 94, 96
  high explosive incendiary (HEI), 87
  M74 Rocket-clip, 95, 99
  M202, 104
  magnesium, 55
  phosphorus, 55
  research and development of, 50, 95,
    97
  SCIFT, 104
  TEA, 95, 96
  TPA, 95
  see also Napalm
India, 5, 6, 13, 90, 140, 157, 158, 172,
    179, 212, 216–18, 225, 229, 231,
    274
  armed forces, 144, 148–54 passim,
    210
  arms production, 150, 173, 176, 178,
    210, 211, 215–19 passim
  and Bangladesh, 136, 137, 139,
    142–6, 176
  Communist Party, 143
  military budget, 147–8, 212
  nationalism, 144
  nuclear weapons, 175, 178, 270
  and Soviet Union, 146, 148, 155
Indian Institute of Defence Studies, 145
Indian Ocean, 163, 168, 206–7
Indochina, 7, 70, 71, 73, 76, 77, 83, 95
Indonesia, 5, 215, 229, 245, 248, 252,
    267
Integrated National Telecommunica-
    tions System, 168
International Business Machines
    (IBM), 37
International Institute for Strategic
    Studies, 15, 193n.
International Monetary Fund, 252, 254
international law, 88, 89, 196, 258–62,
    274–5
International opinion, 8, 9, 14, 52, 81,
    113, 119, 121, 128, 145, 146, 147,

    201, 203, 206, 232, 258, 262, 267,
    273
  and Algeria, 111, 114, 118, 121, 130–3
  censorship, 99
  media, 61, 77, 97
  napalm, 49
  and Vietnam, 29, 36, 40, 55, 253
international peace, 198, 272–3
International Peace Research Associa-
    tion, 1
Iran, 5, 6, 14, 77, 150, 157–79, 212, 215,
    216, 219, 229, 235, 248, 251, 252,
    268, 274
  arms build-up, 157
  armed forces, 160–6
  arms production, 160, 171–5
  military aid (USA), 162–4, 225
  military expenditure, 160, 163, 168
  police, 160, 162, 170
  repression 162–5, 170, 245
  Soviet crisis, 163
Iranian Aircraft Industries (IAI), 171
Iranian Azerbaijan, 163, 164
Iraq, 165, 175, 230, 245
Islamabad, 146
Israel, 6, 62, 77, 79, 84, 99, 169–70, 212,
    215, 216–19 passim, 229, 230,
    251
Italy, 81, 160, 161, 169, 170, 174, 191,
    201, 204, 205, 210, 230, 267, 272
Ivory Coast, 215

Jackson, H., 23, 45
Jag Jivan Ram, 145, 146, 156
Jahoda, M., 16
Janowitz, M., 16, 255
Jarvis, R. C., 48
Japan, 11, 20, 49, 160, 161, 177, 191,
    210, 267
Jensen, G., 177
Jessore, 147, 152, 153
Jinnah, Mohammed Ali, 138
Johannsohn, G., 105n., 108, 109
Johnson, J. L., 16
Johnson, L., 208
Johnson, L. B., 24, 25, 29, 31, 36, 54
Jolly, R., 255
J. A. Jones, Inc., 46
Jordan, 150, 171, 240, 245

Julien, C. A., 134
Junkers, 161–2
jus contra bellum, 259

Kaffir wars, 183
Kahin, G., 44
Kaldor, M., 16, 231
Kalisch, R. B., 44
Karachi, 153
Kashmir, 151
Katorijan, Gen., 172
Kavango, 195
Kavic, L. J., 228
Kennedy, E., 146
Kennedy, J. F., 18, 19, 20, 22, 44, 50
Kenya, 79, 238
Keramane, H., 135
Kessel, P., 135
KGB, 252
Khan, Ayub, 136, 138, 142–3
Khan, Fauman Ali, 152
Khan, Reza, *see* Shah Reza
Khan, Tikka, 152, 154
Khan, Yahya, 136, 143, 145, 147
Khe Sanh, 26, 37
Kidron, M., 229, 230
Kiernan, J. M., 46
Kiesling, H. von, 177
Kissinger, H., 41
Klare, M., 47, 178, 229, 230
Kleber, B. E., 107
Kohri, K., 22
Korea, 210
Korean War, 21, 23, 49, 50, 56, 67, 70, 87, 90, 92
Kriebl, R., 178
Krim Belkacem, 128
Krupp AG, 161
Kukkonen, C., 47
Kurdistan, 163, 164
Kuwait, 175, 230

Lacoste, Y., 134
Lacroix, R., 134
Lambert, M., 230
Lance, 80
Landa, R. G., 134
Lansdale, E. G., 21, 44
Laos, 18, 21, 22, 25, 32–7 *passim,* 41, 60, 61, 63, 253
napalm used in, 51–3
Pathet Lao, 36, 38, 53
Laroui, A., 134
Lasswell, H., 251, 256
lathis, 142
Latin America, 12, 13, 90, 172, 206, 210, 211, 235, 265, 267
Lauppe, E. F., 208
Laurence, M., 177
Lawrie, G. G., 208
League of Nations, 199, 259, 265, 266, 267
Leary, F., 46, 47
Lebanon, 240, 250
Leitenberg, M., 44
lethality index, 64–5
Le Tourneau, R., 134
Lewis, J. W., 44
Lewis, W., 156
Leygues, R., 135
liberation movements, 7, 9, 182, 184, 190, 228, 236, 241, 242
wars fought by, 18, 30, 41, 211, 254, 265
see also individual countries
Libya, 150, 246
Lindquist, A., 156
Lipton, M., 209
lithium, 87
Litton Industries, 168, 171
Lock, P., 215n., 228, 230
Lockheed Aircraft Corporation, 35, 164, 167, 170, 268
Loebelson, R. M., 45
Lotz, W. E., 46
Lucerne and Lugano Conferences, *see* arms limitation
Lumsden, M., 70, 71, 106, 108
Luxembourg, 174
Lynch, J. E., 16

machine guns, 38, 39, 56, 68, 70, 72, 98
Gatling guns, 26, 38
M-16, 220
McConnell, A. F. (Jr), 46
McGarvey, P. J., 46, 47
McNamara, R., 4, 37, 45, 50, 59–60, 76
McNaughton, J., 52, 53, 54

Mahrad, A., 176, 177
Malagasy Republic, 215
Malaya, 17, 21, 32, 240
Malaysia, 215
Malloy, M., 47
Manchuria, 210
Mao Tse-tung, 19, 31, 242
Marx, K., 245, 256
Mascarenhas, A., 155
Maschinen und Turbinen Union
        (MTU), 178
Massachusetts Institute of Technology
        (MIT), 179
Massu, J., 135
Mekong Delta, 18, 36, 225
Mengistu, Lt. Col., 246
Messali Hadj, 111, 112
messalism, 111, 114
Mexico, 215, 248, 265
Mfengu tribe, 82–3
Middle East, 1, 8, 12, 62, 70, 77, 84, 157,
        201, 254, 267
Miles, W. D., 108
militarism, 3–17, 41, 142, 175, 176, 180,
        197, 201, 210, 211, 225, 232,
        234–5, 242, 244, 251, 257–68
        passim, 274–5
    authoritarianism, 3, 6, 13, 112, 232,
        245, 250, 257, 260
    class struggle, 157, 227, 232, 234,
        236, 250, 257, 263
    defined, 232
    dependence, 7, 8, 9, 13, 15, 132, 157,
        165–6, 173, 176, 226, 228, 232–4,
        250, 263–4, 275
    infrastructure, 3, 50, 168, 170, 174,
        263
    protection of investments, 247, 252
    South Africa, 180, 197, 199, 205
military alliances, 14, 201, 202, 267;
        see also CENTO, NATO, etc.
Military Assistance Program (USA), 55
military coups, 4, 14, 25, 138, 238, 245,
        247, 251, 252, 273
military transfer, *see* arms trade
Millspaugh, A. C., 162
mineral resources, 174, 185, 197, 198,
        201, 206, 224, 234, 247, 249, 258
Minty, A., 207

missiles
    air-to-air
        Matra R530, 203
        Sidewinder, 152
    air-to-surface
        AGM-12E Bullpup, 79
        AS-20, AS-30, 203
    anti-ballistic, 104
    anti-tank, 12, 168, 203, 204
    Condor, 169
    man-portable, 274
    shrikes, 40
    strategic, 4, 19
    surface-to-air
        Cactus, 203
        Crotale, 203
        Hawk, 168
        MM-38 Exocet, 168
        Rapier, 67, 172
        Redeye, 45
        Tigercat, 167
        SA-2, 38, 40, 148
        SA-7 Strela, 23, 45
        SAM-2, 136, 149
        SAM-3, 136
        SAM-7/9, 167
        Seacat, 167
    surface-to-surface, 77, 81
    tactical
        SS-12, 168
Monheim, F., 134
Moorer, T., 41
Morocco, 115, 129, 215
Morrison-Knudson, 46
Moslems, 110, 111, 115, 121, 123–30
        passim, 134, 240, 244
    Muslim nationalism, 137–8
Mossadeq, 164
Movimento Popular de Libertação de
        Angola (MPLA), 191, 253; *see
        also* Angola
Moyer, R. A., 208
Mozambique, 235, 236, 253, 273
Mukti Bahini, *see* Awami League
multinational corporations, 6, 11, 13,
        14, 29, 157, 176, 240, 246,
        247
multiple re-entry vehicle (MIRV), 4
Mustin, L., 51, 52, 58, 59, 60

mutual assured destruction (MAD), 262
Myrdal, A., 269, 276

Nairobi Conference, 201–2
Nam Dinh, 61
Namibia, 190, 191, 195, 199, 205, 206, 272
napalm, 45, 49–60, 68, 86–90, 95, 117
  accidents with, 92–4
  effectiveness, 91, 96
  Napalm B, 94
  political controversy, 54, 55, 59, 89, 90, 91
Napoleon Bonaparte, 9, 157, 182, 199, 245
Nasser, G. A., 239
nationalism, 6, 111, 124, 180, 186, 189, 235, 236, 237, 253, 258; *see also* ideology *and individual countries*
National Socialists, 131, 161
naval warfare, 4, 10, 11, 202; *see also* destroyers
Naxalites, 143, 144
Naya, S., 231
Nazari, H., 177
Nepal, 215
nerve gas, 85
Netherlands, 2, 80, 174, 181–2, 206
neutron bomb, 262
New Zealand, 148, 201
Nha Be, 29
Nigeria, 215, 231, 238–9, 240, 241, 242, 248, 250
Nixon, R. M., 32, 36, 40, 41, 42, 146, 147, 268
Noel Baker, P., 16
North Atlantic Assembly, 206
North Atlantic Treaty Organization (NATO), 77, 78, 88–9, 99, 116, 167, 206–7, 254, 271–2, 273
Northern Ireland, 250
North Korea, 5, 215, 252, 270
North Vietnam, *see* Democratic Republic of Vietnam; Vietnam War
Northrop, 79, 167, 171, 178, 230, 268
Norway, 271

Nouschi, A., 134
nuclear energy, 173–5
Nuclear submarines, *see* submarines
nuclear weapons, 2, 6, 7, 18, 40, 58, 64–7, 70, 82, 88, 98, 101, 166, 173, 175, 178, 198, 209, 254, 260–3, 268–70
  as deterrent, 252, 262, 269
  disarmament, 269
  Non-Proliferation Treaty, 174–5, 268–9, 274
  tactical, 270
nuclear weapons countries (NWC), 173, 269
Nur-ul-Islam, 156

Ogot, B., 208
oil, 6, 157, 162, 163, 166, 173, 175, 176, 213, 230, 247, 275
'oil crisis' (1973), 2, 173–4
Oman, Sultanate of, 169, 176
Oran, 131
Organization of Petroleum Exporting Countries (OPEC), 248, 249
Osanka, F. M., 133
Osman Empire, 157–62, 228
OTO-Melara, 230
Ouarsenis, 116
Ovamboland, 195

Pacific Architects and Engineers (PA&E), 30
Pact Government, 186, 187
Pahlavi Dynasty, 159
Pakistan, 14, 90, 136–56, 179, 215, 216, 228, 245, 250
  armed forces, 137–9, 143–7 *passim*, 150, 152, 154
  autonomy movement, 143
  distribution of wealth, 137, 139–40, 154
  foreign aid to, 145, 154, 171
  military alliances, 141
  military expenditure, 149
Papenek, 156
Tsar Paul I, 157
Pave Pat, *see* fuel air explosives
Pearson, J., 107
Pentagon, 4, 22, 23, 26, 29, 35, 37, 38, 40, 50, 57, 80, 99, 109, 170, 175,

Pentagon *contd.*
229, 243
Joint Chiefs of Staff, 27, 29, 38, 41,
51, 54, 58, 59, 60
Pentagon Papers, 44, 45, 46, 52, 63
Peron, J., 211, 217
Perry Robinson, J. P., 16n., 78n.
Persian/Arabian Gulf, *see* Arabian/
Persian Gulf
Peru, 215, 235, 237, 242, 243, 245, 246
Pfeiffer, E. W., 46
Phantom fighter, *see* F-4 *under* Aircraft
Philco-Ford, 46
Philippines, 17, 21, 30, 215, 220, 240,
245, 248, 270
Phou Kout, 53
Phu Gia Pass, 37
Phuoc Long, 42
pied noir, see Algeria
Pike, D., 44
Pirelli, G., 135
Pirow, O., 200
Plain of Jars, 53
Ploger, R. R., 46
Podgorny, 145
Poland, 38
Police, 120, 169, 170, 188, 189, 193, 195,
227, 244; *see also* repression
Portugal, 1, 2, 190, 197, 201, 203, 215,
238–9, 270–4 *passim*
Prenant, A., 134
Presseisen, E., 176
Pretty, R. T., 106, 107
Prokosch, E., 44, 106, 107
Proxmire, W., 47
Prussian army, 158
psychological warfare, 21, 124–9, 172;
see also counter-insurgency
Punjabi, 137, 143, 154

Qadshar dynasty, 159
Quang Tri, 61

Race, J., 45
racialism, 41, 111, 187–8, 194, 264
Rajhasthan, 151–2
Ramazani, R. K., 177
Rand Corporation, 212, 229, 231
Rand rebellion, 186–7

Raymond International, 46
Raytheon, 168
Red Army, 115, 158, 164
Red Cross, International Committee
of, 26, 49, 57, 63
remotely piloted vehicle (RPV), 40
repression, 157, 186, 187, 192, 196–7,
227–8, 243, 250, 255, 257, 259,
263–5, 271–2; *see also* counter-
insurgency
Republic of Vietnam, 17, 18, 33, 50,
171, 212–13
Army of the (ARVN), 17–24 *passim,*
29, 34, 36–44 *passim,* 61
Provisional Revolutionary Govern-
ment, 32, 41, 42
see also Vietnam War
Rheinmetall-Borsig AG, 161
Rhodes, C., 183
Rhodesia, *see* Zimbabwe
Rienzi, T. M., 46, 48
rifles
automatic, 69
M-1, 18
Mauser, 160–1
Robinson, C. A., 105n., 106, 109
Rocard, 135
rockets, 52, 216
microjet, 22
multiple launches, 81
unguided, 70, 72
Zuni, 103
Röling, B., 276
Rolls-Royce, 203, 204, 229
Rommel, E., 200
Roosevelt, F. D., 163
Rothschild, E., 276
Rowe, E. T., 15
Rush, S., 107
Russian Revolution, 158, 238–9

Sabre jet, *see* F-86 *under* Aircraft
Sadat, A., 239
Saigon, 17, 19, 21, 26, 28, 42, 43, 99
Salan, R. A. L., 116
Saudi Arabia, 12, 150, 176, 212, 215
Saunders, C., 208
SAVAK (Iranian secret police), 170
Sayad, A., 121, 135

Schäffer, J., 177
Schmitter, P., 13, 16
von Schulenburg, W., 161
Schwartzkopf, Col., 162, 164
Science Policy Research Unit, Sussex (SPRU), 64n.
Scott, F., 106
Second World War, 5, 6, 11, 21, 22, 28, 32, 70, 76, 82, 83, 85, 90, 98, 100, 112, 115, 162, 163, 164, 180, 188, 194, 200–1, 208, 210, 266
    Nazi Germany, 131, 161, 200
    resistance movements, 110, 131
Senegal, 245
Seventeenth Parallel, 17, 18, 25, 37
Sewell, R. G. S., 107
Shah of Iran, *see* Shah Reza
Shah Reza (Reza Khan), 159–64 *passim,* 169
Shahbaz, 171
Shakargarh, 151–2, 154
Shapley, D., 46
Sharpeville massacre, 189, 191, 193, 196, 198, 203
Sheikh Mujib, 136, 143, 145
Short Bros, 167
Sialkolt, 154
Siemens, 178
Sierra Leone, 238
Silvermine Communications Centre, 206, 207
Simonstown Agreement, 193, 199, 200, 201, 208
Sindh, 153
Singapore, 215, 225, 230, 248, 275
Sino–Soviet split, 236
slavery, 16, 183, 264
smart bombs, *see* guided munitions
Smith, I., 190
Smith, L. D., 45
Smuckler, R. H., 44
Smuts, Gen, 185, 187, 188, 199, 200
Snavely, W. W., 106, 107
SNIAS, 166
Soldiers United Will Win (SUV), 239
Somalia, 251
Soroff, H., 107
South Africa, 12, 14, 176, 180–209, 214, 229, 263, 265
    and Angola, 252, 253
    armed forces, 182–7, 191–6, 200
        generals' rebellion, 186
        native participation in, 182, 185, 188–90, 194–6
    arms production, 172, 173, 181, 201, 204, 205, 215–17, 272
        of nuclear weapons, 179, 205
    embargoes against, 171, 270–4 *passim*
    military expenditure, 191–2
South African Institute on Race Relations, 193
South East Asia Treaty Organization (SEATO), 141, 147
South Korea, 6, 13, 14, 30, 212, 213, 215, 220, 225, 238, 245, 248, 251, 270
Souvanna Phouma, 51, 53
Soweto, 181, 193, 196
Spain, 174, 215, 216, 219, 229
Spence, J. E., 207
Sri Lanka, 215
standardisation, 11, 95
Standard International Trade Classification (SITC), 212, 213
Starfighter, *see* F-104 *under* aircraft
Steffan & Heyman, 160
Stein, N., 178
Stepan, A., 16, 255
Stevenson, T., 107
Stockholm International Peace Research Institute (SIPRI), 3, 63, 156, 176, 192n., 193n., 207, 208, 209, 212, 229, 230, 231, 276
Strategic Air Command, 41
Strategic Arms Limitation Talks (SALT), 270
Stratotankers, 176
    Boeing KC-135, 167
Strauss, J., 47
Student Advisory Committee on International Affairs, 49
submarines, 10, 168, 176, 193, 229
    Daphne, 204
    nuclear, 168
Subramaniam, C., 145
Sudan, 215, 240
Suez Canal, 159, 165
Sullivan, L., 35, 47

Sunderland, R., 65n., 105
Sweden, 49, 57, 100, 162, 267
Sweezy, P. M., 229
Swerrington, 47
Switzerland, 274
Syria, 212, 240, 245

Tabatai, 159, 164
Tahtinen, D., 178, 179
Taiwan, 6, 30, 215, 216, 219, 220, 225, 230, 231, 245, 248
Takman, J., 107
Tanks
   Chieftain, 6, 14, 167, 172
   Leopard, 169, 230
   M-24, 163
   M-41, 191
   M-47, 167
   M-60, 167
   PT-76, 148
   Patton, 142, 164
   Scorpion, 167
   Sherman, 163, 164
   T-54, 95, 153
   T-59, 153
   Vijayanta, 148
Tanzania, 238, 241
Tashkent Declaration (1966), 143
Taylor, Ambassador, 45
Taylor, G. E., 105n.
Tay Ninh, 32
Technology, *see* Weapons
Teherani, A., 177
Tehran, 157, 160, 162, 174
Tenentismo revolt, 238
Terray, E., 16
terrorism, 20, 112, 196
Thailand, 25, 34, 37, 41, 47, 215, 225, 241, 251
Thai Binh, 61
Theal, 183
Thee, M., 63
Thieu, Nguyen Van, 41, 42
Thimmesch, N., 106
Thompkins, J. S., 106
Thompson, L. V., 176
Thompson, R., 21
TNT, 98
Tokyo, 49

torpedo boats, 148, 166
trade unions, 187, 244
Transvaal, 183
Trinidad, 275
Tripier, P., 134
Truong Chinh, 47
turbojet engines, 204
Tunisia, 114, 115, 129
Turkey, 150, 210, 212, 213, 215, 216, 230, 251
Turkmantchai, Treaty of, 158
Tutsi, 240
Tylden, G., 208

Uganda, 235, 238, 239, 241, 267
ul-Haq, M., 155
U Minh, 32, 46
Unemployment, *see* arms trade
Ungar, L., 52
Union of Soviet Socialist Republics (USSR), 2, 4, 80, 108, 109, 133, 138, 175, 205, 207, 267
   and Angola, 252
   arms production, 5, 58, 76, 79, 98, 1
   and China, 236, 253
   and India, 143–55 *passim*
   and Iran, 157–68 *passim*
   and Middle East, 8
   napalm research, 91, 92
   and Vietnam, 34, 38, 39, 40, 57, 62
United Nations, 16, 63, 108, 145, 146, 147, 181, 190, 196, 203, 207, 208, 211, 212, 213, 221, 232, 254, 255, 259, 268
   Charter of, 273
   Security Council, 181, 191, 198, 206, 271–3
   Special Session on Disarmament, 275
   UNCTAD, 211, 212
UNITA (Angola), 273
United States of America, 2–9 *passim*, 14, 89, 92–4, 96, 147, 149, 166, 167, 169, 210, 211, 220, 265
   and Algeria, 115, 117, 131, 133
   anti-communism, 3, 17, 18, 19, 20, 33, 41, 115, 138, 163, 242
   Cold War, 163
   Congress of, 167, 171, 273

United States of America *contd.*
 'containment' policy, 205, 266
 Ethiopia, 267
 and Iran, 157, 162–76 *passim*
 and Israel, 218
 and Korea, 17, 67
 military aid, 100, 150–4, 166, 178, 211
 military expenditure, 231
 military trade, 166–7
 military training, 190, 243, 251
 and Pakistan, 138–9, 141–2
 and Peru, 243
 and Portugal, 271–2
 and South Africa, 200, 201, 205
 and United Nations, 191
 and USSR, 258, 263, 268–70
 and Vietnam, 17–77 *passim,* 110, 235, 252, 253, 258
US Air Force, 21, 29, 38, 39, 71–3, 77, 82n., 85, 87, 96, 97, 98, 99, 104n., 106, 109, 221
US Arms Control and Disarmament Agency, 3, 5, 15, 16, 212, 213
US Army, 15, 65n., 80, 87, 90, 95, 101, 104, 105n., 106, 108
 Limited War Laboratory, 30, 34
 weapons development centres, 22, 56, 64, 80, 88, 93, 98
US Department of Agriculture, 47
US Department of Defense, 47, 51, 52, 59, 60, 63, 70–2, 77, 105, 106, 173, 178, 220
US Department of State, 51, 52, 53, 55, 60, 162, 272–3
US Forest Service, 32
US House of Representatives, 38, 47, 105n., 106, 146
US Marine Corps, 95, 96, 99, 103, 106
US Military Assistance Program, 50, 214, 229
US National Security Council, 22, 51, 288
US Navy, 71, 73, 98, 99, 101–4, 105n., 106, 109
US Senate, 38, 45, 46, 61, 63, 104n., 106, 109, 177, 178, 179
US Signal Corps, 26
US Special Forces, 21

University of Florida, 47
Uruguay, 245, 246, 250
uranium, 68, 83, 179
Ussuri, 90

Vance, C., 53
Van Dinh, T., 44
Van Doorn, J., 16
Vann, J. P., 34, 45, 47
Vatin, J. C., 134
Venezuela, 163, 215, 248
Vergès, J., 135
Versailles, Treaty of, 160
VFW Fokker, 204
Vha Trang, 26
Vickers, 172
Vidal-Naquet, 135
Vien, N. K., 23, 46
Vienna Conference, 260
Vientiane, 52
Viet Cong, *see* Vietnam War
Vietnam Democratic Republic of, 5, 17, 25, 30, 33, 39, 40, 42, 212, 263
Vietnam War, 1, 2, 6, 7, 9, 12, 17–109, 178, 215, 225, 236, 252, 253
 bombing of Laos and Cambodia, 36, 60
 bombing of the North, 22, 25, 48, 54, 60, 88
 civilian contractors, 29
 civilian deaths, 17, 26, 33, 61
 cost of, 2, 25, 27, 29, 31, 33, 34, 37, 38, 59, 60, 70
 defoliation, 32, 33, 54, 67
 Easter Offensive, 61
 Gulf of Tonkin, 25
 Ho Chi Minh Trail, 24, 36–9 *passim*
 Igloo White, 25, 37–40, 76
 morale of troops, 24, 39, 42
 National Guard, 29
 National Liberation Front (NLF), 27, 30, 31, 33, 38, 40, 43, 61, 109
 negotiations, 30, 36, 40, 41
 October agreement, 41
 pacification, 31, 36
 Paris agreement, 41, 42
 Peoples Liberation Armed Forces (PLAF), 25–46 *passim*

Vietnam War *contd.*
  police, 43
  political situation, 7, 9, 19, 24, 41, 225
  racialism, 20, 41
  secrecy, 36, 57, 58
  Spring Offensive, 36, 37, 38
  technology employed, 2, 8, 32, 33, 54, 61, 67, 69, 70, 80–101 *passim*, 110, 168, 228
  Tet Offensive, 36
  Viet Cong, *see* National Liberation Front
  Viet Minh, 17, 18, 19, 24, 43
  Vietnamisation, 37, 39, 43
  weather modification, 32, 33
  withdrawal of troops, 37
Viet Tri, 61
Viksnins, G. J., 231
Vinh, 61
Vinnell Corporation, 46
Vosper Thornycroft, 102

Wall, P., 206
war readiness materiel, 73
Warsaw Pact, 5, 93, 254
Warsaw Treaty Organization, 88–9
Watergate scandal, 42
weapons, 64–109
  cost of, 68, 94, 95, 168–9, 191–2, 218, 274
  effectiveness, 2, 8, 80, 81, 221
  hit-kill probability, 82, 85
  innovations, 4, 7, 22, 30, 33, 34, 82, 85, 87, 94, 180, 218, 221, 244
  and labour, 10, 12, 15
  lethality index, 64–5
  low technology, 18
  moral arguments, 85, 257, 262
  obsolescence, 10, 218
  overkill, 73
  research and development, 50, 59, 64–109, 218, 261
  second-hand, 6, 171, 219
  secrecy, 8, 55, 58, 69, 80, 92, 255, 262
  spare parts, 7, 8, 115, 172
  standardisation, 95
  weapons system concept, 11, 12, 13, 274

weapons technology, 2, 7, 8, 11, 13, 81, 257, 266; *see also* arms trade
  anti-personnel, 25, 67, 68, 85, 87, 93, 94, 99, 262
  area munitions, 67
  communications, 3, 10, 26–8, 117, 206
  disease-causing, 85
  Dum-Dum bullets, 260
  electronics, 3, 11, 27, 35, 168, 202, 216
  fire bombs, *see* incendiary weapons
  gunpowder, 67
  infra-red guidance system, 62
  laser, 62, 168
  massed delivery, 67
  radar, 35, 203
  see also specific technologies, e.g. air-craft, tanks
weather modification, 32, 33, 46
Weiss, G., 45, 46
Weissmann, S., 178
Fritz Werner, 161
West Bengal, 143–4; *see also* Bangla-desh; India
Westing, A. H., 46, 107
Westmoreland, W., 23, 31, 35
Weyand, F. C., 16
Whalen, Col., 106
Wheeler, E., 54
Whittaker Corporation, 105n.
Wildhorn, S., 231
Wilson, M., 208
Wönckhaus, 160
World Bank, 145, 254
Wuillaume report, 135
Wulf, H., 215, 228, 230
Wulff, T., 63
Xhosa tribe, 182
Xuan Loc, 99, 100
Yemen, 215
Yom Kippur War, 84
Yugoslavia, 124, 215, 216, 219
Zaire, 215, 245, 252, 273
Zambia 241
Zavrian, M., 135
Zimbabwe, 190, 197, 201, 202
zirconium, 87